# HANDBOOK
## OF
## CHURCH
# ADMINISTRATION

# HANDBOOK OF CHURCH ADMINISTRATION

by

Lowell Russell Ditzen

NEW YORK

THE MACMILLAN COMPANY

A DIVISION OF THE CROWELL-COLLIER PUBLISHING COMPANY

1962

First Printing

The Macmillan Company, New York
Brett-Macmillan Ltd., Galt, Ontario

Printed in the United States of America

Library of Congress catalog card number: 62-11914

Designed by Hermann Strohbach

TO
THE OFFICERS
THE STAFF
AND
THE PEOPLE
OF

# THE REFORMED
# PROTESTANT
# DUTCH CHURCH

OF
BRONXVILLE, NEW YORK
FOR WHOM
GRATITUDE INCREASES
AND
AFFECTION DEEPENS
AS THE YEARS GO BY

# Introduction

Since the invitation came from the publishing house of Macmillan to write this book, I have often wondered why I should have been asked to take on this project, and why I was so presumptuous as to accept.

There has been some assurance in remembering that my background exposed me to a wide variety of administrative problems and programs of different churches.

The parishes I have served include a rural church that was well attended when twenty people were at worship on Sunday. Then came a period of four years in a congregation numbering about a hundred souls. Following that, several years were spent in a neighborhood metropolitan church whose rolls listed four hundred communicants. Next came a term as assistant minister in a distinguished parish in New York City. Following were seven full years ministering to a congregation of more than fifteen hundred members in a city of a hundred thousand population. For the past decade my ministry has been in a suburban parish that numbers more than three thousand communicants within the orbit of its concern.

Such a background makes me sensitive to the needs of the church where the minister is the complete staff from sexton to secretary to prophet. Having been in that role, I hope that many of the materials presented in this volume will be suggestive to such a pastor and also to the church that may have part-time secretarial help, as well as to clergy and lay officers that minister to large congregations and conduct widely varied activities. I emphasize the word "suggestive." Many forms and illustrations have been made, not as being ultimately suitable for a particular situation, but rather to stimulate the reader to develop a program that is adequate for his specific congregation.

It has been my intention to be particularly aware of churches where laymen play a significant role in administration. Many suggestions have been included with the idea of guiding the thought and activity of dedicated officers of the church. Also, I have worked with the thought that these materials could assist church officers on occasions when the pulpit might be vacant.

I have sought, received, and, I hope, profited by, valuable suggestions from many strong and able churchmen. One, made by my long-time friend and parishioner the Reverend Dr. Samuel McCrea Cavert, was that the material be selective, that only the best suggestions be included. I have been aware of his counsel, and hope that those who turn to the following pages will find a sensitiveness to the criterion of "good discrimination."

A volume such as this does not come to fruition without the co-operation and assistance of many churches. Sometimes I have used precisely a form that has been found helpful in a particular parish. In other instances, it has been reproduced in modified form to be of more interest and help to a wider variety of congregations. In each instance I have refrained from giving specific acknowledgment to the particular parish that provided the original material. The reader will note that, in the vast majority of instances, any church mentioned is simply called "Christ Church." The use of anonymity, I have been led to believe, would better support the over-all purposes of the volume.

Each church that has contributed to the vast amount of material and suggestions, which I have read with care and profit, is hereby accorded my sincere appreciation. In each instance where I have reproduced material from a specific church I believe I have received authorization to use such materials. Where this may not be so, the oversight is unintentional.

Among the large number of churches that have been particularly helpful are the following: Hollywood First Presbyterian Church, Hollywood, Calif.; Immanuel Presbyterian Church, Los Angeles, Calif.; Westminster Presbyterian Church, Pasadena, Calif.; First Presbyterian Church and Point Loma Presbyterian Church, San Diego, Calif.; Community Presbyterian Church, San Marino, Calif.; First Presbyterian Church, Santa Monica, Calif.; The National Presbyterian Church and New York Avenue Presbyterian Church, Washington, D. C.; Christ Methodist Church, St. Petersburg, Fla.; The Presbyterian Church, Arlington Heights, Ill.; First Presbyterian

Church, Springfield, Ill.; Northminster Presbyterian Church, Indianapolis, Ind.; First Presbyterian Church, Wichita, Kans.; First Presbyterian Church, Birmingham, Mich.; Redford Avenue Presbyterian Church and Westminster Presbyterian Church, Detroit, Mich.; Drayton Avenue Presbyterian Church, Ferndale, Mich.; Webster Groves Presbyterian Church, Webster Groves, Mo.; First Presbyterian Church, Haddonfield, N.J.; First Presbyterian Church, New Brunswick, N.J.; Central Presbyterian Church, Summit, N.J.; The Presbyterian Church of Tenafly, Tenafly, N.J.; First Presbyterian Church, Albuquerque, N.M.; First Presbyterian Church of Albany, Albany, N.Y.; Larchmont Avenue Presbyterian Church, Larchmont, N.Y.; Fifth Avenue Presbyterian Church, Madison Avenue Presbyterian Church, Marble Collegiate Church, and Riverside Church, New York, N.Y., Greenville Community Church and Hitchcock Memorial Church, Scarsdale, N.Y.; First Presbyterian Church and Park Central Church, Syracuse, N.Y., First Presbyterian Church, Utica, N.Y., The Church of the Covenant, Fairmount Presbyterian Church, and Parma South Presbyterian Church, Cleveland, Ohio; Lakewood Presbyterian Church, Lakewood, Ohio; East Liberty Presbyterian Church, First Presbyterian Church, and Shadyside Presbyterian Church, Pittsburgh, Pa.; Highland Park Presbyterian Church, Dallas, Texas; University Presbyterian Church, Seattle, Wash.

To the clergy of these congregations and to the many laymen who had a part in developing the fine administration of their parishes I express a deep appreciation.

The Rev. Dr. Paul Austin Wolfe, of the Brick Presbyterian Church in New York, made cogent and specific suggestions. His outstanding administrative skill was, and continues to be, a source of inspiration.

To my fellow members in the Theological Club of Sigma Chi in New York I express appreciation for their comments on an early section of the book. Particularly, my indebtedness must be expressed to the late Rev. Dr. G. Paull T. Sargent, former rector of Saint Bartholomew's Church, New York, and to the Rev. Dr. Lynn Harold Hough, dean emeritus of Drew Theological Seminary. These two members of the circle of Sigma Chi were most gracious in particular counsel and most helpful in the guiding encouragement of their friendship.

Dr. Edwin O. Kennedy, vice president of Union Theological Seminary, New York; the Rev. Dr. L. Wilson Kilgore, of Lakewood, Ohio; the Rev. Dr. George R. Sweet, of Detroit; the Rev. Dr. Harold Paul Sloan, Jr., of Pleasant Ridge, Michigan; and the Rev. Dr. Ray H. Kiely, of Utica, New York, deserve special acknowledgment for the particular time and effort and kindly enthusiasm they have shown toward this whole venture.

This book would never have come to completion without the magnificent group of men that make up the Consistory of the Reformed Church of Bronxville and without the devoted, loyal staff that have such a vital part in carrying on the best in our parish life.

The Rev. Dr. E. Graham Wilson and the Rev. Lee Llewellyn Kester, Jr., associated in the ministry of the Bronxville church, have offered many practical suggestions from the first outline made for this book. Their interest, together with that of our distinguished organist and choirmaster William R. Davis, has been a constant source of support. To them and to the following participants in the work of this parish I express my loving thanks: Richard V. Jones, Director of Christian Education; Miss Karen Beghtol, Assistant to the Director of Music; Mrs. Jean McV. Dupuy, Membership Secretary; Mrs. Russell McCandless, Administrative Assistant; Roy M. Westberg, Financial Secretary; Mrs. Stuart B. Rowe, Director, Nursery School; and Mrs. A. Tomlin Goodman, Jr., Assistant Director, Nursery School; to secretaries Mrs. M. Packard Hubbard, Mrs. Eric Jensen, Mrs. Violet Nahabedian, Mrs. Orden C. Oechsli, Miss Patricia M. Stauffer, Miss Marie L. Tilton, and Mrs. Alfred J. Wahner; to Harry H. Biggs, Superintendent of Buildings; Mrs. Ruth Marshall, Housekeeper; to sextons Samuel Kolesar, Andrew Marcinek, and John Fecsko. Mrs. Orden C. Oechsli has gone the second mile and beyond in her careful transcription and typing of the manuscript.

To these, together with my wife and children and others—of whom, with Paul, I can say, "time would fail me" if I mentioned all—whatever may be of merit in the *Handbook of Church Administration* is most likely due.

LOWELL RUSSELL DITZEN

The Minister's Study
The Reformed Protestant Dutch Church of Bronxville, New York
January 1, 1962

# Contents

# Contents

# HANDBOOK
## OF
# CHURCH
# ADMINISTRATION

# SECTION I

# *Organization of the Parish*

## THE PLACE OF CHURCH ADMINISTRATION

Church administration is a phase of a minister's responsibility for which many clergymen are unprepared. The competence they attain is often on the painful path of trial and error. Rightly, our seminaries give major attention to preparing the clergyman as a preacher and a prophet, as a teacher and religious educator, a psychologist and a counselor. But in terms of the amount of time that the Protestant clergyman must expend in administering the affairs of the church to which he is called, he is without adequate textbook, counselor, or guide.

Of course, the primary business of the church is spiritual. It is the body of Christ. It is commissioned to administer the grace of God by word and the sacraments. But sound theology also affirms that the will of God may be done in any and every area. Brother Lawrence, who performs the scullery duties, shows that the lowliest and most practical task may be done as "unto the Lord," and clothed with glory and dignity. In like manner, efficient administration of the church can undergird its spiritual purpose.

The truth is that administration is an inescapable necessity. Many Protestant congregations have acquired substantial buildings. They own expensive land. Some churches have endowments. The program of many churches has expanded to include weekday education and activities of worship, service, fellowship, and study for persons of all age groups.

The material support of the church becomes important. Without it the wide and varied programs cannot be sustained. To handle

1

the contributions that loyal people subscribe calls for responsible stewardship and careful planning.

Some of us pray as the offering is received: "O God, of whose bounty we have all received, accept this offering of Thy people; and so follow it with Thy blessing that it may promote peace and good will among men, and advance the Kingdom of our Lord and Saviour Jesus Christ. Amen." But that lovely prayer is unfulfilled and God's Kingdom of peace and good will is not advanced unless there is proper and efficient administration by His servants in the use of those gifts.

Indeed, it can be stressed, the oversight of a modern church that is sensitive to the needs of its people and tries to meet them requires competent administration and an able administrator.

The word "administration" comes from the Latin *administrare,* which means "to serve." There is a relationship between the word "minister" and "administrator." The word itself implies that the management and administration of the affairs of the church, the direction and superintendence of its program, the execution of its policies and its principles, though they deal with material matters, provide opportunities for furthering the church's spiritual vitality. And in this role, as in that of prophet or priest, the minister can serve both God and man.

In considering the matter of the organization of the parish, three points should receive careful attention. These are (1) the democratic-representative idea, (2) the ideal of each parishioner's having a part and a place in the ongoing life of the church, and (3) the principle that the clergyman must be the administrative leader.

## THE DEMOCRATIC REPRESENTATIVE IDEA

There are many forms of church policy. Comparable to the patterns in civil government, they range from austere totalitarianism to a free democracy. Within the orbit of the historic Protestant denominations the balancing of the scales comes close to a democratic-representative idea in church administration. The clergy and the laity share in the responsibility for the care and management of the affairs of the church. These leaders, coming from the membership, are ever conscious of informing their fellow members of policies and programs. This great principle needs to be conserved and continuously applied in our church life.

Some churches in the Calvinistic tradition, through carelessness, have permitted the church to be administered either solely by the clergymen or solely by the laity. In one instance, a church now closed was administered by the clergyman who was treasurer and clerk of the session as well as the prophet-teacher of the congregation. In another instance, through lack of proper correction by the Presbytery a church was dominated by one elder who enforced his limitations on the entire congregation. Whether it be within the Anglican-Episcopal-Methodist, Calvinistic, or Lutheran traditions, or among the still freer churches of the Baptist or Congregational polity, the principle of having a series of checks and balances between the clergy and the laity is, in the long run, the most satisfactory.

Democracy has its shortcomings. But if, as churchmen, we share the conviction of Jefferson, who tried to organize our civil life on a basis that provided channels for the expressions of the people's will, coupled with competent leadership, the likelihood of effective administration is greater than if our churches are governed by individuals who rule with the ponderous hand of perpetuity.

The democratic-representative principle provides a channel for the fulfillment of a very important aspect of successful administration. It is rooted in the life of the congregation. It provides a two-way street: it receives the impressions, judgments, and ideas from the people of the parish and at the same time gives the congregation a sense of relationship to the total administration or service of the church. Regardless of its specific ecclesiastical form, a church will have warmth and strength if it maintains the democratic-representative spirit.

## THE PARISH IDEAL—EACH MEMBER PARTICIPATING

A second principle of successful administration is the ideal that every member participate in the life of the church. Dr. Harry Emerson Fosdick recounts overhearing, on Morningside Heights in New York, a little girl saying to her mother, "That man goes to *my* church." Such an attitude is the ideal for our Protestant churches. My Roman Catholic friends appreciate more than any other aspect of Protestantism the fact that we have, as one priest put it, "A greater missionary spirit." One of Protestantism's strengths grows out of the Reformation ideal that "Every man is a priest."

The sense of individual responsibility—for the conduct of his life, for the oversight of the spiritual tone of his household, for implementing Christian principles in his business, and then particularly being a "participating" member in his church—is one of the most provocative and powerful ideas in modern Western history. Cultivated in our churches, it makes them vibrant and strong.

Participation in church life often begins with the recognition of a child's birth. It continues with the reception of a person into the life and program of the church. That ceremony should be one of significance and dignity. The person should be made acquainted with the history of the parish—its organization, its aims, and its program. Personal acquaintanceship with the clergymen and with the staff is important. The person should be introduced to suitable age, service, and fellowship groups within the church and should be challenged to engage in some form of Christian service. He should have an opportunity and a challenge to give of his substance as well as of his time.

One minister, at the reception of new members, says, among other things:

This is *your* church. It will be no stronger in its devotional life than your spiritual expectancy and growth. Its service to the community will be no greater than your sense of service. Its helpful outreach to strangers, to those in need, will be no greater than your tenderness and your responsiveness. Its exaltation of Christ will be no greater than the degree to which you let Christ be manifest in your life.

Another clergyman has been very successful in making his parishioners feel their relationship to the life of the church by sending them with their certificate of church membership a warm personal letter. Within a few weeks he calls on them, and an officer of the church also makes a personal call. After a year the clergyman writes them an anniversary note reminding them of the great principle that every man is a priest and that "they" are the church about whom the outsiders and skeptics would say: "Let me see your Redeemer; let me look at your redeemed."

Many churches inform the entire congregation of personal events in the lives of their members by publishing a parish register or through church publications. One clergyman attests that over the years he has kept many people in close touch with the church by mailing clippings to each church member featured in the local newspaper. With the clipping he sends a note saying that the entire membership of the church is gratified at the particular service or achievement noted in the news. He expresses his personal felicitation and adds that his prayers are with him.

These and many other methods to be discussed later may be used to make a person feel that the church is "his" church. It knows him. He knows it. And he grows spiritually as he participates in its life.

## THE MINISTER AS LEADER

The third point that is fundamental in sound administration is the principle that one person must be the responsible leader. That person must be the clergyman. The strength or weakness of parish organization depends upon whether the minister prayerfully and effectively assumes the inescapable role of administrator.

### "He That Is Greatest"

Building on the broad base of the democratic-representative idea, and then establishing the parish on the idea of each member's participation, one comes to the fine pyramid-apex of administration in the capstone of the clergyman, who must be the "servant in the role of administrator." With humility, docility, and a kindly interest in each parishioner and his service in the church, the minister needs to be familiar with all aspects of the church life. No detail of the care of the fabric of the church, no aspect of the financial life, and no phase of the church program will be outside his concern.

I remember calling on a minister of one of the great churches in the Midwest to seek his counsel on study techniques to develop the mental and spiritual edge. I may have reflected an unhappy attitude toward the administration details laying claim to my time. My counselor responded by saying, "I have devoted the last hour and a half to discussing with the chairman of our Maintenance and Operations Committee and a stonemason the width of a new walk from the cloister to the educational building." He went on to say that it had been his experience over the years that the minister must reconcile himself to the position that all aspects of the church life are part of the building of the Kingdom. He must develop the ability to treat insignificant things quickly but must not be casual about details.

What power there is in humility! The greatest executives have an "open door" to hear the counsel of their associates. And they listen! The president of a large corporation told me: "I go no further with an idea or venture if I can't get response from a group of trusted associates. I've learned to value, and usually act by, their judgments." A minister should do the same. Rather than feel hurt, the minister should appreciate it if sincere and devoted church members question a project. The minister listens and learns. This does not mean that he is to be a puppet. On occasion, in spite of question and objection, he may stand firm for some cause or project. The good leader leads out of strength. One of the greatest facets of that strength is his attentiveness, receptivity, freedom from pride and pique—his humble spirit.

### Vision

A good administrator must have vision. The various long-range plans developed by growing and vital nations like Russia and Red China illustrate the direction and drive that are released when standards are raised and goals are set. I was recently much impressed by the verve, unity of purpose, and enthusiasm aroused in the people of India by the vision of its leaders under Nehru.

I have felt and observed the same kind of positive ferment in congregations where the minister has infused his people with a vision of what they could and should aim to do. The source of one church's strength lies in the annual planning conference of its church boards and organizational officers. Under the chairmanship and inspiration of the minister, aims for the next year are formulated. Goals for a longer period are presented, discussed, and agreed upon. The complete record of the aims becomes the "marching orders" for each group and society. A year later, progress is tabulated and new sights are set.

A stronger religious education program, a more universal prayer life among individuals in the homes of the parish, increasing the outreach of the local church to the nonchurched or in larger missionary service, the paying-off of a church mortgage, or the completion of some building project within a certain period of time—such visions surrounding the people give life. Without the dream, the goal, and the vision there truly is a perishing.

The minister should prove his administrative effectiveness in this area by constantly bringing before his consistory, vestry, session, or governing body, ideas and ways and means to improve, expand, or raise the level and vitality of the church's life. He is the one that should be closest to the total operation and tone of the church. So, logically, he is the artist to paint the vision and inspire the congregation to find a glad, sure way in the composition.

### Thoroughness

Though humility and vision may be the primary attributes of the effective clergy administrator, there must also be *thoroughness*. Vision can come to naught without the persistence and meticulous step-by-step planning and working toward the attainment of that distant goal, whatever it may be. Thoroughness can be a most important means of building security and rapport between church people and their leader. Ministers sometimes reduce their spiritual effectiveness simply by inattention to correspondence. Neglecting to write a note of appreciation may cause ill feelings and doubts that minimize a person's respect for the minister as his spiritual leader.

Promises must be kept. The minister promises: "I will see that you have that material by the day after tomorrow." If the material has not arrived within a week, a parishioner's confidence in his clergyman is weakened.

A clergyman in a large eastern city had one of the most effective ministries in a century in that area. He was not forensically gifted, his scholarly abilities were limited, and his physical appearance was far from prepossessing, yet he had a great influence over countless lives. A student of his character as well as an old friend attributed his success to "a boundless moral obligation to be thorough and meticulous." He added that the minister lived by the principle "Do it now." No word of inquiry or note went without an immediate and a careful response. Persons whose hearts had been seared by sorrow were remembered on the anniversary of their sorrow. No special service was rendered or contribution made to the church that did not receive a word of appreciation. The minister put the spirit of the golden rule into the daily, hourly, momentary working clothes of meticulous attentiveness to the needs, the feelings, the requests, the concerns of his people. The parishioners felt his love as well as his ethical stature in innumerable acts of thoughtfulness, courtesy, and loving attention. Such unfailing response to their needs and actions brought them much closer to the Lord that he loved and served.

### The Organization of Time and Oneself

To become more and more thorough in his administration, the minister must continually evaluate what needs to be done and then organize his time and effort to accomplish it.

Emmet Fox gave practical spiritual advice when he suggested that immediately before going to sleep one outline in his mind the plan for the next day. This has tremendous value. One awakes in the morning with a sense of direction. Many ministers may say, "But my best-laid plan comes to naught because of the innumerable interruptions of the day." In response it can be said that if there is a definitely planned time for personal devotion, study, conferences, visitation, and so on, the interruptions will be managed with greater finesse.

Every minister could profit by doing annually as one effective clergyman does. During each summer vacation he reevaluates the use of his time by the year, the season, the week and the day.

I found in my own church that the clergy were led to a more effective organization and use of their time by keeping a daily record for three weeks, hour by hour, of how their time was spent. In evaluating how each day went they became aware of time needlessly wasted and conscious that devoting time to secondary matters often prevented giving attention to primary ones.

E. Graham Wilson tells of a minister of a generation ago who was visited by one of his church officers. A friend from the West Coast who had greatly admired the minister accompanied him. A note was sent to the clergyman's study asking if he would meet and chat with the admirer from far away. The reply was, "Sorry, but I permit no interruptions when engaged in study and sermon preparation."

E. Graham Wilson also recalls making a cross-country trip on the same train as a leading church statesman. On boarding the train in New York he asked the distinguished clergyman if he might discuss a personal matter with him. Three days later he received word that fifteen minutes could be given to the conference. Out of such discipline, organization of time and protection of it have come the great ministries of Charles E. Jefferson and Robert E. Speer.

There can be no universal blueprint for budgeting and organization of a minister's time for sermon preparation, calling, counseling, denominational responsibilities, marital conferences, administrative duties, and so on. Each minister in the church of Christ has a responsibility, both to God and to the people he serves, to evaluate his primary abilities and emphases and then plan how he can best fulfill his potential. It is vital that he adhere to that plan and interrupt his routine only in an emergency or when a better program or plan presents itself.

In the organization of his time and work the minister should give attention to personal and family affairs. The guiding principle to let all things be done "decently and in order" begins with the minister's home and family. The minister's wife should have a share in planning the economics of family life. One clergyman advised couples on the threshold of marriage as to their spiritual life, their sexual relations, and the importance of keeping their financial affairs in good order. He recommended having a budget and suggested various items, but he never heeded his own counsel. Bills were not paid. His wife never had the security that was her due in sharing in the affairs of the family. Tension and embarrassment crowded out peace and confidence because the minister's administration didn't begin at home.

Because most clergymen have limited incomes, it is doubly advisable that husband and wife share lovingly and intelligently in a plan to make their resources go as far as possible. Their children, the work to which they are dedicated, and their own well-being when the active period of their lives is past are all dependent upon such resourceful planning. In organizing his program time the minister should never neglect his role as husband and father. In his home and with his family he should provide the same attentive leadership that he is called upon to give as leader of the flock.

**Personal Library and Files**

The minister needs an organized workshop. Because of the constant limitations of time, efficiency in the arrangement of equipment, the proper filing of necessary materials, and organization of his library pay needed dividends. Depending on the size of the library and on the time and skill available, there are infinite ways to keep one's volumes so arranged that they may easily be found. There may be a waste of time and frustration if the minister's library is in such a state that he doesn't know where to find the book he needs.

One minister is fortunate in having a wife who is a trained librarian. His books are properly numbered according to the Library of Congress system and catalogued with various cross references in a file that is kept at his desk. Many ministers have placed their books in categories, such as commentaries on books of the Bible, dividing between the Old and the New Testament. A separate section is devoted to church history. Other sections house psychology and philosophy, sociology, the spiritual life, hymnology, sermons, general reference books, such as encyclopedias, and with separate categories for church reports, journals, statistics, and so on. The important thing is to devise a practical method that will make books accessible and thus expedite finding what is wanted.

One minister friend showed me a file he keeps up to date as each new book is added to his library. Using 3-by-5 cards he makes an individual listing and a card for each topic in the book. For example, if there is a section on "Hate" he makes a card for that heading. Then he adds the author, title, publisher, date of the volume, with page numbers where the specific material can be found. The cards are filed alphabetically. Thus material on any particular subject is quickly available.

"Neither a borrower nor a lender be," if not followed inflexibly, should provide the words "caution and care" in both lending or borrowing volumes from personal libraries.

For the enriching of sermons, the keeping of quotations under identifying headings is most helpful. One competent and adept sermonizer keeps two sets of files. One contains 4-x-5-inch cards on which he has entered, over the years, the results of his readings under subject matter. In the upper left-hand corner is listed the subject of the material quoted. Following the quotation there is a full summary of the source, the author's full name, the subject of the book or article, the name of periodical or publisher, the place and date of publication, and the page number. This information is valuable for future reference.

The second file is made up of standard 9-x-11-inch manila folders in which, according to subject matter, are filed clippings, magazine articles, ideas, and so on. This material provides a valuable source for spurring imagination as one comes to particular seasons of the year or faces a sermon or an address on a specific topic.

R. Ames Montgomery, professor of homiletics at McCormick Theological Seminary in Chicago for several years, urged his students to have a "homiletical bias." The idea was to make all one's reading, experience, conversation like grain, which is sifted and then ground in the mill of sermon preparation. This sensitiveness comes to good fruition, for example, if the minister saves a playbill on which he jotted down an idea as he watched a drama. Keep the inspiration from reading a subway card or a thought suggested from random reading.

Stimulations of the mind that come in strange places and at odd times are precious materials. The minister should put all such material in a "Sermon Idea File." Going through the file from time to time is in itself a means of stimulating the imagination and enabling one to gain ideas for future sermons.

The minister should have accessible a working file in connection with the administration of the church. In his desk or near it should be such active files as the following: Religious Education, Governing Body of the Church, Executive Committee, Unfinished Business, Confidential Cases, Individuals to Follow Up, Staff, and so on. If correspondence cannot be handled on a daily basis, there should be an active file of letters requiring the earliest possible attention.

Some ministers keep a record of the sermons they have preached. Information may be arranged in a card file according to subject matter with the key word to the topic in the upper left-hand corner of the card, and below it the title of the sermon, the text, and the date preached. All past sermons should be kept in a chronological file accessible for future reference.

The minister's date book must, of necessity, be his constant taskmaster. It is important that his appointments be arranged so that they may be kept without tension or haste and so that there will be adequate provision for emergencies and for the necessary restoration of physical and emotional energy. Some ministers find a desk calendar invaluable. I have found a pocket-sized date book much more convenient. It enables me, no matter where I am, to look at my schedule and determine when an appointment can be made. Sometimes the minister cannot be reached directly. In such cases, if he has a church office, the church secretary should be informed of the minister's program, so that with a minimum of effort and additional telephoning, appointments can be made for him.

Some clergymen find it helpful to keep close at hand records of weekly attendance and offering at the church services. But each person must arrange his records and calendars and programs to meet the demands and requirements of his own parish. A good principle to follow is to make records and files efficient tools to serve the larger purposes of the ministry. They are not ends in, themselves. If they present a burden of time and effort without a commensurate contribution to the prime aim of the ministry, thought should well be given to discarding or simplifying the system.

## THE GOVERNING BODY

As we consider the wide ramifications of a strong church organization, we must stress the point that the motivating spirit and principle are: "Let whatever is done or planned be done and planned in the spirit of love." If that aura surrounds the clergyman's outlook and action, his ministry will rarely be amiss and there will be a minimum of faulty judgments and actions. This applies as we look at the primary governing body of the church, the session, the consistory, church council, or whatever name it may bear.

This quality radiates from all the facets of Leslie D. Weatherhead's ministry at City Temple, London. His great church has varied activities and emphases with a wide range of administrative problems. The magnificent old edifice was destroyed in World War II, and a new, beautiful church has replaced it. But, in the spirit of the Master, in all Dr. Weatherhead's relationships to his officers and his people, with the programs and plans of the parish, there has been the spirit of a humble, tender, sensitive lovingness. It has made for power, for the development and enrichment of those ties that bind men to one another and to their Maker at the highest level.

### The Selection of Church Officers

This spirit of love should permeate the congregation and the officers as they face the task of selecting, then electing, lay members to share in the over-all leadership of the church.

As a matter of routine a nominating committee should be appointed at the beginning of every church year. The chairman of the committee should be a person who has been associated with the governing body, preferably having had a background of service in that body. The other appointees on the committee should represent the congregation at large, to form a committee of about seven members. The committee may consist of a senior elder as chairman, two elders and two deacons, and two members representing the congregation at large.

The names of the committee members should be publicized in the parish. During the ensuing months all members of the parish should have an opportunity to make suggestions as to worthy church officers. One church places for a Sunday or two in the church pew racks a mimeographed form that reads:

```
┌─────────────────────────────────────────────────────────────┐
│                     CHRIST CHURCH                             │
│              NOMINATIONS FOR CHURCH OFFICERS                  │
│                                              Check One        │
│   Name _____      Elder _____    │
│   Address_____      Deacon _____    │
│   Qualifications: _____      Trustee _____   │
└─────────────────────────────────────────────────────────────┘
```

It can be very helpful to a parish to set standard requirements for church officers. One church makes known to the parish the following duties of an elder:

1. To be himself a spiritual man.
2. To attend church and board meetings regularly.
3. To assist in serving Holy Communion and at the Sacrament of Baptism when requested.
4. To fulfill his committee responsibilities.
5. In our parish zone and district plan, 23 elders are responsible for parish zones, and in this connection guide the work of deacons in their zone.
6. The elder calls in the homes of his zone:
   a. When there is a death, to express sympathy and to offer the help and support of the church.
   b. To deliver baptismal certificates after infant baptism.
   c. To deliver membership certificates when new members join the church, and to become acquainted with the new family in our church. He should be alert to ways of integrating the family into the life of our fellowship and should so notify the church office.
   d. When help is needed in the every member canvass visitation.
7. The elder must at all times be alert to opportunities for fellowship and friendliness. In this connection he will be assigned special duties from time to time—during the Coffee Hour and at the door to greet people on Sundays.
8. The elders, both individually and as the board, encourage, support, and counsel the minister, the associate ministers, the director of Christian Education, and staff members of Christ Church.

Throughout the church year the nominating committee will be receiving from the membership and the governing body suggestions for replacements on the official board or boards. Either through its chairman or through an appointed representative, the committee should obtain full information regarding the persons under consideration, including: (1) full name and address; (2) date of joining the church; (3) record of church loyalty, offices held, church attendance; (4) business, business address, telephone number; (5) standing in the community; (6) contributions or leadership of a cultural or educational nature to the community or nation; (7) spiritual dedication and sensitiveness; (8) facts regarding the candidate's family and their individual relationship to the church.

When the committee meets, the above information and any additional information helpful to the parish should be presented. The committee should understand that all discussions are to be conducted freely and openly but are to be held in strictest confidence by the committee members.

The committee must function impersonally. In selecting its members the minister or whoever is responsible for appointing them must keep this in mind. To spare the members personal embarrassment, the committee should consist of members who have no personal attachment or family relationship to potential candidates. Free from personal bias, the committee will function prayerfully and thoroughly to select the men most competent for the leadership of the church.

The clergyman should sit with the committee as an ex officio member, giving his counsel and judgment. An effective nominating committee may well ask, at its first meeting, for a statement from the minister as to the present composition of the official board and what, in his judgment and experience, are the primary needs of the board with respect to the work of the church. There may be, for example, an acute need for a church officer with a particular skill or training, and this may be significant in considering a candidate. The minister and chairman should review for the committee the standards of the church regarding church officers. Further, the committee should be reminded that the governing body should be representative of the entire parish. Thus the age of a candidate, the location of his residence, or the type of business or profession in which he is engaged may enter into the committee's considerations.

A strong and vital board of a Protestant church should consist of persons of sound judgment, dedicated spirit, openness of mind, aggressiveness of attitude, and with a keen sense of responsibility for building the Kingdom of God.

### Method of Election

The method of election will vary with individual churches. Whatever the method, the election should be conducted with dignity so as to convey to the congregation and to the individual elected its great significance. It is often advisable, after agreement on a nominee has been reached, that the minister and chairman of the nominating committee call on the nominee and personally present the matter of an officership in the church. In such a conference the needs of the church and the opportunities for service can be presented meaningfully. If the nominee then indicates his willingness to be a candidate for an office, the minister may appropriately offer a prayer of gratitude and dedication.

The ordination and installation of the officers should be a highly spiritual experience, planned with meticulous care and conducted with extreme solemnity. Some churches inform their congregation of the background and experience of the newly elected officers. An informal church gathering and reception may be held in their honor and often serves to hallow the ties between the officers and the people.

## Education of Church Officers

Many Protestant denominations have issued effective handbooks giving the historical background and outlining the functions of the officers in the church. A gift copy sent or presented to a new officer with a note or verbal explanation by the minister is always appreciated. New officers should be oriented as quickly as possible so that their work on the governing board may be most effective. If the church has a constitution and local by-laws, they should be promptly placed in the hands of each new member of the board.

One minister has developed what he calls an "orientation program." Each new elder or deacon is brought into direct contact with every aspect and activity of the church. Thus, he visits the church school department, the young people's society, the women's association, the young people engaged in an athletic program, and so on.

To orient and integrate new men properly into their responsibilities, as well as to point up and direct the work of the board, many churches find an annual retreat for church officers highly desirable. On these occasions the needs of the church for the coming year considered, specific reviews of the various committees are held, and the entire group is dedicated in appropriate ceremonies to the work of the Lord in that parish for the coming months.

One or two veteran members of the official board may well convey to new board members that, beyond their specific ecclesiastical duties and responsibilities, the spiritual call to uphold the minister is of prime significance. Friction in a church board may arise if some officers make it their first responsibility to be the self-appointed critics of the minister. So often the minister's role forces him to stand alone. Psychically, emotionally and spiritually he needs the strong, manly support and the friendship of his fellow officers. A very able church administrator made the following request: "Please emphasize: Let our lay officers carry the ball, particularly on unpopular causes. (Too many ministers try to be Jeremiah, going it alone! They suffer from martyr complexes in many cases—and usually get their reward!)"

Bringing the new officers' wives into the picture may be helpful in promoting their understanding and cooperation. An informal evening get-together of the officers and their wives may not only improve fellowship and deepen acquaintanceship among church families but also help inform the ladies of their husbands' work in the church.

The role of church officers in supporting the minister may be increased and effectively demonstrated to the congregation, if an officer serve with the minister in welcoming the congregation at Sabbath service. In one church an elder and a deacon and their wives greet worshipers as they enter the sanctuary for the Sunday service. In the Sunday calendar mention is made of the visitors' table for both church members and strangers. At that table each Sunday there is an officer of the church together with his wife.

When a program such as this is established, with an officer standing with the minister after the church service to greet people and to assist the minister in taking notes on questions raised with the minister, the spirit of concord and togetherness develops among church officers and among the officers and the congregation. And the officers become familiar with the people in the church community.

One of the wisest clergymen of our time has said that he feels that one of the most hopeful signs of Protestantism is the greater participation of lay officers in the work of the church. At the same time he commented that the "entrenchment of the laity" in the leadership of the church also constituted a grave problem. He advised a rotation plan for church governing bodies that has become increasingly widespread and is constructive in vitalizing Protestant churches. The length of the terms of church officers should be considered very carefully. Certain principles should guide the thinking of the local church. The principle of broad education in the life of the church and participation in it will prompt many congregations to establish limited terms of service for their church officers. In this connection, when the names of the official boards are publicized, the dates of their terms of service should also be stated.

One of the most effective ways of educating the church officers, having them understand the parish, and having them vitally related to the individual members is known as the "zone plan." The purpose of the plan is to assist the minister in his pastoral responsibility by assigning a church officer to a specified section of the parish. Some years ago Dr. White Anderson stated that as the parish of St. Cuthbert's Church in Edinburgh increased, the number of elders increased. An elder was assigned to a specified section of the parish and a certain number of families. It was his duty to visit the home of each parishioner prior to Communion and to leave a communion token. Over a period of time he became known as a special spiritual friend and adviser. Through him, particular situations, with individuals and families, were taken care of and special cases were brought immediately to the attention of the pastor.

American churches are finding such a plan and procedure highly meaningful. For example, one denomination outlines this plan, suggesting that the zone leader should serve "as a shepherd" and "as an Evangelist." An effective leaflet outlines the responsibilities as follows:

1. As shepherds
   a. They should visit with each family in their homes often enough to maintain a close friendship. They may have a particular purpose for regularly scheduled calls in the course of the year. They may visit to distribute communion cards, to distribute helps for family or private devotions or to explain about an important project of the church. They should inquire how well the church is serving each member of the family and learn about any problems or any need for help in the home. They should also be on the lookout for talent that the church might be able to use.
   b. They will learn news about their people, such as illness, death, promotion, birth, anniversaries, moves, and so forth. They will give attention to these events and forward word to the pastor.
   c. They will offer help. They may arrange transportation to the church for children or for elderly people, may be called upon to secure blood donors, may aid the distressed, and visit the sick and the shut-ins, and so forth.
2. As evangelists
   a. They are on the lookout for potential Christians in their zones. They

should be concerned about all the unchurched families in their area. These are their responsibility. They should seek out information about those who move into their zones and invite to zone meetings new friends and new neighbors. They should keep the pastor posted on names of those who might be won to Christ. They will always be on the lookout to enlist children in church school.

b. They extend a welcome to new members who unite with the church and live within their district. They seek to help to get them started in the active life of the church. They continually express friendship and interest in the lives of those who are new.

c. They are always alert for signs of decreasing interest. They consider it their responsibility to keep all the families in their district active in the program of the church. They avoid too close a checkup, which might be resented, but are always conscious of the need for fuller participation in the life of the church on the part of all within their district.

3. As representatives

There is a very real sense in which ordained leaders serving as zone leaders are the representatives of the congregation. They are this already by virtue of their election and ordination. However, the close personal contact with members through zone activities encourages them to represent more adequately the church members in anticipating the church's program and in making known the needs and desires of the members at board meetings.

One church, in setting up such a program among its officers, recommends the following five points:

1. Try to get acquainted with all the other members in your zone.
2. Give special attention to the aged and shut-ins.
3. Provide transportation for those who need it.
4. Notify the pastors of any illness, trouble, or sorrow in your zone.
5. Be on the lookout for newcomers in your area. Visit them, invite them to church and tell the church office about them.

## By-Laws

The governing board shall be guided in its meetings and procedure by the constitution of its perfect body. However, where denominational leeway is provided, and where particular parish needs suggest it, many churches have adopted a set of by-laws for the functioning of the board, or boards, of their congregation. The following example will serve as a guide.

BY-LAWS OF THE CORPORATION
"THE TRUSTEES OF CHRIST CHURCH"
ADOPTED BY THE BOARD OF TRUSTEES

### Article I

CORPORATION MEETING

1. *The annual meeting* of the corporation shall be held in the church on a day during the week preceding the last Sunday in January of each year; the exact day and hour to be fixed by the Board of Trustees in each year, or at such adjourned date as those then present may determine.
2. *Special meetings* of the corporation may be called by the Trustees on their own motion, *and must be called on the written request of at least ten qualified voters of the church.*
3. *Notices.* The Trustees shall cause notices of the time and place of special meetings of the corporation to be publicly read by the minister of the church at regular meetings of the church for public worship on the two successive Sundays immediately preceding such meeting. Notices of special meetings shall state the business to be transacted thereat. Notices of annual meetings for the election of Trustees shall contain the names of the Trustees whose successors are to be elected.
4. *Qualification of voters.* Only the following persons according to New York State law may vote: "All persons of full age who are then members in good and regular standing of such church by admission into full communion and membership therewith, in accordance with the rules and regulations thereof, and of the governing ecclesiastical body of the denomination to which the church belongs, or who have been stated attendants on divine worship in such church and have regularly contributed to the financial support thereof during the year next preceding such meeting." Notice of the qualifications of voters must be given at the meeting by the presiding officer.
5. *A quorum* shall consist of at least five per cent of the resident membership of the church qualified to vote.
6. *The President* of the Board of Trustees or the Moderator of the Session shall act as chairman of each meeting. The chairman shall receive the votes, be the judge of the qualifications of the voters, and declare the result of the votes cast.
7. *The Clerk* of the board shall be the secretary of each meeting.
8. *The order of business* at the annual meeting shall be:
   (1) Proof of notice of meeting
   (2) Reading and disposal of unapproved minutes
   (3) Annual reports
   (4) Election of Trustees
   (5) Any other business

## Article II

### TRUSTEES

1. *Number.* Fifteen Trustees shall constitute the board. Five Trustees shall be elected annually by the corporation for three-year terms. A Trustee shall not succeed himself after serving one full elected term. After a period of at least one year from the end of his last tenure of office he may be again elected to the board.
2. *Duties and powers.* The Trustees shall have the custody and control of all property, both real and personal, belonging to the corporation and of the revenues therefrom and shall administer the same in accordance with the discipline, rules, usages, and laws of the denomination and of the State of New York. They shall be responsible for preparing and raising the annual budget. The Trustees shall have no power, without the consent of a corporate meeting, to incur debts beyond what is necessary for the care of the property of the church. The Trustees shall have such other powers and duties as may be prescribed by law.
3. *Vacancies.* If any Trustee declines to act, resigns, or dies, or ceases to be a qualified voter at a corporate meeting, his office shall be vacant and such vacancy shall be filled by the Board of Trustees for the period expiring at the next annual corporate meeting, when the vacancy shall be filled for the remainder of the unexpired term.
4. *Meetings*
   a. Regular meetings will be held on the first Wednesday in October, December, February, April, and June.
   b. Special meetings may be called at any time by the President or by any two members of the board by giving two days' notice to the other Trustees.
   c. An organization meeting to elect officers and to appoint the various committees shall be held immediately preceding the morning church service on the next Sunday following the annual meeting or at such other date as the board may decide.
   d. Five Trustees shall constitute a quorum.
   e. Notices of all meetings shall be given personally or by mail at least three days before the meeting.

## Article III

### OFFICERS

1. *Officers.* The officers shall be the president, vice president, secretary, and treasurer and such other officers as the board may elect for specifically designated purposes and for a stated period of time. The officers shall be elected for one-year terms with the exception of the treasurer, who may be

elected for a three-year term. The president, vice president, and secretary must be members of the board.

2. *President*. The president shall preside at meetings and shall perform all duties that are ordinarily incident to his office or as may be conferred upon him by the board.

3. *Secretary*. The secretary shall be responsible for issuing notices for all meetings, shall keep the minutes, and perform all other duties that are incident to his office.

4. *Treasurer*. The treasurer shall be the treasurer of the church and, under the direction of the board, shall have custody of all corporate funds, shall ensure that regular books of account are kept, and shall perform all other duties that are incident to his office.

## Article IV
### STANDING COMMITTEES

*The Finance Committee* shall consist of four members appointed annually by the president of the board. The church treasurer shall be a member ex officio of this committee. Unless otherwise directed by the Trustees, it shall perform the following duties:

It shall have *general supervision* of the finances of the church.

It shall *define and keep in operation* a consistent policy for raising church revenues.

It shall have *general supervision of all financial campaigns* within the church.

It shall *review all appeals for special offerings* or special campaigns in order that giving to the annual budget may not be endangered.

Due consideration shall be given to such appeals which have been recommended by the board in order that worthy Christian causes outside the budget may be supported. After study, the committee shall submit its recommendations to the board and the Board of Trustees. It shall with the church manager prepare a provisional budget for current operations, missions, and benevolence in June for the following year in consultation with the various departments of the church and the benevolence committee of the board. This provisional budget will be submitted in September to a joint committee which will be composed as follows:

| | |
|---|---|
| Board of Trustees: | President |
| | Chairman of Finance Committee |
| | Church Treasurer |
| Board: | Two representatives |
| Service Board: | Two representatives |
| Board of Christian Education: | One representative |
| Women's Association: | One representative |
| | The Chairman of the Every Member Canvass |
| | The Minister and Church Manager |

The president of the Board of Trustees will act as chairman of this committee. This committee will consider the provisional budget, and after approval a copy of this budget will be mailed to the congregation at the time of the every-member canvass in October.

After the completion of the every-member canvass, a final budget will be prepared and submitted to the Board of Trustees for approval at the December meeting of that board.

*The Building Committee* shall consist of four members appointed annually by the president of the board. It shall with the church manager supervise the maintenance of the church property and be responsible for the submission of recommendations to the board relating to any major renovation or construction which they may consider necessary.

*The Music Committee* shall consist of three members appointed annually by the president of the board. It will be responsible for the general supervision of the musical program of the church.

*The Personnel Committee* shall consist of two members appointed annually by the president of the board. It will be responsible for matters relating to the employed personnel of the church.

*The Parking Committee* shall be a joint committee with representatives as follows:

*Trustees*—Three representatives appointed annually by the president

*Board*—Two representatives appointed by the board

*Service Board*—Two representatives appointed by the Service Board

It will be responsible for all matters relating to parking facilities.

*The President* of the board will serve as an ex officio member on all of the standing committees.

### Article V

#### THE CHURCH MANAGER

The church manager shall be responsible to the Board of Trustees for the day-to-day administration of the business affairs of the church. He shall have the authority to direct, employ, and discharge all maintenance and secretarial staffs of the church. He must approve all purchases before they are made and all bills before they are paid. He or in his absence his delegated assistant on the office staff will countersign all checks. Any request for goods or services outside of the budget shall be referred by him to the board or the respective committee of the board for consideration.

### Article VI

The seal of the church shall be in the form of a circle and shall bear the inscription "The Trustees of Christ Church."

### Article VII

These By-Laws may be amended at any meeting of the Board of Trustees by a two-thirds (⅔) vote of those present provided a copy of the proposed amendment(s) has been included in the notice of the meeting. Notice of any amendment(s) adopted shall be given to the moderator of the session.

The purpose of the by-laws is to give a clear direction to the governing board and continuity to that direction. It is important that the minister and the clerk or secretary of the board see that the actions of the board are in accordance both with the church constitution and with the by-laws.

### Fixed Place, Date, and Hour for Meeting

The minister and the officials of the board should have a definite place, date, and hour for their meeting. The date should be established by majority action of the officers, and strictly adhered to. Most boards function best when a specific day of the week and month is established for the regular meetings. If it is the second Thursday of each month, for example, a list of the calendar dates for the next twelve months should be mailed to the officers. A note from the chairman or secretary of the board might request the officers to note these dates in their books so that they will be clearly apprised of the meetings for the entire year. The dates of the meetings should be changed only on a majority vote of the officers. The place of the meeting is important. Some churches have board rooms. In one such church, dominating the official board room is a small altar on which is a plain brass cross. A recessed light gives a subtle but distinct added illumination to the cross and the table, which from time to time attract the eye of every officer in the room, thus providing both a direct and an indirect reminder of "why we are here." A meeting place that is special or hallowed adds to the constructive tone of the meeting.

The plainest or most inconspicuous room can be made to contribute to the spirit and efficiency of the meeting by cleanliness and the proper arrangement of chairs. There should be a desk for the secretary or clerk, and for the moderator or presiding officer. It is more desirable to hold meetings of the church board in or on the church premises than in a business office or a private home. The board of devoted Christian leaders is to do God's work. If the planning can be done in the spirit of prayer and within the fabric of God's house, that spiritual end is furthered.

Because of limited facilities some church boards must meet in church parlors or club rooms. There are advantages in arranging the room for business rather than for informal chatting. If the furniture is too comfortable and informal, it may lead to desultory and casual conversation rather than to alert thinking about the matters at hand. Firm, straight chairs, not painfully uncomfortable, arranged so that the entire board will face the chairman of the meeting, are practical. Reports and agenda, if available, should be distributed in advance of the meeting, and a note pad and a sharpened pencil should be at hand for each member.

The hour of the meeting should be determined by the personal programs of the majority of the board members. In some areas the meeting may be in the late afternoon. Suburban communities may have to schedule their regular meeting in the evening. If the hour set is 8:00 P.M., the chairman of the meeting should open the meeting with prayer promptly at that time. Where there is a lack of meticulous attention to this point the minutes reveal that the meetings open later and later. A prompt beginning serves to remind possible latecomers that they will be tardy if they are not there by 8:00 P.M.

It is equally important to close at an appointed hour. One governing body has set the adjournment time at 9:30 P.M. The result is that the members' remarks have become increasingly relevant and concise. Reports that once were unprepared and rambling are now presented in written form and often are mailed to the officers in advance. Even with an approved time of adjournment, special occasions may arise that merit a time extension. The chairman can and should entertain a motion that the meeting be extended for a specific period of time during which the remaining business can be transacted.

Beginning and ending the meeting on time makes for a more dedicated interest and attendance of church officers, who, in the main, are men of wide responsibilities and whose time is budgeted with discretion. There is a growing respect for the church that thus values its corporate time and energy. From the psychological standpoint, increased attentiveness and interest can make for more intelligent decisions and actions. If the group spirit and the group mind are channeled in a defined period for "consideration of the Lord's work," the quality of that work is enhanced.

### The Executive Committee

Many parishes will benefit by setting up a small executive committee to work with the minister. The governing body may delegate authority to this committee to act on behalf of the board, within limitations, between the regular stated meetings. Depending on the size of the parish and its needs, this committee may meet regularly in the intervals between the regular board meetings, or it may meet at the call of the chairman and/or the minister of the church.

An executive committee may be organized on one of two bases. It may have as its constituent members the chairmen of the major committees of the governing body. Such a committee would obviously represent the major areas of the church life. Alternately, the committee may be constituted on the basis of representative officers of the church whose loyalty and judgment are known and respected.

The first plan provides a committee particularly effective in viewing over-all policies of the church that will have long-term or major importance. The alternate plan is supportive to the minister as he presents problems, thoughts, or needs for the enrichment or the development of the parish.

There may be a modification of the two ideas, in which case the committee would have a cross section of leadership from the major committees but would be organized also as a committee that would be particularly effective in evaluating fresh ideas or untried projects.

The committee can be of great value to the minister in screening his thoughts before he presents them to the larger church body. Loss of time and needless discussion are avoided. Ill-formed or worthless ideas may be previewed in a limited council and thus avoid later embarrassment. Ideas or thoughts that are valid will have a solid core of backing and enthusiasm when they are presented to the official board.

The committee should function informally. The minister's study, if large enough, is a good place to meet. Though the group is informal, it is advisable to have a secretary record the minutes. The chairman of the committee should present its decisions to the official body at its next meeting. The executive committee, if given responsibility to act in the interim between official board meetings, should report its actions at the next meeting.

### Division of Responsibility

A governing body functions best when each officer shares in the over-all work of the church. The board should support the minister and work with him in supervision and strengthening of the entire church program and the congregational life. There should be major assignments in the role of leadership. The minister, the counsel of the executive committee, and then the judgment of the governing body itself should survey and approve major committee appointments and assignments. The minister should recommend assignments, seeing that no man has two or more major tasks while another officer has none. In making assignments he should take into consideration a man's years of experience in the church and in the governing body. Major tasks should be assigned to a man of greater maturity or vigor rather than to an inexperienced new officer or to one whose energies are limited or whose physical disabilities would make a particular assignment burdensome.

Almost every governing board should have certain officers. If it is traditional that the minister serve as moderator or president of the governing body, there should usually be a vice chairman, clerk, or recording secretary and treasurer, with their necessary elected assistants. As these persons are duly and constitutionally elected at the first meeting of the governing body, each one should receive in writing or in mimeographed forms the name and the home and business addresses and telephone numbers of all the members of the governing body. Two copies of this list should be sent to each officer, one for use at home and the other for the office.

The list might profitably include the names of the officers of the governing body with their addresses and telephone numbers, then the entire roster of the governing body arranged alphabetically with telephone numbers and addresses. According to the needs of the parish and the board members, then may be listed the names of the chairmen of major committees together with addresses and telephone numbers.

In addition to the above information, a governing body will find useful a list of the members of the staff, including their office or function and their church extension and home telephone numbers.

### Standing and Special Committees

A committee has been defined as "a group of people who individually can do nothing and collectively decide that nothing can be done." In a vital church organization the committee is an indispensable instrument for decision and action. It provides opportunity for education and participation of church members in the detailed and intimate life of the church. The organization of the governing body into committees is a significant step in developing the efficiency of that board.

Each church should plan for committees most needed in the work of its board and congregation. It is usually advisable to have at least two kinds of committees, standing committees and special committees, which may be appointed annually. In the course of a given year it may be feasible to have temporary committees to deal with specific questions. Such special committees may be appointed at one meeting of the board and asked to report back at the next.

It is essential to keep in mind certain principles:

1. The purpose of the committee should be clearly defined.
2. In terms of its function it should be composed of the most capable persons available. In this connection, certain committees may very well, with the approval of the board, include representatives of the congregation at large.
3. The chairman of the committee should be advised as to appropriate times for meetings and informed of dates when reports are expected by the governing body.
4. With few exceptions the minister should be considered an ex officio member of all committees.
5. All committees should be instructed to keep a record of their meetings and actions.
6. When a special or temporary committee's function has been completed, the committee should be dismissed or dissolved by the action of the governing board.
7. Committees should be appointed annually, preferably at the first meeting of the newly constituted board.
8. The principle of rotation in committee appointments should be continually considered by the minister and the board. It is a sound principle to consider the constitution of major committees always one, two, or three years in advance. The minister will oversee the committee appointments with the idea that certain persons will be preparing for the chairmanship of their committee in subsequent years.

One church sets up committees and lists the duties of each committee as follows:

The following standing committees of the board, whose terms shall run for one year, will be appointed by the chairman in consultation with the moderator and shall consist of at least three members of the board:

**Benevolence:**   Shall review missions and benevolence needs, local, national, and world-wide, including Christ Church–supported missions, and shall prepare the annual Missionary and Benevolence Budget, and shall have general supervision of the Benevolent Funds.

**By-Laws:** Shall be responsible for keeping up to date the By-Laws as amended from time to time by the board, and for providing complete copies of such revised By-Laws to members of the board at appropriate intervals.

**Membership:** Shall consider ways and means of expanding the membership of the church; shall supply committees for the reception of new members; shall encourage church members to take an active part in the church program; and shall have general charge of the visitation of the membership.

**Property:** Shall supervise the use to be made of the various church properties; shall inquire into the property needs of the church; and shall, in consultation with the church manager and the pastors, make recommendations to the board with regard to Memorial Funds, and refer board recommendations to the Trustees.

**Pulpit Supply:** Shall provide supplies for the pulpit during temporary absences of the pastor; shall review the order of worship with the pastor and consider appropriate changes.

**Sacraments:** Shall provide for and supervise the Communion Service, assist in the administration of infant baptism, and provide for the ordination of elders.

**Social:** Shall cultivate the social life of the church, supervise the social activities, and resolve conflicts in dates between the various church organizations.

**Denomination:** Shall consist of the ministers and one elder or alternate, who shall attend regular denominational meetings and report to the board.

**Board Organization:** Shall consist of three active officers. It shall present recommendations for officers for the coming year to be elected by the board. It shall consider the proper committee organization of the board, and recommend changes whenever appropriate.

**Nominating:** Shall consist of three elders, one of whom shall be designated as chairman. It shall prepare lists for the board of those who in its judgment merit consideration as members of the board. It shall also make all arrangements in connection with the elections at the annual meeting of the church.

Another church has a simpler organization because its congregational life is less complex. Five standing committees are regularly appointed as follows: (1) committee on finance and properties, (2) committee on missions, (3) committee on Christian education, (4) committee on stewardship and promotion, (5) committee on spiritual life.

Another church has found that it functions most effectively with its committees organized as departments, as follows:

**Christian Education:**   Audio Visual Aids, Adult Education, Children's Work, Church School Administration, Library, Recruitment, Social Education and Action, Youth Work.

**Membership:**   Assimilation, Care of Members, Historical Records, Hospitality, New Life Calling, Preparation of New Members, Reception.

**Organizational:**   Board of Deacons, Area Council of Churches, Men's Club, Denominational Village, Spice Club, Thirty-Up Club, Women's Association, XYZ Club.

**Policy:**   Church Council, Long-Range Planning, Nominations, Personnel, Public Relations, Use of the Building.

**Stewardship:**   Benevolences, Every Member Canvass, Joint Budget, Memorials, Special Gifts.

**Worship:**   Arts and Chancel, Church Service and Music, Communion, Ushering.

In another church that has a widely varied program, the supervision of the church is organized into six departments with committees in each major department. In the complex organization of such a large church, where there is a multiple ministry, one of the ministers or a staff member is appointed adviser to each department. (See the chart, opposite.)

The interest and emphases of the church are to be found reflected in the committee setup and organization. It cannot be overemphasized that the nature and purpose of the committee should be clearly and concisely stated. The following illustration states the specific responsibilities of each commission:

**Worship:**   The Worship Commission plans and directs the total worship program of the church, which includes the sacraments, all services of divine worship, weddings, funerals and all special services. This commission through its subcommittee on Music directs the total music program of the church. The following staff personnel are responsible to the board through the Worship Commission: the ministers, the administrator, the minister of music, the organist, and the soloists. The Clerk of the Board is automatically a member of the Worship Commission and is responsible for planning all details relative to the sacraments, reception of new members (reception teas shall be planned by the Group Activities Commission), and the schedule for greeting worshipers in the narthex on Sunday mornings.

**Christian Education:**   The Christian Education Commission is responsible for the total education program of the church, which includes child, youth, and adult education. The staff member responsible is the Director of Christian Education.

| Departments | Committees |
| --- | --- |
| | Administration |
| | Methods |
| Christian Education | Leadership |
| Advisors: Rev. Smith | Weekday Activities |
| Mr. Jones | Church School |
| | Curriculum |
| | Special Program |
| | |
| | Promotion and Education |
| | Benevolence |
| | Special Projects |
| Missions | Missions Conference |
| Adviser: Rev. Walker | Local Missions |
| | Prayer and Communion |
| | Literature and Publicity |
| | Guidance Committee |
| | Displaced Persons |
| | |
| | Communion |
| | Music |
| Worship and Music | Ushers |
| Adviser: Mr. Cooper | Greeters |
| | Prayer |
| | Radio and TV |
| | |
| | New Life |
| Evangelism and Integration | Enlistment |
| Adviser: Rev. Roberts | Social Fellowship |
| | Organization Integration |
| | |
| | Church Rolls |
| | Special Visitation |
| | Citizenship |
| Membership and Visitation | Deacons |
| Adviser: Rev. Baker | Men's Work |
| | Christian Life Seminar |
| | Special Shut-in Calling |
| | |
| | Trustee Representative |
| | Every Member Canvass |
| | Budget |
| Stewardship and Finance | Annual Meeting |
| Adviser: Mr. Allen | Education and Promotion |
| | Church Property |
| | Personnel |
| | Auditing |
| | Legal |

**World Missions:**   The World Missions Commission is responsible for planning and directing all missionary education throughout the congregation. This commission shall create the annual Benevolence Budget and shall make recommendations regarding special offerings for others.

**Social Education and Action:**   The main responsibility of the Commission on Social Education and Action is to communicate to the board the pronouncements of the denomination in this field. It is to remind the local church that it has a responsibility for the total community. While the main function of this commission is one of education, at the same time it should be ready to lead the congregation in taking a definite stand against any social injustice that may arise, either locally or nationally.

**Group Activities:**   The Group Activities Commission will be responsible for the work of the various organizations in the local church, such as Women's Association, Men's Club, Mr. and Mrs. Club, and so forth. Also, this commission will make all recommendations regarding the use of the church buildings by outside groups. It will plan the physical details of the new-member teas.

**Evangelism:**   This commission will plan and direct the program whereby our local congregation reaches out into the community to win men, women, and young people to a Christian commitment and active participation in the life of the church. It will be in charge of the prospect list and will plan all fellowship and visitation-evangelism programs.

**Christian Nurture:**   The basic responsibility will be to help new church members grow in the Christian life and become assimilated in the work and responsibility of the local congregation. The Christian Nurture Commission will plan and direct all communicant classes for adults. It will look into the status of disinterested members with the purpose of winning them back to active participation. It will create a zone plan in which each elder, along with a deacon, will be responsible for a specific area of the parish. This commission will work closely with the Board of Stewards in planning and promoting stewardship education of time, talent, and money, and with the Commission on Christian Education for leadership recruitment. It will appoint those who are to speak at the meetings when new members are received.

In planning the church organization, committees should be conceived of as instruments to further the established program of the church. The moment a committee ceases to function or to be needed, it should be dismissed or its purpose reformulated. "Working committees" that are active in the vital thrusts of the church build morale and enthusiasm, and have an infectious quality of vitalizing other areas of the church work. Contrariwise, "purely-on-paper" committees that never report or function are a drag on the vitality of other nuclei interests and responsibilities.

The persons who should be most effective in keeping the committees active and forward-moving are the minister and the adviser assigned to the committees. By a word to the chairman as to particular needs or by a reminder that a report is due at the next board meeting the minister can keep a committee active. Each committee meeting should have a definite purpose, and every committee member should leave the meeting with the feeling that the meeting was worth while.

### The Agenda for the Board Meeting

Many board meetings flounder for the lack of advance planning. Every church officer should have a mimeographed agenda sheet similar to the following:

AGENDA FOR BOARD MEETING

8:00 P.M.

    I. Opening prayer
   II. Excuses for absence
  III. Minutes of past meeting
   IV. Executive Committee—Mr. Smith
    V. Clerk's Report—Mr. Jones
   VI. Treasurer's Report—Mr. Abbot
  VII. Reports of Standing Committees
        1. Finance—Mr. Johns
        2. Benevolence—Mr. Cole
        3. Music—Mr. Ellis
        4. Pulpit Supply and Lenten Service—Mr. Wyatt
        5. Operations and Maintenance—Mr. Phillips
        6. Christian Education—Mr. Davis
        7. Communion—Mr. Perry
        8. Ushers—Mr. Cooper
        9. Publicity and Public Relations—Mr. Hughes
       10. Endowment—Mr. Phelps
       11. Auditing—Mr. Douglas
 VIII. Reports of Special Committees
        1. Nomination—Mr. Spencer
        2. Historical Records and Archives—Mr. Hall
        3. Denominational Representative—Mr. Spencer

        4. Sermon Publication—Mr. George
        5. Committee on Memorials—Mr. Frazer
  IX. Report from Women's Society
   X. Ministers' Report
        1. Mr. Jones' report
        2. Dr. Morehouse's report
        3. Monthly report to the board regarding the status of the church
  XI. Old Business
 XII. New Business
XIII. Date of next meeting (announce)
XIV. Adjournment

(The following reports of assistant ministers are appended in mimeographed form to the agenda.)

*Assistant Ministers' Report to the Board*

Report of John L. Jones, Jr., for monthly period from_____ to _____.

All ministers take equal responsibility in general duties, such as the prayer phone, morning prayer services, weekly meetings of the staff, and weekly ministers' conferences.

A. *Regular Duties*

| | | | |
|---|---|---|---|
| Meetings attended | 18 | Baptisms | 0 |
| Home calls made | 16 | Funerals | 5 |
| Hospital calls made | 119 | Committal | 1 |
| Personal conferences | 11 | Weddings | 1 |
| | | Board Meeting | 1 |

B. *Special Activities*

Concluded my lectures on "The Tenets of Our Faith."
Assisted regular Sunday worship.
Assisted Maundy Thursday service.
Conducted two Good Friday services.
Conducted 8:00 A.M. Easter Sunday Communion.
Assisted Easter Baptism service.

C. *Comments*

In process of reorganizing the outreach program, which will extend arm of the church into every neighborhood.

Shut-ins and hospital patients received Easter Chancel lilies through Good Neighbor Committee of Women's Society. Chancel flowers continue to go to hospital every Sunday.

*Minister of Education's Report to the Board*

Report of Dr. Harold N. Morehouse for monthly period from _____ to _____.

All ministers take equal responsibility in general duties such as the prayer phone, morning prayer services, weekly meetings of the staff, and weekly ministers' conferences.

A. *Regular Duties*

| | | | |
|---|---|---|---|
| Meetings attended | 30 | Baptisms | 0 |
| Home calls made | 9 | Funerals | 0 |
| Hospital calls made | 3 | Weddings | 0 |
| Personal conferences | 9 | Denominational meetings | 1 |

B. *Special Activities*

Took part in the Lenten Service on Wednesday, March 18.

Conducted Wednesday morning Lenten Service, March 25, for young people.

Took part in Maundy Thursday Communion Service, March 26.

Conducted 1:00 P.M. Good Friday Service, March 27.

Conducted Easter Sunrise Service, March 29.

Supervised breakfast for young people following the Easter Sunrise Service.

Officiated at overflow congregation in the Assembly Room at the 11 A.M. Easter Sunday Service.

Took part in Easter Baptismal Service.

Showed films for Senior Men's meeting.

Attended Women's Society meeting, Wednesday, April 8.

C. *Comments*

About 575 young people attended the State Youth Rally at our church.

Two of our Boy Scouts completed the work for the God and Country Award, which was given them in the church worship service.

I was recently elected to the Board of Managers of the Family YMCA which serves this area.

Mailing a statement of the agenda to the church officers prior to the meeting is helpful. One church consistently mails such a statement a week before the meeting in the same envelope with the minutes of the previous meeting. Several purposes are served. The board member is reminded of the forthcoming meeting. He has the record of the past meeting to refresh his memory and to peruse for possible corrections. But beyond this he is able to ruminate a bit on points that may come up for group discussion and decision at the board meeting.

At one small church where the minister is part sexton and full-time secretary, as well as prophet and priest, there is no time for mimeographing. Instead, the agenda are written on a blackboard, and as the members enter the room they can readily see the items that are up for consideration.

### Conduct of the Meeting

The meeting of the official board should be a spiritual experience. Its tone should be set with the opening prayer offered by the minister or else by an elder or a church officer duly notified in advance. The opening prayer should be thoughtfully and carefully prepared so that with reverence and consecration the minds and hearts of the members will be committed to their specific tasks.

Some boards, after the opening prayer and the call to order, set a brief period for stressing some spiritual truth. Each minister with his officers must decide on the most suitable and helpful means for inspiring, uplifting, and educating the board to its central purpose. The procedure should be concise, relevant, and consecrated.

In most churches the minister himself serves as moderator, chairman, or presiding officer of the meeting. His direction of the meeting should be decent and orderly if his preparations have been careful. One minister with the services of a good secretary prepared an instruction sheet reminding the secretary to proceed as follows:

On the day of the meeting please check the following: The room is in order, the chairs are properly placed, and a table for the secretary and presiding officer are suitably arranged. Put on the table for the clerk and presiding officer:

1. The minute book
2. Copies of the minutes of the last meeting
3. Attendance sheet. (This is a simple mimeographed sheet listing the names of the officers. The secretary may put opposite their names "p" for present, "x" absent but excused, or "a" absent.)
4. The names of those who asked to be excused, together with any written notice from them
5. Copies of any papers to be distributed to the board
6. Regular monthly copy of the statistical report of the parish
7. Pads of paper
8. Pencils
9. Copies of church publications or literature, or special denominational materials for distribution to church officers
10. List of new members
11. List of members to be dismissed, or who desire letters of transfer

After the preliminaries the meeting proceeds according to the agenda. The chairman should invite questions or comments on major reports, but he should aim to have the meeting progress without undue delay. If reports are clearly understood as presented, a motion for approval should be immediately welcomed.

A fine balance is needed in the timing of questions and discussion and then moving the matters to a conclusion. In the main, the chairman must take the initiative in prompting pointed discussion and moving matters to completion with dispatch. If the attitude is too laissez-faire, irrelevant comments and unwarranted questions may annoy and tire the members.

A good moderator should know when to refer items of new business on parish welfare to standing or special committees for judgment and consultation. It is ill advised to discuss among fifteen or twenty officers an item that should receive the quiet evaluation of a small group appointed to deal with a particular area of the church life. Such judicial referrals not only save time but also ensure to the board a sounder opinion and more considered judgment.

Not only major reports but also seemingly minor assignments should be put in written form. One church, for example, makes assignments among its church officers to assist the minister in the public greeting of church worshipers. An assignment sheet listing the dates, the hours, and the names of the officers who are to serve is distributed at the board meeting. Any changes are made and noted at that time. Each officer then has in his hand as well as in his mind a list of his duties for the days ahead.

It is highly important that the governing body have each month a statistical summary of the life and activities of the church.

Individual departments can be very helpful to the governing body if in their reports they tabulate specific items and arrange them clearly and concisely so that the point of the report may readily be determined.

Though the unfailing attitudes for a fruitful meeting are gravity and spirituality, lightness and good humor have their place. Dr. William Pearson Merrill, long-time minister of the Brick Presbyterian Church in New York, spoke nostalgically of the monthly board meetings. Minister and elders made it a point to relate at those meetings some humorous experience they had had since they last met as a group. A deep camaraderie and a good spirit made for an atmosphere of togetherness and cooperation for progress. How like President Lincoln, who, in the dark and tragic days of the Civil War, deliberately tried to relieve and vitalize his Cabinet meetings with humor!

All reports and papers should be dated. The chairman of the meeting should request that all committee and other special reports submitted to the board in writing be dated in the upper right-hand corner. This simple procedure makes for orderly filing and facilitates reference work. This is true especially when a congregational survey, a study or the annual audit is undertaken.

## HOW TO DISCOVER NEEDS

A vital congregation constantly seeks to understand and to minister to the needs of the total membership. These needs are discovered by various means. Individual contacts with church members are indispensable and basic. The ministers, church officers, and staff members must listen to what people say. Devoted church members may note deficiencies in the church or be aware of opportunities. In loving directness or even in seemingly roundabout or negative ways their expressions can lead to constructive evaluations and worthy opportunities. Church officers and leaders should live by the admonition of the Saviour, "He that hath ears to hear, let him hear."

The every-member canvass and other church-wide calling programs, in which selected officers and representatives contact the entire membership, provide an excellent opportunity to "feel the pulse" of the entire parish. On such occasions, canvassers or callers should be urged to note and report comments or suggestions made by parishioners. These comments and suggestions will then be sorted and compiled and brought to the attention of the minister and the church board for consideration and action.

An annual questionnaire sent to the entire membership may bring desirable results in some parishes. If the church has a public relations committee, it should be consulted before the questionnaire is prepared and mailed. The questionnaire should be clearly worded, brief, and to the point. In one such attempt I invited the newer members of the church to indicate the church's shortcomings as they saw them, and I proposed that their replies would form the basis for the teaching and preaching ministry of the local church. It was clearly stated that the church wanted to improve the effectiveness of its ministry by speaking to their needs rather than "answering questions that people are not asking." The response was exceptionally fruitful.

Parish needs are frequently discovered in church group experiences. The women's society in its program of activity, or the meeting of the mothers of children in the nursery school department, in an informal atmosphere, may uncover needs that the church could constructively meet.

In the church that I serve, several strong projects and programs have grown out of informal meetings held to inquire whether a certain service of the church would be meaningful or helpful. For example, a nursery school was organized as the result of a meeting of the mothers of three- and four-year-olds. I wrote to them that the consistory of the church had authorized me to inquire whether the young families in our church desired a day nursery school. An informal meeting was held at ten o'clock in the morning when young mothers could come. The notice of the meeting stated simply that their judgment and personal reaction were needed. An invitation to that meeting was sent to approximately sixty mothers. About thirty-five were present. Others who could not come expressed interest. Here was a clear indication of interest simply by response. The meeting followed a simple and informal agenda, raising such questions as: Is there a need in your family for a church nursery school? What kind of nursery school would be most helpful to your child and to your family? What hours would be most desirable? Where should the school meet? Would you be willing to give some time to the supervision of the school and participate in its life? It would be necessary to pay for leadership. What monthly contribution would be possible for you and your family? What kind of leadership would you like to see in the school?

Sufficient interest, response, and direction were gained from this one meeting to win the governing board's approval of the idea and to appoint a committee, related to that governing body, which developed a plan for the establishment of the nursery school.

Sometimes needs can be discovered and the program to meet those needs indicated by a small special commission or committee appointed to study a particular aspect of the community or congregational life.

If the question is raised, "Is there a need for a senior (retired) men's program in the parish?" the best way to get an answer is to assemble the retired men of the church and obtain their judgment and reaction. Many projects for young people fail because the young people themselves have not been consulted and their judgment has not been brought to bear on the question.

Not only is need discovered and direction pointed out among such specific groups, but, more significant, out of such a survey comes a vitality of interest that will give impetus to the program and leadership for it once it is established.

If the congregation has been prepared in advance, a congregational meeting may prove helpful in obtaining a widespread reaction to a program or project. Of course on major programs, such as a new building, the entire congregation should be consulted, either through public meetings, group discussions, or individual surveys.

Consider the results of a survey made by the chairman and his committee to determine the facilities and the program of a church needed for recreational and congregational activities. The committee wanted to begin outlining a program that would enlarge the activities of the parish within a "versatile congregational hall." The chairman shared with his committee the following letter:

*Dear _____:*

Many interesting points of view were expressed in answer to my letter of December 19, and I should like to summarize and share some of them with you in order that we may arrive at some conclusions on this matter when the committee meets next Sunday, January 5, at 3:00 P.M.

"Programs and activities planned and executed by groups of all ages within our church family should be strongly encouraged."

"Our new facilities should be used by our own people as much as possible at all times."

"Could the school have occasional access to the new hall?"

"Stress quantity of local participation over quality of production; that is, do not let professional groups take over to a point where our amateurs might become mere spectators rather than participants."

"Our own church programs should take precedence over community programs and community programs over outside programs."

"Limited athletic programs might include Ping-pong, volley ball, mixer games, stunts, and so forth."

"Encourage travelogues, art exhibits, lectures, musical programs."

"Try young married-couple programs planned by themselves."

"Why not weekend programs for children?"

"Folk dances and square dances are good fun for all."

"All ages love dramatics."

"Adult educational programs are 'sure-fire,' as the school has found out."

"A strong sense of Christian fellowship can be achieved when members find joy in the experiences they share. Our Church must help fill the lives of members in this busy, noisy world with satisfying activities that afford individual expression through dramatics, music, arts and crafts."

I look forward to seeing you in the minister's study at the church on Sunday afternoon. We plan to start promptly at three o'clock.

Faithfully,

*Chairman, Committee on Congregational Hall*

Such a report vitalizes and directs interest and prepares an appointed group to sift ideas and come to united conclusions.

## HOW TO DEVELOP PROGRAMS AND THE SUPPORT TO MEET NEEDS

When there is sufficient indication to convince the church leaders that they should move in a specific direction, several preliminary steps are advisable. From the beginning the official board should be completely informed, and its approval should be obtained for every step to be taken.

### Survey

A detailed survey in written form is then in order.

One church sent the following questionnaire to all older adults:

RECREATIONAL INTEREST INDICATOR

Name _____ Address _____ Phone No._____
                Phone listed under name of _____

I. Things you would be interested in seeing Christ Church plan for older adults:
  1. Special activities at the church on certain days
     *a.* One day a week _____
     *b.* If you prefer activities once or twice each month please indicate____

    *c.* Which day would you prefer? Indicate day of week _____

    *d.* Which time would be best? (Morning, afternoon, all day?) _____

  2. A club room for games, reading, visiting, and so forth, open at stated hours during the week _____

  3. Other suggestions _____

II. What are some of the activities you would suggest?

  1. Table games _____ What kind? _____

  2. Group games _____ Have you some to share? _____

  3. Handicrafts _____ Any special one? _____

  4. Conversation and visiting _____

  5. Group singing _____

  6. Luncheon meetings _____

  7. Dramatics _____

  8. Hobbies _____

  9. Other suggestions _____

III. My hobby is (Please place "X" beside your hobby.)

  1. Collecting (What?) _____    9. Flower arrangements _____

  2. Woodcarving _____    10. Playing piano _____

  3. Making furniture _____    11. Other instrument (Which?)__

  4. Singing _____    12. Memorizing and reciting

  5. Painting _____       poetry _____

  6. Cooking _____    13. Telling stories _____

  7. Writing poetry _____    14. Reviewing books _____

  8. Gardening _____    15. Handwork _____

                             16. Others _____

IV. Some people have indicated their willingness to furnish transportation to the church for special activities for those who need it. Will you need transportation? (Yes or No) _____

Do you have friends who would be interested in these activities? Please use the reverse side of this sheet to list names, addresses, telephone numbers, and other suggestions.

Please fill out this sheet and return it to Christ Church as soon as possible. Your answers are needed to help us plan the best program possible for our older adults.

This questionnaire occupied only one letter-size page, which is advantageous. Brevity and clarity are highly effective in bringing about the return of filled-in questionnaires. The results of a survey should be carefully tabulated, and a statistical summary made. Out of such summary, and its careful analysis, interests are determined, programs established, and leadership for them is gained.

More and more churches make valuable surveys by asking their new members at the time of their public reception to record their interests and experience. The following form, with infinite variations according to the needs and the program, is used:

Please answer the following questions:
1. Have you held an office on a board or organization in another church? Yes _____ No _____ State position. _____
2. Have you ever taught in public or private school? Yes_____ No_____ If yes, in what capacity? _____ For how long? _____
3. Have you ever taught or served in a church school or Bible class? Yes _____ No _____ If Yes, give age group _____ Boys_____ Girls _____ For how long? _____
4. Regardless of previous experience, would you be willing to teach regularly? _____ Periodically? _____ As a substitute? _____ On a trial basis? _____
5. Check any of the following in which you have had experience: Vocational guidance _____ Social work _____ Counseling _____ Type __ _____
6. Have you ever assisted in any youth organization program, such as scouting, young people's church groups, and so forth? Yes _____ No __ _____ If so, indicate type and extent. _____
7. Regardless of previous experience, would you be willing to assist in our youth programs? Yes _____ No _____
8. Which musical instrument(s) do you play? _____
9. Would you sing in a choir if accepted? Yes _____ No _____ Have you ever led a choral group? Yes _____ No _____ Led an orchestra? Yes _____ No _____
10. According to time available, would you join with others in personally informing friends, neighbors, and newcomers of the life and work of the church? Yes _____ No_____ Check means you would be willing to use: Personal call _____ Telephone call _____ Personal note with printed leaflet _____
11. Would you be willing to invite neighboring families into your home occasionally for study and fellowship? Yes _____ No _____ If Yes, under your own guidance? _____ Under the guidance of the minister or others? _____
12. Would you be willing to assist in planning and carrying out a church social function? Yes _____ No _____
13. Have you ever given a book review? Yes _____ No _____
14. Regardless of previous experience, would you be willing to review an appropriate book for a group of the church? Yes _____ No _____
15. Would you be willing to speak informally on your occupation, business,

or profession? Yes_____ No_____ Would you try with a small group?
Yes _____ No _____

16. Aside from home and business, what are your main interests or hobbies?
_____

17. Are you interested in Men's Work? Yes _____ No _____ Women's Work?
Yes _____ No _____ Mariners' Club? Yes _____ No _____ Young
Adults? Yes _____ No _____

18. Miscellaneous. Check all activities in which you have had any experience. Double-check activities in which you would be willing to devote some time to the church.

_____ Church library                          _____ Typing
_____ Ushering                                _____ Duplicating machine
_____ Visiting the sick and shut-ins          _____ Bookkeeping
_____ Dramatics—coaching-acting-writing_____ Sewing
_____ Storytelling                            _____ Cooking
_____ Painting or illustrating                _____ Menu planning
_____ Church interior decorating              _____ Landscaping church property
_____ Handicrafts                             _____ Nurse
_____ Games and recreation supervision        _____ Reader
_____ Writing and editing church paper        _____ Song leader
_____ Operating movie or slide projector      _____ Pianist or organist
_____ Coaching (athletics) Type?              _____ Photography
_____ Lifeguard
_____ Providing flowers for worship one Sunday each year

The accumulation of such information from the entire parish creates a body of material from which leadership may be found to develop particular programs. It is very important that the resultant statistics be compiled and fully shared with the governing body. No program will gain the desired support unless all potential participants are in possession of complete details regarding it and unless the information is presented to them in such a way as to arouse their interest and desire to support the program.

### Stimulation of Creative Ideas

Often a meeting of church people to deal with a specific topic is unproductive because of inadequate stimulus to creative ideas. Alex F. Osborn's book *Applied Imagination* has many suggestions for the church administrator who seeks the maximum creative response from church people. Mr. Osborn has developed techniques known as "brainstorming." Under his plan a group of people assemble to deal with a specific question or problem. Thirty minutes are to be devoted to the topic. The rules are: (1) Begin and close with prayer; (2) deem no idea too wild to be expressed; (3) quantity of ideas is wanted, so every idea coming to any member's mind should be expressed; (4) combination and improvement of ideas are highly desirable; (5) criticism or negative discussion regarding any idea is absolutely forbidden.

A recent issue of *Church Business* makes suggestions. The ideal number of participants in a brainstorm session is seven. The procedure calls for a strong moderator. The approach is to be positive. No one is to interject a criticism or negative thought. A person may add to a point made by another or seek to improve it. A light, happy, and, eventually, an exciting spirit seems to develop, and often many vital ideas flow forth. A secretary, preferably one who can take shorthand efficiently, should record all comments and suggestions.

### Formulating the Plan

It is a good thing for a group to have ideas and to be in agreement on a particular need, but no steps should be taken until a working plan has been decided. For example, if a Golden Age group is being considered, the procedure for organizing the group, the conducting of meetings, the election of officers, the place and time of meeting, and so on, must be agreed upon, prepared in written form, and approved by the group as a whole. In these initial stages the counsel and support of the minister are indispensable. After tentative and final details have been determined, they should be approved by the governing body and be placed in its files.

### Oversight and Reports

Every activity in the church, each area of service, and all organized groups will be strengthened by contact with the church's leaders. The senior minister, a staff member, or a church officer should maintain an active relationship with each working project or established organization. The minister who is ever sensitive to the program of the nursery school or the senior women's organization of the church wisely maintains the "life-line relationship." Regular reports of the work of the group should be made to the central governing body of the church. Many congregations wisely expect an annual report of each activity and organization in the church at the annual meeting. When this procedure is not followed, occasional reports, at stipulated times, should be placed on file with the governing body which has approved and seeks to maintain oversight of the particular society or activity.

## LINES OF RELATIONSHIP

In our churches, with their boards, committees, commissions, and various organizations and activities, it is important to have clear-cut lines of responsibility. Who is responsible to whom? An outstanding church administrator follows the motto "Keep the lines straight!" How valid this is!

The chart opposite shows the lines of relationship in one of our great churches.

Often it will be up to the minister, as the senior administrator of the church, to see that "the lines are kept straight." If the committee on buildings and properties is directly responsible to the board of trustees, and through them to the church corporation, the minister should not presume to make decisions that can be made only by the board of trustees. Also, if the Christian education committee is primarily responsible to the minister of education, the senior minister should not interpose himself between that committee and the minister of education. *The lines should be kept straight!*

## LONG-RANGE PLANNING

The church program should be considered not for the current week alone or even for the church year, but with a "long view" to the future. Some congregations have a standing long-range planning committee. Others appoint a committee from time to time and receive its reports for suggestions and ultimate evaluation and decision by the major governing body.

An evaluation once every five years or so of the entire church program and activity in terms of its direction and the results in the past and the projection into the future is wise. Having long vision

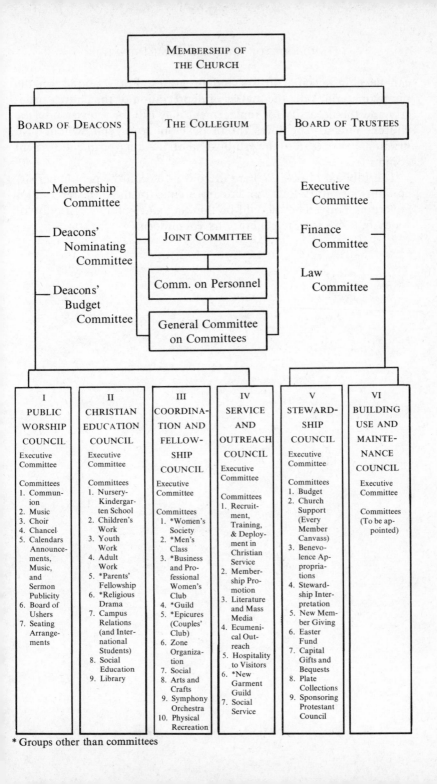

**MEMBERSHIP OF THE CHURCH**

**BOARD OF DEACONS**

**THE COLLEGIUM**

**BOARD OF TRUSTEES**

Membership Committee

Deacons' Nominating Committee

Deacons' Budget Committee

**JOINT COMMITTEE**

**Comm. on Personnel**

**General Committee on Committees**

Executive Committee

Finance Committee

Law Committee

**I PUBLIC WORSHIP COUNCIL**

Executive Committee

Committees
1. Communion
2. Music
3. Choir
4. Chancel
5. Calendars Announcements, Music, and Sermon Publicity
6. Board of Ushers
7. Seating Arrangements

**II CHRISTIAN EDUCATION COUNCIL**

Executive Committee

Committees
1. Nursery-Kindergarten School
2. Children's Work
3. Youth Work
4. Adult Work
5. *Parents' Fellowship
6. *Religious Drama
7. Campus Relations (and International Students)
8. Social Education
9. Library

**III COORDINATION AND FELLOWSHIP COUNCIL**

Executive Committee

Committees
1. *Women's Society
2. *Men's Class
3. *Business and Professional Women's Club
4. *Guild
5. *Epicures (Couples' Club)
6. Zone Organization
7. Social
8. Arts and Crafts
9. Symphony Orchestra
10. Physical Recreation

**IV SERVICE AND OUTREACH COUNCIL**

Executive Committee

Committees
1. Recruitment, Training, & Deployment in Christian Service
2. Membership Promotion
3. Literature and Mass Media
4. Ecumenical Outreach
5. Hospitality to Visitors
6. *New Garment Guild
7. Social Service

**V STEWARDSHIP COUNCIL**

Executive Committee

Committees
1. Budget
2. Church Support (Every Member Canvass)
3. Benevolence Appropriations
4. Stewardship Interpretation
5. New Member Giving
6. Easter Fund
7. Capital Gifts and Bequests
8. Plate Collections
9. Sponsoring Protestant Council

**VI BUILDING USE AND MAINTENANCE COUNCIL**

Executive Committee

Committees
(To be appointed)

* Groups other than committees

can develop specific thrusts and programs. For example, on the purely material side, the matter of depreciation of the church property and the necessity for replacement may call for a revision of the church budget. The foresight in developing an endowment program may well lead to the establishment of a long-term endowment committee.

The Biblical phrase "Where there is no vision the people perish" contains a century-long validated principle for the minister and his governing body. They should be thinking and building not only for today but also for the generations yet unborn.

# Parish Activities and Programs

The minister and the governing body should have oversight and be directly associated with all the activities, interests and programs in the parish. As our churches develop increasing activities to meet the needs and interests of their people, their leadership will profitably ponder the words "Keep all phases of the church life distinctly Christian!" The mark will have been missed if the church finds its activities turning into, as one competent observer termed it, "another Rotary club."

A sound doctrine of the church is indispensable both for the minister and for his church leaders and groups. By teaching and example the minister should seek to make every church activity a channel for the application of religious principles or an opportunity whereby the Holy Spirit may breathe new life into the parish.

One means of keeping such aims and objectives before all church organizations is to hold at least one annual meeting with all officers of all church activities and programs. The purpose of such a conclave would have before it the following definite aims: (1) to make each leader conscious of the fact that he is an agent of his program for extending Christ's kingdom and doing, within the limits of the program set before his group, the work of the Lord; (2) the establishment of aims and goals for the year in keeping with the overall purpose of the church as a means of implementing this basic interest and concern.

The dedicated and well-administered church will not be what Robert N. Rodenmayer described in his little book *We Have This Ministry:*

... the organizational beehive of the parish which is so activated, departmentalized, structured, and constantly in motion that the fast-clicking machinery seems to be an end in itself. There is a place for everybody, and everybody is in it whether he likes it or not. There is no quietness here, no peace, but lots of activity.—In a town where I once lived, there was a local church which served meals at a tremendous clip to numerous groups and societies at work there, and apparently all the time. The figures, proudly published, on suppers and luncheons served up and disposed of in the course of an active year, were overwhelming. One of the oldsters of the town once remarked, "That's not a church, it's a restaurant."

Indeed, the church we seek to build should avoid that condemnation. It may have activity, but each phase of the activity should be motivated to bring men to Christ or to interpret some aspect of "the great and living Christian tradition."

## BRINGING INDIVIDUALS INTO THE CHURCH AND TO THE CHURCH'S CHRIST

Throughout this book the approach to strangers, newcomers, and prospective members will be considered in detail. One cannot look at the matter of the activities of the parish without giving thought to the initial contacts with newcomers into the community or with those who come for the first time to the worship services.

### The Recognition of Visitors

The entire church congregation will be aware of the presence of visitors, newcomers, and strangers who come to worship. A greeting in the narthex by an officer of the church and courtesy and attentiveness on the part of the usher are of prime importance in welcoming the stranger who comes to the church for the first time. Some clergymen attest to the helpfulness of a word of greeting printed in the order of service and perhaps emphasized in the worship service itself.

Some churches provide identification for guests or visitors. One church uses a printed card, shown at the top of the following page. Pinned to the card is a red ribbon 2½ by ¾ inches in size. On the red background, printed in contrasting gold, are the words "Our Guest Today." Members and officers noting the ribbon should make a point of extending personal greetings to the wearers.

---

WELCOME TO CHRIST CHURCH

We are happy to have you worship with us. We would like to know you better.

So that you may be recognized as a visitor, please wear the attached ribbon where it may be seen. Also, please fill in this card and leave it on the seat so that the usher may pick it up after the service.

Name _____ Phone _____

Address _____

Church Member?   Yes _____   No _____

Where? _____

Would you like a caller from the Church? Yes _____ No _____

---

There are various ways of seeking the name and address of the newcomer. A visitors' book, in charge of a member of the church, at a convenient point in the entranceway may attract the interest and signatures of visitors and strangers. Many churches have found it very helpful as a form, either attached to the Sunday bulletin or as a separate card in the pew, for the visitor to sign.

One such card is as follows:

---

CHRIST CHURCH

"Every Visitor Is an Honored Guest"

We are happy to welcome you to the worship and fellowship of our church. Please give us your name, address, and other information in order that we may serve you better.

☐ I am a member of _____ Church
☐ I am not a member of any church
☐ Desire to unite with church
☐ Desire to have pastor call
☐ Remarks on reverse side

Name _____

Address _____

Phone _____

☐ Adult        ☐ College        ☐ High School

Visitors' Reception in Parlor Following 11:00 A.M. Service

---

Note that this church makes a further effort in hospitality to the stranger or visitor by an informal reception. For such a reception, regarding refreshments, hosts and hostesses, and so on, a fitting plan will have been made.

One church housing a large worshiping congregation each Sunday has devised the following card:

---

I AM A VISITOR TODAY     Date _____

Name _____

Address _____

City _____ Phone _____

☐ I am a member of _____ Church

    in _____ City, _____ State

☐ I would appreciate a pastoral call at my home.

PLEASE READ OTHER SIDE

---

On the reverse of the card the visitor reads the following statement:

Our Church has a tradition of friendliness, and we are certain that you will find a warm welcome while visiting here. To assist our members in recognizing visiting friends, you are urged to register on the reverse side of this card, and to wear the attached Pennant this morning.

You are also urged to visit the patio following the morning services. You will be greeted at the foot of the patio ramp, and, if you wish, you will be directed to that section of the patio where most persons of your age or interest group congregate. The wearing of the little Visitor's Pennant will greatly assist you in meeting new friends.

Attached to the card is a triangular white pennant, approximately three inches in length. Printed on it in navy-blue letters are the words "Visitor, Christ Church."

Another church expresses its warm, hospitable spirit on a greeting card as follows:

CHRIST CHURCH

Card for the Ritual of Friendship and Loyalty

Name _____ Telephone _____

Address _____ Date _____

Check ☐ correct statements below

☐ I am a member of this church.

☐ I am not a member of this church.

☐ I am a member elsewhere at the _____
Church, located at _____

☐ I desire to unite with this church.

☐ I desire to talk with the minister.

☐ I would appreciate an early pastoral call.

☐ I suggest a call be made on the sick, or otherwise needing
a call, whose names I am writing on the reverse of this card.

The reverse of the card reads:

THE RITUAL MEANING

We pause for a moment in our service of worship that each worshiper—whether member or guest—may register his name on this card. We do this as an act of worship, identifying oneself with his fellow worshipers. The card is then laid upon the offering plate with the offering for this day. Thus we make this act a token of our dedication of self without substance to our Lord and Saviour Jesus Christ.

_____

_____

This card combines the responses of visitors and strangers with those of all the members of the congregation. For certain churches this type of approach is highly commendable. It does not embarrass the stranger or newcomer by making him feel "different." It also helps the minister and the church office to keep up to date on changes of address of the members, and serves as an indication of church attendance.

Whatever the means used to obtain the names of visitors and strangers, certain principles should be followed: (1) Let there be warmth and sincerity with dignity. (2) Individuals appointed as greeters should clearly understand their function. A mimeographed sheet may be used to explain the duties of a greeter, and specify what information he is to obtain from newcomers. (3) If cards are used, the printing should be large enough to be readily legible. (4) Request the minimum of information. Name, address, telephone number, and present church connection are often sufficient. A card is more likely t be signed if it is simple and if it requests a minimum of information.

### Information Leaflet

Many newcomers to a church are interested in facts about that church. Numerous ways of preparing material for strangers and newcomers will present themselves to the minister and associates responsible for the introduction of the church to visitors and strangers. A number of churches use attractive "kits."

Single-page mimeographed sheets or more elaborate one-fold printed leaflets describing the church activities and services can be placed in one or two pockets inside a single-fold leaflet.

One such kit has a picture of the church on the cover. As the leaflet is opened there appears across the "pocket" the following:

#### AN INVITATION

This packet is designed to introduce you to Christ Church. We trust that you will read the material presented here, and find the information that may help you find your place in the fellowship of our congregation. The facts can be printed, but the spirit of the church you will discover only as you become a part of her life.

To you who live in this area we extend a most cordial invitation. We invite you to worship with us, to enroll in the church school, to attend our many activities. You are invited to call upon the ministers whenever they may be of help to you.

To you who are without a church home in our community we extend a sincere invitation to unite with Christ Church and to join with us in our confession of Christian faith and in our service for Christ and His Kingdom.

In the left-hand pocket of this kit are two leaflets bearing the titles, together with Biblical verses, as follows:

### THE MINISTRY OF SACRED MUSIC

"Serve the Lord with gladness!
Come into His presence with singing!" (Psalm 100:2)

### THE WORSHIP SERVICES AND PASTORAL MINISTRY

"That Christ may dwell in your hearts through faith." (Ephesians 3:17)

In the right-hand pocket are three leaflets, denoting the following together with their Scriptural verses:

### THE ADULT PROGRAM

"His disciples came to Him . . . and He taught them" (Matthew 5:1, 2).

### THE YOUTH DIVISION

"Remember also your Creator in the days of your youth" (Ecclesiastes 12:1).

### THE CHILDREN'S DIVISION

"Bring them up in the discipline and instruction of the Lord" (Ephesians 6:4).

These leaflets are of the same width, namely, 4½ inches, but the length varies so that the reader opening the kit will see the titles of the leaflets one above another. The reader can easily take from the kit the leaflet that interests him most.

In preparing printed matter for strangers or visitors the church should emphasize that the church is the center of spiritual force and power. Often those who prepare the leaflet are so much engrossed in giving information about the various activities of the church, from crib care to senior folks' programs, that this leaflet presents the church as merely a place "where things hum." The fact that the church is essentially a "spiritual citadel" may be lost amid the clutter of items about committees.

One simple leaflet pictures the exterior of the church on the first page. Then it makes, as the page is turned, a photograph of its worshipers at prayer within the sanctuary the focal point of emphasis. The motif of the leaflet should be the Scriptural passage, which appears prominent: "Except the Lord build the house, their labour is but lost that build it; except the Lord keep the city, the watchmen waketh but in vain" (Psalm 127).

The introductory leaflet must not become a compendium of church history. Historical material can be better presented in a special and different form.

One impressive folder is a one-fold mimeographed leaflet. On the outside are the name, address, and telephone number of the church. On the inside is a warm greeting in Christ's name followed by details concerning (1) Sunday worship services; (2) the Christian education program, with room numbers and locations for children and adults; (3) Sunday-evening fellowship; and (4) group activities during the week. The leaflet is unpretentious, simple, and brief, and therefore appeals to the reader.

If the budget permits its preparation, a leaflet showing photographs of the church activities with a minimum of explanatory statements and a maximum of specific information will be both interesting and useful.

The church administrator should avail himself of the experience and judgment of church members active in the fields of publicity and public relations. Format, diction, use of illustrations, colors, and so on, are important factors in making a leaflet interesting and readable. A simple statement regarding the background of the church, its denominational affiliation, and a sentence or two regarding its emphases may be in order, but such material should be concise.

### The Invitation

If the newcomer to the community has been welcomed and informed regarding the church, the administrator may be moved to invite him into the membership of the congregation.

By anticipating questions in people's minds, and also to stimulate their desire to join the church, some parishes have printed material ready in advance. The church bulletin, too, should welcome strangers and visitors, and a simple statement regarding membership may immediately stimulate interest in such an association. One church carries on the cover of the Sunday bulletin a statement of its participation in various local, national, and international councils of churches, followed by: "We believe in the equality of all Christians before God, and we receive into our fellowship all those who love, obey, and follow Christ."

When inviting people to join, many churches send them a brief statement describing the procedures for becoming a member. One four-page leaflet reads as follows:

*Page 1*

## An Invitation

Christ Church extends to you a most cordial invitation to become a member of its fellowship.

(Small picture of the church printed here.)

"And Jesus said unto them, I am the bread of life: he that cometh to me shall never hunger; and he that believeth on me shall never thirst . . . and him that cometh to me I will in no wise cast out."—John 6:35, 37

*Page 2*

### YOU MAY JOIN BY THE PROFESSION OF YOUR FAITH

We welcome into our membership all those who are willing to answer Yes to the following:

1. Do you acknowledge yourself to be a sinner in the sight of God, justly deserving His displeasure, and without hope save in His sovereign mercy?
2. Do you believe in the Lord Jesus Christ as the Son of God and Saviour of sinners, and do you receive and rest upon Him alone for salvation as He is offered in the Gospel?
3. Do you now resolve and promise, in humble reliance upon the grace of the Holy Spirit, that you will endeavor to live as becometh the followers of Christ?
4. Do you promise to support the church in its worship and work to the best of your ability?
5. Do you submit yourself to the government and discipline of the church, and promise to study its purity and peace?

*Page 3*

### YOU MAY JOIN BY
### CERTIFICATE OF TRANSFER

By a Church Letter we will receive anyone into our membership who is in good and regular standing in any evangelical church.

We do not require rebaptism but accept as valid any baptism administered by an ordained minister in the name of the Father, Son, and Holy Spirit regardless of the mode used.

Our church office will be happy to write for your certificate of transfer.

### YOU MAY JOIN BY THE
### RESTATEMENT OF YOUR FAITH

Those who cannot secure a certificate of transfer (some denominations do not grant letters to churches outside their own communion), or who have been inactive and wish to make a fresh beginning in the Christian life and rededicate themselves to God, are received on the restatement of their faith, without rebaptism.

When a persons unites by restatement, he is asked to reaffirm, in the presence of the board, his faith in Jesus Christ and to renew the vows which he took when he first united with a Christian church.

*Page 4*

PROCEDURE IN

RECEPTION OF MEMBERS

In this denomination it is the responsibility of the board to examine and receive new members. The board meets following each Sunday morning worship service (or following the Midweek Service by request) for this purpose.

At a meeting of the board the applicant presents his Church Letter or makes a restatement of his faith or takes the vows of membership for the first time, as the case may be. If his profession or credentials are satisfactory, the board votes to receive him into full membership.

If a new member has not received the ordinance of baptism, he is baptized by sprinkling after taking the vows of membership.

A recognition service for new members is held at a stated time in connection with the Sunday morning worship service. On this occasion the new members are seated in a reserved section and accorded a public welcome. You will be notified of this recognition service in advance.

Considerable thought should be given to organizing classes to prepare people for church membership. An example of a helpful presentation of this aspect of church membership is suggested by the following four-page leaflet printed by one church:

*Page 1*

We Invite You

to Consider Membership with Us

(Small picture of the church printed here.)

Christ Church

(Address)

*Page 2*

a cordial welcome

Before the reception of new members on each Communion Sunday we offer an introduction to the life and work of Christ Church. It is our purpose to discuss the following topics in the four sessions:

1. What we believe—*Our Faith*
2. Where we came from—*Our History*

3. How we work—*Our Organization*
4. What we do—*Our Program*

Although attendance is not required for membership, we hope that you will plan to attend all four meetings. The Rev. John Smith, Associate Minister, is the teacher.

*Pages 3 and 4*

SCHEDULE OF MEETINGS FOR ADULT NEW MEMBER CANDIDATES
19–

| | | |
|---|---|---|
| (1) January 11 | | February 4 |
| (2) January 18 | | Reception of New Members |
| (3) January 25 | | February 8 |
| (4) February 1 | | Communion Sunday |
| | | |
| (1) March 15 | | April 8 |
| (2) March 22 | | Reception of New Members |
| (3) March 29 | | April 12 |
| (4) April 5 | | Communion Sunday |
| | | |
| (1) May 17 | | June 10 |
| (2) May 24 | | Reception of New Members |
| (3) May 31 | | June 14 |
| (4) June 7 | | Communion Sunday |
| | | |
| (1) September 6 | | September 30 |
| (2) September 13 | | Reception of New Members |
| (3) September 20 | | October 4 |
| (4) September 27 | | Communion Sunday |
| | | |
| (1) November 15 | | December 9 |
| (2) November 22 | | Reception of New Members |
| (3) November 29 | | December 13 |
| (4) December 6 | | Communion Sunday |

All meetings to be held on Sunday evenings at 7:30 in the Junior Department Room (third floor) of Christ Church.

The church administrator should provide prospective members with information regarding the denomination, the Christian heritage, and the Christian life. Many Protestant denominations have on hand excellent printed material to answer promptly and convincingly such questions as: "What is the Reformed Church?" "Where can I get a brief history of the church?" "What is the difference between the Protestant and the Roman Catholic church?" "What is expected of me as a member of the church?" "What are the main emphases of this denomination?"

There are many application forms for church membership. One church has found the following simple card effective:

---

Christ Church welcomes into its fellowship all who love our Lord and desire to be associated with His Church.

It is the purpose of this church to provide a Christian fellowship in which service to the Kingdom will find joyful expression and all of us will grow in the likeness of our Lord.

ENLISTMENT IN THE CHURCH

I am willing to subscribe to this covenant and desire to unite with Christ Church,              (address)

Name _____

Address_____

☐ By Profession or Reaffirmation of Faith

☐ By Letter from _____ Church

in _____

---

The reverse of the card contains the Covenant.

---

MY COVENANT WITH GOD AND THE CHURCH

I. In uniting with this church I subscribe to the following declarations:
   1. Believing Jesus Christ to be the Son of God, I accept Him as my own personal Saviour and acknowledge Him as my Master and Lord (Luke 12:8).
   2. Trusting in the Holy Spirit for guidance and grace, I shall seek to lead a consistent Christian life, honoring Christ in all my relationships (John 15:14).

II. As a member of this church I accept the following responsibilities (Mark 8:34):
   1. I shall strive to be faithful in my attendance upon its services (Hebrews 10:25).
   2. I shall endeavor to render some form of Christian service (II Timothy 2:15).
   3. I shall give regularly to the support of the church and its benevolences as the Lord shall prosper me (II Corinthians 9:7).
   4. I shall pray regularly for myself, for others, and for my church (Luke 11:9, 10).

---

## Welcoming the New Member

The reception of the new member into the church should be a significant spiritual experience. In churches that receive members by action of the official board, the occasion should be carefully planned. The minister should present to the members the joys, the privileges, and the responsibilities of church membership. The officers assisting in the election and reception of members should take this opportunity to express the warmth of the entire congregation.

The public acknowledgment of new members on a Sunday morning is an occasion when the ties of new relationship and potential loyalty can be strengthened into the congregational life. It is desirable to publish the names and addresses of new members for distribution to the congregation. Often, publishing them in the Sunday bulletin will suffice. Where there is an annual directory of church members a printed insert for the membership booklet may prove more useful.

Many churches issue a certificate of church membership. It may be a one-fold leaflet with a picture of the church on the outside, a brief statement of the confession and promise of the new member on page 2, and on page 3 a simple statement as follows:

---

This is to certify that

_____

was received by Reaffirmation of Faith
into full membership in
Christ Church
Washington, D.C.
on the _____ day of _____ 19–
_____*Minister*
_____*Clerk*

---

Certificates read: "Reaffirmation of Faith," "Confirmation of Baptism," "Confession of Faith and Adult Baptism," or "Letter of Transfer."

One church issued a one-fold certificate of membership on the back of which is "Steps in Christian Growth," adapted from literature of the Presbyterian Church, U.S.A.:

#### STEPS IN CHRISTIAN GROWTH

1. Have a planned study of God's Word and a regular habit of prayer.
2. Faithfully attend the services of your Church.
3. Sacrificially support the work of Christ.
4. Live a life that is consistent with the will of Christ.
5. Share with others your faith in Jesus Christ.

Not many Protestant churches require identification cards for their members, but churches whose facilities are constantly crowded at worship services have various means of identification for parishioners. One identification tells the usher that the holder is to have preferential seating until five or ten minutes before the worship hour. A new parishioner will undoubtedly appreciate having a printed card signed by the pastor stating: Mr. (or Mrs.) ——— is a member in good standing of Christ Church. Such identification has occasionally been helpful to travelers in distant places. In this connection, Dr. G. Paull T. Sargent, former rector of St. Bartholomew's Church in New York, reports that he gave to each member of his parish who was about to travel such an identification card, together with a statement, signed by himself, that any assistance to that parishioner away from home would be appreciated.

Many churches present to their new members a booklet, or simply a mimeographed compilation, listing the departments of the church and giving the names, addresses, and telephone numbers of their leaders. One church accompanies its material with the following brief statement:

#### INTRODUCTION

Prayerfully and diligently the church leaders and staff are always seeking ways in which *you the members* can be best served.

Historically, one of the major problems of a large church is to keep its membership properly advised of facilities and services available to them.

God has blessed Christ Church with equipment, facilities, services, and resource materials. We have compiled a list of them in booklet form for your convenience.

The staff is here to help you so that together we may better serve our Lord and Saviour, Jesus Christ.

Your Pastor,<br><br>————————

Another church uses a modified form of the "kit" idea. The outside page contains, in part, the following statement:

> The spiritual benefits of your Church to you and your family are commensurate with your participation and your contribution of time, talents, and treasure. The more you give of yourself, the greater your rewards will be. The attitude of the parents toward the Church largely determines the interest and devotion of the children and their ultimate Christian ideals. The family that prays together really does stay together.

In a pocket inside are mimeographed sheets different in color and in size so that the headings stand out one above another. The sheets are entitled "Key Directory, 19–" "Christian Education," "Financial Information," "Youth Activities," "Ministry of Music," "Couples, Groups, Young Adults and Family Activities," "Christ Church Women and Churchmen." Facing this pocket and immediately visible is a mimeographed statement welcoming the new member. It is signed by the minister, and reads as follows:

> A hearty welcome to the new members of our Christ Church.
> In this brochure, and in this material, there are documented the various ways in which you may participate in the rich life of our church.
> It is important that you do participate, for there is little advantage to you, or to your church, if you remain merely a name on the roll. Church membership is a growing experience, not merely a matter of addition.
> The organizations are anxious to welcome you; the Church Services and Church School Services are in duplicate, for your convenience, at 9:30 and 11:00 on Sunday morning. The ministers and the staff are available for counseling and service of many kinds.
> It is a privilege, in the name of the officers and the members and the staff of this church, to welcome you into our fellowship, a community-church fellowship, but primarily a fellowship of Christians.

One of the concerns of a new member may be his lack of familiarity with the church and the church people. To "open the door" one church sends the new member a note from the official board. It states that, though the church is traditionally friendly, the church family is so large that the board asks the new member to use an enclosed identification ribbon reading "New Member." The wearing of the identification will prompt the older members of the church to offer their services and friendship readily. It is suggested that the identification be worn to church functions and that it be kept in purse or billfold for ready use.

### Integration of the New Member

Many persons join the church with great enthusiasm, but their expectations are dulled if integration into the life and fellowship of the church has not been thoughtfully planned. Either the minister or an officer of the church should see that a personal call is made at the home of the new member within a week or ten days after his reception into the congregation. On this occasion he may be given information that was not presented to him at the time of reception, and in face-to-face contact he may express his interests. Such information should be passed on to the church office and, through a designated person, to the department of the church life where the new member might find work or association meaningful. For example, if, in the call, the elder or minister learns that the new member is interested in music, he will note that fact on a card and pass the card to the organist or choir director. The following card is an example:

---

Follow-Up Card for Reference and Use by
Elders in New Member Interviews

(To be returned to the church office within ten days
from assignment.)

Name _____

Address _____

Telephone No. _____

*Remarks:* _____

_____

_____

_____

---

Many new members will appreciate at this time material as to the best ways to cultivate the Christian life and develop their faith. Several denominations have carefully selected, attractively printed material that may be obtained from their departments of evangelism or spiritual advance.

One church assembled four or five leaflets put out by its denominational headquarters in an attractive folder. This folder is left at the home of a new member. Among the titles of the leaflet are: "Steps to Christian Maturity," "Being a Church Member," "Twelve Rules for Christian Living," "How to Pray," and "Your Place in His Church."

The person who calls on the new member should emphasize the spiritual development groups in the church. Obtaining specific information regarding the service and participation interests of the new member at this time is most important. Often this is more productive in gaining his direct interest than an elaborate statement of possibilities for service at the time of his reception into the membership. If the "enlistment sheet" is presented at the time of reception, the new member may give it only cursory attention and he may be hesitant about indicating his past or future interests. But in the quiet of a home the minister or elder may speak directly about opportunities for church service and elicit a more "committed response." He may find it advantageous to have with him an outline of opportunities for service. He may not bring it conspicuously into the picture during the call but may make notes on it later.

Some churches may never have made a careful analysis of the church backgrounds and interests of their members. If that is the case, it may be advantageous to make a thorough membership survey.

One church seeking to obtain comprehensive information regarding its membership used the following questionnaire:

CHRIST CHURCH, MEMBERSHIP SURVEY, April, 19–
(This questionnaire is to be filled in and returned as soon as possible.)

Name _____

Address _____

_____

Home Telephone Number _____

Marital Status            Married                    Single

Date of Birth _____

Occupation _____

     If retired, please check here      and list former occupation above.

Firm Name _____

Business Address _____

Business Telephone Number _____

| | | Yes | No |
|---|---|---|---|
| Education | High School | | |
| | College | | |
| | Other _____ | | |
| | Major field of Study _____ | | |

Please list children living at home:

| *Name* | *Date of Birth* |
|---|---|
| _____ | _____ |
| _____ | _____ |
| _____ | _____ |

Please list, as closely as possible, the date when you united with Christ Church _____

Method of uniting with Christ Church:

☐ Confession of faith
☐ Reaffirmation of faith
☐ Transfer from another church

If you belonged to another church before joining Christ Church, please list name and denomination.

_____

Please list church leadership positions which you have held. List such things as elder, trustee, deacon, teacher, officer in men's, women's, or youth organizations, scout leader, and so on.

Leadership positions held in Christ Church:

_____
_____
_____

Leadership positions held in other churches:

_____
_____
_____

If you are now participating in one or more of the activities listed below, please check in the "Active" column opposite the activity or interest. If you are interested in participating but are not now active, please check in the column marked "Interested." If you may be interested in participating at some future time, please check in the column marked "Future Interest."

| | Active | Interested | Future Interest |
|---|---|---|---|
| **Services—General** | | | |
| Ushering | | | |
| Operating sound system | | | |
| Slide or movie projection | | | |
| Audio-visual librarian | | | |
| Work on church newspaper | | | |
| Working in check room | | | |
| Telephoning | | | |
| Providing memorial flowers | | | |
| Baby sitting | | | |
| **Educational** | | | |
| Teaching: | | | |
| High School—10, 11, 12 grades | | | |
| Junior High—7, 8, 9 grades | | | |
| Junior—4, 5, 6 grades | | | |
| Primary—1, 2, 3 grades | | | |
| Kindergarten | | | |
| Nursery—3-year-olds | | | |
| Nursery—1- and 2-year-olds | | | |
| Nursery—Infant | | | |
| Assistant teacher | | | |
| Librarian | | | |
| Assistant librarian | | | |
| Pianist | | | |
| Organist | | | |
| Nursery School visitor | | | |
| Vacation Church School | | | |
| Teacher in training | | | |
| Junior Church helper | | | |
| **Office Work—General** | | | |
| Typing | | | |
| Mimeographing | | | |
| Addressograph operation | | | |
| Graphotype operation | | | |
| General clerical | | | |
| Private secretary | | | |

Active    Interested    Future Inter

**Visiting**
  Prospective members
  Social calls
  Every Member Canvass
  Visiting shut-ins with church
    service records
**Music**
  Sing in choir
  Piano accompanist
  Choir mother
  Play instrument
  Which instrument
**Youth Group Leaders**
  Boy Scout leader
  Girl Scout leader
  Recreation leader
  Youth Group sponsor
  Camp counselor
**Transportation**
  For Youth groups
  Members to Sunday service
**Women's Projects**
  Women's Association
  Sewing
  Serving in dining room
  Women's Bible Class
  Wedding receptions
**Men's Projects**
  Men's Organization
  Traffic direction
  Dishwashing
  Men's Bible Class
  Conducting church tours
  Donating blood to Christ Church
    blood bank
  Serving in kitchen

|  | Active | Interested | Future Interest |
|---|---|---|---|
| **Participation Interests** | | | |
| Youth Group | | | |
| Young Adult Group | | | |
| Adult Social Activity | | | |
| Drama Guild | | | |
| Square Dance | | | |
| Marriage Clinic | | | |
| Camping | | | |
| **Study Interests** | | | |
| Prayer Group | | | |
| Child Study | | | |
| Bible | | | |
| Family Living | | | |
| Church Government | | | |
| Theology | | | |
| Comparative Religions | | | |
| Church Music | | | |
| World Events | | | |
| Christian Beliefs | | | |
| **Special Skills** | | | |
| Art Work | | | |
| Photography | | | |
| Handicrafts | | | |
| Storytelling | | | |

Please use the space below to make comments or suggestions which you feel may be helpful to your church, that it may serve all its members well.

Many churches have an organized group of parishioners who serve as sponsors for new members. When the sponsor has accepted the assignment of a new member, he is personally to assist in that member's integration. He is expected to fill out a report and return it to the church office in one month's time. A sample report is on page 70.

Sponsor's Report for New Member Received

_____

(Name of New Member)

Will you kindly fill out the following and return it to our office in the enclosed envelope?

| Have you been able to— | Yes | No |
| --- | --- | --- |
| sit with them in church and introduce them to others? | ____ | ____ |
| invite them to some study group? | ____ | ____ |
| bring them to a family night? | ____ | ____ |
| have them in your home? | ____ | ____ |
| invite her to Women's Association? | ____ | ____ |
| have her placed in a circle? | ____ | ____ |

| What was their response to your efforts? | Good | ____ |
| --- | --- | --- |
| | Not interested | ____ |

_____

(Sponsor Sign)

Every church member should be alert for new people to be brought into the life and worship of the church. Where a new member is received into the church the minister should point out that one of the duties and privileges of church membership is to bring others into the fold of Christ. Each member is a missionary in his profession or his business, in his home and in his neighborhood. A program that points this up may find its direction in the following:

Realizing that evangelism is the challenge to every Christian, I hereby dedicate myself to the discipline of praying for one person and doing all I can to bring him into the fellowship of Christ and the Church.

Signed _____

Date _____

"The harvest is plentiful, but the laborers are few; pray therefore the Lord of the harvest to send out laborers into his harvest."
—Matt. 9:37, 38.

At the time of public worship each member of the congregation is asked to give careful and prayerful thought to making such a commitment. The cards are received and fittingly dedicated.

The idea of a loving personal outreach to others through the use of a prospect suggestion card, if properly introduced, can serve a most useful purpose. The form for such a card is as follows:

```
┌─────────────────────────────────────────────────────────────┐
│                  PROSPECT  SUGGESTION                        │
│  I believe _____  │
│                            (name)                            │
│  _____  │
│        (address)                            (phone)          │
│  is a good prospect for membership in the                    │
│     ☐  Church                                                │
│     ☐  Church School                                         │
│     ☐ _____ group                                     │
│  Church background _____  │
│  Religious attitude _____  │
│  Occupation and interests _____  │
│  Why a good prospect _____  │
│  Suggested by _____  │
│                               (signature)                    │
│  (Use other side for more information)                       │
└─────────────────────────────────────────────────────────────┘
```

Let us turn now to various parish activities that can deepen the interest and participation of members in active congregational life.

## DRAMATIC PROGRAMS

Drama had its origin and infant relationships within the Christian church. There are evidences in the twentieth century of attempts to return to that alliance beween spiritual values and their portrayal through the drama.

The survey of church members will uncover persons who are interested and experienced in drama. Oriented with prayer and direction to further the life of the congregation, both on the spiritual and the fellowship side, a properly conceived program may be enriching.

The drama program should be aligned with the governing board, and that body should have oversight of the dramatic activities through a designated church officer or through a committee delegated to report to the minister and the governing body.

If a church desires to institute a dramatic program, the first step is to call a meeting of all those interested. Such a meeting, which brings together many members, will also reveal leadership for the program. One congregation developed a splendid dramatic interest in the church through the initial enthusiasm of four people.

Opportunities should be presented to the group not only for special and major dramatic production but also for leadership in dramatic programs by children and young people, as at Children's Day and at Christmastime. Also, the drama group may fittingly offer its services to the adult organizations, such as the women's society, which may desire a special type of presentation for an annual or special meeting.

The drama group may attract persons of widely varied interests and abilities. Some, of course, are interested in acting in the dramatic presentations. Others may be interested in writing, directing, producing, designing and constructing sets, making costumes, managing stage properties, producing sound effects, lighting, and so on. Others again are interested in preparing the program, publicity or posters, or in handling the tickets.

Whether the dramatic group plans to offer major presentations, such as *Family Portrait* or *The Concrete City*, or simpler presentations, such as anniversary pageants and special programs for the high seasons of the church year, success or failure will depend mainly on organization and administration.

Besides a clear understanding of the division of authority between the governing body and the dramatic group, leadership is most important. Though the minister may not be directly or regularly involved in planning the activities of the drama group, he must have a constant interest in them and be ready with his counsel and guidance.

## CONGREGATIONAL DINNERS

Where facilities are available, a meal for the whole congregation is a valuable opportunity for parishioners to become acquainted with one another in an informal atmosphere and to share in some phase of the spiritual life. Many churches have family buffet suppers during Advent and Lent. Both in rural and metropolitan areas occasions when families eat together and then participate in a special worship service may stimulate regular church attendance.

Many congregations have successfully combined family suppers with a lecture series. Often during the Lenten season clergymen give sermons of spiritual and educational significance. Some churches have classes in various subjects appealing to different interests after the evening dinner.

To be successful the congregational dinner must be efficiently organized. The following plan has proved successful: Working under a chairman and a co-chairman or vice chairman should be the following committees: flower, table setting, decoration, preparation, and clean-up. Several women should supervise the preparation of the food. Other helpful committees include reservations, hospitality, music, table hosts and hostesses, and waitresses. Often junior and senior high school students serve as waitresses.

## LECTURES

The purpose of this book is to discuss not the substance of church programs but the administration of these programs. The principles recommended for future programs are as follows:

*a*) There must be a purpose for the lecture—educational, inspirational, or informative—to deepen the spiritual perceptiveness of the parish.

*b*) The lecture should be held at an hour convenient for the majority of those likely to attend.

*c*) Careful attention should be given to the place of the lecture. If the audience is likely to exceed the accommodations, extra chairs should be provided for a possible overflow. Contrariwise, if a small attendance is expected, a smaller room should be used.

*d*) The lecture should be announced well in advance. If it has community interest, the use of newspapers, posters, advertising, and publicity should be considered. If tickets are needed for admission, the place for obtaining them should be clearly mentioned, and responsible persons should be placed in charge of them. Public interest in the lecture will determine whether or not ushers are needed.

*e*) It should be determined in advance whether there will be an opportunity for questions, and if so, whether questions are to be addressed to the lecturer orally or in writing. If they are to be in writing, provisions must be made for collecting them.

*f*) It is important that everyone be able to hear. If the hall is large and the acoustics doubtful, a public address system tested before the lecture should be used, with someone responsible for its proper functioning.

*g*) The lecture room should be properly ventilated. A person appointed in advance should open windows whenever the room becomes oppressively warm and uncomfortable.

*h*) Prior to the lecture the chairman and the lecturer should have determined the time limit for the talk and for the question period. The audience should understand and abide by these arrangements. Often a lecture suffers in effectiveness because it is too long or because the question period is not properly limited. If at the time for adjournment there are still questions, the chairman should nevertheless call the meeting to a close and, with the approval of the speaker, invite individuals either to come forward or to meet the lecturer at an appointed place to discuss their questions.

*i*) The lecturer should be introduced suitably but briefly.

*j*) Individual lectures and lecture series should be planned with the counsel and judgment of the governing body. Lectures should be given for the purpose of furthering or undergirding some need in the church life, and their timing is very important.

*k*) Arrangements should be made by correspondence for the lecturer's transportation to and from the place of the meeting.

*l*) If an honorarium is to be paid, that matter will have been cleared with the governing body so that the compensation may be handed to the lecturer at the time of the lecture.

*m*) Depending upon circumstances and the lecturer's wishes, a reception may be held before or after the lecture. The lecturer may wish quiet and solitude before his presentation. Some speakers may appreciate the opportunity to meet members of the church either before or after the lecture; others may wish to leave immediately. These details will have been arranged with the lecturer before the appointed evening.

## MUSICAL AND OTHER CULTURAL EVENTS

Some churches serve their parish and the community by bringing major cultural and musical events into the orbit of the church.

The church I serve seeks annually to invite a major figure who has made notable contributions to the aesthetic and cultural life of our time. On one memorable evening Robert Frost was the guest. Because of Mr. Frost's popularity tickets were distributed in advance, and ticketholders were given preferential seating.

The organization for the evening included: (1) a general chairman; (2) three vice chairmen, forming, with the general chairman and the two other officers, an executive committee; (3) a treasurer and ticket chairman; (4) a chairman of hospitality; (5) a chairman of ushers; (6) the ministers of the church who presented Mr. Frost to the congregation; (7) the sextons who saw to the arrangement of the stage, seating, lighting, and ventilation; (8) and a person in charge of the sound system.

Leaders of our Bronxville Church experimented in bringing significant musical events to our congregation and community. An announcement of these events went to the congregation and to other interested people in the community. It read:

### It Is Coming to You!

December 11, 1959—YEHUDI MENUHIN—World-famous violin virtuoso will present a program. 8:30 P.M.

February 3, 1960—The complete CLEVELAND SYMPHONY ORCHESTRA with George Szell conducting. 8:30 P.M.

May 6, 1960—GEORGE LONDON, leading American bass-baritone of the Metropolitan Opera Company. 8:30 P.M.

Three great evenings of fine music are coming to you!

There will be no necessity for city trains or garage space for cars. It will all be right here in the Congregational Hall of Christ Church at State Street and Center Avenue in Crestville.

This fine music is coming to you for $15 per person for the three concerts. (There will be no single tickets sold for an individual concert.)

Seating space is limited. Get your tickets now from—

   Mrs. John Jones, 1 Washington Road, Crestville, N.Y., Ce 2-7159

   Mrs. James Fenton, Christ Church, Crestville, N.Y., Ce 2-5540

Checks are to be made payable to Christ Church.

Printing and mailing courtesy of Crestville National Bank and Trust Company of Crestville. (Help from commercial organization.)

The organization for a venture of this nature is necessarily involved, including a general chairman; committees on hospitality, patrons, tickets, publicity; an advisory committee; representatives of the women's society, the ushers' association, the evening group, and other groups of the church. In planning events of this kind the minister and the governing board must determine that they are in keeping with the over-all purpose of the church and are furthering its basic Christian ministry to the parish and the community.

## SERMON PUBLICATIONS

The able preacher will receive requests for copies of his sermons. Supplying these copies may prove a burden on the minister and his secretary if he is fortunate enough to have one. Sermons may be reproduced in various ways. Mimeographing them on 9-by-11-inch paper is comparatively easy, but the bulk and size of mimeographed copies is a disadvantage. A leaflet 5-by-6 inches containing four sermons would fit easily in a lady's purse but not so easily in a man's coat pocket. A 3-by-7-inch publication has the advantage of easy insertion into a legal size envelope, but a 2½-by-4½-inch leaflet of about sixteen pages could easily be mailed in a regular-size envelope.

The sermon publication program can be supported in one of several ways. Some churches provide in the annual budget a stipulated amount for sermon reproduction and distribution. Other churches have no set program, and action is taken by the governing body according to the number of requests for copies. Sometimes members of the congregation who have been helped by a particular sermon will volunteer to defray the cost of reproducing it.

If the governing board feels that the distribution of sermons will serve to enlarge the ministry of the church, it should devise a plan for the distribution.

A plan to print ten or twelve sermons a year, under the direction of the board and supervised by a sermon publication committee, is worthy of consideration. The project may be supported by voluntary contributions.

Some churches publish sermons and the church magazine on a subscription basis. This policy should be the last recourse. If the project is worth while, it should be available without subscription to a large number of people, not only parishioners but also interested outsiders.

The following procedure for a sermon publication project is recommended: (1) The plan should be approved by the governing board. (2) The chairman of the sermon publication committee should be a member of the official board. (3) The committee should include two other active officers of the board—an elder and a deacon. The other members should be parishioners selected for their regular attendance at worship, their interest in sermons, and their intellectual and spiritual development, their church loyalty, or their experience in publicity and public relations. (4) The names of the members should be published several times a year, and the congregation should be invited to make suggestions to the committee as to which sermons should be published. (5) The committee should meet every two to three months to select the sermons for publication. (6) The sermons should be mailed monthly to all members of the church, particularly to students away at school or college, to members serving in the armed forces, to ministers and chaplains, and to others who have requested copies. (7) Whenever possible, the sermons should be mailed with other church publicity, such as the monthly magazine. The sermons should also be placed on the literature tables throughout the church for strangers and visitors. Additional copies should be placed regularly at distribution points in the local hospital. (8) The project should be supported by the voluntary gifts of those receiving the sermons. A request should be sent out annually as follows:

DEAR FRIEND OF CHRIST CHURCH:

Herewith we send you a sermon preached from our pulpit by Dr. Smith, another sermon selected by our committee.

These printed sermons are distributed to our students, members of the church in our armed forces, to chaplains and schools across the nation and throughout the world.

The project is supported by the voluntary gifts of those who are interested.

It has been more than a year since we have invited friends to share in this work. We do so now.

If you wish to contribute to this ministry, will you please use the enclosed envelope to send your contribution for our work.

Thank you in advance for your support.

Yours faithfully,

*Chairman, Sermon Publication Committee*

Each sermon sent out should contain the following statement:

This sermon is published in the interest of extending the influences of Christianity and strengthening the spirit of all Christians who chance to read it. When you have finished reading this copy, please pass it to a neighbor that he too may be enriched by its message.

A particular aim of the Sermon Publication Committee is to make selected sermons available to shut-ins, young people away at school, members of the armed forces and any others who are unable to attend church. If you know someone who wishes to receive these publications regularly, please inform the Christ Church Office, Newtown, New York.

This is a self-supporting project of Christian work. Voluntary contributions make its distribution possible.

Gifts and communications should be directed to:

> John H. Smith
> Sermon Publication Committee
> Christ Church
> Newtown, New York

In reproducing the sermons, the date and place of the preaching of it should be clearly indicated. If there is an established program such as the one outlined above, each sermon should be numbered for future reference. The year should be indicated by a volume number, and the sermons in numerical order.

## FINANCE COMMITTEE, ITS WORK AND RESPONSIBILITY

Responsibilities and duties of the finance committee should be specified in written statement or by-law established by the governing board. The "standing rules" of one church read as follows:

The Finance Committee shall be composed of nine (9) members, at least three of whom shall be appointed from the new members of the board each year. The committee shall report to the board at each regular meeting. They shall have the management and supervision of all financial affairs of the church. They shall ascertain the financial needs of the church for the coming year and prepare a budget embodying the same and present it to the board at its October meeting for its approval. Upon approval of the budget by the board, the Finance Committee shall devise ways and means of raising the money to meet the same and take charge of the canvass of the congregation or any other plan that may be adopted by the board to raise the needed funds.

In some church organizations the auditing committee is an adjunct or subcommittee of the finance committee, but the auditing committee should be a separate standing committee responsible directly to the governing body.

Among the most important responsibilities of the finance committee are the handling of gifts and contributions to the church, the keeping of necessary records, and the suitable distribution of funds under the authority and direction of the governing body. Many churches overlook the importance of proper procedures for handling offerings and gifts.

One congregation outlined the procedure for the handling of church funds as follows:

### PROCEDURE FOR HANDLING COLLECTIONS

I. Sunday Collections

A. *First Sunday Morning Service*. Collections are to be carried by two persons—the captain of ushers for the day (or an usher appointed by him) and another usher—from the chancel to the Consistory Room and placed in the canvas bag(s) with attached lock, checking in the process for any notes which should be delivered that day to the ministers. The canvas bags should then be locked and placed in the treasurer's compartment of the vault, leaving the treasurer's compartment unlocked. The ushers should then lock the vault by throwing the combination.

*Note:* Ushers will please look on the floor and elsewhere to be sure no money has fallen off the plates.

B. *Second Morning Service*. Repeat above procedure. One usher and the consistory man on duty for the day must remain until the Church School Treasurer places her locked Church School money bag in the treasurer's compartment. This usher and the consistory man should then lock the treasurer's compartment and the vault itself by throwing the combination.

C. *On Monday Morning*

1. The bookkeeper (who has the combination of the vault), the Church School Treasurer (who has the key to the treasurer's compartment) and the volunteer (who will assist with the counting) will take out of the vault the Church School collections and give them to the Church School Treasurer.

2. Both the bookkeeper and the volunteer will take the locked bags to the bookkeeper's office, the office secretary who has the keys to the locked bags will open them, and the bookkeeper and the vol-

unteer (calling upon outside help where necessary) will proceed with the count.

3. In counting, the following must be observed:

   a. Two persons must always be present.

   b. The work may not be divided with one person doing half of the job all of the way and the other person the other half. One must count while the other observes, and then the original observer recounts while the original counter observes.

   c. The results of the count should be recorded in ink on the cashbook sheet which must be initialed and dated by both counters.

   d. *Envelopes.* First sort them numerically and break by hundreds. Each group of one hundred is to be treated separately; each envelope opened separately, the contents counted, amount noted on the envelope and recorded in the cash book in ink. Each group of one hundred should be proved by the double-count method and by footing in the cash book. After this the proved section may be merged with the loose plate.

   e. *Deposit.* Make up the deposit slip in duplicate. Wrap cash and coin as per the bank's instructions. Both individuals will prove the cash check to the deposit slip and initial the copy of the deposit slip and duplicate tape of checks. Both individuals will take the deposit to the bank.

II. *Thursday Lenten Services and Other Special Services at Which a Collection Is Taken.* The same procedure as above should be followed for special collections.

III. *Daily Mail.* Any mail (which is opened by anyone on the staff) containing cash or checks should be counted by the bookkeeper and an assistant, and the results entered in ink in the cash book, checked, and initialed by both parties.

IV. *Distribution of Controls*

*Vault.* Bookkeeper has key or combination. He does not have the key to the treasurer's compartment or to the locked bags.

*Key to the Treasurer's Compartment.* An assistant who does not have the combination to the vault or the keys to the locked bags.

*Keys to the Locked Bags.* Another assistant who does not have the key to the treasurer's compartment but does have the combination to the vault.

The treasurer of the church should be either an appointed or exofficio member of the finance committee. His duties should be clearly stated, and his work should have the double control of both the finance committee and of the governing body. The treasurer should make a report at each regular board meeting. In the annual audit of the church, his working procedures should be fully reviewed, and the counsel of the professional auditor should receive careful consideration by the governing body.

One church stipulates the duties of the treasurer as follows:

### TREASURER

1. The board shall annually elect a treasurer, who need not be a member of the board. The treasurer shall attend all meetings of the board and shall be a member ex officio of the Finance Committee. Before he enters on the execution of his duties, he shall, together with two sufficient individual sureties, or a surety company, to be approved by the board, execute a bond to "Christ Church" in the sum of ten thousand dollars, conditioned for his prompt and faithful discharge of the trusts reposed in him. The premium on any such bond shall be paid from the funds of the church.

2. The treasurer shall have the custody and safekeeping of all bonds, mortgages, deeds, maps, and other papers and evidences of titles to lands, and other property belonging to the church, and shall not deliver the same, or any of them, out of his possession, except on an order of the board and then only against a receipt therefor. He shall, however, aid the officers of the board and the members of all committees, standing or special, with all such information as he may possess relating to the subjects committed to them.

3. The treasurer shall, under the direction of the Finance Committee, collect and receive all the income and revenues of the church; pay all taxes and assessments payable by the church; effect from time to time fire or other insurance on or in connection with the property of the church and pay for the same; pay the fixed salaries of the ministers and employees of the church; and make only such other expenditures as may be authorized from time to time by the board.

4. He shall deposit in the name of the church all funds of the church in such bank or banks, trust company or trust companies as the Finance Committee shall approve. He shall keep proper and detailed accounts of all his receipts and disbursements, and all financial transactions, subject at all times to the inspection of the board or any committees designated by it.

5. On the days of the stated meetings of the board, the treasurer shall balance his cash books, and lay before the board his accounts of receipts and expenditures, showing the balance in the treasury. At the stated meeting of the board on the second Thursday in January in each year he shall render full and particular accounts of all his transactions as Treasurer for the preceding fiscal year.

Under the section "Personnel," particularly under the duties of financial secretary, other considerations regarding the treasurer and his office are enumerated.

One important responsibility of the finance committee is the supervision of ways and means to pay the bills and obligations of the church.

Another duty, in most of our churches, is the preparation of the annual budget and the planning for the every-member canvass.

In one parish the finance committee has subcommittees engaged in the improvement of the church finances and the stewardship life of the parish. One committee is set up in four sections, with every member assigned to a specific department of the finance work. The committee includes the chairman, under whose leadership are appointed: (1) Every-member-canvass chairman, a subcommittee with a chairman and two other members. (2) Concerns the Capital Fund Follow-up, with a chairman and two supporting members. (3) Concerns the Financial Committee from the congregation, with a chairman and supporting members. In this particular church, the Financial Committee from the congregation is a parish-wide organization engaged in the actual annual every-member canvass. It functions throughout the year, educating the congregation as to the needs and the programs of the church. (4) Includes advisory members, a worthy section of the finance committee. This group also includes the treasurer of the church, who serves ex officio, senior and outstanding members with sound judgment, long experience in financial affairs, or their capacities for major financial support of the church. Meeting with the finance committee from time to time in the church year, these advisory members provide not only good counsel but also general support for the total work of the committee.

The finance committee is responsible for the preparation of the church budget. Depending on the size and complexity of the church life, this may involve considerable detail. Far in advance of the every-member canvass, the standing committees that have charge of phases of the church life where moneys are expended should be given an opportunity to submit their budgetary estimates for the coming year. Estimates should be submitted by the music, benevolences, maintenance and operation, and Christian education committees. The pulpit supply committee and the personnel or leadership committee, if that is a separate committee, should also submit, at an appointed time, a proposed budget for the coming year.

The chairman of the finance committee, with the treasurer, should not only receive the budgetary proposals of the several departments of the church but also should, if necessary, discuss the requirements and suggestions with the chairmen. The finance committee should request a carefully itemized budget in each case. Where necessary, there should be an explanation, either written or verbal, for including a particular item in the budget.

After receiving the various recommendations and suggestions from the several departments, the finance committee as a whole must study and prepare the total budget for the coming year and submit it to the governing board for consideration and approval. If the denomination demands congregational approval, this requirement must be met.

If a congregational meeting is not required, the parish leader will thoroughly familiarize the membership with the budgetary needs of the church.

Under circumstances where it is desirable, the finance committee should pass on to the parish certain items of information regarding contributions to the church. For example, some members may wish to make their contributions in the form of securities rather than cash. The finance committee of one church supplies the following advice to members in this position:

GIVING SECURITIES TO CHRIST CHURCH

If you decide to give the church securities in payment of a pledge for the Annual Church Expense Budget, please note:

The security should be made payable to you personally. Do not endorse it in any way.

Use a stock assignment form (the church will supply these forms if wanted) made out in blank, listing the security. Sign the form personally. Have a bank guarantee the signature and also have it witnessed. If you bank by mail, send the stock assignment to your bank to have your signature guaranteed, and then have the stock assignment returned to you. It is not negotiable by itself.

Send a letter to the church treasurer as follows:

"Christ Church Treasurer                                   "Date_____
"Marion, Ohio

"I am delivering to you herewith Certificate No._____, for_____ shares of_____stock of the_____Company, registered in my name, as a gift to Christ Church for its general purposes.

Signed_____"

Send the letter and the stock certificate to the church treasurer in one envelope but send the stock assignment in a separate envelope to the church treasurer. Neither the stock certificate nor the stock assignment is negotiable by itself, and you will avoid excess postage.

If the letter is sent in duplicate, the church treasurer will note its receipt on the duplicate and return it to you. If it is not in duplicate, an official receipt will be sent to you by the church treasurer. Thank you, in advance.

The finance committee has the great privilege of educating the congregation in Christian stewardship. This should be a year-in, year-out project. If the church has a public relations committee, the chairman of the finance committee together with the public relations committee should devise a program which, throughout the church year, will keep the church members informed of the work of the church and will foster the proper attitude toward Christian stewardship.

## EVERY-MEMBER CANVASS

The every-member canvass provides an occasion when the entire church membership may be reached and, by adequate preparations, direction, and spirit, may be a means of invigorating the spiritual tone of the whole parish. Every member is asked to give. This can be an educative opportunity and an experience of deep dedication. Since nearly every major Protestant church body has prepared material that is readily available and ideally suited for the program of stewardship on the local congregational level, there is little need to duplicate that effort here.

## THE CHURCH BUILDING COMMITTEE

As a church faces the prospect of structural addition, a new church building or parish house, or relocation, the appointment of a suitable committee becomes imperative.

Many denominational headquarters, as well as the offices of the National Council of the Churches of Christ, can offer guidance and suggestions to churches facing such projects. Fuller details regarding this aspect of the church program are considered in Section IV, particularly on pages 283–284. The basic principles for the establishment of a building committee are discussed below:

*a.* The building committee should be appointed by the governing board.

*b.* Its major purpose should be to study the needs and the programs of the parish, and submit a report on whether or not new or modified facilities are needed.

*c.* If the report recommends additional buildings and the official board approves the recommendation, the matter should be presented to the congregation. The question should be asked: "Shall we proceed at this time to investigate the specific type of structure needed and the cost thereof?"

*d.* If the governing body and the congregation decide in the affirmative, the original building committee may be dismissed or reconstituted and another committee be appointed to answer the next question.

*e.* It is advisable to prescribe the limits of the committee's authority and the limit of the funds it may expend to gain the desired information.

The committee should consult the staff members, the department heads, and the leaders of the programs that might be affected by the new building project. What are their suggestions? And, in their opinion, what are the primary needs? What are their specific suggestions and counsel as to how their work and the work of the church as a whole may be made effective through the proposed building program?

*f.* At this point, with a general outline of the needs of the parish and suggestions for meeting them, the committee would do well to consult the department of architecture of its denomination and to correspond with the appropriate department of the National Council of Churches.

*g.* An architect may be engaged to make sketches from the general specifications that have been prepared. The fee to be paid and the limitations of the commitment of the church to the architect should be stated in writing.

*h.* The purpose of preliminary sketches is to inform the congregation visually of the proposed building and to provide rough specifications on which responsible builders may base estimates of costs.

*i.* With the indication of the needs, with some architectural proposal as to how those needs can be met, and with estimates of the cost by responsible builders, the committee should present a report to the governing board and, with its counsel, to the congregation. The question now is, "Shall we engage an architect to prepare definite plans and proceed to raise funds for the church building?"

*j*. At this point the governing body may again dismiss the committee or reconstitute it for the work at hand.

*k*. The committee should be composed of representatives of the major departments of the church. The minister should, from the beginning of the project to its consummation, be an ex officio member of the committee. The committee should be divided into subcommittees determined by the nature of the building program.

One church-wide committee that was engaged in a project to expand its educational and congregational facilities, as well as to plan for chancel renovations, including a new organ, had the following setup: a chairman and a co-chairman, and a chairman for each of the following departments: education and survey, worship, music, finance and promotion, church administration, recreation, plans and construction, women's activities, furnishing and equipment.

Once established, the church building committee should be maintained, if possible, without change of personnel until the project is completed.

*l*. It is advisable that it remain in existence for at least a year after the completion of the project. A subcommittee on financial follow-up or any capital program may well be maintained for several years.

*m*. All records, correspondence, blueprints, and minutes of the church building committee should be placed in the church archives upon completion of the committee's work.

## CHOIRS AND CHOIR GUILDS

Sacred music being one of the "ministries" of the church, the proper administration of this significant phase of the church life is highly important. The understanding and backing of the official board and the minister are essential to its success. Close relationship between the pastor and the director of music should be encouraged and cultivated. A harmony of thought and conviction between them will enrich not only the major worship occasions in the sanctuary but also the mutual supportiveness throughout the church life.

The music committee of the governing body should be chaired by a church officer competent in the art of music or genuinely interested in and devoted to the ministry of music in the over-all program of the church. The music committee should be responsible to the governing board for the oversight of all phases of the ministry of sacred song. It should report periodically to the governing body regarding the statistics of the choirs, the morale, and the needs for the program, and should prepare the budget for the music department for submission to the finance committee. It should have authority to seek replacements in the music department personnel and to recommend them for approval by the governing body.

As an agency of the official board the members of the music committee can undergird the entire musical program by their interest in it. They may occasionally attend choir rehearsals. In some churches, particularly in those that have a volunteer choir, the committee may improve the morale of the director and the singers by arranging an annual dinner or reception at which the appreciation of the official board and the entire congregation is expressed.

The music committee together with the director of music should study the needs of the church, and devise activities and offer musical opportunities commensurate with those needs for every member of the parish. The committee should be sensitive to the fact that participation in choral work provides an opportunity for spiritual education. It should further cooperation between the music department and the Christian education program by enabling the director of music to assist the church school in selecting hymns for departmental services and in providing special musical counsel and support for all opening exercises and special church school events.

Churches should seriously consider organizing youth and children's choirs. If there is an interest in such a program, the music committee, with the music director, should plan to set up a program.

The music director, the chairman of the music committee, and perhaps the leading representative of the Christian education department will work together to determine the hours for rehearsal; the type of music to be taught; the occasions for public appearance; the type of robes to be worn, the method of obtaining them, and their care; and the advisability of an organization of church members to support the director in the development of the choir or choirs.

Where a church has a multiple-choir ministry, an organization for the senior, or chancel, choir has proved beneficial. Particularly significant may be an organization of interested mothers in a choir guild.

One church ten years ago had two choirs. Owing to the interest of the governing body, an active music committee, and a devoted director of music, it now has eight music groups. The organization of the chancel, or senior, choir and the choir guild are outlined below.

A.  *The Chancel Choir:*

Mr. John Johnson, president, 1959–1960

Mrs. Francis Brown, retiring president

*Purpose:* To promote instructional, educational, and social activities within the Chancel Choir and in cooperation with other departments and organizations within the church.

To conduct routine business matters pertaining to the Chancel Choir and for the Chancel Choir.

*Executive Committee* of Chancel Choir consists of the president, secretary, and treasurer. Chancel Choir funds are derived from a one-dollar assessment of each member and are dispersed for the purposes of the choir's social commitments, flowers to hospitalized members, flowers to funerals involving members and families, memorial gifts, and so on.

*Committee of the Congregation for the Chancel Choir*

Mrs. Henry Brown, chairman, 1958–1959 and 1959–1960

Mrs. Burton Smith, vice chairman

*Purpose:* Recruitment of singers; help with care of Chancel Choir robes; Chancel Choir suppers; interest in and concern for morale and the well-being of the choir; public relations and publicity.

B.  *The Choir Guild*

1. Name: The Choir Guild of Christ Church
2. Object

The purpose of the Choir Guild is to strengthen the music program by supporting the choirs through public relations and promoting and caring for the mechanics of the activity so the directors can concentrate on the musical aspect of the work.

3. Membership
   The membership is to be composed of parents of choir members, music directors, and chaplains.
4. Executive Committee
   The Executive Committee is to be composed of general officers, the music directors, the chaplains and a representative of the Chancel Choir.
5. General Officers and Duties of Each:
   a. President
   b. Vice President: To work cooperatively with the president and share the responsibility of her work; to be responsible for the direction of social functions of the Choir Guild; and to keep the inventories of the choir properties.
   c. Recording Secretary: To record the minutes and attendance of the Executive Committee meetings.
   d. Corresponding Secretary: To write letters for the Executive Committee and to be responsible for the preparation of birthday cards for the Carol, Children's, Junior, and Boys' choirs.
   e. Publicity Chairman: To write articles concerning Choir Guild activity with the approval of the directors, president, and vice president.
   f. Chairman of each group in the Choir Guild: Each group may have its own corresponding secretary (telephone), robing chairman, and hostess chairman if, at the discretion of the group's chairman, these specific officers are deemed necessary. Each chairman is asked to confer with the director in October and prior to the award services.

Clearly conceived administrative details of such an organization and program are seen in the following memorandum:

MEMO TO: Parents of Choir Members
FROM: The Music Department

1. *Services:* Each choir will take part in various church and church school worship services throughout the year. Specific preparation for these occasions is made in the rehearsals immediately preceding. In general we feel a child cannot get the most out of choir participation without thorough preparation. A group can only perform at its best with instructed members. Therefore choir members are not to sing in services unless they have been present for the rehearsal immediately preceding the service and two other rehearsals when the music was being prepared. In case of injustice in this ruling, consultation with the director is invited.

2. *Rehearsals:* A rehearsal schedule is distributed to the members of each choir in the fall. We want the children to enjoy their choir role and, at the same time, to feel that they are learning to be of service. With this in mind, we ask that at each rehearsal they enter God's house prepared for a spiritual experience, neat in appearance and in keen anticipation of the task of the hour ahead.

3. *Dress:* Beautiful robes are provided for each choir. The function of the robe is twofold: signifying the chorister as a leader in worship and providing a harmonious group appearance. Without conformity of dress, a choir may provide distractions to the worshiper. Therefore the following regulations have been designed:

| *Little Girls* | *Older Girls* | *Boys* |
|---|---|---|
| Hair ribbons, if necessary, small and white | No crinolines | White shirts |
| | No hair adornments | Dark four-in-hand ties |
| No bracelets | No bracelets | Plain dark socks |
| No crinolines | No earrings | Dark trousers |
| White socks | Dark shoes | Dark polished shoes |
| Dark shoes | | |

4. *Awards:* Toward the end of the year, an award is given each child with a good attendance record (hence the value of excuses) and cooperative behavoir. The award is worn on a ribbon over the choir robe. A wooden cross is added to the award ribbon the fifth year that a child receives an award, and a hymnal is presented the sixth year.

5. *Absences:* We like to have written excuses when children are ill or are out of town. This not only helps us to keep your child's choir record straight, which is important in the giving of awards, but helps us to understand a child's response and interest in the choir program. Absences due to forgetfulness or indifference are not considered excusable.

WILLIAM M. MERRILL
*Director of Music*

A choir newsletter may be significant in arousing interest and furthering a healthy morale among choristers. The following sample reveals the care and thoughtfulness of a well-administered choral program:

### CHOIR NEWSLETTER
#### CHRIST CHURCH, WINSTON, OHIO

Issue

10

Father, sing in my heart that I may pray.
I cannot pray till I have heard Thy song:
sing in my heart a song of hope. There
are moments in which Thou speakest only
in song. I do not ask a revelation; I do not
ask a lifting of the night: I only ask a light-
ening of the heart which refuses to be defined.
Music proves nothing, but it helps me to
prove all things. Give me Thy music therefore, O my Father! —GEORGE MATHESON

September

1959

#### CHOIR SUPPER

Next Thursday, October 1, at 6:30 P.M. in the Assembly Hall

Price $1.00 per person

Chicken royale (stuffed breast with sauce)
Spiced peaches
Whole tomatoes
Hot bread
Lady Baltimore cake
Coffee

You know Ruth! So you know the above menu doesn't in any way indicate
the really great cooking she provides. Where else could you dine as well for
a dollar?

You are welcome to bring guests, especially choir prospects.

Reservations for the supper must be made by Monday noon, September 28.
We request your dollar at the time your reservation is made. You recognize,
we're sure, that the suppers are run on a tight budget. We cannot return money
if you find you cannot attend after the food is ordered on Monday afternoon.

Christ Church, Winston, Ohio
Music Department

I wish to make _____ reservation(s) for the Choir Supper on Thursday, October 1, at 6:30 P.M.

Enclosed is my check ☐          cash ☐ at $1.00 per person.

Signed _____

Our first page presents both spiritual and material food. So will the Chancel Choir supper, for Mr. Merrill plans to speak on "The Beauty of Holiness." This phrase is one which we have said with our lips and sung with our lips all our lives. It may be time to pause and consider its meaning. We who take an active part in the worship of a congregation should be aware of its significance.

Another ingredient of the Chancel Choir suppers has not been mentioned. Sociability! Especially after a long absence from our work together, it will be pleasant to sit down together for the chitchat that goes a long way toward helping people to sing in tune with happiness.

We are a disparate group, come to think of it! Teachers, lawyers, housewives, businesswomen, senior citizens, students, doctors' assistants, businessmen, and a decorator. In other words, we are representative of the various forces that make the world go round! As aides to the worship of a large congregation and an extension of that congregation into the Chancel, disparate is exactly what we ought to be! Nice to know we are right in this respect.

Our first two rehearsals have been thrilling. Never before have we begun a season with such a good sound!

. We welcome our new members: sopranos Margaret Brown and Mary French; alto Kay McMillan; the return of our tenor Fred Jones; and basses Frederick Mason and John Martin. There is some very real ability in this group of new members. We are proud to have them with us. Let's all make them welcome, and help them to enjoy their work with us.

Mary and her husband are on Cape Cod enjoying a belated vacation; we miss the Smiths; Mary Barton has a job getting all the demands of their nursery school satisfied, but she hopes to join later; you've been reading about Bob Major in the newspapers, so his absence is self-explanatory, trying to do a good job for us in Washington. Florence Davis, with four boys in school, was asked to boost the PTA, and she felt conscience-bound to do it—hers meets two Thursdays a month, and she feels badly that it could not be changed.

There will be a beautiful Music Department exhibit at the Congregational Dinner on October 2. Mary Poe has lent us some museum-piece treasures to spark our display, and Frank Harris, chairman of Operations and Maintenance of the Church, is helping with the mechanical aspects of the display. Do be sure to take it in.

President: Henry Malcolm
Secretary: Carla Johnson
Treasurer: Mary Andrews
Chairman of Music Committee:
   Edward Arnold
Chairman of Chancel Choir Committee: Joan Carter

Mary Barry has a new job teaching public school music. Congratulations and all good wishes for success. Mary is also playing the organ in Youth Chapel this year at 11:00.

William Merrill is giving six lectures at the Theological Seminary on Parish Music, starting this week.

Organ Recital: On October 25 at 4:30 in the Church, Bill will play three of Mozart's organ sonatas with strings, the Mendelssohn first Sonata and Franck's A Minor Chorale.

## NURSERY SCHOOL

On finding the need within their parish for the care of preschool children, many churches are developing effective nursery schools. These are not only significant in the lives of younger children but also constructive to the homes of young parents.

The nursery school may be organized and developed on several bases:

1. It may be placed in the hands of persons who will operate it outside the jurisdiction of the church. They will be provided with the facilities for the school and will make agreed compensation to the church.

2. The nursery school may be organized as an adjunct of the church program. The staff will be, by means of the religious education committee, employees of the church.

3. Some nursery schools have operated with relative effectiveness on a cooperative basis. In such schools, by mothers sharing in the leadership and responsibility, the school operates without a professional staff and at minimum cost to participants. The cooperative type of nursery school should be considered carefully and cautiously. It requires a great deal of administrative time and organizational talent and the continuous attention of an appointed staff who will take full responsibility for the development of the program and activity. Special supervision by the minister and the Christian education committee is advisable.

4. A modified form of cooperative school established with the approval of the governing board and operated under the supervision of the Christian education committee has much to recommend it. The staff are considered church employees and are therefore subject to the same privileges and/or restrictions as other church employees. But the participating and cooperative aspects are maintained through the formation of a mothers' board, which is responsible to the Christian education committee and is commissioned to concern itself with all problems related to the administration and activity of the school.

Following is a set of by-laws of a nursery school operated in a church where there is a mothers' board.

By-Laws of Christ Church Nursery School

## Article I

### NAME

The school shall be known as Christ Church Nursery School.

## Article II

### PURPOSES, POLICIES, AND FUNCTIONAL ORGANIZATION

*Section 1.* PURPOSES: To guide children to play together happily; to develop good social habits; to create companionship and friendship with other children; to train children to respond to discipline outside the home, and so to develop habits of behavior that will strengthen character. It also aims to develop coordination of the senses to increase tactile skills and to instill a feeling for cooperation and fair play in group activities; to give each child a happy and normal understanding of religious values; and to deepen a respect and love for the church.

*Section 2.* GENERAL POLICIES

*a.* The Nursery School is an integral part of Christ Church for all respects and purposes and as such is under the jurisdiction of the Official Board of the Church.

*b.* The direct liaison between the Church Board and the Mothers Board shall be the Christian Education Committee of Christ Church aided by the Minister of Christian Education.

*c.* The Mothers Board shall have direct supervision of all operational details of the school and shall have such general responsibilities as provided in Article V, Section 6.

*d.* The Mothers Board shall make monthly reports to the Official Board of the Church through the Christian Education Committee on the condition and general operations of the school.

*e.* The financial and fiscal control shall be under the Church Treasurer as more particularly provided in Article XI.

*Section 3.* FUNCTIONAL ORGANIZATION. The functional organization shall consist of the Minister of Christian Education, the Official Board of the Church, the Committee of Christian Education, a Board of Mothers, a teaching staff, an enrollment of pupils and a body of parents.

## Article III

### ENROLLMENTS

*Section 1.* NUMBER. The number of pupils shall be determined by the Minister of Christian Education, the Christian Education Committee, and the Mothers Board.

*Section 2.* REGISTRATION. Registration of children shall be made through the Corresponding Secretary of the Mothers Board.

*Section 3.* AGE LIMITS. Children shall be eligible for enrollment only for the two years directly prior to the school year established by law in existence at date of enrollment for their acceptance into kindergarten of the local public school.

*Section 4.* ENROLLMENT PREFERENCES

*a.* Children currently enrolled in the Nursery School shall have first preference for the following year.

*b.* Children of whom at least one parent is a member (active or affiliate) of the church shall be given second preference in chronological order of enrollment until March first, prior to the opening of the fall session of that calendar year. The substance of this rule and the March first deadline shall be published in the January and February editions of the church publication or in the church bulletin at least three times between January first and February fifteenth.

*c.* After March first, pupils shall be accepted for the following school year in chronological order of enrollment regardless of church affiliation.

*Section 5.* FINAL ACCEPTANCE. No child shall be finally accepted until after a conference has been held by the teaching-director with the mother *and* the child prior to the opening of school. The teaching-director may refuse acceptance to a child who, in her opinion, would be unable for any reason to maintain the level of the group, or to a child who, in her opinion, would require more individual care and attention than the average child.

*Section 6.* WITHDRAWALS. Notice of a withdrawal shall be in writing. One month's notice shall be required.

## Article IV

### FEES AND CHARGES

*Section 1.* TUITION. The tuition shall be decided by the Minister of Christian Education, the Official Board and the Mothers Board.

*Section 2.* ENROLLMENT FEE. Upon acceptance, a $10.00 enrollment fee for each child shall be paid, which fee shall be deducted from the first month's tuition, and which shall not be refundable, except in cases covered by the last sentence of Article III, Section 5.

*Section 3.* PAYMENTS. Tuition shall be payable monthly, with the exception of the first month when tuition shall include payment for the first and final months. If a child is withdrawn prior to the end of the school year, the final month's tuition shall be forfeited.

*Section 4.* REDUCTIONS

*a.* Children of Christ Church ministers and the head of the Department of Music are eligible for a reduction of one half of the tuition.

*b.* Other reductions in tuition for individual cases may be granted at the concurrence of the Mothers Board and the Christian Education Committee.

## Article V

### MOTHERS BOARD

*Section 1.* A. PERSONNEL. The Mothers Board shall consist of five officers who shall also be directors, and a maximum of five additional directors. In addition, the president of the Mothers Board for the year immediately preceding shall attend meetings ex-officio.

B. EXECUTIVE COMMITTEE. The Executive Committee shall consist of the following officers: president, vice president, treasurer, recording secretary, and corresponding secretary. The Executive Committee shall have all the powers of the Mothers Board between meetings. The minutes of the meetings of the Executive Committee shall be submitted to the Mothers Board at the next meeting.

*Section 2.* ELECTION

*a.* Members of the Mothers Board shall be chosen by the current members of the Mothers Board at the April Board Meeting preceding the fall semester and shall be submitted for approval to the Minister of Christian Education and the Christian Education Committee.

*b.* Any member of the church other than employees or wives of ministers or employees who has a child currently enrolled in the school shall be eligible for election to the Mothers Board.

*c.* Insofar as practicable, half of the members of the Mothers Board shall be mothers of three-year-olds (who shall automatically remain for two years on the board) and half shall be mothers of four-year-olds.

*d.* Newly elected members of the board shall be invited to attend the June meeting preceding the fall in which their children enter the Nursery School.

*Section 3.* VACANCIES. Vacancies among officers or directors may be filled by a majority vote of the remaining members of the Mothers Board with the approval of the Minister of Christian Education. Persons so elected shall serve until the expiration of the original term of office.

*Section 4.* MEETINGS. The Mothers Board shall hold regular monthly meetings from September through June. Special meetings may be called by the president and shall be called upon the written request of three members of the board.

*Section 5.* ABSENCES. Each member of the board shall notify the president of her absence from a meeting and shall send a written report when necessary.

*Section 6.* GENERAL RESPONSIBILITIES. The Mothers Board shall be responsible to the Minister of Christian Education, the Official Board, the Christian Education Committee, and the parents of school pupils for the over-all organization and administration of the school.

*Section 7.* QUORUMS. A majority of the members of the Mothers Board shall constitute a quorum.

*Section 8.* VOTES. A majority vote of a quorum will be required to carry any matter at any meeting under these By-Laws unless otherwise specifically provided.

*Section 9.* SUPPLIES AND EQUIPMENT. See Article VII, Section 6.

### Article VI

#### DUTIES OF OFFICERS

*Section 1.* PRESIDENT. The president shall be responsible for the over-all supervision of the Mothers Board and shall call and conduct all meetings. She shall attend all Christian Education Committee meetings or appoint some other officer or director of the Mothers Board to represent her. She shall also have the powers and duties as set forth in Article XI, Section 4.

*Section 2.* VICE PRESIDENT. The vice president shall assist the president and shall assume the duties of the president in her absence.

*Section 3.* TREASURER. The treasurer shall have the duties as set forth in Article XI, Sections 3, 4, 9, and 10, and shall present to the regular meetings of the Mothers Board the financial statements referred to in Article XI, Sections 6 and 7. She shall consult with the church treasurer and the church financial secretary as to financial matters from time to time and as required.

*Section 4.* RECORDING SECRETARY. The recording secretary shall keep the minutes of all regular and special meetings of the board and of the Executive Committee. She shall keep these minutes in quadruplicate—copies being for her files, for the president, vice president and for the Minister of Christian Education.

She shall maintain a file of essential records which shall be transferred to her successor at the close of her term of office.

She shall handle all correspondence of a general nature.

*Section 5.* CORRESPONDING SECRETARY. The corresponding secretary shall be responsible for keeping a correct classified list of the names, addresses, birth dates, and church affiliations of all enrolled pupils and those on the waiting list. She shall be responsible for the complete procedure of enrollment of pupils.

## Article VII

### DUTIES OF THE COMMITTEES OF THE MOTHERS BOARD

The committees shall be responsible within their number for the following:

*Section 1.* INDOOR AND OUTDOOR MAINTENANCE. Cooperation with the Operation and Maintenance Committee through the Christian Education Committee in the upkeep, maintenance, and appearance of the portion of the church building and grounds used by the Nursery School.

*Section 2.* PROGRAM. The program planning of the PTA meetings and for any other social occasion.

*Section 3.* PUBLICATIONS. The publishing of a periodic newssheet and Nursery School articles in the church publication, in cooperation with the director of the Nursery School.

*Section 4.* PUBLICITY. The notices in the Church Bulletin and local newspapers including the notices required by Article III, Section 3 (*b*).

*Section 5.* SUPPLIES. The purchasing of all school supplies and equipment, subject to the provisions of this subsection. All expenditures for equipment or supplies must be approved by the Mothers Board. When the bills for any supplies or equipment are rendered, they should be approved by signature of the president or treasurer of the Mothers Board and forwarded to the church treasurer or church financial secretary for payment as more particularly provided in Article XI, Section 4. If purchased with cash, an appropriate signed memorandum shall be so furnished to the church financial secretary in similar manner. Any expenditure for supplies and equipment which would bring the total for the fiscal year of the appropriate budget classification to a figure in excess of the budgeted amount must first be approved as an over-budget item as provided in Article XI, Section 5.

*Section 6.* EQUIPMENT. The repair and maintenance of all toys and equipment.

*Section 7.* LIAISON. A committee consisting of: president, vice president, and whenever possible the Minister of Christian Education to consult monthly with director on the program and conduct of the school.

### Article VIII

TEACHING STAFF

*Section 1.* PERSONNEL. The teaching staff shall consist of a trained nursery school teacher-director and as many other trained teachers and/or untrained assistants as the Minister of Christian Education, Mothers Board, and teaching-director together deem necessary. There shall be a minimum of one teacher for every ten children, as required by law.

*Section 2.* APPOINTMENT. The teaching staff shall be appointed jointly by the Minister of Christian Education, the Christian Education Committee, and the Mothers Board and the director.

*Section 3.* AGREEMENTS. Upon employment, a written agreement stating the terms of employment shall be signed by the teacher, the Minister of Christian Education, and the president, representing the Mothers Board. The agreement shall be for one year and will be subject to renewal in March for another school year to the satisfaction of all parties.

*Section 4.* DUTIES
*a.* The teacher-director shall be responsible to the Minister of Christian Education, the Official Board through the Christian Education Committee, and the Mothers Board for the over-all organization of the Nursery School in all matters relating to curriculum, teaching methods, daily and yearly planning, and delegation of responsibility to other teachers.
*b.* The teachers and their assistants shall be responsible to the teaching-director for these responsibilities delegated to them by her.

*Section 5.* ABSENCES
*a.* A teacher shall advise the director when she will be absent. If a teacher is absent for two weeks in any school year through sickness, the Mothers Board shall pay the salary of the substitute teacher. For a period of time longer than said two weeks, the teacher shall pay the salary of the substitute teacher.
*b.* A teacher may be given leave on occasion, upon consent of the Mothers

Board, to visit other nursery schools, or to participate in projects directly related to Nursery School activity.

Section 6. WAGES. Wages of teachers and assistants shall be determined by the Minister of Christian Education, the Official Board, the Christian Education Committee, and the Mothers Board.

Section 7. MEETINGS. The teacher-director shall meet with her staff daily to discuss matters concerning the internal program of the school.

Section 8. GENERAL

a. The teacher-director shall maintain communication with parents through a periodic newssheet.

b. The teacher-director (and/or her staff) shall have a minimum of one conference with each pupil's parents per school year.

## Article IX

### HEALTH

Section 1. The school shall operate under Article X on Day Nurseries of the Sanitary Code of the County Health Department.

## Article X

### P.T.A.

Section 1. The Mothers Board shall arrange a minimum of two meetings a year for the purpose of giving the Minister of Christian Education, parents and teachers an opportunity to meet together.

Section 2. Payment of outside speakers at P.T.A. meetings shall be determined by the Mothers Board.

Section 3. Parents shall be free to visit the Nursery School at any time convenient to the teacher-director and her staff.

## Article XI

### FINANCIAL OPERATION AND FISCAL CONTROL

Section 1. BOOKS OF ACCOUNT. The books of the Nursery School shall be taken over and maintained by the financial secretary of the church and shall be under the jurisdiction and control of the church treasurer.

Section 2. BANK ACCOUNT. The administrative account of the Nursery School shall be kept in a separate bank account under the title "Christ Church Nursery School."

*Section 3.* BILLING AND DEPOSITS. The billing of tuition fees shall be done by the treasurer of the Nursery School, and tuition checks shall be returned to her. A return envelope with her name and address shall be used for such purpose. The treasurer of the Nursery School will make deposits of such tuition fees and any other general funds from time to time in the above-designated account, giving the financial secretary of the church a duplicate deposit slip showing the source of the funds, whether from tuition, special gift, and so on.

*Section 4.* DISBURSEMENTS. All disbursements from the account "Christ Church Nursery School" (including wages to teachers) shall be made by check which shall be prepared by the financial secretary of the Church and signed by any one of the church treasurer, the assistant treasurer, or the chairman of the Finance Committee. The treasurer of the Nursery School or the president of the Mothers Board shall approve each bill or other disbursement for payment by placing her signature on the bill or other memorandum. No checks will be drawn on the aforesaid account to pay any bill unless the signature of either of the foregoing two persons appears on the bill or other memorandum. (See Article XI, Section 10 for wage checks.) The authority to order materials, supplies, and so on within the budget of the Nursery School shall be as provided in Article VII, Section 5.

*Section 5.* OVER-BUDGET ITEMS. Any over-budget item shall be presented to the Official Board for approval through the Christian Education Committee and must be approved before payment is made.

*Section 6.* MONTHLY STATEMENTS. At the end of each month the financial secretary of the Church shall prepare monthly statements in the usual form on a cumulative basis showing the income account and the balance sheet of the Nursery School account. Three copies thereof shall be forwarded to the treasurer of the Nursery School and two copies to the secretary of the Christian Education Committee and a copy shall be handed to each member of the Official Board at its next meeting.

*Section 7.* ANNUAL STATEMENTS. The church financial secretary shall prepare an annual statement which will be in the same form as the monthly statement, summarizing the results for the entire year.

*Section 8.* FISCAL YEAR. The fiscal year of the Nursery School shall be changed to a calendar year so as to coincide with the church fiscal year.

*Section 9.* BUDGET. The treasurer of the Nursery School shall submit by October 1 of each year a budget for the ensuing calendar year showing estimated disbursements in the same account analysis as in the Cash Journal and showing estimated receipts. Such budget shall be channeled through the chairman of the Christian Education Committee.

*Section 10.* PAYMENT OF TEACHER-DIRECTOR AND TEACHERS. The teacher-director and teachers shall be paid twice a month by checks drawn and signed as provided by Article XI, Section 4. At the beginning of each school year the Nursery School treasurer shall provide the church financial secretary with a list of the teacher-director and teachers, showing monthly salary of each, address, and social security number, if any. The Nursery School treasurer shall see that the church financial secretary is notified as to any change in salary approved as provided in Article VIII, Section 6.

*Section 11.* WAGE REPORTS—INCOME TAX WITHHOLDING. Wage payments to all employees of the Nursery School shall be reported for all purposes in the respective reports filed by the church. Income tax shall be withheld at the source and included in the usual church quarterly and annual summary reports. Forms W-2 shall be prepared in the name of the church and so filed with the annual church return. The church treasurer shall assure that the proper exemption certificates on Form W-4 are procured for the purpose of withholding.

*Section 12.* SOCIAL SECURITY. Since the Nursery School teachers became employees of the church upon adoption of the resolution by the Official Board on April 1956, they then became subject to social security as "new employees" of the church by virtue of the waiver of exemption filed by the church on Feb. 11, 1954, and no further election or waiver of exemption need be filed. Social security taxes must therefore be withheld in the future from their wages and the same should be included in the usual church reports and returns. All subsequent employees and teachers after April 1956 are automatically subject to social security without further action and shall be so advised. The Nursery School budget shall include the employer's social security tax and the cost of any other fringe benefit or tax. Employees should be directed to procure social security numbers.

*Section 13.* ANNUAL AUDIT. The accounts showing the operations of the Nursery School shall be included in the annual church audit by its regular auditors beginning with the audit for the calendar year 1956.

*Section 14.* CHANGE OF ACCOUNTING AND FISCAL PROCEDURE BY CHURCH TREASURER. The church treasurer is empowered to change from time to time the accounting and bookkeeping methods, the procedure or machinery for the making and recording of deposits, the procedure for the indication of approval of bills or memoranda upon the authority of which checks are drawn, and the procedure or machinery for the making of and accounting for disbursements.

## ARTICLE XII

### THE OFFICIAL BOARD

*Section 1.* The chairman of the Committee of Christian Education of the Official Board shall represent the Mothers Board on the Official Board. In general, wherever Official Board action is required, a recommendation shall be made to the Official Board by the Christian Education Committee. The Official Board may delegate to the Christian Education Committee power to act for it in any matter requiring Official Board action under these By-Laws and failure to take direct action shall be deemed to constitute such delegation as to the specific matter involved.

## ARTICLE XIII

### INSURANCE

*Section 1.* The following types of insurance shall be carried in coverage of the Nursery School either separately or as part of the over-all coverage of the church in amounts to be determined by the Minister of Christian Education, the Official Board, and the Mothers Board:

    *a.* For the children in case of accident or injury while in school
    *b.* For the teaching staff in case of accident or injury while in school
    *c.* For all employees in case of accident or injury while in school

## ARTICLE XIV

### OPERATING RULES

*Section 1.* The Mothers Board and the Minister of Christian Education may adopt from time to time such operating rules as are not specifically inconsistent with the provisions of these By-Laws and may amend the same.

## ARTICLE XV

### AMENDMENTS AND RULES OF ORDER

*Section 1.* Except as provided in Article XI, Section 14, the By-Laws may be amended by the majority vote of a quorum at any meeting of the Mothers Board subject to approval of the Official Board.

## ARTICLE XVI

### ANNUAL REPORT

*Section 1.* The president shall present annually in writing to the chairman of the Committee on Christian Education a report on the activities of the school during the year immediately past or shall make such report orally at a meeting of the Christian Education Committee which shall be included in the Minutes of such Committee.

Adopted by Mothers Board on
June 14, 1956
Adopted by Christian Education
Committee on
September 27, 1956
Adopted by the Official Board on
——————— , 1956

The study of the above by-laws will indicate the many administrative details that are involved in a strong and effective nursery school program.

In the development of any carefully conceived and executed church activity there may ever be the necessity of clarifying methods for procedure. I recommend particularly Article XI above as offering suggestive points for other types of church organizations that receive and disperse funds, especially for salaries.

Papers and reports prepared by various nursery schools and distributed to parents are advisable only if they will genuinely further the aims of the program. One church nursery school occasionally puts out one small sheet that carries detailed announcements regarding dates and special school activities, gives information about the teachers and about plans for conferences of teachers and staff, and reports on projects of the church school and special activities. Such a paper provides a splendid opportunity for guidance of families in the spiritual enrichment of their homes and families. It may contain graces suggested for mealtime or may mimeograph songs or hymns that the children are learning and may enjoy singing in the home.

There may be advantages in preparing a leaflet for interested or inquiring parents. One particularly appropriate leaflet presents on the outside page smiling faces of children in the school, with the caption "We Like Day Nursery School." Further information on page 1 includes the name and address of the church and the school hours.

Page 2 reads as follows:

### Parents Like Day Nursery School

because—

1. This period of early childhood is one of growth—physical, mental, emotional, social, and spiritual—unequaled during any other period of life.

2. It is a supplement to, not a substitute for, the home by providing regular association with others of the child's own age in an environment especially planned and equipped for him.

3. There is loving guidance of persons trained to promote his best development.

4. Creative expression through clay, sand, painting, drawing, building, pasting, music, and drama.

5. Guided indoor and outdoor play.

6. Establishment of health, rest, eating, play, and toilet habits.

7. Many opportunities for parent participation: "get-acquainted" coffees, study courses, open-house programs, and Mothers' Council.

8. Visitors are always welcome by appointment.

Page 3 contains five pictures with the following captions: Housekeeping; Rhythms; Christian Daily Living and Learning; Play; and Activities, picturing simply certain of the main emphases of the school.

Page 4 contains the following information:

The Nursery School is a regular part of the educational program of Christ Church and is open to all children of the community. All are invited to attend Sunday Church School classes.

The school year begins and ends with the public school year with the same holidays observed.

Since the school is a nonprofit organization, the tuition rates are lower than the average: 3 days per week, $22.00 per month; 5 days per week, $30.00 per month.

Tuition is payable one month in advance. Due to low cost, no refunds are made for absences or holidays. Where two or more children from one family attend, a 10 per cent discount is granted.

A parent conference with the director is necessary to enrollment. A physical examination by family physician is required at entrance. Thereafter a daily check is made at the school.

The staff consists of director, accredited teachers and substitute teachers, secretary, bookkeeper, custodians.

For further information write or telephone

Christ Church<br>
Address<br>
Telephone

Such prepared material may be very helpful in answering the questions of prospective parents, saving time for the staff and serving as a vehicle of good public relations.

## DEDICATORY AND ANNIVERSARY OCCASIONS

The thoughtful administrator will utilize the significant anniversaries in the church and occasions for dedication to hallow the precincts of the church, to exalt the spirits of the parishioners, and to leave a deep imprint of the "things of the Lord."

The planning and the outlining of the most minute details are basic. The Rev. Dr. Edward L. R. Elson of the National Presbyterian Church told of the great care and detail that went into the planning of the visit of Queen Elizabeth II and Prince Philip to the National Presbyterian Church as guests of President and Mrs. Eisenhower on October 20, 1957. Mr. Eisenhower did not delegate in any casual way any details regarding the occasion. With the minister of the church and representatives of security agencies and his staff, every aspect of the occasion was covered with minute concern. Dr. Elson, recounting the experience, said that the care and detail of preparation made the "entire occasion seem free of any mechanics." This is the underlying purpose behind care in planning for significant occasions in the life of the church.

Let us suppose that a new church building is to be dedicated. The minister, perhaps with an appointed committee, should carefully go over all aspects of the service, visualizing every detail, considering it, and putting it on paper. If necessary, printed details should be given to all having any responsibility for the occasion, so that they may know where they are to be, at what time, and what is expected of them.

Confusion over "Where is my order of service?" "Isn't there a hymn book for me?" "Where am I to sit?" can be intrusive and detrimental elements to an occasion that should be marked with high dignity and meaning.

A detailed outline of a dedication service meaningful to all participants is as follows:

CHRIST CHURCH

DEDICATION SERVICE OF THE

EDUCATIONAL BUILDING

AND

CONGREGATIONAL HALL

The Tower Bells
Processional Hymns

1. Austrian Hymn—Haydn
2. The Old Hundredth Psalm—Bourgeois
   (Congregation and Choirs)

Call to Worship

Invocation

Anthem

Responsive Reading

Gloria Patri

Scripture Lesson—Revelations 21:10–27

Hymn—For All the Saints—Sarum, Barnby

The Call to Prayer

The Pastoral Prayer

Announcements

Anthem—Two Chorales with Trumpets and Tympani—J. S. Bach

Dedicatory Sermon

Act of Dedication

   (Presentation of Keys by the Builder and Architect to the Chairman of the Physical Expansion Committee)

*Chairman:* For as much as this congregation has set its hands to the building of this Congregational Hall and Educational Building for the worship and service of Almighty God, I now deliver to you the keys thereof, and pray you to lead us in its dedication.

*Minister:* Let us not doubt that God will approve this act of devotion, and that he will graciously accept our work.
   (The people will rise at the call of the minister.)

*Minister:* God our Father having graciously moved us to the preparation of this house, and having brought us to this joyous occasion, let us now proceed to set it apart to its proper and sacred uses, to the praise and honor of his holy Name.

O God, who art present in all places of thy dominion and dost graciously rejoice in the services of all thy children; hear us, we humbly beseech thee, as we dedicate this house.

To thy glory, O God;
To the honor of Jesus Christ;
To the praise of the Holy Spirit;

*People:* We dedicate this house.

*Minister:* For the worship of God in prayer and praise;
For the teaching of the gospel message;
For the fellowship of the people one with another;

*People:*      We dedicate this house.

*Minister:*   For ennobling all honest toil;
              For quickening civic righteousness;
              For promoting peace and justice in all the earth;

*People:*      We dedicate this house.

*Minister:*   For the opening of minds to thy truth;
              For the consecration of all earthly powers to thy glory;
              For the furtherance of brotherhood and unity;

*People:*      We dedicate this house.

*Minister:*   For the founding and hallowing of the family;
              For the nurture and guidance of children;
              For the enlistment of youth in Christian service;

*People:*      We dedicate this house.

*Minister:*   For the carrying of the gospel unto the uttermost parts of the earth;
              For the giving of hope and courage to those who labor in the Lord;
              For the consecration of life and service;

*People:*      We dedicate this house.

*Minister:*   In grateful remembrance of those who have gone before us;
              In gratitude for the fellowship we have in the service of this church;
              For the blessed hope of a house not made with hands, eternal in the
                  heavens;

*People:*      We dedicate this house.

*All:*         We now, the members and friends of this church and congregation,
               mindful of the inheritance into which we have entered, and the
               glorious company, seen and unseen, whose communion we share;
               and deeply sensible of those bonds by which we are bound to the
               Lord of all life and to each other, do covenant together in this act
               of dedication, offering ourselves anew to the worship and work of
               our heavenly Father; through our Lord Jesus Christ.
                        (Here let the people be seated.)

*Minister:*   Let us pray.

               Almighty and ever living God, whom the heaven of heavens can-
               not contain, much less these temples made with hands, graciously
               accept, we beseech thee, this place of thy dwelling, and ourselves at

home therein, which we have consecrated to the honor and glory of thy blessed Name.

Grant, we pray thee, that all who come within these walls may feel thy nearness and hear thy voice within their hearts, and be moved by thy Holy Spirit into ways of righteousness and peace. As thy gospel is taught in this place, may it become power unto salvation to all who receive it. Here let thy people come to seek thee in spirit and in truth; and seeking, find the forgiveness of their sins and the peace of thine acceptance. Grant, O heavenly Father, that all who turn their steps to thee in this place may receive that grace most needful, the ordering and establishing of their earthly days, and, at length, their perfect consummation in the life everlasting.

Father of all mankind, we pray that to these buildings all thy children may ever be welcomed. Let thy grace fill this place. Hither may little ones delight to come, and young men and maidens be strengthened. Here may the strong be moved to consecrate their lives to thee. Hither may age turn its footsteps to find rest and light at eventide. Here may the poor and needy find friends. Here may the tempted find victory; the sorrowing, comfort; and the bereaved learn that over their beloved, death has no more dominion. Here may they who fear find courage, and they who doubt have their faith increased and their hopes confirmed. Here may the careless be awakened to their folly and guilt and be turned to repentance. Here may oppressed and striving souls be assured of the mercy that triumphs over evil and be brought off more than conquerors; through him that loved us, even Jesus Christ our Lord.

*Minister:*  Therefore with angels and archangels, and with all the company of heaven, we laud and magnify thy glorious Name, evermore praising thee, and saying:

*People:*  Holy, Holy, Holy, Lord God of hosts; heaven and earth are full of thy glory. Glory be to thee, O Lord most high. Amen.

The Hand Bells—Vesper Hymn
Recessional Hymns
Benediction
The Tower Bells

Such a service reveals careful planning with organist and choir master, consultation with the individuals associated with the building projects and meticulous attention to worship materials and their proper presentation by means of the order of service and printing.

An individual church will consult with the sensitive and creative members of the parish in arranging the observance of special and anniversary occasions.

To deepen fellowship among its members at an open-house evening following the dedication of a new building, one church presented to its members ribbons of different colors to indicate the periods during which they had joined the church. Those who had joined since 1950 wore a yellow ribbon, those who had joined during 1940 to 1950 a blue one, and those who had joined during 1930 to 1940 a silver one. The charter members wore a gold ribbon. By this means the purpose of the gathering, which was that the members recognize one another and pay special tribute to charter members, was efficiently and happily fulfilled.

The dedication of an organ presents an opportunity for the use of beautiful liturgical materials and for the education of the congregation in the place and function of sacred music. A brief history of the organ as a musical instrument may be followed by the story of the new church organ being dedicated. In the planning of the dedication program the director of music and the minister must bear in mind that the majority of the church members are probably not technically educated in music, that therefore a simple, interesting explanation will be most effective.

One Southern church, on the occasion of the dedication of its enlarged and beautified property, put out a pamphlet with the theme "How God Brought It to Pass." One of the subheads reads: "The Building Committee and Trustees Built Christ Church." Another reads: "An Altar Built Christ Church," and under it is a photograph of the altar together with the scriptural verse "How lovely is Thy dwelling place, O Lord of hosts!" The theme "How God Brought It to Pass" is repeatedly elucidated with photographs and Scriptural quotations. Among the factors that helped "bring it to pass" were the members, the staff, the choirs, guest preachers, the ushers, Christian will, worship, prayer, fellowship, sacrificial giving, the Good Samaritan spirit. The booklet closes with the great answers that summarize all the other answers: "The Gospel really built Christ Church," and "The Christ of the cross and the open tomb built Christ Church."

Anniversary and dedicatory occasions present opportunities for developing a great theme that involves all aspects of the church life.

The following principles will serve as a guide in the administration of observances of important occasions.

1. A reverent feeling for the past.

2. A sensitive recognition of all who have made possible the glory of the moment.

3. The creation of exaltation through great music, noble prayer, and inspired speaking.

4. Unity, order, and movement, with an emphasis on conciseness and brevity.

5. One person who is in charge of all aspects of the program.

## RELIGIOUS LITERATURE AND THE CHURCH LIBRARY

The reading of spiritual material should be increasingly encouraged in the parish. For this purpose a literature committee responsible for the purchase and distribution of Christian literature may be authorized by the official board. It should have the following responsibilities:

1. To select suitable pamphlets and leaflets with the approval of the minister.

2. To devise ways and means, if necessary, with the approval of the Official Board for the purchase of such material.

3. Place literature racks or tables at suitable locations in the church.

4. Inform the parish of the materials available.

5. See that the literature racks or tables are neat, properly supplied with literature and made attractive to the passerby.

6. If contributions are made in a coin box or on an offering plate, see that such contributions are collected frequently and turned over to the treasurer of the committee.

7. If a specific contribution is expected for certain items, the committee will mark such items accordingly.

8. The committee will ask the prayer and spiritual-life groups and other study groups for suggestions as to helpful literature.

9. The committee will call attention to its work and service by periodic announcements to various church societies and organizations at their regular meetings.

10. The committee will keep an inventory of its materials and at its meetings will authorize, after discussion, the purchase of additional stock and/or new materials.

11. The committee will encourage various departments, such as stewardship and Christian education, to use supportive literature to further their activities.

12. The committee will find it helpful to maintain a file of publishing houses, denominational headquarters, and bookstore sources from which literature may be obtained.

A church may find it worth while to develop a church library to serve the parishioners and parish activities. This may be done by setting aside in the church office or at a convenient place in the church a shelf for selective religious books. One person is placed in charge of checking out books borrowed and receiving those returned at the time of the regular Sunday worship service.

If there is a possibility of going beyond such a simple arrangement and where the church desires to establish a working library for the parish, the following suggestions for procedure may be in order:

1. The matter should have the approval of the official board. Tentative ways and means for the purchase or obtaining of books should be outlined. Further, a plan for the maintenance and operation of the library should be assured. One church, with official approval and with beautiful space available, went one step further.

2. It asked the music and drama departments, the study group, the spiritual-life committee, the Christian education committees, the women's society, and so forth, to recommend books that would be helpful in their programs. With these suggestions there was formed a church-wide committee that had the following subresponsibility: (a) a selection committee to determine the books to be acquired for the library; (b) a committee responsible for the arrangement and cataloguing of the books; (c) a committee to staff the library and supervise the care of the books and the library; (d) a committee to engage in the project of obtaining funds to purchase certain books. This project enabled the committee to defray certain costs of its procedure. With the list of books recommended by the various church departments the selection committee drew up a statement of the purpose of the library. It was the committee's judgment that the library should be devoted mainly to religious material but should also serve the needs of the parish and its active departmental and program life.

The library was to be essentially for laymen, not a research library for theologians. Since the funds were limited, the list of books desirable for the library was circulated among church people known to be interested in religious books. The letter that accompanied it read as follows:

Christ Church has a splendid room completed for the housing of a library. It will be devoted essentially to the field of religion and with the prime idea of serving the individual and the various study emphases of groups within this church.

We've asked leaders of various departments and organizations of the church to indicate books that would be helpful, in their judgment, for inclusion in the library.

That list is enclosed.

On behalf of the Library Committee, it is being sent to you with the thought that you might possibly have some of these titles which you might be willing to donate to the program here.

The committee has limited resources and cannot, at the beginning, purchase all these books. Any book that is given enables the committee to spread its purchases for additional volumes.

Thank you for considering this request.

Yours faithfully and gratefully,
*Minister, Christ Church*

Where there is no underwriting of the project by the church budget the committee may seek, with the official board's approval, individual contributions for the purchase of books that cannot be donated. It is advised that each major department include in its annual budget a sum for the purchase in the coming year of books that would be helpful to its program and that could be added to the library. Once the library is established and its supervision provided for, the church members should be kept informed regarding it. The church magazine and Sunday bulletin may be used to emphasize additions to the library or to recommend books suitable for Lenten or Advent reading or for other important occasions in the church year.

A survey made by Audience Analysis for the *Christian Herald* and Protestant Church in 1948 presented some interesting material regarding rooms or church libraries in American churches. The following questions and answers of the survey will be of interest to anyone considering the establishment of a church library:

*How many Protestant church libraries?*

31.8 per cent of the 200,000 churches have libraries for a total of 63,600.

*How many books do they have?*

The average per church is 437 books. One church reported a library of 1,508 volumes and a quarterly magazine used to acquaint readers with the titles available.

*What types of books?*

The following list shows the per cent of churches that have books in each classification:

|  | *Per cent of total churches* | *Average number of books per church* |
|---|---|---|
| Religious | 93.0 | 133.8 |
| Bible commentary and reference | 89.5 | 31.7 |
| Inspirational | 94.1 | 53.8 |
| Fiction | 87.7 | 48.1 |
| Nonfiction | 71.9 | 37.3 |
| Children's | 87.7 | 103.3 |
| Other | 7.0 | 14.0 |

*Is the church library market expanding?*

Yes, 12.3 per cent of the churches reporting libraries state that they are a year old or less.

*Are recommended reading lists used in these libraries?*

Recommended reading lists are used in 64.9 per cent. The following list shows the purposes for which the lists are used:

|  | *Per cent* |
|---|---|
| In choosing titles to be purchased | 27.0 |
| For guidance of readers | 32.4 |
| Both | 40.6 |

*Approximately how many books are added to these libraries each year?*

|  | *Per cent* |
|---|---|
| 25 or less | 59.6 |
| 26 to 50 | 10.5 |
| 51 to 100 | 10.5 |
| 101 to 250 | 3.5 |
| 251 to 500 | 3.5 |
| Budget of $100 | 1.7 |
| No answer | 10.5 |

## STUDENTS AWAY FROM HOME

An effectively administered parish, concerned with all its members, will devise a program for contact and assistance to students

attending school away from the parish limits. The following suggestions should result in the development of a desired program.

1. On the occasion of graduation from the local grammar school
or high school the minister will write to each graduate, congratulat-
ing him on his achievement and expressing his hope for "the next
educational step." The note will also request the student to keep
the church office informed of his new address if he goes away to
school.

2. If the church publishes a magazine or paper, a section of one
of the fall issues may appropriately be devoted to "Our Student
Members Who Are Away at School." Names, complete addresses,
and the name of the schools attended should be given. It is fitting to
add that the church prays for the students and follows their careers
with loving concern.

3. The names of students should be placed on the church mailing list, and all meaningful church literature should be sent to them.

4. Some churches, through an "Away at School Committee," ask
the students to send brief items which in turn are printed on a news
sheet and circulated to all the students away at school.

5. The church is soundly advised to develop an "Away at School
Club." During holidays and vacation times, with a simple organization of student leaders guided by the Christian education committee,
activities in the way of get-togethers can be planned.

6. Students away at school may be invited, while at home, to address assemblages at the church school and the youth groups, and
may be especially helpful under an organized program of offering
Christian guidance and counsel for other young people who will
be leaving home for their higher education.

7. Once a year at least the pastor should send a personal note of
loving thoughtfulness to all students who are away from home.

8. If there is a Christian foundation or activity on the campus or
in the environs of the school or college, the person in charge there
may assist the student in keeping ties with his home church meaningful if he is told the student's name and background. Passing the
name of the student on to the pastor of a church of a similar denomination in the location of the school may lead to a helpful association
for the student away from his home church.

9. The minister, church officers, leaders in the Christian education department should let the students know that they are avail-

able for counsel and assistance at any time during the school year, and should make themselves available for conferences with students at holiday and vacation times.

10. The minister, Christian education chairman, or director may make a meaningful occasion for young people who are leaving home if a special service prior to their departure is planned in the church. In some parishes a dedication service, with the sacrament of Holy Communion, has been highly meaningful. A family service, prior to the opening of a school, when special invitations are sent to students known to be leaving home, and their parents, may be an occasion to leave a deep and constructive influence.

## MEMBERS IN THE ARMED SERVICES

Many of the steps suggested above may be followed with regard to parishioners serving in the armed services. Additional points that may be considered are as follows:

1. The preparation of a dignified list of all members of the church in the armed services maintained in some suitably prominent place in the church building.

2. The occasional printing in the Sunday bulletin of the names of parishioners known to be in the armed forces. The minister may, on such an occasion, which might be suitably at some civil anniversary, offer a prayer for those in the service of their country. A copy of the bulletin, together with a brief note from the minister, may be deeply meaningful to a young person far from home and in a strange atmosphere.

3. The minister and the staff should make a point of greeting individuals on their return from serving in the armed forces.

4. The counseling service of the church should be ready to help and support young people in making any necessary adjustment to the home, community, church, and to their civilian life and responsibility.

## CHURCH FAIRS

A church fair may be a happy occasion in the life of the parish, when friendships are widened, when many people engage in definite activities, and where some of the joy and happiness of congregational life is readily evident. One of the fine by-products of a church fair is the sense of "all of us together, working, having fun, men and women, boys and girls." Of course, without a proper concept and aim and without adequate administration, such church activities may result in considerable irritation and frustration. Each local parish, with guidance of its governing board, will determine how often it should have a fair. Some churches have found an annual fair fits well into their program. Others make the fair an occasion only once in several years. The parish is well advised to stress infrequency rather than frequency.

A major principle to be put before the congregation, by the minister and the governing board and by those in charge of the fair, is to keep the fair Christian and to remember that its purposes are to further such spiritual aims as deeper and happier friendships, a wide acquaintance among parishioners, and contribution to some cause or agency that will further the work of Christ.

The following organization for a church fair is recommended: A general chairman, six vice chairmen, a chairman of teas, a treasurer, an assistant treasurer, and chairmen of the following committees: decorations, arrangements for booths, church dinner, children's program, white-elephant booth, snack bar, fancy-article table, post office, cookbook and bookshelf, cake and food, donations from corporations, auction, flowers and greens booth, reading of handwriting, carousel and other entertainment for children, housewares, antiques, art committee, art sketches and program book.

In addition to the above, the following steps should be taken in the administration of the fair: (1) The maximum participation of every member of the parish is required. (2) Instructions for every activity in the fair should be clearly drawn up and delivered in due time to the persons responsible. For the cookbook and bookshelf booth at one church fair, committee members and their helpers were recruited six months in advance. Favorite recipes were requested from the women by members and friends of the church. These were duplicated on 3-by-5-inch cards, and filed. Once a week for several weeks the members of the committee met at the home of the chairman and collated these cards, placing them in the decorative recipe boxes purchased for this purpose. In the meantime, used books for the bookshelf donated by interested people were brought to the assembling point or were collected from homes by members of the committee. Before the opening of the fair the books were grouped according to type and price, and arranged attractively in the booth, where they were accessible to those wishing to browse. On the day of the fair each member of the committee served as a "salesman" for a specified number of hours. (3) The fair should be opened with prayer and, if at all possible be closed with a prayer of thanksgiving. (4) It is important that the congregation feel the interest and support of the minister and the governing board. The fair is a valuable means of promoting a warm relationship between church leaders and parishioners that can lead to deeper spiritual instruction and guidance.

## CRADLE ROLL AND INFANT CARE

In the church's consideration for its infants and small children several procedures have proved satisfactory.

1. One church has set up a plan for remembering the birthday of each child from one to three years old under its care. The details are as follows:

### CRADLE ROLL PROGRAM

I. On receiving the information of the birth of a child, the following information is to be sent to the parents:
  1. Letter announcing the fact that the child is being placed on the Cradle Roll. Included also will be an invitation to bring the child to the Toddlers' Department until the age of three, when he (or she) is eligible to join the Nursery Department. Further information is to be included about the "Crib Care Program."
  2. A copy of the folder "Dear Baby."
  3. A copy of the folder "What Baby Needs."
II. Several days before the child's first birthday (to be mailed in sufficient time for it to be delivered on or before the birthday), the following material is to be sent to the parents:
  1. A copy of the folder "Dear One-Year-Old."
  2. A copy of the folder "What Baby Is Learning."
III. Several days before the child's second birthday (to be mailed in sufficient time for it to be delivered on or before the birthday), the following material is to be sent to the parents:
  1. A copy of the folder "Dear Two-Year-Old."
  2. A copy of the folder "Companionship with the Two-Year-Old."

IV. Several days before the child's third birthday (to be mailed in sufficient time for it to be delivered on or before the birthday), the following material is to be sent to the parent:

1. A copy of the folder "Dear Three-Year-Old."
2. A copy of the folder "When the Little Child Goes to Church."
3. A letter inviting the parents to enroll the child in the Nursery Department of the Sunday school and informing them that he (or she) is no longer listed on the Cradle Roll.

2. A permanent Cradle Roll board or tablet might well be displayed in a prominent place in the church school building. Each month, a list of new babies is compiled from information obtained from hospital lists and the church office and members of the church. On the first day of the month, a plate giving the name and birth date of a new baby is placed on the Cradle Roll board. The plate stays there until the child is three years old, when it is removed. Thus the board is always up to date, containing only the names of children under three years of age.

3. Details regarding the baptism of the child and consequent relationships are noted under "Baptism," page 156.

4. Under the direction of the Christian education department a Cradle Roll superintendent should be appointed.

5. Under his direction a program of personal contact with the child, the home, and the family will be carried out.

6. Many churches have found it rewarding to have in the Cradle Roll department older women with experience and understanding. These women may call on young mothers in their homes often and can give them practical assistance in their needs and problems.

7. It is often desirable to have one or two special services during the church year for Cradle Roll parents and children. One such service that has meant much to homes and families took place during the Christmas season. At four o'clock on Christmas-Sunday afternoon the little children and their parents gathered in the church for a service that lasted only twenty minutes. The high point of the worship, which included Scripture reading, a prayer, an anthem by the children's choir, and a very brief message, came when parents brought their children forward to the chancel rail to be blessed individually by the minister. Then a modified form of the confirmation statement "Bless, O Lord, this Thy child (or these Thy children) that they may continue Thine forever . . ." was uttered. Each child received a small memento picturing Jesus as the Good Shepherd.

8. The church administration may well study the need of Cradle Roll parents for classes for young parents and for social and fellowship activities.

9. It is often advisable to publish the names of all Cradle Roll children in the church bulletin on one particular Sunday in the church year. On this occasion a special prayer or a liturgy may be used. The essential purpose of such an occasion will be to deepen the congregation's responsibility for the nurture and care of the infants and small children. Parents who have children on the Cradle Roll will receive a special invitation to participate in the service.

## CHILDREN AND YOUTH ACTIVITIES

The wide and important field of the church program for children and youth has many ramifications. Among the items that should be on the check list of the church board that desires an effective program for its children will be the following:

1. The religious education committee or commission will be composed of strong and dedicated and creative leaders.

2. The official board will, by attention to and cooperation with this committee or commission, let it be known that it believes that the work for children in the parish is of primary importance.

3. The staff or appointed representatives to oversee the church school program will prepare a careful organizational chart that shall show the position of each participant in the religious education program.

Two such organizational charts are presented on pages 121–123.

4. The leadership of the children's and youth program will constantly be evaluated through reports and counseling and, on occasion, testing the effectiveness of its program. There should be occasional intimate sessions between the minister and the leaders in the Christian education program on such questions as "Where are our weaknesses?" "How much should we be improving?" "In what direction should we be moving?"

One such session came up with a number of highly significant and most helpful suggestions.

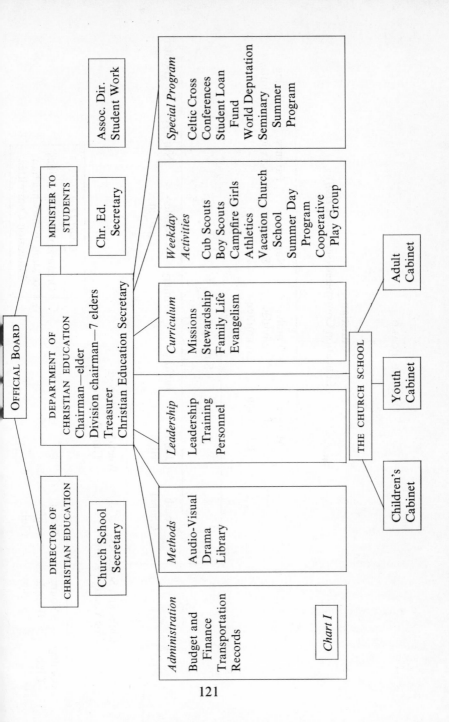

OFFICIAL BOARD

DIRECTOR OF CHRISTIAN EDUCATION

MINISTER TO STUDENTS

DEPARTMENT OF CHRISTIAN EDUCATION
Chairman—elder
Division chairman—7 elders
Treasurer
Christian Education Secretary

Assoc. Dir. Student Work

Chr. Ed. Secretary

Church School Secretary

*Administration*
Budget and Finance
Transportation
Records

*Methods*
Audio-Visual
Drama
Library

*Leadership*
Leadership Training
Personnel

*Curriculum*
Missions
Stewardship
Family Life
Evangelism

*Weekday Activities*
Cub Scouts
Boy Scouts
Campfire Girls
Athletics
Vacation Church School
Summer Day Program
Cooperative Play Group

*Special Program*
Celtic Cross
Conferences
Student Loan Fund
World Deputation
Seminary
Summer Program

THE CHURCH SCHOOL

Children's Cabinet

Youth Cabinet

Adult Cabinet

*Chart I*

121

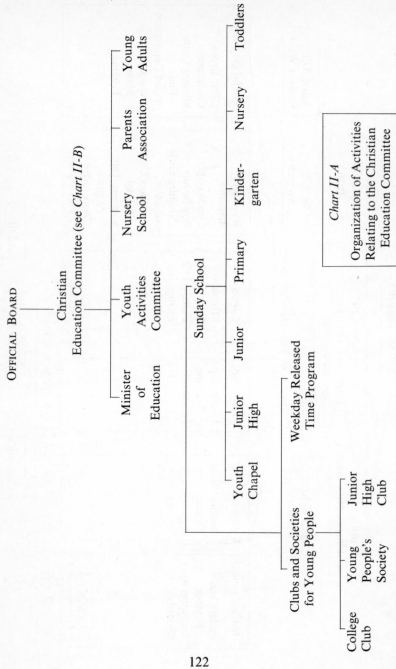

OFFICIAL BOARD

Christian
Education Committee (see *Chart II-B*)

Minister of Education — Youth Activities Committee — Nursery School — Parents Association — Young Adults

Sunday School

Youth Chapel — Junior High — Junior — Primary — Kindergarten — Nursery — Toddlers

Weekday Released Time Program

Clubs and Societies for Young People

College Club — Young People's Society — Junior High Club

*Chart II-A*
Organization of Activities Relating to the Christian Education Committee

**Chart II-B**
Christian Education Committee
—Organization—
Subcommittees and Duties

CHAIRMAN Mr. Jordan
VICE CHAIRMAN Mr. Shelton
SECRETARY Mr. Bowen

| Subcommittees | Executive | Personnel and Leadership | Parents Assoc. | Curriculum | Nursery School | Steward-ship & Budget | Library | Youth Clubs | Youth Activities |
|---|---|---|---|---|---|---|---|---|---|

(Names of members of all of these divisions should be listed below particular heading)

DUTIES

| Executive | Personnel and Leadership | Curriculum | Steward-ship & Budget | Library | Youth Clubs | Youth Activities |
|---|---|---|---|---|---|---|
| To consider aims and purposes of the Christian education com. To suggest policies. To evaluate effectiveness of programs and activities in operation. | To discover and select personnel (supt., teachers and substitutes). Limit terms of service. Remove misfits where necessary. Maintain information contacts with teachers. | To deal with any curriculum needs. To study available materials. To evaluate utilization of material being furnished. To insure maximum benefit is being received from money spent. | To consider the annual Christian education budget, the stewardship and benevolent program and financial policies. To also promote the consciousness of stewardship in the program. | To recommend book and audiovisual materials (other than curriculum) for use in the program. To co-operate with the church library in evaluating existing material and recommending new material. | To be concerned with all phases of the youth program outside the Sunday school. To promote and conduct extra-curricular social activities. | To develop a program of arts and crafts and popular scientific interests amongst the young people to be conducted on Saturdays. |

SUGGESTIONS FOR THE IMPROVEMENT OF THE
RELIGIOUS EDUCATION PROGRAM OF CHRIST CHURCH

1. Definite goals and objectives should be established and a sincere effort made to accomplish these aims.

2. The present curriculum and materials should be evaluated by the director of Christian education, the Christian education committee, the superintendents and teachers to determine if we are employing the very best tools available. It is suggested that a thorough survey be made, class by class, and department by department.

3. A teachers' training program should be established on a permanent basis for instruction to both old and new teachers with special emphasis on current curriculum.

4. The field of visual aids (movies, slides, filmstrips, maps, and so forth) should be explored very carefully and specific recommendations made to teachers for use in their respective classes. Teachers should be encouraged to make maximum use of these facilities.

5. The Christian education program should be developed to the point in which participation by the children will become a thrilling experience.

6. The opening exercises in each department should be evaluated, and every effort made to improve upon them to make them exciting and meaningful.

7. A "new-life program" should be instituted with a concerted effort made to enroll all children in the community who are not affiliated with other churches.

8. Children should be encouraged to attend church school regularly (every Sunday—not only when the "spirit" moves them) and every effort made to instill within them a sense of obligation and loyalty to their God and church.

9. Young people (especially of high school age) should be encouraged to take a more active part in the over-all church program—Sunday school, choirs, summer camps, interchurch conferences, and so forth.

10. Regular meetings of departmental heads, teachers, Youth Chapel Board, and other organizations within the Christian education program should be held. Problems should be freely discussed and action taken to help improve the entire program.

11. Greater parent cooperation and participation should be encouraged.

12. A specific and intelligent program on church music should be instituted. "Good" hymns should be taught. Choir participation in the opening exercises should be encouraged. A course on Protestant sacred music should be instituted.

13. Greater emphasis should be placed on Christian stewardship. Young people should be encouraged to contribute more generously of their time and resources.

14. The Youth Fellowship, Junior High, and other youth groups should be carefully reviewed. Specific objectives should be established for each group and programs planned with the view to complementing the regular church-school instruction. Every encouragement should be given for greater and fuller participation.

15. The physical setup of the assembly hall could be improved upon greatly in order to create a more worshipful atmosphere for Youth Chapel. It is recommended that a "real" chapel be constructed in the assembly hall complete with pews (portable if necessary), an organ, pulpit and lectern, choir loft, and a completely refurbished chancel. Under the present arrangement it is very difficult for young people to be reverent and to acquire the "spiritual lift" which the service should provide. People should be restrained from using the assembly hall as a passageway between the main sanctuary and the educational wing of the church, particularly during the actual Youth Chapel service.

16. A recognition program should be instituted for perfect (or near perfect) attendance; outstanding achievement in areas of religious education; for teaching or participation in the religious educational program; and so forth. An award might be considered for the outstanding senior boy and girl who have been active in youth groups (including choir participation) and who in their personal lives have exemplified true Christian principles.

17. A study on the specific qualifications of teachers could be helpful in the assignment of classes. The more qualified and experienced teachers should be assigned generally to the older and more critical age groups.

18. With respect to released time, a program should be instituted which would not overlap but complement the regular Sunday periods of instruction.

19. It must be recognized that religion must be "sold." We should not be content to sit back and merely "hold our own." We must and can make progress both quantitatively and qualitatively. We should continuously review and evaluate our program, experiment with new ideas, place no limitations on what we can do, and make every effort to develop a program which will make ours the model for the entire Protestant Church.

20. Our young people should be taught fully to understand and appreciate our great Protestant heritage, particularly as it relates to our own personal lives. They should be made aware of the spiritual, moral, political, and cultural significance of our Protestant faith.

In condensed form the program of the church for children and youth should be frequently placed before the entire church membership.

One West Coast church, in Sunday calendars and bulletins, such as at Eastertime, devotes a page to the presentation of the entire program of the church. The items for children and youth appear as follows:

CHRIST CHURCH PROGRAM

Children's Division

| | | |
|---|---|---|
| Sundays | 9:30–12:15 | Crib and Toddlers' Rooms for child care |
| | 9:30–12:15 | Church School, Nursery through Junior |
| | 10:00 | Primary Choir rehearsal |
| | 11:30 | Junior Choir rehearsal |
| Weekdays | 9:00–12:00 | Weekday Nursery School, Monday through Friday |
| During year | 9:00–11:30 | Vacation Church School, June 22 through July 3 |

Youth Division

| | | |
|---|---|---|
| Sundays | 9:30 A.M. | Jr. Hi, Niner, Sr. Hi, College Ch. Sch. Classes |
| | 12:15 P.M. | College Coffee Hour—Brides' Room |
| | 5:00 P.M. | Confirmation Class—Sr. Hi Chapel—at stated times during a year. |
| | 5:30 P.M. | Jr. High Westminster Fellowship—3rd floor, Parish House |
| | 6:15 P.M. | Westminster Fellowship Supper—Youth Lounge |
| | 7:00 P.M. | Westminster Fellowship Group Meetings—Parish House |
| Mondays | 7:00 P.M. | Boy Scout Troop—Scout Room |
| Tuesdays | 3:10 P.M. | Girl Scouts—home of Mrs. John Jones, 10 Ridge Street |
| Wednesdays | 3:30 P.M. | Westminster Fellowship Activities—Parish House |
| | 4:30 P.M. | Christ Church Bell Choir Rehearsal |
| Wednesdays | 6:00 P.M. | Westminster Fellowship serves the Midweek Dinner |
| | 7:00 P.M. | Westminster Fellowship Fun Night—Youth Lounge |
| Saturdays | 10:00 A.M. | Senior High Boys in Gym |
| | 10:00 A.M. | Palo Girls' Club—Parish House |
| During year | | Jr. Hi Vacation Church School, June 22 through 27 |
| | | Outings and Retreats |

5. To develop an active program that lets volunteer as well as professional leadership know where it is going and what is to be done, clear-cut information regarding specific duties and assignments should be given. An example of this is the following paper

sent out early in the fall or at the end of the summer to all teachers and participants in the church school program:

1955–1956

SCHEDULE OF CHURCH SCHOOL EVENTS
MARK THEM DOWN ON YOUR CALENDAR

| | |
|---|---|
| Sept. 6 | New teacher coffee hour |
| Sept. 11 | Opening of Church School |
| Sept. 13 | Teachers' Meeting at the church—8:15 P.M. |
| Sept. 20, 26, | Oct. 4, 11, 25—Teacher-Training Course, church |
| Oct. 14 | Parents Association Family Night (grades 1–6) at church |
| Oct. 18 | Departmental Teachers' Meetings (place to be announced) |
| Nov. 29 | Teachers' Meeting at the church—8:15 P.M. |
| Dec. 25 | Christmas Day, no classes—all go to church |
| Jan. 3 | Teachers' Meeting, departmental (place to be announced) |
| Jan. 27 | 7th and 8th Grade Parents Association Party |
| Feb. 7 | Teachers' Meeting at Church—8:15 |
| Feb. 17 | Snowflake Ball (Parents Association) 9–12 graders |
| March 13 | Teachers' Meeting, departmental (place to be announced) |
| April 1 | Easter Sunday, no classes—all in church |
| April 29 | Choir Festival |
| May 1 | Teachers' Meeting at church—8:15 |
| May 4 | Parents Association—Mother-Daughter Dinner |
| May 25 | Parents Association—Father-Son Outing |
| June 10 | Church School Day |

VISITATION OF DEPARTMENTS TO THE REGULAR
CHURCH SERVICE (9:30 TO 9:50 OR 11:00 TO 11:20)

| | |
|---|---|
| Grades 9–12 | Oct. 30, Dec. 4, Dec. 25, Feb. 5, March 4, March 25, April 1, May 6, June 10 |
| Grades 7, 8 | Oct. 30, Dec. 25, Feb. 5, March 25, April 1, June 10 |
| Grades 4–6 | Oct. 30, Dec. 25, Feb. 26, April 1, April 29, June 10 |
| Grades 2, 3 | Dec. 25, March 25, April 1, June 10 |

Such an outline enables the teachers to make adequate plans for the program and to participate with the minimum number of uncertainties.

6. Not only the teachers but also the young people who have responsibilities must have full details about the program, such as "When? where? how? to whom? what?" and so forth. In one church,

junior elders and deacons in its high school department are appointed to assist in the worship service. To such young people the following material was sent:

ELDERS ON DUTY IN YOUTH CHAPEL

1957–1958

| Team 1 | Team 2 | Team 3 |
|---|---|---|
| Henry Dunn | George Merritt | Clark Cooper |
| Sue Jones | Sarah Bowen | Mary Hodges |
| Nov. 3 | Nov. 10 | Nov. 24 |
| Dec. 29 | Jan. 5 | Jan. 12 |
| Feb. 23 | March 2 | March 9 |
| April 2 | April 27 | May 4 |

| Team 4 | Team 5 | Team 6 |
|---|---|---|
| Nancy Ellis | Diana Douglas | Philip Marsh |
| Mary Sweet | Harold Otis | Virginia Darrow |
| Dec. 1 | Dec. 8 | Dec. 15 (or 22) |
| Jan. 26 | Feb. 2 | Feb. 9 |
| March 23 | March 30 | April 13 |
| May 11 | May 25 | June 1 |

*Sunday Duties of Elders*

1. Be at church by 10:45 A.M. on the day you are to serve.
2. Put on robe.
3. Assist in the Worship Service.

*Note:* A practice session with the Director of Religious Education will be held on the Saturday morning at 10 prior to the Sunday on which you are to serve. If this time is inconvenient, another time can be arranged.

Be sure to arrange for a substitute if you cannot serve on the day you are scheduled. Give the name of your substitute to Dr. Smith by Wednesday so that the correction may be made on the Youth Chapel Bulletin, which is prepared on Thursday.

You will receive a reminder card early in the week before the Sunday you are to serve.

### DEACONS ON DUTY IN YOUTH CHAPEL

#### 1957–1958

Following are the teams of deacons and the dates each team is to serve. Please keep this schedule handy and serve when you are scheduled. You will receive a reminder card early in the week before the Sunday you are to serve.

| *Team 1* | *Team 2* | *Team 3* | *Team 4* |
|---|---|---|---|
| Nancy Brown (Captain) | James Farrell (Captain) | Robert Allen (Captain) | Jennie Ballou (Captain) |
| Harry Smith | Virginia Drew | Donald Morse | Barbara Baer |
| Lynn Fellows | Susan Barrows | Melinda Nash | Stephen Jones |
| John Rebeck | John Barr | Carol Peake | Frank Joel |
| Carol Warren | Frances Scott | Elaine Brown | Joyce Crandall |
| Richard Friend | Lee Winters | Bill Cannon | Pamela Waters |
| Nov. 10 | Nov. 24 | Dec. 1 | Dec. 8 |
| Dec. 15 (or 22) | Dec. 29 | Jan. 5 | Jan. 12 |
| Jan. 26 | Feb. 2 | Feb. 9 | Feb. 23 |
| March 2 | March 9 | March 23 | March 30 |
| April 13 | April 20 | April 27 | May 4 |
| May 11 | May 25 | June 1 | |

*Sunday Duties of Deacons*

The captain should see that the deacons do the following:

#### Before the Service

1. Place a hymnbook on every other chair.
2. Place a Youth Chapel Bulletin on every chair.
3. See that the drapes by the study cubicles are closed *before* the service begins.

*Note:* The captain should take care of the following items personally or appoint a deacon to do them:

1. Light the candles on the altar.
2. Be sure that four offering plates are on the altar.
3. Place the hymn numbers on the hymn board. (Check Bulletin for hymn numbers.)

*Following the Service*

1. Collect all hymnbooks and place them on the shelves at the rear of the assembly hall.
2. Collect all left-over Bulletins and place them in the wastebasket.

*Note:* Everything done following the service *should be done quietly* so as not to disturb classes.

All deacons should report to their team captain not later than 10:40 A.M. so that the above duties can be carried out in sufficient time before the service begins.

7. The vital church will consider the formation of a parents' association to support the over-all program for children and youth and to educate the parents in that program.

8. "Family-centered activities" are part of the program of the youth and children's division of the church. Much may be gained, both directly and indirectly, when the church sponsors family nights to which the whole family comes for recreation, fellowship, or constructive activities. Family dinners, square dances, and father-son and mother-daughter banquets are types of recreational and fellowship activities that may be considered to further the church's aim to strengthen the unity of the home and family.

9. The church should take advantage of the released-time program in cooperation with the local schools. The Director of Religious Education outlined one successful program in a letter to all parents concerned:

DEAR PARENTS:

Plans are being made to expand the Tuesday Released Time Program for high school students (Grades 9 through 12) of Christ Church in the fall. The program will be held at Christ Church each Tuesday at 11 A.M., when students are permitted to leave the public school to attend religious classes.

In addition to the Young People's Choir for boys and girls of Grades 9 through 12, the following Christian-education classes will be a part of the program:

1. Boys and girls of the 9th and 10th grades will make "A Study of the Gospels" during the first half of the year. The course of study for the second half of the year will be entitled "Our Part in the World-Wide Church."
2. Boys and girls of the 11th and 12th grades will study "Christ's Life and Ours."

The courses of study and the texts being used are recommended by the Division of Christian Education of the National Council of Churches of Christ in the United States. This type of weekday Christian education is being carried on in over 3,000 communities in the United States with over 2,000,000 children and young people enrolled.

Thus, for 1961–1962, our Tuesday Released Time Program will include:

The Hand Bell Ringers—7th and 8th Grade boys

Chapel Choir—7th and 8th Grade girls

Young People's Choir—9th through 12th Grade boys and girls

Christian-education class—9th and 10th Grade boys and girls

Christian-education class—11th and 12th Grade boys and girls

This letter, with the enclosed card, is being sent to all parents who will have children in Grades 9 through 12 next year. I would appreciate it greatly if you would fill out the enclosed self-addressed card and return it to me by June 15. No postage is necessary. If you have any questions, please feel free to get in touch with me.

Thanking you for your kind attention to this matter, I remain,

Sincerely yours,

(Minister's signature)

10. Among the organizations and programs suggested are weeknight boys' club, girls' club, communicant class, vacation church school, Sunday-evening programs, summer weekday activities where the church may have facilities. All such programs and activities should be referred to the governing board. One person should be responsible for devising a program that will meet with the approval of the board. The program will then be administered under the supervision of the person placed in charge.

## YOUNG ADULT ACTIVITIES

Specific programs for the young adults should be developed on the basis of the number of young adults within the parish, their interests and needs. Particular consideration should be given to the locale of the church. Are there perhaps young adults in the area that have no home ties or church home?

One metropolitan church developed a program directed to the particular parish and locale. A condensed outline of that program, in an attractive leaflet is available to newcomers and strangers. The

leader in any local parish may find in it stimuli for consideration
in his own church:

### LAMPLIGHTER'S PURPOSE

To foster Christian Fellowship.

To promote a living, working faith in the lives of the members.

To provide opportunities for this faith to be put into action through group
participation and leadership, in the total program of the Church, in the
home, community, and the world.

Art. II, Lamplighters' Constitution

### LAMPLIGHTER'S SONG

We bear the flame of truth and right
And with all Lamplighters
Light the Lamp of Faith,
The Lamp of Hope,
The Lamp of Charity.

We send our beam into the night,
And we'll be Lamplighters
'Til the path to God is bright
For all the world to see.

### LAMPLIGHTER COMMITTEES

*Executive* . . . Our officers and committee chairmen meet monthly to exchange
ideas, coordinate the work of all our committees, and make plans for furthering the purposes of Lamplighters.

*Program* . . . We look for interesting speakers, movies, and plan musical programs and discussion forums. We ask our members to play piano, lead hymn
singing, sing solos, and lead our devotional time.

*Service* . . . Our purpose is to discover places where we can be of help. We
find them through appeals from the Church, civic organizations, and information from our own members. We then make plans for meeting these needs
within the resources of Lamplighters.

*Membership* . . . Our pleasant tasks are greeting and registering newcomers,
and introducing them during the meeting to the group. We also distribute
name tags to our members and guests, and invite them to return. Once a
month we introduce our new members to the group at a regular meeting.

*Social* . . . Our responsibility is planning a monthly party—the time, the place,
games, food, and decorations. We plan a variety of events to please as many
as possible. Besides this, we recruit someone to be in charge of snack time,

and K.P. after our meetings. We also help plan and cooperate in events such as the Coffee Hour on Sundays and the platter party each month.

*Room* . . . We set up chairs and distribute programs and hymnals before every meeting. After the meeting we return the room to order. We also run the projector for movies, and help arrange any props, lighting, and equipment for a special program.

*Publicity* . . . All of our committees are responsible for writing articles about their activities. They are printed in the *Fellowship News,* Sunday bulletin, and the *Messenger.* In addition to this, posters are often needed to advertise a special event, program, or project.

## WELCOME!

Every Sunday evening we have a home-town greeting ready for any young adult new to Lamplighters. We're from most of the 50 in the United States, and parts beyond.

This means that few of us have known each other very long. We're always busy learning new names to match new faces. That's why we wear name tags faithfully. What we hope you'll like about us is our smile and friendly handshake. We want you to feel at home, and to come back again soon.

*Let's Have Fun* . . . Besides our enjoyment of casual conversation, we enjoy many active and spectator sports; also less strenuous forms of recreation, like singing around the piano, and sun bathing at the beach. We have great enthusiasm for weekend retreats, record parties, and such.

*Our Purpose* . . . Making friends and sharing fun activities are only part of our purpose in being Lamplighters. We want to know how our role as young adults, in our relationships at work, at home, and in citizenship, can be better understood and enriched by a closer relationship with God.

As we grow in Christian faith, we want to reach out beyond ourselves and help others in some way. Whether we lead singing, have devotions, work on a committee, or simply do K.P., our efforts become identified with the aims of Lamplighters.

We attempt to have some kind of project with a need we can fulfill. Singing carols to shut-ins at Christmas, donating blood, donning jeans to paint an old church, or giving to feed the hungry—these activities mean more to us because we're doing them together.

*We Invite You* . . . If you like us and our aims of friendship, devotion, and service, we want you to be a member! All we ask is that you continue your faithful attendance, and indicate your desire to share in attaining our Lamplighter purposes.

If you express your desire to be a member, we will introduce you to the group at a future Lamplighter meeting. We want you to feel that becoming a member is a special occasion for us, and for you!

GENEVA FELLOWSHIP—Young Adults 23–35

| | |
|---|---|
| Breakfast Class | singles—Sunday morning—breakfast 9:00—class 9:30—Youth Lounge. |
| Clippers | couples—Sunday morning—class 9:30—3rd-floor Parish House |
| Lamplighters | singles and couples—Sunday evening—program 8:00—Geneva Room |
| Presbyweds | couples—first Friday evening of the month—meetings announced |
| Activities | Coffee Hour after church . . . Fun Night, with volleyball, Ping-pong, and square dancing, on Tuesday night . . . *Geneva News* published monthly . . . Geneva Players on the stage . . . Platter Party monthly |

## ADULT ORGANIZATIONS

The numerous and varied adult organizations that may worthily support the purpose of the local church include: (1) women's society; (2) men's council or club; (3) adult Bible classes, as a part of the church school program; (4) study groups; (5) prayer groups; (6) business and professional women's evening society; (7) social service groups; (8) sewing committees, engaged in preparing materials for hospitals, orphanages, and so forth; (9) crafts and art programs; (10) physical and recreational activities, such as bowling leagues, an annual golf day, and so forth; (11) "School of Religion" or "University of Life," whose programs will be devoted to education and information on a selected number of dates within the church year; (12) in certain metropolitan areas a noon luncheon club for businessmen (a similar club may be considered for professional women); (13) the couples club for young married people; (14) music and choir participation. A great many service and planning committees within the work of the church, such as the every-member canvass, the calling program on new members, will claim the attention of the good church administrator. He will see to it that adults feel a sense of relationship to the work of the church through participation here.

Familiarity with the background, interests, and needs of parishioners is of vital importance to church leaders. These can be obtained by personal contact, by church-wide surveys, and through "interest sheets" to be filled in by new members. Above all, this information should be carefully compiled in the church office. Through it and the background that led to acquiring it church leaders will have the basis for sensing needs and for "tapping" the abilities of parishioners to meet them. The following questionnaire has proved very satisfactory in providing a basis for an adult program:

I HAVE SPECIAL TRAINING, APTITUDE, AND/OR EXPERIENCE IN/AS:

GENERAL OFFICE WORK
- [ ] Accounting
- [ ] Filing
- [ ] Mailing
- [ ] Receptionist
- [ ] Secretary
- [ ] Typing

WRITING
- [ ] Book Reviews
- [ ] Creative Writing
- [ ] Editorial Work
- [ ] News Reporter
- [ ] Proof Reading

FUND RAISING
- [ ] Budget Review
- [ ] Canvassing
- [ ] Organizing
- [ ] Program Planning

PUBLICITY, PUBLIC RELATIONS

CHURCH WORK
- [ ] Bible Study
- [ ] Choir
- [ ] Couples' Clubs
- [ ] Council of Churches
- [ ] Denominational Boards
- [ ] Food Service
- [ ] Men's Work
- [ ] Official Boards or Committees
- [ ] Parish Calling

- [ ] Prayer Group
- [ ] Social Action
- [ ] Teaching
- [ ] Ushering
- [ ] Women's Work
- [ ] World Service
- [ ] Worship Program Planning
- [ ] Youth Activities

CHILDREN'S WORK
- [ ] Camp Counseling
- [ ] Crafts
- [ ] Dramatics
- [ ] Gym—Sports
- [ ] Kindergarten
- [ ] Nursery
- [ ] Storytelling

SOCIAL WORK
- [ ] Administration
- [ ] Case Work
- [ ] Club Work
- [ ] Geriatrics
- [ ] Group Work
- [ ] Institutional Visiting
- [ ] Recreation

PUBLIC SPEAKING
- [ ] Dramatics
- [ ] Entertainer
- [ ] Lecturer
- [ ] Master of Ceremonies

- [ ] Radio
- [ ] Television

MUSICIAN
- [ ] Conductor-Director
- [ ] Instrumentalist
  _____ (which?)
- [ ] Singer
  _____ (which voice?)

ART
- [ ] Chart Making
- [ ] Drawing
- [ ] Illustrating
- [ ] Painting
- [ ] Photography
- [ ] Poster Making

FOREIGN LANGUAGE
_____ (which?)

CRAFTS
- [ ] Bookbinding
- [ ] Needlework
- [ ] Pottery
- [ ] Sewing
- [ ] Woodwork
  _____ (others)

DOCTOR, NURSE
_____ (Degree)

RECREATIONAL ACTIVITIES
_____

OTHER ABILITIES
_____

TYPES OF VOLUNTEER SERVICE THAT WOULD INTEREST ME AT CHRIST CHURCH
OR IN THE COMMUNITY: _____

_____

I could be available _____ per week, month, or for specific assignments
                        (hours)
day
evening _____
           (which day?)
Present (or former) volunteer commitments (in church or community):

_____

_____ Amount of time per week _____

CHIEF INTERESTS
Favorite Hobbies, Recreations, Sports:
Residence Abroad—or Extensive Travel:
Previous Employment (during the past ten years): Firm Names _____

_____

Types of Work _____

## SENIOR MEMBERS' GROUPS

One minister writes about senior members' groups as follows:

We are rejoicing in a group we call "The XYZ Club"—extra years of zest
and energy. Such a name probably wouldn't be successful everywhere. But it
has been helpful in our bailiwick. We purposely place the minimum age at
sixty-five. I think it's most important to have some younger oldsters to give
the program adequate leadership. My thinking here has been abundantly
substantiated, and we now have a fine group of persons sixty-five years of
age and over.

Steps in the formation of a program for senior members are the
following:

1. Permission from the governing body to survey the need;

2. A meeting, called by the minister or an appointed leader, of
known individuals in the senior age group. Consideration should
be given to separate groups for men and women.

3. At the initial meeting the following question shall be raised:
"In your judgment is there a need for a senior members' program?

If so, what kind of program? How often should the group meet? Where should the meeting be held? How will the program be organized and administered so that it will have continuity?" The raising and answering of these questions may lead to surveys, discussions, and additional meetings.

4. If the consensus is that there is a need for a program, a temporary chairman, possibly with an advisory committee, may be appointed by the governing board to hold the first meeting.

5. Those consulted in the original planning and survey will have the responsibility of spreading the word, personally inviting eligible friends.

6. The church office will have prepared a list of church members known to be in the senior age group. These persons will be asked in writing and/or by personal contact to attend the first meeting.

7. That meeting should be planned to point out the benefits of entering upon a senior members' program.

8. The plans and thoughts thus far developed should be presented.

9. Reactions, limited as to time, should be elicited from the group. If the consensus seems to favor going ahead, the time for the next meeting should be agreed upon.

10. If necessary to solidify the organization, individuals or committees such as program, nominating, constitution and by-laws, ways and means, should be appointed.

11. A member of the church staff or a lay member of the official board should be designated counselor or adviser to the group.

12. This counselor would perhaps serve as the liaison with the official board, reporting to the board regularly on the work and program of the senior group and in turn receiving counsel from it. Then he may serve to keep the senior group aware of the larger work and the program of the church.

## THE INVITATION COMMITTEE

Besides the minister and possibly other staff individuals devoted to inviting outsiders into the life of the church, a group of lay people dedicated to this purpose may be of great service.

One congregation, for more than a quarter of a century, has brought a sizable percentage of new people into its life year after year. The minister attests that the agency largely responsible for this is the strong church-wide invitation committee, which meets for a single supper prior to each midweek service. At this time, assignments are made for calling on prospective individuals, and reports are received of all calls made. The occasion is used for a brief period of encouragement, inspiration, and instruction.

Other churches have found it desirable to assign this support of the church's ministry to a board of deaconesses. The minister of another well-administered parish has formed a women's service committee, which in addition to calling on prospects, assist the minister in visiting shut-ins, new mothers, and new members.

In planning for the administration of such a program the steps are as follows:

1. Divide the parish into geographical sections.

2. Assign one, two, or more visitors to each section. The visitation members should, if possible, be residents of the area assigned to them.

3. Have a regular meeting time for education, inspiration, the receiving of reports, and the assignment of new callers.

4. Place responsibility for the program in the hands of: (*a*) general chairman, (*b*) an assistant or co-chairman to serve in the absence of the chairman; (*c*) a secretary to receive information from visitors and channel it to the church office or the minister.

5. Prepare a mimeographed sheet giving all details of the program. Offer definite suggestions as to how to make a visit, and give specific instructions regarding the information desired from the call.

6. Thoroughly acquaint each visitor with the organization of the church and its activities, particularly with regard to the ways of joining the church, the date for the reception of new members, and so on.

7. Place in the visitors' hands material they may leave with the persons on whom they call. The assignment cards for callers should be adequate but clear and brief, as in the example on page 139.

## THE MEMBERSHIP COUNCIL

Often the governing body may be greatly assisted by a membership council that works with it in keeping in touch with all church

```
┌─────────────────────────────────────────────────────────────┐
│            PROSPECT  AND  ASSIGNMENT  CARD                   │
│  Name _____  │
│  Address _____  │
│          Reasons for being on our responsibility list       │
│  ____ Member of Sunday School   ____ Attends Church Service │
│  ____ Child in Sunday           ____ Wife or Children Mem-  │
│        School                          bers                 │
│  ____ Baby on Cradle Roll       ____ Attends some Women's   │
│                                        Meetings             │
│  ____ Survey—Prefer our         ____ Attends Young People's │
│        Church                          Society              │
│  ____ Member Elsewhere          ____ Contributor            │
│  Other reasons or information _____  │
│  _____   │
│  Called on by _____ Date _____   │
│  Report and Follow-Up Recommendations _____   │
│  _____   │
└─────────────────────────────────────────────────────────────┘
```

members and integrating them into the life of the church. The following program, called "The Under-Shepherd Plan," is assigned to the deacons of the church:

### THE UNDER-SHEPHERD PLAN

The genius of the Protestant Church is fellowship—fellowship with one another and with God. Fellowship is the crucial problem of the large church and must be approached from every angle. One approach is the under-shepherd plan, wherein the congregation is divided into geographical units under lay supervision. The following suggestions may help you in making this ministry more effective.

1. The entire parish is divided into geographical zones, each under the supervision of an elder.
2. Each zone is subdivided into districts, each under the supervision of a deacon. The deacon will call personally in every home prior to each quarterly communion service to deliver the family communion token and extend a personal invitation to attend the service. It is important that these calls be personal and that each deacon get to know his people well. It is of inestimable benefit to all concerned.

3. The deacon should keep informed of the activities, programs, and problems of the church. Situations may demand that he be able to handle problems arising among his people, and he should be prepared to give intelligent, constructive, and positive answers.

4. The deacon should be alert to the problems and needs of his people and refer such to his elder or the pastors.

5. Deacons may suggest home Communion for invalids and shut-ins, and submit names of such to the pastors.

6. It will be most helpful if each deacon makes a personal evaluation of each person in his district, noting such things as the degree of interest and activity and leadership abilities.

7. From time to time deacons will be called upon to recruit manpower for specialized services. Knowing your people will help immeasurably.

8. Deacons may feel free to conduct district social gatherings either in a home or at the church. The elder with his deacons should plan at least one zone social gathering each year. The church staff may be called upon to assist, and should be notified of all such meetings.

9. A deacon may be called upon from time to time to render special services to persons within his district.

10. Each deacon should report to the church office those persons known by him to be inactive and unresponsive. These names will be turned over to the roll revision committee of the board.

11. The goal of each deacon should be to promote an active church interest on the part of each person committed to his care. There is no substitute for the personal contact you will have with your people. Make the most of it.

If there are many indigent or shut-in persons in the parish, the official board may organize a special group to help these members. One parish reports that a board of deaconesses with this special function has been most meaningful. In one church such deaconesses are nominated by the governing board, elected by the congregation at the annual meeting, and meet at a given time each month to report on their work. Each deaconess is assigned five or more shut-ins. Representing the church, the deaconesses call regularly on the shut-ins, send them birthday cards and holiday remembrances, and render any service that may be helpful. They also call on church members who are convalescing from a serious illness or operation.

A report of the invitation committee and the membership council or the board of deaconesses should be made annually, not for the governing body alone but for the entire membership. It should state the names of the district leader and his co-workers. Alongside each name, in two columns, should be recorded the number of calls assigned and the number of calls reported. The totals will be impressive. With an additional statement by the chairman, such a report vividly points up for the entire membership the validity of the program.

For the program of supervision of the membership, some churches have a continuing church roll committee. Authorized and delegated by the governing body and working in conjunction with the minister, the committee may have the following responsibilties:

1. The consideration of all applications for transfer of membership to other churches and recommendation to the board concerning these applications or requests.

2. Scrutiny of the roll of the church and the sending of letters to churches in communities concerning those who have moved to other areas.

3. The direction of the sending of letters to those who have been away from the church for over two years and those who have failed to attend or contribute to or take part in the activities of the church. To ascertain their desire concerning their relationship to the church.

4. To recommend to the board those who should be suspended from the active membership of the church.

5. To see that the rolls of the church are kept up properly and in accordance with the directives of the denomination.

6. To see that the rolls of the church are kept up to date in respect to addresses and telephone numbers, deceases, or removals from the roll.

7. To consider all matters of discipline concerning members and make recommendation to the board.

One such program is known as "Shepherding." The statement regarding the program is made under the Scriptural heading "Shepherding the Church of God which he has bought with His own blood" (Acts 20:28). The administrative outline follows:

### SUGGESTIONS FOR SHEPHERDS

1. Hold at least one meeting of his flock a year.
2. Call on each family once or twice a year, personally or by telephone.
3. Report:
   a. All cases of sickness to the minister's office. (Call on the sick or shut-ins of your group when possible.)
   b. Deaths and sorrows. (A card of "consolation" would be greatly appreciated.)
   c. Nonchurch members of your families who might be won to Christ.
   d. All prospects for church membership in your group.

4. Call on church membership prospects who sign communion cards but have no church membership in the city.
5. Encourage the attendance of members in your group at all church services, Sunday school, and the midweek service.
6. Help assimilate members into the various organizations of the church according to their ages.
7. Report promptly all removals or changes of address to the church office.

### SUGGESTIONS FOR FLOCK MEETINGS

The Shepherd should:
1. Secure a home in which such a meeting can be held.
2. Arrange a date convenient to himself, the host, and the minister.
3. Get a pianist for the evening and have sufficient chairs. Song sheets are provided.
4. Get in touch with each family, extending a personal invitation. The minister sends a general letter, *but it should be supplemented by telephone calls, and if possible by personal calls. Satisfactory attendance at these Flock Meetings depends very largely on the efforts of the Shepherd.*
5. The host and hostess may or may not serve refreshments. This matter is purely voluntary and the success of the meeting does not depend on this feature. The host and hostess need not plan a program. The minister will be responsible.

On page 143 is the annual report.

## HOSPITALITY PROGRAM

Some churches appoint individuals or a special committee to develop a hospitality program for prospects and new members. This activity is separate from the invitation committee, whose task is essentially evangelism, and from the membership council or shepherding program, which is the oversight of members already in the church. The hospitality program aims to present the interest and friendly warmth of the church to the stranger or visitor. This interest may be expressed by having a regular tea or hour of hospitality for newcomers in the church or in the manse or parsonage.

Once a year the membership and hospitality chairmen of every organization in the church should be called together. Under a united plan, the minister or the officer in charge of the program will instruct and counsel these leaders as to the best method of greeting the people

SHEPHERD'S REPORT

Name _____

From _____, 19___ to _____, 19___

I.  A FLOCK MEETING held _____, 19___ Number present ___

II.  PERSONAL CALLS made at homes _____

III.  TELEPHONE CALLS made

    1.  To encourage attendance at:    *Number*
        Flock Meetings           _____
        Church services          _____
        Church school           _____
        Prayer meeting          _____
        Women's meetings      _____
        Other meetings         _____

    2.  To report:
        Sickness                _____
        Death and sorrow      _____
        Prospects for membership  _____
        Change of address     _____

               Total number of calls  _____

IV.  COMMUNICATIONS
    1.  Letters promoting Flock Meeting  _____
    2.  Seasons' greetings sent      _____
    3.  Consolation notes sent      _____
    4.  Sick cards sent          _____

        Total number of communications  _____

V.  OTHER SHEPHERDING WORK DONE

who come to participate in their activities. Suggestions will be made by the various representatives. A plan whereby each membership and hospitality chairman will report to the church office the names of new members, visitors, and strangers will be devised and put into operation.

## USHERS

A planned and well-administered program for ushers may be a significant factor in dignifying the order of worship, preparing worshipers for the solemn adoration of Almighty God, and may be of inestimable meaning to the stranger and visitor.

One church outlines its procedure of instruction for ushers as follows:

### INSTRUCTIONS FOR USHERING

It is a well-recognized fact that a church usher plays a very great part in the religious life of the people who attend services of divine worship. The usher is usually the first person the worshiper meets, and the manner in which he greets people and welcomes them into the church sets the mood and spirit for those who have come to worship. With this thought in the background, a few helpful suggestions may be offered in the interest of a more effective service.

1. Ushers should always move in an easy and unhurried manner, speaking softly and respectfully so as to foster and maintain an atmosphere for worship.
2. Ushers always "request" and never "tell" a worshiper in giving directions. They never argue or become irritated.
3. All ushers should report for duty at least twenty minutes prior to announced time of service. The usher captain is responsible for such matters as:

   a) having bulletins on hand and inserts, if any.
   b) checking on temperature, ventilation, drafts, and order of the sanctuary.
   c) seeing that washrooms are open.

4. In the event of bulletin inserts, first-service ushers should collate inserts for second service during the first service.
5. Six ushers are assigned to the main auditorium, with two stationed in each of the two center aisles, and one in each outside aisle. Three ushers are assigned to the balcony—one for each aisle. Whenever the Fellowship Hall is used for overflow, extra ushers will be assigned to this location.
6. Worshipers should be ushered to a pew and then presented with a bulletin. Usher should wait at pew end until worshipers are seated.
7. Ushers should always precede guests, never follow—this applies both to the auditorium and to the balcony.
8. Parents bringing small children may leave them in the nursery. Ushers should know where these places are. Otherwise, ushers should encourage parents with children to sit in the balcony.

9. The four (4) tallest ushers present should be assigned to the two center aisles in the main auditorium with shorter men on the outside aisles. At the beginning of morning prayer the outside ushers should stand immediately behind the two taller ushers in their respective center aisles. At the signal of the minister the two separate bodies of three ushers will march in unison to the altar, forming a straight line one (1) foot from the bottom step. At the conclusion of the minister's offering sentence, the two end ushers will go up three (3) steps while at the same time converging to the middle. After the minister hands them the plates, they will turn to the inside, go down one (1) step and pass the plates to the other ushers. When each usher has received his plate the men on the outside will turn and proceed to their assigned sections, with the original two (2) end ushers working the center section and the other sets of two ushers working the east and west sections. Ushers will carry the plates in both hands at all times, with the forearms parallel with the floor. Money should never be rattled on the plates, or transferred from one plate to another in the sanctuary. This should be done in the vestibule, after the doors are closed. In taking attendance, each usher is responsible for counting only those worshipers in the pews in which he starts the collection plate. Each usher then reports his total to the deacon in charge, who totals the attendance slip and places it on the collection plate. The deacon in charge is to count the deacons and the members of the choir. After the offertory music, the plates are returned to the minister in much the same fashion as they were received.

10. Worshipers should be ushered to seats at only such times as indicated on the bulletin. Rear doors to the sanctuary should be closed during those periods when we "refrain from ushering," but should be opened immediately thereafter, so worshipers can be seated without delay.

11. One usher shall be appointed at each service as keeper of the wardrobe to protect articles hung in the lower vestibules. Keeper of wardrobe will open outside doors at close of service.

12. During the fall, winter, and spring service, ushers should wear dark suits. During summer services, light suits will be acceptable.

13. Ushers are expected to obtain their own substitutes for scheduled services they cannot attend.

14. No portable chairs are permitted to be placed either in the main auditorium or in the balcony—such action is contrary to the state insurance laws. Standees are permitted, however, but not to such an extent as completely to block any of the aisles.

15. On Baptismal Sunday one deacon will be assigned to assist and direct those having children to be baptized.

16. Ushers, with exception of keeper of wardrobe, should remain in sanctuary during sermon period in case of an emergency. Usher captain will assign one usher on each center aisle to open vestibule doors at close of service.

17. Ushers are requested to attend coffee hour to greet people and assist wherever possible.
18. Crib room for infants and nursery for toddlers up to three years of age in Room 203 on the main floor of the education building. All other children should go to the educational office for room assignment.

The individual church will adopt its usher program in terms of the size of the worshiping congregation, the arrangement at the pews, and the order of worship. But the attentive service and anticipation of congregational needs expected of ushers should be clearly outlined so that each new usher may be fully instructed as to his duties.

Organization of the ushers, if not a function of the active official board, should be handled by an ushers' committee that will be responsible to the governing board and that will serve as overseers of the ushers and as counselors in their work.

In considering the usher program, the following points may helpfully be followed:

1. A member should be invited to become an usher not only by the ushering body but also by the minister as a leading member of the governing body. So, by word and deed, it is conveyed to the prospective usher that his work is important. It is related to the primary purpose of the church, which is the worship of God and the entrance into his presence.

2. The ushers may well be given the responsibility for taking the Sunday attendance. One form for this purpose is the following 3-by-5-inch mimeographed card:

```
        ATTENDANCE
     MORNING SERVICE
                    (date)
   Sunday _____
   Choir _____
   East Section _____
   Center _____
   West Section _____
   Balcony _____
   Ushers _____

   Total _____
```

Each usher should receive an usher's schedule showing his assignments. It is recommended that the name, address, and telephone number of each usher appear on the sheet. The captain of the ushering team may keep a record of attendance of ushers on a simple form like the following:

CHRIST CHURCH

*Attendance of Ushers*

TEAM: _____ CAPTAIN: _____

PERIOD: _____June 4, 19—_____ to _____June 25, 19—_____

| NAME | 6/4 | 6/11 | 6/18 | 6/25 |
|------|-----|------|------|------|
|      |     |      |      |      |
|      |     |      |      |      |
|      |     |      |      |      |
|      |     |      |      |      |

Ushers should be instructed as to what to do in emergencies and in unusual circumstances. One church supplies each usher with a mimeographed copy of an ushers' manual with the following instructions:

1. *Illness*
There is a couch in the Bride's Room for those who wish to use it if they become ill.

If someone faints or otherwise becomes unconscious, ask others to move so the stricken person can lie on the pew seat. Then summon a doctor from the congregation or notify the Church Office to get a doctor.

Doctors in the congregation are being asked to make themselves known to the head ushers, so one may be known to be available in an emergency.

2. *Fire*
If a fire starts, the head usher should have ushers open all doors to evacuate the congregation, and he should report the fire to the Church Office immediately. As soon as the sanctuary is empty, all doors are to be closed to restrict the fire. Fire hoses are strategically located throughout the structure.

### 3. *Communion*

After a Communion Service, the glasses are to be collected and taken to the sacristy. They break easily, so please handle carefully. Cloth is to be removed from altar, care being taken to avoid wrinkling.

Communion linen is to be folded and placed in box in sacristy. Ushers will assist elders with Communion if requested to do so, but otherwise will remain seated at the rear of the sanctuary during Communion.

### 4. *Chapel-Overflow*

If the attendance is so large that it cannot be accommodated with extra chairs in the back, the late arrivals are to be told that they can go into the chapel, which has a public-address system that will bring the service into the chapel.

If there are people that go into the chapel, an usher should be assigned to the chapel to seat people, and to look out for them generally.

This same usher will take up the collection, using one of the extra collection plates that will be found on the west table in the sanctuary.

After the service the chapel is to be cleaned up like the sanctuary, lights turned off and the door closed.

### 5. *Extreme Crowds*

On some occasions there will be extra-large crowds, and a single row of chairs can be placed in each side aisle. These chairs can be obtained from the Fellowship Hall. Should some event be taking place there, ask the Church Office for additional chairs.

### 6. *Absence*

If you find you will be unable to attend when your team is scheduled, notify your head or assistant head usher and arrange for a substitute.

### 7. *Extra Services*

Be sure to check your schedule for extra services. The head usher should make a special contact with his team on such occasions.

### 8. *New Ushers*

When a new man joins a team, he should be assigned to work with an experienced man, so he can learn quickly. Starting on the side aisle has proved to work out quite well in most cases.

Heads or captains of the ushering groups will find it helpful to remind all ushers of their duties and make up a check list of responsibilities for themselves. The following procedure is used in one church:

#### DUTIES OF CAPTAINS

Prepare ushering schedule for Sundays on which team serves and assign specific duties to each man. Make assignments for special services as required.

Check that church is ready for services, including:

| | |
|---|---|
| Lights on | Offering plates in chancel |
| Bulletins distributed | Pews reserved, as required |
| Ventilation | Floor mats on rainy days |
| Ushers' flowers | Ministers' capes available |
| Extra folding seats | First-aid equipment in order |

Hearing aids in working order

See that any special instructions from minister or chairman are executed.

Train new usher and refresh team on duties and practices as required.

Put lost property in safekeeping in board room or church office.

Make sure that accidents, damage to church property, or complaints requiring official attention are reported to chairman.

See that decorum is maintained in narthex and outside church during services.

Maintain constant watch for comfort and safety of worshipers. See that important messages are delivered, suggestions passed on to proper authority, strangers made welcome. Try to anticipate problems before they arise and solve them quietly and smoothly.

Make it a point to know where a doctor is located at each service.

Brief team on special duties that occur infrequently, such as assisting the elders at Communion, handling overflow crowds, and other departures from routine.

Keep alert to possible improvements in ushering routines and encourage suggestions from team.

Keep on lookout for new usher candidates.

The captain, or his deputy, has sole responsibility for assignment of duties, determination of such matters of judgment as when and where to use extra chairs, releasing men before end of service, and other decisions involving departure from routines spelled out in these instructions.

Captains of ushers, in reminding ushers of their responsibilities, can helpfully emphasize these items:

Familiarize yourself with the location of telephones, rest-room facilities, and the church school offices so you can direct inquiries intelligently. Questions about church activities that you may not be able to answer should be referred to the captain or to the deacons on duty at the guest book in the board room.

Learn where the *First aid* kit is kept and familiarize yourself with its contents. However, don't attempt to give assistance beyond your skill. There is usually at least one doctor in church. Content yourself with making the victim comfortable and keeping others around him calm. If you need the *help* of another usher, *raise your arm over your head*. If you see this signal given, proceed *immediately* to the man, unless you see another usher already on his way.

If a worshiper falls or injures himself in any way, when you have rendered whatever assistance you can, obtain his name and address and report it to the captain. This is important so that the church can express its concern and so that our insurance company can be properly notified.

Read "Principles of Church Ushering" carefully and refresh your memory occasionally on the little niceties and techniques that will help us to maintain our high standards of service to our church.

## MEMORIAL AND ENDOWMENT FUNDS

One aspect of the well-administered parish that not only concerns its present activity but may also have an influence in strengthening its future life is the planning and execution of certain memorials and endowments.

It is advisable that the governing body appoint memorial and endowment committees from the congregation. As with all other committees, the memorial and endowment committees will be responsible to the governing body.

Memorial funds are established in various ways:

1. The memorial committee may advise the congregation that certain parts of the church fabric or furnishings may be presented to the church by individuals or groups of individuals as memorials. These include such major items as a section of the church building or an organ, or smaller items of church furnishing and equipment. The committee may find it helpful to list for the congregation, in a letter or leaflet, items that are suitable for memorials. In the case where a new church building is being erected, the list may include windows, a pulpit, a lectern, a communion table, a baptismal font, a cross, chancel pews, a *prie-dieu,* a candelabra, a pulpit Bible, and so on. The congregation will be given the names, addresses, and telephone numbers of persons to be reached. The committee may find it desirable to state the approximate prices of such memorials. Some committees have avoided doing this and have, instead, welcomed questions from the parishioners and indicated that they would share, in confidence, any specific information with questioners.

2. Many churches have established a tribute or memorial fund that is given to the church in lieu of floral tributes to a deceased person. One church that has such a fund explains it to the congregation as follows:

THE TRIBUTE FUND

You have probably been troubled because of the inadequacy and fleeting nature of the floral gifts presented on the solemn occasion of death.

Many members and friends of our congregation have expressed a desire for a means of expressing friendship and sympathy that would be of a more lasting and significant nature. To this end Christ Church has established the Tribute Fund. Contributions may be presented to this fund in loving memory of a friend who has passed into the other world.

Tribute Fund gifts may be designated by the donor for some specific purpose in the church. The donor may wish the gift to be used for the Building Fund to help erect our new sanctuary, for the work of the Board of Foreign Missions, for new equipment in our Church School, or perhaps for sending some underprivileged child to a summer camp. In a multitude of ways a Tribute Fund gift of remembrance will go on living by the benefit it brings.

When a memorial contribution is made through the Tribute Fund a suitable acknowledgment is sent to the family of the person honored by the gift. (No reference is made to the amount contributed.)

---

A GIFT HONORING

_____

has been made to

THE TRIBUTE FUND

of

CHRIST CHURCH

by

_____

---

When a number of gifts have been presented in memory of some deceased member or friend of this parish, the bereaved family may wish to suggest how the total undesignated gifts should be used. When no designation is made by the donor or the bereaved family, the board will use its best judgment as to where and how the gift will do the most good or serve the most urgent need.

The officers of Christ Church would commend to our members and friends this permanent and useful expression of Christian remembrance and sympathy.

If you wish to make use of the Tribute Fund, kindly phone the church office
Checks should be made payable to the Tribute Fund of Christ Church. The
mailing address is Christ Church, 2436 Fairfield, Ferncrest, Maryland.

Memorial gifts should be acknowledged and the bereaved family should be informed about it. Below is a form used for acknowledgment to the donor.

The following form is sent to the family or next of kin of the person in whose memory the gift was presented.

Gifts to the Tribute Fund provide a lasting and significant remembrance of
those the gifts honor. In certain instances, the donor may specify the use of
the gift as a contribution toward our building fund or for the purchase of
some needed equipment for our church. Again, gifts may be designated to fill
an urgent need in a remote mission field or a Christian neighborhood house.
Gifts may make possible a period at summer camp for some underprivileged
child, aid to some young person in training for Christian service, or healing
and comfort for the sick and aged. In a multitude of ways these gifts go on
living, honoring those for whom they were given, rather than being merely a
fleeting remembrance.

> The TRIBUTE FUND of the
> CHRIST CHURCH
> 2436 Fairfield
> Ferncrest, Maryland

---

THE  TRIBUTE  FUND
OF
CHRIST  CHURCH

Acknowledges with Deep Appreciation a Gift
from

_____

As a Tribute to

_____

_____

Clerk of the Board

---

3. The governing board may initiate a memorial project for a
specific purpose and may invite special "living gifts" at specific

times or for specific occasions. One such program invites the congregation to make contributions for the floral decoration of the chancel at special church seasons such as Easter or Christmas. The governing board, through a memorial committee, informs the congregation that a portion of the funds (perhaps half) will be used for the beautification of the church at the designated season. The remainder of the fund will be used for a specific purpose outlined by the governing body. This may be along one of many lines: (*a*) For the immediate support of some benevolent project; (*b*) for a permanent memorial fund, the income of which is to be used for a specific purpose, such as the maintenance of the church grounds, the support of the children's activities, or a scholarship for a student who is a candidate for the Christian ministry. These suggestions will open up innumerable possibilities. This type of program is a modified memorial-endowment fund and may have a particular appeal because of its perpetuity.

Not only should all gifts be acknowledged, but a permanent record of such gifts should be maintained in the church office and by the archives committee. (In the section under Records, page 295, suggestions for the maintenance of such records are outlined.) The governing body and the memorials or endowment committee may provide a "Book of Remembrance" in which all such gifts are recorded. Consideration should be given to the housing of the book and its exhibition for the parish.

Programs for the endowment of the church should be thoroughly outlined and be presented to the parish at least once a year. Rules governing the endowment funds should be established by the official board and should be published for all parishioners to read. One church has prepared the following statement:

RULES GOVERNING THE ENDOWMENT FUND
AS APPROVED BY THE GOVERNING BOARD

1. The Endowment Committee under authority of the Governing Board will invest and reinvest all money in the Fund, and will generally supervise all money and securities given or bequeathed to the Fund.
2. The principal of all bequests and "living" gifts to the Endowment Fund received prior to January 1, 19__, and where specified or requested after that date for memorials or other purposes, shall at all times remain intact. Otherwise, after a period of twenty-five years the Governing Board in its discretion may appropriate and use the principal of the Fund in such man-

ner as it deems best to advance the work of the church, not however in excess of 5 per cent of the principal in any one year. Except where the donor specifically desires principal to be kept in perpetuity, the Governing Board believes that this provision is a safeguard which at the same time allows a new generation to make its plans about the future. The income from investments may be used as voted by the Governing Board for the ongoing work of the Church.

These provisions are made to regulate the administration of the Endowment Fund, and also to assure contributors that their donations or bequests and the income earned thereon will be of maximum assistance in the work of the church.

The Endowment Fund provides a means to establish a perpetual memorial for loved ones or for those to whom special tribute would be given. The Endowment Committee and Consistory is pledged to regarding the intent of all such gifts and specially designated bequests.

The statement should give to the members of the parish the names of the endowment committee, and a statement welcoming questions by any member of the parish should be made.

Forms of bequest may be worded as follows:

---

FORMS OF BEQUEST

Restricted bequest:

To Christ Church of Pleasantville I give and bequeath the sum of _____ dollars ($_____) to be added to its Endowment Fund. (Note: Additional appropriate language can, of course, also be added if the bequest is intended for some specific purpose.)

General bequest:

To Christ Church of Pleasantville I give and bequeath the sum of _____ dollars ($_____).

---

Certain members of the parish will respond to and appreciate an occasional report of the endowment fund. The committee should list the assets of the fund, such as cash, bonds, and stocks, and the liabilities, such as legacies, "living" gifts, and miscellaneous memorials, and state the market value of the stocks. At the same time, the committee should publicize in its literature the names of individuals who have provided legacies and living gifts to the church.

Certain institutions have adopted a dignified but aggressive program inviting church officers and members to provide for the church in their wills and to notify the endowment committee of their intent and action. It is advised that the endowment committee have in its membership, when possible, a lawyer or another person acquainted with the drafting and execution of wills who could give direct, constructive assistance to the parishioners in this matter.

One church, to encourage certain parishioners to do likewise, has gone so far as to reveal to the governing body and to the congregation the names of living members of the parish who have already made provision in their wills for the parish. The details of such a program must be considered with great sensitiveness, good taste, and caution by the governing body and its endowment committee.

## THE SPIRITUAL LIFE COMMITTEE

The heart of the church life is in the spiritual nurture and maturity of its members, which are the prime commitments of the ministers. The governing body may feel that this aspect of its life should have the support of a strong spiritual-life committee constantly to stimulate the membership to the disciplines of Bible reading, prayer, and the enlargement of their religious understanding and commitments.

Such a committee may be assigned other responsibilities, but only on the advice and specific judgment of the governing body. Among such responsibilities may be the formation of and supervision of prayer cells within the church and the furtherance of adult study classes in the Bible study, prayer life, or some aspect of church history, theology, or the relationship of spiritual tradition and teaching to modern needs.

One church, under the stimulation of the spiritual-life committee, has engaged in a church-wide program of daily prayer by each parishioner. Another has prepared in mimeographed form prayers for children and for young people, graces and general prayers for the home and family.

The spiritual-life committee may serve to bring together in occasional meetings the devotional chairman of all the church groups to study means of lifting the spiritual tone of each group. It may offer guidance as to the most suitable way to conduct a devotional service, and may suggest prayer materials for the opening and closing of meetings. Such meetings may stimulate over-all aims to enrich the spiritual life of parishioners through each activity of the church. The chairman of the committee, or some appointed member of it, should constantly be on the lookout for devotional material suitable for the spiritual life chairmen of the various societies of the church.

## BAPTISM

Guided by the constitution, the official board of the church will appoint occasions for the public baptism of infants, children, and adults, and will establish policies regarding private baptisms.

One minister writes:

It was my custom to call on the mother of a new baby while she was still in the hospital. I got the name of the baby and the date of birth. I then wrote a simple note to the baby and enclosed it in a small white New Testament with the child's name on the fly leaf, and then delivered the Testament usually in person to the mother. This often resulted in an early baptism, and quite often the parents united with the church.

Such prompt, loving concern of the church leadership is a suitable beginning to bringing the infant into the orbit of the church life. Baptism is an occasion when the minister together with the church officers can deepen the understanding and the dedication of the parents and the families. The event requires careful planning and execution. The minister should have the information shown at the top of page 157. Such a record may suitably be in the minister's hands at the time of baptism and be filed with other church records. For the baptismal occasion itself the following preparations should be made:

1. The sexton or another person in charge of the church and the baptismal font will have been notified of the hour of baptism.

2. The church will be in order, properly ventilated, and lighted.

3. Water will have been placed in the font.

---

INFANT BAPTISM RECORD

Baby's Name _____

Father's Name _____

Mother's Name _____

Place of Birth _____

Date of Birth _____

Date of Baptism _____

Church Affiliation _____

Address _____

Telephone _____

---

4. The parents and infants will have been notified where to go and how to proceed.

5. There should be a quiet place where the child's and the parents outer garments may be left.

6. Prior to the baptism, in the church or in the home, the minister may speak to the parents on the meaning of Christian baptism, reminding them of their responsibilities in the Christian nurture of the child.

7. A certificate of baptism will have been prepared and after the baptism will be signed and presented to the parents.

8. Some churches have a beautiful or an unusual symbolic baptismal font. A little leaflet, or even a mimeographed paper, telling the history and symbolism of such a font may be appreciated by parents and other participants in the baptismal service.

9. The minister will have directed parents and godparents or sponsors, if such there be, where to stand and how to proceed at the baptismal ceremony. A word of assurance by the minister that all will be well at the ceremony may put anxious parents at ease and open their hearts and minds more readily to the deep spiritual experiences of the occasion.

10. It would be in order to present to the parents reading matter concerning the meaning of baptism. Some denominational headquarters and their boards of Christian education have put out very helpful material regarding the child in the home, as, for example: "Why We Baptize *Our* Children," "What Baptism Means." If the

church has plans for the pre-churchschool child in the life of the parish, the occasion of baptism is a suitable time for delivering the information to the parents.

The certificate of baptism should be a beautiful and appropriate memento. When it is practical, the church may well issue a certificate showing a significant aspect of the church and having a direct relationship to the individual baptism. One attractive certificate has on the cover "Certificate of Baptism." On the inside, one page bears a photograph of the baptismal font in the church, and the opposite page has, in dignified print, the certificate to be filled in and signed by the minister and an elder and spaces for the signatures of the godparents or sponsors.

The church should be prepared to grant statements of baptism. The following form, typed on church stationery, is recommended:

---

*To Whom It May Concern:*

This is to certify that _____
was baptized in the above-named church on _____
by the Reverend _____
The record of this baptism is to be found in Book Number _____, page _____, of Christ Church.

Church                    _____
Seal                                    Signature

---

If there are godparents, helpful material may be directed to them, accompanied by a statement giving the name of the godchild, the date of birth, and the date of baptism. The following statements serve as a reminder and as a guide for the godparents:

My Duties to My Godchild Are:

1. To be a Christian myself and assume Christian responsibility in the church and in the community in which my godchild is to grow up.
2. Pray for my godchild daily.
3. Remember the anniversaries of my godchild's baptism in the following suggested ways:

    *a.* Attend church and renew my obligation as a godparent.

*b.* Give him a religious book or picture.

*c.* Give him a Bible or Book of Common Prayer.

4. Discuss with his parents, at least once a year, my godchild's Christian training.
5. Cultivate continuous Christian relationship with my godchild through companionship and discussion of his faith and life.
6. See that my godchild is presented for confirmation.
7. Be present at my godchild's confirmation and receive with him at his first Holy Communion.
8. After confirmation, see that my godchild is established in the life of the church.

## WEDDINGS AND MARRIAGES IN THE CHURCH

Careful foresight and the preparation of adequate material for marriage participants and their families will save considerable time in the parish.

Simple marriages require a minimum of preparations on the part of the minister. When there are only the bride and the groom and two witnesses, and no music or guests, the marriage ceremony can be performed intimately by the clergyman. But when the wedding is elaborate, including a wedding party and many guests, with music and decoration of the church, many items must be seen to in advance so that the wedding may proceed with the dignity, beauty, and symbolism it deserves. Items significant in the administration of a wedding ceremony are as follows:

1. When a couple approach the church to plan their wedding, they should be asked to supply the information required by the Marriage Record shown on page 160.

The date and the hour for the wedding should be checked with the church calendar to avoid conflicts.

2. The bride and the groom will have many questions. The church will be wise to anticipate the questions and prepare in advance answers that may be placed in the hands of the bride and her family. One church has prepared a very helpful leaflet in mimeographed form under the title "A Wedding Guide for Christ Church." The Scriptural verse "Whom therefore God hath joined together let no man put asunder" is prominently displayed. The table of contents on page 160 shows the points discussed in the leaflet:

CONTENTS

MARRIAGE RECORD

|  |  |
|---|---|
| Groom _____ | Divorced _____ |
| | Children _____ |
| Address _____ | |
| Age _____ Phone _____ | Member? _____ |
| | |
| Bride _____ | Divorced _____ |
| | Children _____ |
| Address _____ | |
| Age _____ Phone _____ | Member? _____ |
| Wedding _____ _____ Time _____ Place _____ |
|      Day     Date | |
| Rehearsal _____ _____ Time _____ Organist _____ |
|      Day     Date | |
| Minister _____ Reception _____ Flowers left? _____ |
| No. of attendants _____ Bridesmaids _____ Ushers _____ |
| Best man _____ |
| Maid of Honor _____ |
| Single or double ring? _____ Music in Service _____ |
| New Address _____ |

The following wedding arrangements of a particular church indicate the areas that require attention in planning the wedding and suggest the wording of information for the bride:

## YOU AND YOUR WEDDING
### AT
### CHRIST CHURCH

Christ Church is eager to make your wedding a beautiful and memorable occasion. The following information is given to help you plan for this important event. After reading through this leaflet, will you please fill out the attached form and mail it to the Membership Secretary at the Church Office?

### Setting the Wedding Date

Before a definite date is planned, please telephone the Membership Secretary at Christ Church to make sure the church and the minister are available. The Marriage Service at Christ Church should be performed by one of the ministers, or someone delegated by the minister. In every case the minister or his representative will be present to direct and take part in the service.

### Rehearsal

A rehearsal date should also be set. The best time for this is between 5:00 and 7:00 the evening before the wedding. Forty-five minutes to one hour should be allowed for the rehearsal. If organ music is to be provided for the wedding, it is recommended that the organist play for the rehearsal.

### Invitations

In ordering invitations, the suggested form for the address of the Church is: Christ Church, 1100 Middle Road, Pleasantville, Maine.

### License

It is recommended that the marriage license be obtained at least one week before the wedding. You are asked to bring the license with you to the rehearsal, or see that the license is delivered to the minister the day before the wedding. Note that your marriage cannot be performed until twenty-four hours have elapsed from the time the license is issued.

### Premarital Conference

A significant phase in preparation for the wedding is the conference of the minister with the prospective bride and groom. Please telephone the minister's secretary to make an appointment for this most important conference.

### Music

Organ music at all services shall be rendered by the organist of Christ Church. He will be happy to discuss with you a program of music to be played at your wedding. If you wish to select the music, please telephone the organist at the Church Office at least one week before the wedding. Otherwise, he will choose a program that he believes will be suitable. It should be noted that the Music Committee of the Official Board has made the specification that only religious and classical music should be played in the church.

The church soloists may be engaged to sing at your wedding. If you wish a soloist, the organist will make arrangements for one upon receiving your request.

## Tower Bells

Should you wish the tower bells to be played, the Membership Secretary at the Church Office will obtain a bell ringer for you. The bells are usually played for ten minutes, as a summoning to the church, beginning thirty-five minutes before the wedding, and then are played again after the recessional.

## Photographers

Photographers are requested to refrain from taking flash pictures during the wedding ceremony. Time exposures can be taken from the balcony or the narthex entrance to the church.

## Decoration of the Church

Arrangements for floral decorations should be made through the florist of your choice, except at Easter and Christmas seasons, when arrangements should be made with the Church Flower Committee to use the church decorations. In this case, the bride's family makes a contribution to the fund providing the decorations.

Most of the local florists are acquainted with our church and will be able to suggest various decorations for your consideration. If your florist is not familiar with our church, he should be told that it is not permissible to put nails or tacks into the woodwork of the chancel. Also, wires or strings may not be tied to the carved woodwork of the chancel. Flowers on the communion table should not exceed the height of 25 inches. Please ask your florist to communicate with the Membership Secretary before making final plans, to make sure that the church will be available and open at the hour desired for setting up the decorations.

Florists are expected to supply the flower containers. However, if the church flower containers are particularly desired, permission for their use must be granted by the Church Office. Requests for them should be directed to the Membership Secretary.

If you wish to leave your floral decorations at the church, the church will be happy to make use of them, either in the chancel for Sunday-morning services or in other parts of the church. Please inform the Membership Secretary of your wishes in this regard.

Other Arrangements

Aisle ribbons, carpeting for the aisle, or white crash to be unrolled over the carpeting can be ordered by your florist or from a chair company. A canopy for the main entrance to the church can be ordered through _____ Company.

The church provides a *prie-dieu* for the kneeling of the bridal couple at the Benediction, should this be desired. Also available, if desired, is the church's pair of seven-branched candlesticks. The Church Office will obtain the candles for them.

Sexton

The services of the sexton are needed to prepare the church for the ceremony and to clean it afterward. Also, he must be on duty if a rehearsal is held.

Expense

The church makes every effort to assist in keeping costs at a minimum. Weddings, however, involve some extra services which the church is unable to underwrite. The Church Office serves as your agent in compensating the individuals whose services you have desired. Immediately after the wedding, a statement will be mailed to you itemizing the expenses of your wedding. These can be paid for in one check made out to "Christ Church."

There is no charge for the services of the clergyman. If the groom wishes to make a gift to the minister, it is usually presented by the best man before or after the wedding. Other charges are as follows:

1. Use of the Church. *No Charge for Members and Adherents*. Others are expected to make the following contributions:

> *a.* The Church                          $35.00
> *b.* The Chancel only                    20.00
> (guests seated in choir stalls—
> limited to 60 guests)

(These contributions apply only where principals are not members or supporters of the church.)

2. Music

> *a.* Organist (including rehearsal)          $35.00
> Organist (if no rehearsal is held)       25.00
> *b.* Soloist                                 25.00
> *c.* Tower bell ringer                       10.00

3. Staff member who conducts rehearsal          10.00

4. Sexton (including rehearsal)           10.00
    Sexton (if no rehearsal is held)       5.00

5. Fourteen candles for church candlesticks     4.00

Please fill out the enclosed form, indicating which of the above services you wish to have arranged for you, and mail or deliver it to the Membership Secretary at the Church Office:

Bride's name _____
Bride's address _____ Tel. no. _____

Name and address of bride's parents. (If statement of charges is to be sent to someone other than parents, please indicate to whom it should be sent.)

_____

Groom's name _____
Date of wedding _____ Hour of wedding _____
Rehearsal date and time _____

Please order the following services for my wedding:

Church _____     Bell Ringer _____
Chancel only _____     Rehearsal _____
Organist _____     Sexton _____
Soloist _____     Candles (14) _____

One church uses the following wedding information sheet:

WEDDING INFORMATION

CHRIST CHURCH

1234 Washington Road
Telephone Number

Bride: _____ Date of Wedding _____ _____
                                           (Date)    (Day of week)
Groom: _____ Time of Wedding _____
Minister: _____    Place of Wedding:
                                            _____ Sanctuary
Organist: _____    _____ Chapel
      (If church organist is not available)
Hostess: _____
          (To be provided by church)
Address of Bride: _____ Phone: _____
Address of Groom: _____ Phone: _____
Rehearsal: Date _____ Day of Week _____ Time _____
Reception _____
                   (Indicate Place)

Conferences (to be arranged with the minister):

Wedding Plans—Attendants:

| | | |
|---|---|---|
| Bridesmaids _____ | Florist _____ | |
| Ushers _____ | Cateress _____ | |
| Junior Bridesmaid? _____ | Recordings Desired? | |
| Flower Girl? _____ | Tape     Records | |
| Ring Bearer? _____ | How many _____ | |
| Single or Double Ring? _____ | Send to _____ | |

Music:
    Soloist? _____ Duet? _____ Other _____

Witnesses—List two
    1. _____ (Best Man)
        Address _____
    2. _____ (Maid or Matron
                                                                of Honor)
        Address _____
Future Address of Couple, if known: _____
Other Details (use reverse side if necessary):

(Please complete and return this form promptly to the church.)

After such information has been received, the staff member responsible for the arrangement of marriages will do the following:

1. Obtain the minister's approval of the date and hour of the ceremony.

2. Make or confirm arrangements with the organist, when requested, and pass on to him and to the minister information pertinent to the wedding.

3. Set the date for the rehearsal and clear with the church calendar, the minister, the organist, and the sexton that the date is satisfactory; arrange for the premarital conference with the minister.

The rehearsal will have been planned as nearly as possible prior to the hour of the wedding itself for clarity and efficiency. One church has prepared the following list of the steps in the wedding procedure for the guidance of the participants in the wedding party:

### THE WEDDING PROCEDURE

1. The bridal party assembles in the lower east narthex.
2. At wedding time an usher brings the bridal party to the upper east narthex.

3. The head usher escorts the groom's mother down the aisle and seats her in the first pew on the right-hand side of the church as one faces the communion table.
4. The head usher escorts the mother of the bride and seats her in the first pew on the left-hand side of the church facing the communion table.
5. The solo is sung.
6. The ushers walk forward in step and bring back the carpet.
7. The wedding march begins, immediately followed by the entrance of the minister, the groom, and the best man, who take their places at the chancel.
8. The ushers proceed down the aisle in time to the music.
9. The mother of the bride stands and so do all the guests.
10. The bridesmaids proceed down the aisle in time to the music.
11. The bride proceeds down the aisle on the arm of her father and, arriving at the chancel, lets go of her father's arm as she takes the arm of the groom.
12. The mother of the bride and all guests are seated.
13. Following the benediction the bride and groom proceed down the steps and down the center aisle and then the maid of honor and best man go out separately.
14. The mother of the bride and all guests stand and remain standing until the bride and the bridesmaids have proceeded down the aisle. Then the bride's mother and other guests are seated.
15. The ushers proceed down the aisle.
16. The head usher returns to escort out the mother of the bride followed by the father of the bride.
17. The usher returns to escort out the mother of the groom followed by the father of the groom.
18. The ushers escort out other honored guests.
19. The ushers indicate where the reception is being held, if held in the church.

The distributing of material such as this to participants in the wedding will be most effective in explanation, and possibly of discussion at the time of the rehearsal.

The minister should see that the bridal couple receives an appropriate wedding certificate. An engraved certificate combined with the marriage service in book form is both appropriate and attractive.

The couple should be informed of all the civic aspects of a marriage. If a marriage license is issued by a local clerk and the law requires that the officiating clergyman return it within a limited time after the ceremony, the minister should so inform the couple and advise them to obtain a photostat of the license.

After a wedding the records in the church office should be brought up to date. One local church has outlined for its church office the following procedure to be used after the marriage of a parishioner:

WEDDINGS

Add to Statistical Report

If a male member of the parish:
1. Add wife's name to his McBee card.
2. Change Addressograph plate to include Mrs.
3. Notify Denominational Life of change of status.
4. Change master card to read Mr. and Mrs.
5. Change zone card to read Mr. and Mrs.
   Change zone list to read Mr. and Mrs.
   Notify zone Leader of change.
6. Make necessary notations in board card file.

If a female member of the parish:
1. Remove Addressograph plate.
2. Notify Denominational Life to remove her name from their mailing list if she married a member of the denomination. If her husband is not a member, notify them of her new name and address.
3. If she is a member of the Women's Society, notify that association.
4. If an officer of any organization, change black book and notify organization.
5. Change zone book—notify zone leader.
6. Record in parish register.
7. Make proper notations on card file.

If the mechanics of the wedding are worked out in advance, they will not be evident during the ceremony. The aim is to make the wedding a high spiritual experience for all who participate in it. In addition to the counsel of the clergyman and his associates, the young couple may benefit by suggestions and materials for their spiritual guidance in their future together. One church includes with its material for the marriage service the following statement:

SUGGESTIONS FOR A HAPPY MARRIED LIFE

God in the Home

It is no secret why very few Christian homes are broken up. The reason is that when God is brought into the home his own qualities of kindness, helpfulness, and thoughtfulness accompany his presence. His Spirit makes each person sensitive to the needs and desires of the other.

God himself is the Author of marriage, and since he has ordained this relationship between two lives, it is reasonable to believe that he should have a central place in the affairs of the home.

God is the author not of confusion but of peace. It is his will that the home shall be filled with happiness. But to achieve this there must be a right attitude toward him, his Church, and his service. Happiness is the fruit of a united faith.

Then let God be the Head of your home. Let Christ be your Saviour. Take your place in his Church. Only so will you lay hold on your rightful heritage in the home that is to be.

## THE FUNERAL

The parish would be wise to formulate its counsel and judgment regarding the conducting of funeral services. Often the minister's position is strengthened if the official board has issued a statement of attitude and policy. One church publishes the following statement:

### THE FUNERAL
### AND
### CHRIST CHURCH

The funeral is a precious part of a minister's relationship with his people and a mediating influence involving the entire parish and often the community. This outline of procedures is prepared with the hope that all concerned with the funeral may make of it an occasion of comfort and satisfying strength to the bereaved.

The ministers of the Christ Church are available for funerals of such bereaved families as are connected with our church either as members or as relatives of members or simply those who look to Christ Church as their church home. The request for and presence of a minister brings the service within the influence of the church and makes the emphasis uniquely Christian.

Ordinarily, in the case of members and those closely related to the church, the ministers will have knowledge of the impending death and will sometimes be of assistance in the actual funeral arrangements (e.g., the order of service, Scripture, music to be used). They deem this a proper function of their total ministry.

The sanctuary and the chapel of Christ Church are available for funerals and memorial services for members of the church at no charge. There is but one regulation: If the casket is present in the service it be and remain unopened.

Nonmembers of the church may also use the sanctuary and chapel of Christ Church under the same conditions and under the further provision that one of the ministers of Christ Church be in charge of the service. A nominal charge for organist and custodian may be made at the discretion of the board of the church.

There is no fee or honorarium charged or expected for the services of the ministers. This is part of the ministry of the church that they serve. It is hoped that this may be made quite clear to the bereaved by the mortician, and in no case should the services of the minister be made a part of the funeral bill. If the family wishes to express its appreciation in a monetary way, a gift to the church that makes possible the minister's service would be appropriate. A memorial fund, a tribute window, and many special items at the church have had the benefit of such gifts.

Because there is misunderstanding upon this point of funeral fees, especially among the nonchurch families, further elaboration may be necessary. A funeral involves much more than the preparation and conducting of a memorial service and the interment. Always there is at least one call and usually several calls upon the family between the time of death and the service, and always at least one call after the service. The service itself, sometimes requiring an interment at a distance, takes not only the minister's time but time away from his duties at the church that is entitled to his time.

Beyond this, however, is the further consideration of the funeral ministry itself. If the minister has adequately done what he is trained to do in the spirit of the God he serves, he has deepened the dependence of the church family and he has influenced the nonchurch family toward closer relationship with the church. The fee or honorarium becomes an intrusion upon this delicate relationship, while a financial response to the church itself may be a part of a proper response.

One further matter needs to be mentioned, one upon which both the morticians and the ministers must surely be in agreement: The wishes of the family are the major determining factor. Among Christians, funeral practices differ: for example, the disposition of the body by burial or cremation, the floral tribute or memorial gifts in lieu of floral tributes, the open or closed casket. In these matters the ministers will usually give support to the best judgment of the family and will be happy to confer with morticians if requested to do so. Surely each problem involving funeral procedures may be solved decently and in accordance with Christian principles.

Discussion of these or other matters connected with the Christian attitude toward funerals and Christ Church practices in connection with funerals will be welcomed by the ministers.

Approved provisionally by the board, April 4, 19—.

The church will have established a definite procedure for recording the death of a parishioner. One church outlines its procedure as follows:

BURIALS

On receiving word of death of member of the parish take these steps:

1. Send information to senior minister, who will give an information slip to be circulated as he indicates.
2. Remove name immediately from Rolodex of each staff member. If a married person, be certain other member of family is left in Rolodex.
3. Leave notification on desk of each staff member indicating that you have removed Rolodex card.
4. Remove card from McBee file. If married, indicate on survivor's card the date of death.
5. Remove from master card file.
6. Remove from Addressograph.
7. Remove from "active" to "out" file in clerk's safe. On card indicate date of death.
8. Remove from zone book and records. Notify zone leader.
9. Record in parish register.
10. Add to statistical report.
11. Notify treasurer.
12. Remove from any official list in the black book.
13. Notify denominational magazine and ask that name be removed from mailing list.

Other parishes will devise methods to meet their particular needs. The above is simply a guide.

Information regarding all deaths and burials should be noted for the church record. The form on page 171 is one suggestion.

Such information is kept permanently in the church records for future reference.

## THE SACRAMENT OF THE LORD'S SUPPER

In churches where the sacrament of the Lord's Supper is offered monthly, bimonthly, or quarterly, attention should be given to the registration of the congregation. Communion cards placed in the pew to be signed will prove helpful in keeping church records

CHRIST CHURCH

FUNERAL RECORD

Name _____

Address _____ Telephone _____

Date of Birth _____

Date of Death _____

Date of Funeral _____

Time of Funeral _____

Place of Funeral _____

Church Affiliation _____

Officiant _____

Undertaker _____

Interment _____

Arrangements made by _____

Address _____ Telephone _____

Near Relatives _____

Address _____

straight, in noting the attendance of communicant members, and in supplying the names and addresses of visitors and prospects. Two forms of the communion card are suggested below:

COMMUNION REGISTRATION

☐ I am a member of this church.

☐ I am a member of _____ Church.

   in _____, _____

               City                State

☐ I have no church affiliation.

☐ I am interested in uniting with this church.

Name _____

Address _____

CHRIST CHURCH

Date _____

It was my privilege to partake
of Communion today.
Name _____
Address _____
Telephone _____
If you are a member of this church,
                              Check here_____
If you are a member of some other church,
                              Check here _____
If you are considering membership in
    this church,                Check here _____

In churches where the communicants come to the altar rail for the sacrament, the ushers or appointed church officers will have been carefully instructed in the manner of indicating to the members of the congregation the time when they should proceed to the altar rail. Care and foresight in this matter will make for the smoothness of the ceremony and the avoidance of intrusive mechanics.

Where elders assist the minister in serving the elements, additional instructions and care must be exercised.

After determining the physical procedure for the conduct of the service and the sharing of the elements with the communicants, the communion committee should have an occasional rehearsal with the minister. The appointed places to stand can be very carefully indicated, and the elders, if newly introduced to this aspect of their leadership, will feel greatly at ease.

New officers who will assist in this sacrament should be carefully instructed by the chairman of the communion committee. For the guidance of its elders one church has prepared detailed instructions. The points covered may serve as a guide for the consideration of other churches:

### CHRIST CHURCH

#### CONCERNING THE COMMUNION SERVICE

It is the high privilege and distinctive duty of the Board of Elders to handle the administration of the Lord's Supper. This is the most explicitly Christian action of the church, and it is well that the elders are so largely in evidence in connection with it.

The communion service requires careful planning and perfection of mechanical details if it is well done, and the elders can make or mar it for the worshipers.

For this reason it is very important that every elder know his own part or place without any confusion or consultation when the service begins.

For your assistance we present a standard procedure to follow in administering, with dignity, the Lord's Supper and for the purpose of preserving at all times the real spirit and meaning of the sacrament.

*Attendance:*

As you know, there are 15 men on the board. However, 18 men are necessary to serve the two communion services, so it is important that members of the board plan to serve at *every* communion service, at either the first or the second service.

If you have promised to serve and then find you cannot come, please notify the chairman of the Worship Committee in advance so a replacement can be obtained.

*Punctuality:*

Please report to the Business Manager's Office at least fifteen minutes before the Worship Service.

*Dress:*

A dark suit and modest tie are recommended.

*Precaution:*

It is recommended that the bread trays be carried with one hand, but it is very important to use two hands to carry the wine trays and to use extreme caution when "negotiating" the steps to the chancel.

PROCEDURE

*Proceed to First Row:*

During the singing of the processional hymn, proceed behind choir to the first row from the position and in the order indicated at point *A* on the chart on page 175. If the choir does not enter in processional manner, go forward during the processional hymn to first row indicated at point *B*.

*Proceed to Altar:*

During the singing of the second verse of the communion hymn, the ministers meet and go to the altar followed by the elders who will take places indicated by point C. You will get your signals from the No. 1 man in the post position.

The congregation is seated at the conclusion of the hymn, but the ministers and elders remain standing in place for the reading of the words of the institution and blessing of the elements with prayer.

The ministers will then pass the bread trays to the elders. The ministers are then seated. The elder in the No. 1 post position then serves the minister on his side of the altar, as noted by point D, and then returns to his post position.

*Serving the Elements:*

The elders then leave the altar and go to their appointed positions as indicated on attached chart. Elders of odd numbers go to side-aisle locations and those with even numbers take positions in the center aisle. Please do not start to serve the elements to the congregation until all elders have reached their proper positions. The elders in the center aisle serve the first row; the elders in the outside aisles the second row, and so on.

The No. 3 and 4 elders serve the front section back to and including a center pew which is identified by buttons on both front and back side.

The No. 1 and 2 elders serve the back section, starting with the row back of the center pew marked with button. Be sure to serve people standing in rear of church and those sitting on ushers' benches.

The No. 5 elder serves the choir at both services.

Never go to the altar for additional trays of the elements. These will be available on the table at back of church at location marked E.

Exception: The elder serving the choir may have to come to the altar to replace the wine tray.

Serve the ministers the elements at both services. Serve organist and choir director at second service only.

When the congregation has been served, the elders will then go to back of church and get in new positions at location F with No. 4 men in the lead.

Remember that while you have been serving the congregation, elder No. 5 has been serving the choir, so do not proceed forward to the altar until the choir has been served. Elder No. 5 is the only one that may receive any additional elements as needed from the minister at the altar.

When the elders return to the altar, the ministers will take the trays. The elders will then kneel in unison on signal from No. 1 post men and be served by the ministers and then remain in silence for a moment.

The elders will then rise and ministers will pass the wine trays to the elders. The ministers are seated and then served by the No. 1 post men. The congregation is then served in exactly the same procedure as the bread trays were served.

POSITION CHART

ALTAR

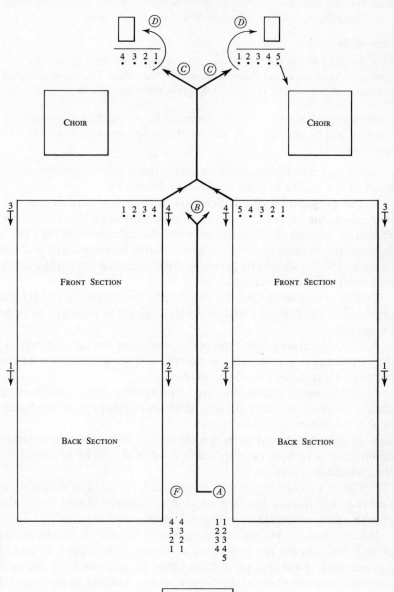

CHOIR

CHOIR

4 3 2 1        1 2 3 4 5

1 2 3 4    4    4 5 4 3 2 1    3

FRONT SECTION        FRONT SECTION

BACK SECTION        BACK SECTION

4 4    1 1
3 3    2 2
2 2    3 3
1 1    4 4
      5

175

*Note:* It is the minister's custom to quote Scripture during the serving of the elements. Proceed on schedule; it will not disturb him.

*Close of the Service:*

At the close of the service, during the singing of the final hymn, the ministers go to the back of the church followed by the elders. The elders are asked to remain at the back of the church to greet the congregation.

The Worship Committee of your Board of Elders sincerely hopes these instructions will be helpful to you, and we always welcome your comments and suggestions.

Other points to have as a check list for the conducting of the sacrament of the Lord's Supper may be the following:

1. The preparation of the elements. If there is a chancel committee responsible for the care of the communion ware, that committee should be notified of all occasions when the sacrament of the Lord's Supper will be administered. When possible an annual schedule of dates and hours should be given to the committee so that they may make suitable arrangements.

2. The sexton of the church should also be informed, and if he is responsible, the furniture within the chancel will be arranged prior to the service.

3. Consideration of the type of decoration or the use of flowers at the communion service will be determined with the advice of the minister. Deviations will not be made.

4. If the church follows the use of liturgical colors, consideration should be given to the minister's stole and perhaps other ecclesiastical appointments in the chancel.

5. A diagram should be prepared for the chancel or preparation committee as to how the communion table should be arranged for the communion service.

6. Elders to assist in the service should be notified in ample time, and the chairman of the communion committee should notify the church office which elders will participate.

Information regarding the communion service should be in the church bulletin for the benefit of strangers and visitors. It should answer such questions as, is it an open Communion, or are only communicant members of the denomination welcome to participate? How is the service administered? Answering these questions may spare embarrassment to the stranger or visitor.

A chart together with full instructions for elders at their various stations will have been given to each elder at the beginning of the church year. Additional copies will be readily available prior to the worship service when the sacrament is to be administered.

Some parishes have found it valuable to have an officer of the church call at the homes in his district of church families prior to the administration of the sacrament of the Lord's Supper. The governing board may consider a plan comparable to, or modified from, the old Scottish tradition of leaving a "communion token" which the parishioner brings to the church when he comes to partake of the Lord's Supper.

## CHURCH CAMPS

Since only a few churches own their own camps, little comment is necessary. However, more and more churches are developing a summer-camp program for their children, young people, or families. Whether the church owns a camp or rents a camp for a specified period, its program will be effective only under the following conditions: (1) The purpose must be clearly stated, and it must be a worthy one. Stated briefly, the main goal should be the development of Christian character and leadership. Of course the purpose is also to have a good time and to engage in a constructive and creative experience that will make for the happiness and health of the participants. But, unless the primary purpose is spiritual, a camp project might better be left to other institutions. (2) Detailed information should be given to participants and their families. One church with long experience in camping issues the following information to the parents of prospective campers:

### PRECAMP POINTERS FOR PARENTS
*The Camp Periods*

All camp periods are two weeks in length. Campers may register for a two-week period or for the entire month. If your child has never been to camp before, we recommend that he be registered for a two-week period only. We encourage the parents of an experienced camper to consider a four-week stay, as the results in wholesome all-round growth are most desirable.

| *Boys' Camp* | *Girls' Camp* |
|---|---|
| June 24 to July 8 | July 23 to August 6 |
| July 8 to July 22 | August 6 to August 20 |

### Age

Camping at Christ Church Camp is for all boys and girls from 10 to 16 years of age.

If your child is not 10 years old by the opening of camp, but will be 10 during 19–, he or she is eligible.

### Rates and Registration

Two weeks—$40.00
Four weeks— 70.00

Rates include insurance and transportation to and from camp.

A registration fee of $5 must accompany the registration, and the balance, $35 or $65 in addition, is payable before the camper enters camp. Checks should be made payable to Christ Church and sent to the Boys' and Girls' Camp Director.

Campers leaving before the expiration of the camp period for which they are registered will receive no refund.

### Health Certificate

A certificate of health must be submitted by the applicant, based upon a thorough medical examination made by the child's family physician within ten days of entering camp. At the proper time the camp will mail out to those enrolled a medical certificate. This should be brought to camp on the opening day.

### The Camp Bank

The camp bank is operated for the convenience and security of the campers. All money is deposited upon arrival in camp. There are few opportunities to spend money while at camp, except for camp crafts or for ice cream and soft drinks at the camp store.

### Mark Belongings

To avoid loss or confusion, all bedding and clothing should be marked with name tapes and a complete list of personal belongings listed in the camper's trunk.

*The camp is not responsible for lost articles.*

The camp is not equipped to do any laundry for the campers.

### Visiting Day

Parents and friends are requested to limit their visiting to Saturdays only (1 to 5). If a child is inclined to be homesick, any visiting is discouraged. It is further requested that campers not be taken from camp by parents except for very special reasons. Permission must then be obtained from the Camp Director.

*What to Bring*

| | |
|---|---|
| 4 large towels | T-shirts or blouses |
| 4 sheets and 2 pillow cases | Shorts and slacks or jeans |
| Washcloths and soap | Socks |
| 1 piece of plastic or oilcloth 3 x 6 ft. | Pajamas |
| Kleenex | 1 pair old but sturdy shoes |
| Toothbrush and paste | Swim suit or trunks (2) |
| Comb, brush, and mirror | White shorts and white blouse for |
| Raincoat or poncho | Sunday (girls only) |
| Boots or rubbers | Bible and notebook |
| Heavy sweater or jacket | Pen or pencil |
| Tennis shoes | Flashlight |

*Transportation*

The cost of transportation by bus to and from camp is included in the camp fee.

Notice will be sent to all campers telling where to take baggage to be shipped and time of departure for camp.

*Camp Post Office Address*

Christ Church Camp
Portland, Pennsylvania
Telephone Number

*Daily Schedule*

| | |
|---|---|
| 7:30 | Reveille |
| 7:55 | Flag Raising |
| 8:00 | Breakfast |
| | Chapel |
| | Campus Clean-Up |
| 10:00 | Tribe Games |
| 11:00 | Swimming instruction or crafts |
| 12:30 | Dinner |
| 1:15 | Free Time |
| 2:00 | Rest Hour |
| 3:00 | Swimming or Crafts |
| 5:25 | Flag Lowering |
| 5:30 | Supper |
| 6:15 | Free Time |
| 7:00 | Special events and entertainment |
| 8:30 | First Call |
| | Bed Preparation |
| 9:00 | Cabin Devotions |
| 9:30 | Taps |

On Sunday the program is modified in harmony with the spirit of the Lord's Day.

Some churches have leased a camp for a season and have found it beneficial to develop a "family camping experience." This is along the line of experiments in various fields and directions of a family-centered program. The details to be established and presented to possible participants answer the following questions: (1) The date? (2) Who is eligible? (3) What is the purpose of the project? (4) What about facilities? (5) What about the program? (6) What does it cost? (7) How do I register? (8) From whom may I obtain further information? (9) What deposit is required? (10) What is the latest date for application?

## SPECIAL MINISTRIES AND PROGRAMS

At the head of the list of special ministries and programs should be a program to encourage daily and universal prayer by the church members. Below is the administrative setup for a program followed in one church.

GENERAL OUTLINE OF THE CORDON OF PRAYER
CHRIST CHURCH OF MAYWOOD

March 6, 19–

*Colonel* _____ You have 20 Captains, each having a "block."

| | | | |
|---|---|---|---|
| 1. | 6. | 11. | 16. |
| 2. | 7. | 12. | 17. |
| 3. | 8. | 13. | 18. |
| 4. | 9. | 14. | 19. |
| 5. | 10. | 15. | 20. |

*Captain* _____ You have 10 Lieutenants

| | |
|---|---|
| 1. | |
| 2. | |
| 3. | |
| 4. | |
| 5. | |
| | 6. |
| | 7. |
| | 8. |
| | 9. |
| | 10. |

*Lieutenant* _____ You have 7 "Pray-ers"

| | |
|---|---|
| 1. | 5. |
| 2. | 6. |
| 3. | 7. |
| 4. | |

The *Colonel* sends out (in writing) to the Captains the requests for prayer.

The *Captains* send out (in writing) to the Lieutenants these requests for prayer.

The *Lieutenants* send out (in writing) to the Pray-ers these requests for prayer.

Of course the Colonel, the Captains, the Lieutenants, and the Pray-ers will *all* join in prayer for those sending in requests. If *all* members of this Cordon of Prayer actually were notified and prayed, there would be 1,621 praying people lifting to the Throne of God in prayer those for whom prayer was asked.

Report back to any officer if you know that there is no need of further prayers for certain purposes (if the prayers obviously have been answered).

Also, report any requests which *you* feel should go to the Cordon of Prayer as a whole.

Also, check addresses of those to whom you send requests at least once every two months.

Report removals and disinclinations of any who constitute a part of the Cordon as outlined above. Will you not help us to keep the Cordon intact and functioning effectively?

"More things are wrought by prayer than this world dreams of."

"The effectual fervent prayer of a righteous man availeth much."

An arts and crafts program has proved beneficial to some parishes and the communities in which they are situated. One such program is as follows:

### ARTS AND CRAFTS PROGRAM OF
### CHRIST CHURCH

The Arts and Crafts program offers many opportunities to members of the Church and the community. Through the various classes one may discover and develop a latent talent, and gain the satisfaction that comes through creative work. In the congenial company of those with similar interests, the student can fashion with his own hands objects both beautiful and useful. Here one may develop new interests, and find the true relaxation of turning to something different from his daily occupation.

Preceding each semester an exhibit is held to show the work of teachers and students and to feature demonstrations of various crafts. These exhibits provide an opportunity to meet the staff and discuss the classes.

Twice a year an evening is planned around a program devoted to some phase of the arts. Following the program, students, staff and members of the church join in a social hour which offers a chance to meet others with similar interests.

Those who wish to do so may register at the October exhibit for the year or for the fall semester, and at the February exhibit for the spring semester. Registration on an annual basis is preferable. However, semester registrations are accepted in most classes.

Those who wish to register by mail should write to the Arts and Crafts Committee at the church, enclosing a self-addressed envelope and requesting a registration card. To avoid delay, the student should fill out the registration card completely and mail it to the Arts and Crafts Committee with a check covering the full amount of the tuition. (See section below on Charges.)

If registrations fall below the minimum needed to maintain a class, the Arts and Crafts Committee will arrange transfers to other classes or refund the money paid.

|  | Unit Course 7 lessons | Semester 14 lessons | Annual 28 lessons |
|---|---|---|---|
| Registration Fee: | $2.50 | $5.00 | $10.00 |
| Waived for Christ Church members |  |  |  |
| Tuition: |  |  |  |
| Unit course | 7.00 |  |  |
| Two-hour course |  | 11.00 | 22.00 |
| Three-hour course |  | 16.50 | 33.00 |

In some classes a small fee will be charged for special services. Most of the materials which are needed can be purchased during class time at the church.

A limited number of lockers are available for a small charge. The committee cannot be responsible for materials or work left after thirty days following the close of the semester.

All charges are to be paid by the second session of the class. No refund is made except in those instances where the Arts and Crafts Committee withdraws or discontinues a class because of insufficient registration or other administrative considerations.

A schedule of classes gives the dates and hours of meeting and the name of the instructor.

Courses that have proved interesting include bookbinding, ceramics, drawing and composition, flower arranging, weaving, jewelry making, glove making, enameling on metal, letter work, painting (in oils, water colors, tempera, and so on), photography, rug making, sewing, tray decoration.

One church prepares an annual classified directory of professional and business members. Being a Methodist church, it bases its presentation on the counsel of John Wesley and early Methodism to patronize one another "by doing good, especially to them that are of the household of faith, or growing so to be; employing them preferably to others; buying one of another; helping each other in business; and so much more because the world will love its own and them only" (*The Discipline,* p. 35, 1952). This is followed by the admonition; "As we have therefore opportunity, let us do good unto all men, especially unto them who are of the household of faith" (Galatians 6:10). In the directory under the name of each business and profession listed alphabetically from "Adding Machine" to "Welding" are printed the name, address, and telephone number of each church member engaged in that business or profession.

The special ministries and programs may be the creative edge of the church. The official board should be sensitive to needs and courageous in trying to meet them. Their efforts may lead to developments ranging in variety from a foundation for the application of religious truth to modern business to the formation of a stamp club.

The questions that the minister and the official board must ask and answer are these: (1) Will a special program further the Christian faith and the application of its teachings to modern life? (2) Will it be constructive, in the name of Christ, to our parish and community? (3) Is there competent leadership to organize and administer the program? (4) Are there sound means of meeting the financial obligations of the program? (5) Will the program compete with or duplicate an activity as effectively, or more effectively, carried on by another institution?

# SECTION III

## *Personnel*

The majority of Protestant churches have a full-time minister. A survey of 200,000 Protestant churches in the United States revealed that more than 90 per cent of the churches were served by a full-time minister, and the remaining 10 per cent by a part-time minister. In that sizable group of churches 14 per cent had assistant ministers, 19 per cent a minister of music, 73 per cent an organist, 50 per cent a choir director, 47 per cent a pianist, 15 per cent a director of Christian education, 2 per cent a business manager, 45 per cent an office secretary, and 89 per cent a custodian or janitor.

These statistics readily indicate that the majority of churches have, in addition to the minister, one or more full-time or part-time salaried or volunteer functionaries on the staff. The optimum size of the staff in terms of the church membership is debatable. The situation in a parish in one community may be entirely different from that in a parish of similar size in another location. In a study made in May 1957, John H. Shope came to the following conclusions on which there was general agreement. He affirms that (1) multiple staffs are needed in city churches with over 500 members, and (2) churches with a scattered membership need the assistance of a multiple staff more than do churches with a compact membership. However, the data do not show that increasing the size of the staff will automatically enhance the effectiveness of the church.

As the result of another study the Rev. Dr. Robert W. Young made the following recommendations:

RECOMMENDED CHURCH STAFFS
(for congregations of sizes shown)

300 members
  Minister
  Part-time sexton
  Part-time leader of music, unless volunteers are available

600 members
  Minister
  Part-time sexton
  Part-time musical leadership, unless volunteers are available
  Part-time secretary
  Part-time treasurer

800 members
  Minister
  Full-time sexton
  Full-time secretary
  Part-time musical leadership
  Part-time student assistant
  Part-time treasurer

1,200 members
  Minister
  Director of religious education
  Secretary
  Sexton
  Part-time to full-time secretary
  Part-time parish visitor
  Part-time organist and choir director
  Part-time financial secretary or treasurer

1,600 members
  2 ministers
  Director of religious education
  2 secretaries
  2 sextons
  Full-time organist and choir director
  Part-time financial secretary

The size of the parish, the program it seeks to develop, the geographical distribution of the membership, the financial resources of the congregation, the attitude of its clergy leadership, and its plans for the future must all enter into a decision by the minister and the church officers as to the most suitable staff for the parish.

## THE CHURCH STAFF

If the governing body decides that additional staff assistance is needed, a definite procedure should be followed for selecting salaried or volunteer personnel for specific responsibilities. (Denominational traditions, rulings and requirements, with few exceptions, are available for the guidance of the parish in the selection of ministers.)

### Selection

The governing body must find the person best qualified to render the service required.

*The Personnel Committee.* If the governing body is composed of more than six members, it may appoint a personnel committee to find a candidate suitable for the position to be filled. Where there is a multiple staff, the personnel committee may well be maintained as a permanent committee. Some committees authorize the maintenance and operations committee to oversee this phase of the church life. The personnel committee should be in charge of the employment and, if necessary, dismissal of employees subject to the approval of the board. The terms of employment should be filed with the secretary of the official board.

The composition of the personnel committee should be carefully considered. The ideal chairman would be a person with administrative experience, a knowledge of the needs of the parish and its methods of operation, a spirit of Christian good will and tolerance, and a willingness to support the church employees. Persons with experience in office procedures, in organizational work and activity, in public relations, would be particularly useful on the personnel committee.

*Determination of Qualifications.* In considering an applicant the personnel committee will be interested in the following details: age, education, experience, family, personality, religious orientation and experience, and, most important, aptitude and experience for the specific task. The statement of requirements may read:

Christ Church is seeking a woman 35–50 years of age, preferably with a college education, for part-time employment as a general office secretary. Business training and experience are not essential, but would be helpful. The candidate must be a competent typist and preferably should have skill in shorthand. We are seeking someone with a strong Protestant background, preferably a member of our own church and community, with a cooperative spirit, a pleasing disposition and the ability to adjust to many varied situations, individuals, and requirements.

The minister should be an ex officio member of the personnel committee, and his counsel should be sought and related continually to the committee's work, since new staff members will be working largely with him and will be responsible to him.

*Screening of Applicants.* One or two individuals should conduct the first interview and screen the applicant. Reducing the number of applicants expedites the selection of the right person. The applicant fills out an application form from which the committee can evaluate the qualifications and form an opinion.

---

### CHRIST CHURCH, MAYVIEW
#### APPLICATION FOR EMPLOYMENT

Name _____

Address _____ Telephone _____

Marital Status _____ Children _____ Age _____

Education (Please list schools, dates attended, and type of
    course.) _____

_____

_____

Business experience (Please give dates of employment and name
    of supervisor.)

_____

_____

Church affiliation _____

Special interests or hobbies _____

_____

References _____

---

The applicant's references should be carefully checked, preferably in personal conferences. In view of the fact that the personnel committee has a major responsibility, there should be no reluctance to use every means of obtaining pertinent information. If the references are checked by correspondence, specific questions should be asked. In personal interviews or conversations there should be no hesitation in asking the references to give personal, even intimate information that might be of assistance to the personnel committee. Of course, it will be understood all such information, written or verbal, will be held in the strictest confidence.

Where it is possible or necessary, as, for example, in the case of the employment of an organist or an assistant minister, the personnel committee would do well to visit the church or institution where the applicant is presently employed. Such visitation should be made with the greatest tact. Every effort should be made to avoid embarrassment to the applicant under consideration, and nothing should be done to jeopardize his relationship in his present position.

*The Interview.* The procedure in conducting an interview with an applicant is as follows:

1. Preferably two individuals should meet the applicant after basic information has been obtained. The initial interview should be very informal, since a large committee might embarrass the applicant and cause the interview to be strained and unnatural.

2. An informal, neutral atmosphere should be created if possible.

3. The interviewers need, in addition to the information they already have from the application form and the references, answers to the following questions: (*a*) Has the applicant a definite interest in our position? (*b*) Does he appear to have the capacity for growth and the initiative to go "the second mile?" (*c*) Does our impression from the interview confirm the information we have obtained in written form from the application and the references? (*d*) Have we answered fully the questions the applicant may have in mind? (*e*) Does the applicant have an accurate concept of what will be expected of him? (*f*) If we decide to employ this applicant, when will he be available? (*g*) If the applicant is moving to our parish from a distant place, what arrangement can be made for transportation and for housing on arrival? If the personnel committee is to take the initiative or responsibility in this area, that fact should be clearly stated, and certain individuals should be appointed to take care of the details. (*h*) What is the interviewer's judgment regarding the personality of the applicant? How will he react to pressure? To strain? (*i*) Difficult though it

may be, the interview should seek to evaluate the applicant's spiritual maturity, his feeling about the church, and the balance of personality as a Christian.

*Specifics of Responsibility.* The personnel committee or the designated interviewers should give the applicant a detailed outline of the responsibilities of the position to be filled. The specific items will vary with the position. Obviously the requirements of the assistant minister differ greatly from those of a choirmaster or a sexton. Before he starts working, the new staff member should understand exactly what is expected of him. To avoid misunderstanding, or perhaps a disaster later, both the employer and the employee should have, preferably in writing, a list of the duties of the new incumbent. The personnel committee of the local church faces problems that may not arise in a highly organized business or professional office. The needs will vary; the program may change. The demands are varied and unexpected because of the intimate, personal needs of so many human beings. Therefore the interviewer should emphasize to the applicant the need for cooperation, understanding, and versatility.

*Details of Employment.* When the personnel committee is ready to hire a person the terms of employment should be discussed and be verbally agreed upon. The church should state its position in regard to the following: (1) Salary to be paid. (2) Pay period—weekly, bi-weekly, or monthly. (3) Hours of employment. (4) Vacation. (5) Policy regarding sickness and sick leave. (6) Pension program, hospitalization and group insurance. (7) Holidays. (8) To whom the employee will be responsible. (9) Is the employment for a definite term? Is there to be an "experimental period" in which employer and employee will "try each other out"? If the term of employment is indefinite, will the personnel committee periodically evaluate the service of the employee and his satisfaction with his position? (10) Does the employer assume any responsibility for housing? for moving? for transportation? (11) By whom are social security taxes to be paid?

*Final Approval.* The maintenance committee and personnel committee, with mutual approval if required, then present to the governing body the recommendation for the employment of the applicant under consideration. The official board authorizes the employment.

The governing body may have delegated to the personnel committee authority to proceed with employment within certain financial limits. With larger church staffs the procedure for the employment and dismissal of employees may be so well established that the personnel or another designated committee may merely report its action to the governing body and then file the details of its actions. If the new employee's salary has not been included in the annual budget, the personnel committee should consult the finance committee before reporting to the governing body. If there are insufficient funds, the governing body should request ways and means for raising the required sum.

*Contract or Call in Writing.* The invitation to join the staff should be conveyed to the applicant in writing by the minister or by the chairman of the personnel committee. Since the minister is the chief administrative officer of the church, the letter of invitation should go out over his signature on behalf of the official body of the church with a warm invitation to join the staff. It should outline the details of the employment and specifics of responsibility. A copy should be given to the treasurer or the financial officer to apprise him in writing of the salary to be paid. If there is a continuing personnel committee it too should have a copy. The secretary or clerk of the governing body should have a copy for his files. The minister will retain a copy in his personal file under the heading "Employment" or "Staff."

The employee should acknowledge the written call, or contract, by letter. His written acceptance should be handed to the secretary of the official board for permanent filing. Those who will have some relationship with the new employee and those who have received copies of the contractual letter should also be notified of the acceptance.

### Introduction of the Staff Personnel

The first impression and introduction to his position and his work may have a lasting influence on the new employee and may serve as an effective springboard into his tasks and the life of the church. The introduction should be made to each of three groups within parish life.

*Introduction to Other Staff Members.* The new employee will work closely with the minister and with other staff members if there are any. If there are only the minister and the new employee, the two should become acquainted with each other as human beings and should develop a good rapport in their positions. They may accomplish this by spending an hour together in informal chatting. A meeting in the home, where the family of the minister and the family of the new staff member can get to know each other, may result in bonds of understanding that come only from being with each other "at home."

If there is a larger staff, the minister should make every effort to see that the new employee is introduced to each member. A moment to mention what the new employee is to do and what the older employee is doing, accompanied by a friendly word, should be sufficient.

Some church staffs have an occasional luncheon together or a "tea break" in the afternoon. This is an excellent opportunity to introduce the new staff member to the group as a whole. Telling the group about the person's background, interests, and something personal will help him become known and accepted.

*Introduction to Responsible Church Leaders.* The personnel committee may feel it advisable to introduce the new staff member to the official board. This may be done with the board's approval at the meeting following the employment. If the new staff member is to work with leaders in the various organizations, an informal tea may be one means of helping him feel at home. Everything should be done to identify him so that those most active in the church and those who will work most closely with him will know what his work is and how they may cooperate. At such occasions informality and a light spirit should prevail. If the group is rather large the minister may say a few words when presenting the new employee. The newcomer may or may not be moved to make a brief response. The tone of his words should express humility, gladness, and "good anticipation."

*Introduction to the Parish.* The personnel committee and the official board will, as in all matters, wish to inform the parish of the new addition to the staff. Depending on the size of the church and on the type of position, the minister may, from the chancel at a Sunday worship, tell the worshipers the salient facts regarding the new staff member. At that time the employee in person may be presented to the congregation from the chancel in a dignified and restrained manner. If the task of the new member concerns the spiritual life of the church, it may be appropriate to offer a prayer for that work, dedicating it to the service of the Saviour.

The public relations committee should be informed of changes in staff membership, and the personnel committee may advise that such information be relayed to the membership, either in the Sunday bulletin or in the monthly magazine, if there is one. One church, even though it has a large staff, consistently informs the parish of every change in employment with a vignette of the background of each employee.

The committee in charge of personnel will be committed to "the way" of making every member of the staff feel at home in the church, and will give him the assurance that the parish appreciates his work and considers it important.

### The Sense of Cooperation

Not only before a person is employed but also continually throughout his employment the minister and the church leaders assigned to personnel should stress the importance of cooperation. The staff is to serve the Lord in the work of that particular parish. This cannot be done without perceptiveness of and prompt responsiveness to the needs of the individuals and groups in the parish. There will be many occasions when one department is burdened with heavy responsibilities and demands when another may be comparatively free. The spirit of our pioneer forefathers, who lived in scattered cabins and who came to one another's assistance in time of need, should animate the modern pioneering church. It is well described in the slogan "All for one and one for all". If job specifications and requirements are not too rigid, this means, in practice, active cooperation.

### Personal Counseling with Staff Members

The personnel chairman and the senior minister should be available at any time to counsel staff members regarding any phase of their work. Of particular importance to the new employee will be the first counseling session after he begins working.

As administrative overseer of the church, the minister can greatly advance the Lord's work by his kindly, constructive counsel to the new employee. It should be understood that the minister's door will always be open for the discussion of a personal need or problem or of any aspect of employment.

### Regular Staff Worship Period

To strengthen the ties of togetherness among staff members and to provide spiritual direction for their daily work, a regular period for worship together is recommended:

*a.* The staff may meet informally, perhaps in the minister's study or office, for about five minutes before beginning work, to read a few verses of Scripture, listen to a guiding thought, and say a prayer for the parish and for the work of the day.

*b.* The church may hold a ten-minute service of devotions and prayer at 8:20 or 8:50 each morning in a meditation room, small chapel, or in the church itself. Staff members are urged to participate. Usually such a service is conducted by the minister. It may consist of a few scriptural verses, a prayer of invocation, followed by a Scripture reading, and perhaps by a word of meditation emphasizing a special thought for the day. Then may follow prayers for the staff and for the men and women and boys and girls of the parish. The minister may wish to include a brief prayer of confession, adoration, thanksgiving, and dedication as well as petitions and intercessions.

The entire parish may be welcome to attend, and both staff and parish may be invited to request special prayers for individuals or special needs. This daily prayer service must be kept within the time limit. Staff members who attend the service must reach the church ten minutes earlier than their regular office hour.

*c.* Some churches may prefer to the daily worship a weekly service at an hour when all staff members can be present. One church has a weekly staff luncheon, prior to which, at twelve o'clock, the staff members meet in the chapel for a fifteen-minute worship service. Such a service may be directed, in Scripture reading and meditation, to the needs of the staff members. The minister should use discretion in referring to the personal problems or deficiencies of staff members during the meditative period of the worship. Suppose that on the preceding day a staff member had been ill-tempered. If at the next worship service the minister delivered a homily on self-control the "guilty" person might interpret it as unfair censure. He may use the theme "self-control" more effectively a few weeks later.

*d.* Some churches have a program of staff worship in which each member occasionally has a role in the service, perhaps that of reading the Scripture. Such a policy should be adopted only with the approval of all the members. In all cases the minister should have control of the planning and the execution of the service.

However, one minister says that he has found merit in having a staff member read a few verses of Scripture and offer (or read) a prayer when the church office opens. The minister is available to give suggestions to the staff member appointed to conduct the meditative service, which is held next door to the office from 9:00 to 9:05. Staff members are not asked to arrive before the regular opening hours of the office. One person tends the switchboard while the others are at prayer.

### Staff Meetings

Following the principle that communication and understanding between staff members should be continuous, staff members should meet at appointed times so that each member may understand the functioning of the other members in the over-all program and needs of the parish. The following items are to be considered in developing effective staff meetings:

*a.* Once the time and place for meetings have been agreed upon, all staff members should be expected to attend every meeting. For example, if the minister, assistant minister, director of religious education, and organist decide to meet in the minister's study every Tuesday morning at ten-thirty, that will become a regular appointment throughout the year. If a member cannot be present he should notify the senior minister. If the minister must be away on an emergency, he should notify the others that the meeting is postponed.

*b.* In churches where there are only one or two staff members besides the minister, perhaps a part-time sexton and a part-time secretary, these three persons may plan an occasional meeting. Though sometimes such meetings seem to accomplish little in the way of administration, they are occasions of "togetherness" for presenting ideas, counsel, or problems. The regular getting-together draws attention to the work of each member and thus gives him a feeling of participation in the church program.

*c.* With the approval of the majority a larger staff may hold a weekly luncheon on a day when full attendance and participation may be expected. If possible, a simple, nutritious lunch should be provided at cost. The staff of one particular church meet for luncheon once a week from 12:20 to 1:30. A hot tasty meal is served at a price lower than that of a similar meal at public eating places. By careful management the modest payment that each member makes for his lunch results in a small surplus at the end of the year. This money is applied to an annual social function.

*d.* During the meal the tone should be light and pleasant. Conversation promotes friendship and understanding. A person with a good story or joke to tell should "have the floor" while the food is being served.

The minister or the chairman will then direct the agenda planned for the meeting.

*e.* The purposes of the staff meeting, beyond fellowship, are to inform members about church activities, to exchange ideas and present suggestions; to discuss problems and means of solving them. The agenda may include the following matters: (1) Department heads may make announcements regarding future events. (2) The person in charge of the church calendar may make suggestions or raise questions of general interest. (3) Unidentified long-distance telephone calls may be clarified. (4) The minister may report any decisions and attitudes of the governing body. (5) Problems concerning the functioning of the staff or their total welfare may be discussed. A problem regarding procedure may be discussed and settled. (6) Notes should be taken of the meeting, particularly on decisions regarding procedures or projects. (7) The minister should note recommendations from the staff to be presented to the governing body.

*f.* The minister should inform the governing body of the church that staff meetings are being held. If any item on the agenda involves a committee or department under the jurisdiction of the governing body, it should be reported and cleared. If the sexton is to prepare the room and the housekeeper to serve for the meeting, these assignments should be approved by the maintenance and operations committee.

*g.* Each staff member should receive a copy of the minutes of the meeting and file it in a notebook or folder. He should note any matter that requires action on his part or that should be reported at the next staff meeting.

### Staff Social Events

An occasional social event for staff members may be salutary, but the question may be asked, "Why have a social event?" What is the purpose? What will be achieved? If it is decided to have one, the following questions must be considered: (*a*) What will be of most interest to the staff—a picnic? a theater party? an evening together in a home? (*b*) Shall husbands, wives, or sweethearts be invited? (*c*) Who will be in charge of the arrangements? (*d*) How will costs be met?

### Annual Staff Conference

When the staff has more than three members, an annual conference away from the parish to plan the work for the coming year has decided advantages. The success of such a conference will be determined by the following factors:

*a.* Location is significant. The conference should take place in an atmosphere different from that of the church, such as a YMCA camp, a denominational summer meeting compound, a farm where facilities are suitable.

*b.* The official board will usually see the validity of such a program and should be asked to authorize the payment of expenses.

*c.* Someone should be appointed to make arrangements with the officials at the camp or other place agreed upon. Staff members should be notified well in advance of the date, place and time of departure and return.

*d.* The conference should preferably last two days and one night. If the members leave the church about 9:00 A.M. on a Tuesday, for example, they should be back about 5:00 P.M. on Wednesday. If the meeting place is within two hours' traveling distance from the church, the conference can open before noon on the first day and close in the middle of the afternoon on the second day. With adequate preparation a great deal can be accomplished in this period.

*e.* To be successful, the conference must be planned weeks, or perhaps months, in advance. A good time for the conference is late spring between June 15 and June 30. But each department will have been alerted in February, and at the regular staff meetings the leaders will have been urged to be outlining the problems they have met during the current year together with suggestions for improving the work of the church in the year ahead. All such notes are to be taken to the conference.

*f.* One member of the staff should be responsible for bringing to the conference such supplies as paper, pencils, perhaps a typewriter, the church calendars for the current church year and for the year ahead, and any records of the departments that are to be revised.

*g.* An agenda sheet should be placed in the hands of each staff member. One church has the following agenda:

TENTATIVE PLAN FOR STAFF CONFERENCE

June 15, 16, 19\_\_

*Wednesday, June 15*

| | |
|---|---|
| 8:30 A.M. | Leave church |
| 10:00 A.M. | Arrive Windsor Estates, room assignments, etc. |
| 10:30 A.M. | Opening prayer and introduction to conference— Dr. Jones |
| 10:45–11:45 | Outline of program |
| 12:30 | Lunch |
| 2:00 | Conferences |
| | A. Clergy and Music Department |
| | B. Office, Financial and Administrative Departments |
| 3:30–4:00 | Reports |
| 4:00–6:30 | Free time |
| 6:30–8:00 | Dinner |
| 8:00–9:00 | Conference of entire staff (or groups, depending on needs) |
| 9:00–9:30 | Movie |
| 9:30 | Evening Prayer—Dr. Enloe |

*Thursday, June 16*

| | |
|---|---|
| 7:15 A.M. | Rising time |
| 7:45 A.M. | Morning watch—Mr. Lester |
| 8:00–9:00 | Breakfast |
| 9:00–9:30 | Meeting of entire staff |
| 9:30–11:30 | Conferences |
| | A. Office, Financial & Administrative Departments |
| | B. Christian Education and Music |
| 11:30–12:00 | Reports from conferences |

| | |
|---|---|
| 12:00–12:30 | Free time |
| 12:30–1:30 | Lunch |
| 1:30–3:00 | Final conference of entire staff |
| 3:00–3:15 | Closing chapel—Dr. Graham and Dr. Jones |
| 3:30 | Leave for home |

*h*. Rest and recreation are important and may contribute much to the *esprit de corps*. One person should be in charge of the planning group activities, but no one should be urged to participate in any one activity. Alternate possibilities should be offered, such as a walk in the woods, a swim, a game of volley ball, or "just sitting for a time."

*i*. Separate conferences should be arranged for the discussion and solution of problems arising from the interrelationship of church departments. Suppose, for example, that the nursery school, which operates weekdays, has a problem with regard to its supplies and equipment in relation to the church school program on Sunday. The director of religious education should meet with a representative of the nursery school and perhaps with the custodian of the church property discuss and resolve this problem.

*j*. All decisions and recommendations should be presented to the staff as a whole. With the tacit approval of the entire staff, all these suggestions and recommendations will be formulated into a full report of the staff conference. Among the matters one successful staff conference covered were the following: special worship services, nursery school, special lectures, adult Bible classes, membership interests, music in the church school, vacation Bible school, communicant class, public relations, sermon mailings, tentative dates, organization of work—office assignments, office hours, office etiquette, office arrangement.

*k*. When a decision is reached at the conference, the minutes should include the name of the person that will be responsible for the action to be taken.

*l*. Each member of the governing body should receive a copy of the minutes.

*m*. Any item that belongs in the province of the governing board or of any of its standing committees should be referred to the board for final decision.

*n*. In the course of the ensuing church year, the recommendations of the staff conference should be reviewed from time to time to see whether the decisions made have been implemented.

## SALARIES

The governing body should aim to pay church employees a decent compensation for their services. Some ministers declare that not only for those in the ministerial category but also for employees at other levels, such as secretaries and sexton, some church officers will approve a low and inadequate salary scale that would not be tolerated in their own field of industry or business. The Christian spirit, which seeks the well-being of each of God's children, would sanction nothing short of adequate compensation for the work of each church employee.

### Principles Governing the Salary

The salary of a church employee should be determined on the following basis:

*a.* The prevailing wage rate for similar job classifications in business and industry or institutions in the regional area served by the church.

*b.* The experience of the employee.

*c.* The general competence of the employee.

*d.* The age of the employee.

*e.* The church budget.

*f.* The value of the employee to the over-all ministry of the church.

*g.* The years of service and the talents, abilities, and quality of work of the employee. Once these factors are determined, the governing body should see that the employee is regularly compensated at the established salary. If there is to be any deviation from this policy, the employee should be informed.

*h.* The personal obligations and responsibilities of the employee.

### Plan of Increment

In the well-administered church the governing body, through its personnel or maintenance and operations committee, will have adopted a program of salary increases. Each employee should be informed of the plan at the time of employment.

*a.* The governing body follows the principle that on the anniversary of the employee's coming to the church, the proper committee will review his work and authorize an increase in his salary within understood limits.

*b.* If there is a salary-increment plan, provision should be made in the annual budget for increases.

*c.* Some churches feel that there should be no precise plan, that salary increases should be based primarily on ability. Individuals of outstanding competence should be given salary increments commensurate with the quality of their work. This plan has advantages and disadvantages. Let us suppose that of two women serving as secretaries one is 25 per cent more competent than the other. It would seem fair to pay the more competent secretary a proportionately higher salary. However, it is difficult to make an unbiased judgment in such situations. Personal likes and dislikes may be stronger factors than pure competence. Under such conditions the employees have no dependable basis for anticipating or estimating an increase. This may cause discontent and jealousy.

*d.* Another program has a salary scale for each type of position in the church and a stipulated percentage increase on the anniversary of employment. Under this system each employee knows what he may expect if his work has been satisfactory at the end of a year's service. This plan does not preclude the granting of additional compensation for outstanding service.

Each parish should develop a program that will be feasible in its particular situation and that will give the prospective employee a satisfactory answer to the question "What is the church's plan for salary increases?"

### Method of Payment

Employees may be compensated weekly, biweekly, or monthly, depending on their needs. Payment should be made by an accredited officer of the church, preferably in the form of a check, which serves as a record, and should be delivered to the employee in a sealed envelope.

Because of an emergency an employee may request payment in advance or a change in the pay period. The governing body should permit such adjustments in emergencies. However, before making payment in advance the pay officer should explain the circumstances to the official board and ask its approval. In general, payment in advance should be discouraged.

### Handling of Salaries

The governing body, through its finance and personnel committees, must be informed of the salary of every employee. It should hold this information in the strictest confidence and should not permit the disclosure of the salary schedule of its ministers and other employees to individuals or to other churches without its approval.

The officers should guard against indiscriminate disclosure of the salary schedule to parishioners. In the annual budget submitted to the parish the salaries of the ministers and the staff might advisedly be incorporated in over-all terms rather than individually listed. For example, in preference to the item "Salary of the Director of Religious Education," followed by an item for each subordinate of the directors, there should be one over-all impersonal item such as "Leadership and office assistance for the Religious Education Department." The treasurer or financial secretary who makes out the salary checks should guard against their being seen by any employee other than the one whose name is on the check. Otherwise there may be hurt feelings, possibly envy or jealousy among fellow workers, which might undermine the *esprit de corps* of the staff.

## SOCIAL SECURITY AND RETIREMENT PLANS

The church should cooperate with the United States Government and the local social security office. The clergy are not automatically included in the social security program, but they may enter it on their own initiative.

The chairman of the personnel committee should see that social security taxes are paid promptly and that all details are handled according to Federal regulations. He may discuss with the clergy their possible participation in the social security program.

Retirement programs are established by many of our denominational headquarters, not only for the clergy but also for all full-time employees. The officers of the governing body should consider the over-all plan of its denomination with respect to their own church employees. Giving a feeling of security, both for the present and the future, will make for greater contentment and efficiency among employees. The church must bear in mind the competition of business and industry in the matter of retirement plans for employees. The principle of the church's doing no less but, if possible, more than the commercial world should appeal to the minds and hearts of church officers. The minister and the chairman of the personnel committee should not hesitate to bring this matter up for consideration by the officers.

The conscientious supervisor of a pension project will evaluate the denominational plan and other plans and, after consultation with staff members, will recommend the most beneficial program for adoption by the governing board. More and more churches, feeling their responsibility to employees at retirement and, in some instances, paying them a salary for many years after retirement, realize that the well-being of the church, from the economic standpoint, is happily served by a retirement program. It eases the mind of both employer and employee.

## GROUP INSURANCE

Increasing numbers of employees in various fields participate in a group insurance program. The plans vary. Usually the employer and the employee each pay part of the premium on the employee's life-insurance policy. Under group insurance plans the over-all premium rate is lower per average than that on individual policies.

Group insurance should be considered by church boards in situations where there are several employees on the staff. If a group insurance plan is in effect, the church's obligation to the survivors of a deceased employee is satisfied in large part by the insurance benefit. Many employees gratefully avail themselves of group insurance to add to the protection of their homes and families. An informal study of the matter by the church and a survey of the staff on an informal and "noncommittal" basis will usually furnish the answer as to whether or not the church should adopt such a program.

## HOSPITALIZATION PLAN

The personnel committee should familiarize itself with government provisions for employee compensation in the event of accident while "on the job." The matter of employee insurance by the church is discussed elsewhere (page 202). The personnel committee should make sure that the church's insurance policies cover employees injured or permanently disabled in the performance of their duties, and should be familiar with the local Workmen's Compensation laws. The governing body, the staff, and the personnel committee should also consider a group hospitalization plan for church employees. Blue Cross is universally known, and detailed information is readily available at any of its local offices. Hospitalization plans are a form of group insurance in which employer and employee participate. The "dues" are deducted periodically from the employees' salaries and are forwarded in a lump sum to the insuring association. If the church participates in such a program, its policy regarding sick leave may be adjusted in terms of the hospitalization coverage.


## HOLIDAYS AND VACATIONS

With the approval of the governing body, the maintenance and operations or a similar authorized committee should prepare a list of the holidays on which the church office will be closed and the staff members, with a few exceptions, will be free of their usual responsibilities.

In an annual memorandum for all employees one church states its policy regarding holidays as follows: "The following legal holidays will be observed: New Year's Day, Washington's Birthday, Memorial Day, Independence Day, Labor Day, Armed Forces Day, Thanksgiving, Christmas Day. . . . In the event that it is necessary for a member of the staff to work on a holiday, a 'lieu' day will be allowed either in the week before or after."

Vacations of staff members should be provided for as follows:

*a.* The governing body should establish a vacation policy along the following lines: If an employee has worked for the church less than six months, no vacation with pay is granted. If he has been employed between six and nine months, one week's vacation with pay is granted. After a full year's service two week's vacation with pay is granted. Some churches increase the vacation allowance on the basis of additional years of service. For example, after two full years of service, the employee may be entitled to two and a half weeks' vacation, and after three years' service to three weeks' vacation with pay. Except in the case of the ministers three weeks is the maximum vacation period with pay.

*b.* The governing board should make a ruling regarding time off or vacations without pay. When an employee needs time off for a special reason, the personnel committee should handle the matter with the individual concerned.

*c.* The vacation schedule should be established well in advance of the normal season to ensure that the church will have ministerial service and that basic programs will not be interrupted. The switchboard must always be tended, and the church office must always be open to serve the parish.

## THE DETAILS FOR PARTICULAR STAFF WORKERS

### Associate or Assistant Minister

If a parish becomes so large that its one minister is overburdened, it may consider the employment of an associate or an assistant minister. To find the right person the following procedure is suggested:

*a.* With the approval of the governing board a statement should be issued, preferably in writing, indicating the duties and the services expected, the preferred age, experience, and background, and the areas to which the new assistant is expected to devote his time and energies.

*b.* With the counsel and participation of the minister, a "net" may spread to "catch" the right person. Denominational headquarters, the officers of various presbyteries and dioceses are sources from which the names of qualified candidates may be obtained.

*c.* If the conference with the candidate is satisfactory, and if his references are good, the candidate will be invited by the governing body to serve as assistant minister and will be welcomed by the church. His work should be supervised by the senior minister, to whom he will be primarily responsible. There must be only one senior minister of the church. Experience has taught that "two pilots at the helm can get the ship easily off its course."

*d.* All ecclesiastical details with regard to the denominational body will be fulfilled.

*e.* A suitable installation service will be held.

*f.* The duties of the assistant minister will depend on the needs of the parish. One church has prepared the following statement:

A SECOND MINISTER

SOUGHT BY

CHRIST CHURCH

The Church
Approximately 1,500 members, 500 in church school
$93,000 yearly budget
Two services of church and church school
Active, united, progressive

The Staff
Minister, Dr. John Freeman
Director of Christian Education, Miss Marjorie Hall
Director of Christian Service, Mr. Frank Johns (layman, trained in Business Administration)
Organist, Choir Director, Mr. George Allen
Secretarial and maintenance staff

Facilities
Attractive church and church house located in residential uptown area
Additional building facilities to be erected in the near future

City of Pleasantville
Population of over 100,000 in incorporated city
Including outlying area, 125,000
Home of Pleasantville College, Glen Valley Technical Institute
Industries—General Electric, Maryland Pneumatic Tool, Brown Aviation, near Reef Air Force Base

Proposed Job Analysis for New Position
Worship Services—sharing regularly in worship leadership
Occasional pulpit responsibility to be worked out with the individual
Pastoral Work—sharing in prospect and membership calling, hospital ministry, shut-ins, counseling, and so on

Adult Education—sharing in new-member and communicants' class responsibilities, Bible classes, leadership training, spiritual life groups, and so on

Funerals, baptisms, weddings, home Communions, as requested

Publicity—assume responsibility for the monthly church newspaper plus other publicity media

Additional responsibilities to be determined by abilities and interests

Remuneration

Probable starting salary, $5,000

House or apartment to be supplied by church, plus pension

If interested in applying or suggesting a person for the position, please contact:

Dr. Roy M. Klieman, Christ Church, Pleasantville, Ohio

or

Mr. Howard Miller, Chairman of the Board Committee, Camerin, Ohio

### The Minister of Visitation

A church may grow to the point where further division of ministerial leadership is required, and it may therefore seek an additional clergyman to serve as "minister of visitation" or "minister of evangelism" or "parish minister." His responsibilities may include: (1) obtaining the names of prospective members for the church; (2) maintaining an accurate prospect file; (3) calling on new people, prospects, and strangers to develop a closer relationship to the church; (4) preparing new members for reception into the church; (5) contacting agencies through which the names of people moving into the area may be obtained; (6) forming a committee of church members to welcome or call on new people in the area.

The church must determine whether the minister of visitation should be responsible for calling on and the caring for the shut-ins and those who are hospitalized. Every minister must have adequate office and work space, and the governing board, through its personnel committee, should provide the equipment and secretarial assistance needed for efficient service.

### The Ministry of Education

*Director of Christian Education.* Often the main province of the assistant or associate minister is supervision and direction of the Christian education program. The chief qualifications for this office are: Christian maturity and dedication, technical training, knowledge and experience in the principles of religious education, a love for children and youth, competence in inspiring in children and young people an interest in and love for the church and encouraging their participation in its service and in the service of the Master.

The specific duties of the director of Christian education will be determined by each church. They should include: (1) enlisting teachers and staff and training them for the church school program; (2) supervising the young people's and youth societies; (3) arranging for leadership when necessary, outlining the program and supervising at all points the activity and development of the children's and youth programs; (4) ordering religious education supplies; (5) keeping records of classes, enrollment, offerings, and so on; (6) supervising the religious education budget under the authorization of the Christian education committee; (7) counseling related activities, such as a Christian Parents' Association, the nursery school, crib care, and so on; (8) cooperating with the senior minister, the music department, and the maintenance staff in all phases of the church life, and seeking to develop a strongly integrated program between children, youth, and adults.

*Assistant and Other Employees.* Depending on the size of the church school and the variety of activities under the Christian education committee, the director of Christian education may have the services of an assistant or another compensated employee. The Christian education committee, in cooperation with the personnel committee, will see that the director has a good office with a telephone and other necessary equipment and the secretarial help he needs.

If the church school program is highly organized, the director may need an assistant, on a part-time, full-time, or volunteer basis. Perhaps he is not experienced in dealing with children under primary age. In this case a woman with a background in education, and preferably experienced with small children, may be hired on a part-time, if not a full-time, basis to develop this area of the church life. Or perhaps the director cannot supervise the weekday released-time program or the Vacation Bible School or some other activity. In these cases if the religious education committee feels that the programs are needed to strengthen the spiritual life of children and

young people, it should employ one or more persons to direct these
activities on a part-time basis.

Again, if a church conducts a crafts or an art program or has
club activities—for example, a stamp or a coin club or other hobby
groups—these may be the straw that breaks the camel's back for
the head of the religious education department. Ideally all such activities should be under the direction of the minister of religious
education and the Christian education committee, but persons
skilled in these areas may be employed to advantage.

### The Ministry of Music

The "ministry" aspect of the music department deserves emphasis. Leadership in the educational and inspirational aspect of sacred
song is akin to the prophetic, priestly, and sacramental functions in
the church. The governing board should place a high premium on
the spiritual qualities of the person who heads this department.

In seeking the minister of music, the committee and board should
be guided by the following suggestions:

1. The needs and the program of the parish should be analyzed.
What does the congregation expect of a sacred music department?
What does the governing board desire in the way of educational
leadership from the music department for adults and children? Answering these and similar over-all questions will enable the employing group to select the best qualified person for their parish.

2. The committee should not employ a director of music without
the enthusiastic approval of the clergyman. A close and harmonious
relationship between minister and choirmaster is essential for the
conduct of worship and for the spiritual enrichment of the parish.

3. General traits of personality should be considered. The director
of the music program should have a demonstrated ability to work
understandingly and sympathetically, with individuals and with
groups.

4. The musical education and competence of the individual should
be considered.

5. The organist and/or choirmaster should be given an opportunity to see the facilities and equipment of the church for musical programs.

6. It should be clearly indicated to whom the director of music
will be responsible. From the administrative standpoint, his line of

responsibility may pass through the music committee to the official board. The employing committee might say, in effect, to the director of music: "Two persons will be especially interested in your work and will be available for counsel and guidance. They are the chairman of the music committee and the minister of the church. These are the persons you must specially aim to satisfy."

In this arrangement the director of music has a varied relationship to the official board and to the congregation. Here, and in every other administrative setup, simplicity is desirable. If the music director is to be responsible both to the chairman of the music committee and to the minister, cooperativeness cannot be overemphasized. He should apprise both parties of his policies, programs, and ideas. The minister should be ex officio member of the music committee. Usually he is more readily available for consultations than the chairman of the music committee. If there is a meeting of minds and of spirit, these three individuals will respond as a unit to the suggestions and counsel of the congregation and of the governing board.

7. Arrangements should be efficiently made for the development of the music department. The following questions should bring an affirmative reply: Is the organ satisfactory? Is there a program for its care and maintenance? Does the minister of music have suitable office space? Are there adequate rehearsal rooms and facilities for housing the music library? Is there a choir guild or another supportive organization within the music program to assist the director in administrative details if necessary?

As a music program develops, it may be necessary to have more than one person in charge. If a church has a multiple-choir program, involving several groups of children and adults, the music committee and the official board should provide the necessary assistance for keeping records, rehearsing the groups, maintenance of robes, and so on.

In a church where there are both an organist and a choir director, it should be understood that the choir director is the responsible director of the music program.

### Administrative Assistant

As churches increase in size and in complexity of organization and program, many of them employ either a clergyman or a layman to relieve the pastor of some of his administrative burdens. One church has as "administrator" a layman who had a business education at college and who was experienced in the commercial world. With a deep love for the church he has found in his full-time employment as church administrator the most rewarding role for his particular abilities.

Since the duties of this office vary from parish to parish, it is important that the minister, the personnel committee, and the governing board outline the duties of the administrator. Areas which the administrator can handle not only to relieve the senior minister of "peripheral duties and responsibilities" but also to coordinate church activities are indicated in the following outline.

### DUTIES OF ADMINISTRATIVE ASSISTANT

1. *Office.* Schedules and supervises the work of the Church Office: mimeograph work, preparation of mailings, maintenance of mailing lists, various records, clerical work, etc. (This does not include the work of the minister's secretary.) Plans special work during summer: membership directory; Christian education directory; preparation for every-member canvass; other special clerical jobs. Coordinates office records; provides suitable storage for blueprints and for historical records.

2. *Grounds and Buildings.* General supervision of the work of the chief custodian and assistants; general responsibility for condition of grounds and buildings. Schedules cleaning and maintenance work in cooperation with chief custodian; obtains information on special room arrangements for meetings and plans details with chief custodian; schedules special repair and maintenance jobs to be done by custodians.

Attends all Trustees' meetings; works closely with committees responsible for grounds, buildings, furniture and equipment to carry out plans for repairs and improvements; contacts local workmen; obtains bids when necessary; follows through to see that jobs are properly done; obtains approval (when necessary) for payment of bills.

Attends meetings of Long-Range Planning Committee; coordinates current repair and maintenance work with long-range plans to avoid conflicts and duplication of expense if possible; works out long-range plans for maintenance jobs, such as painting, landscaping, and so on.

3. *Use of Buildings.* Prepares and maintains year's schedule for use of rooms and equipment by church and outside organizations; contacts representatives of outside organizations and obtains applications for clearance with the governing board; passes along instructions for room arrangements to custodians; constantly revises schedule and issues typewritten copy of

scheduled meetings each week to members of staff and chief custodian; posts schedule of meetings each day on blackboard at church house entrance.

4. *Contact with Official Boards.* Follows through to carry out actions of the board between meetings; coordinates records of the board with office records. Attends meetings of Trustees (see above).

Attends meetings of stewards when necessary. Coordinates plans for every-member canvass with office procedures; assists with records on canvass; receives and records pledge cards turned in after first day; passes to financial clerk; keeps interested persons advised periodically of total pledges received.

Attends meetings of church staff; reviews schedule of meetings for current week and following week; makes any necessary revisions.

5. *Purchase Orders.* Investigates sources of supply for various supplies needed. Prepares and issues purchase orders; follows up for delivery, checks to see that right material has been received; approves and audits bills; sends to financial clerk for payment.

6. *Budget.* Supplies various boards with data needed for preparing annual budget figures; consolidates estimates from various boards and prepares total budget for approval of board. Obtains monthly report from treasurer and prepares for distribution to board and Trustees. Keeps track of special expenditures during year and coordinates with appropriations made by Trustees to avoid overspending budget.

7. *Personnel.* Working closely with Personnel Committee of board, employs custodians and clerical help for office (not including minister's secretary); supervises their work and handles any problems or grievances. Prepares semimonthly and monthly time sheets and sends to financial secretary for payment.

If some of the above functions are already being performed by others, the administrative assistant may be assigned other duties. He may, for example, assume responsibility for personal contacts with new people in the community. Other duties will suggest themselves for inclusion among the administrator's responsibilities, depending on the needs of the parish.

Another church, with a different organization and needs, has outlined the position of administrative assistant in this fashion:

DUTIES OF ADMINISTRATIVE ASSISTANT IN CHRIST CHURCH

A. In the Religious Education Department to work in consultation with the director and the minister and with the approval of the Religious Education Committee in areas that will develop the church school program and free the Religious Education Director to give increasing time to the training of teachers, to individual conferences with teachers and parents, to the strengthening of the spiritual and educational program of the school. Some of those areas are:

1. Cooperation with the Parents Association in the special activities of the year, such as Father-Son, Mother-Daughter banquets, the Class Parents' program, the coffee for parents of Church School students, and so on.

2. To develop a program for following up absentees.

3. To develop a program for the recognition of, follow-up of, and supervision of the Cradle Roll Department.

4. To work with the director in furthering other areas within the church school administration that will develop as the program is considered in greater detail.

5. Assistance in the recruitment of teachers and in giving particular attention to the nursery, kindergarten, primary, and junior departments with regard to their over-all program.

B. The Administrative Assistant is to work with the minister in areas of administration that will relieve him and, at the same time, will serve to further activities and programs that will enrich the entire congregational life. (The Administrative Assistant will be considered, in every way, a member of the staff, share in the weekly staff luncheons, and participate in the formation of over-all policies and programs that will develop out of those meetings, as well as in the annual staff conference.)

1. Particularly, the Administrative Assistant will serve as liaison officer of the staff in developing activities in the Congregational Hall. Some of those that are worthy of consideration and development are the following:

   a. One or two major annual church dinners.

   b. Serving as the minister's representative in the oversight of, or liaison officer to, recreational programs that will be established.

   c. Serving as hostess and assistant in organizing and furthering significant musical, dramatic, or other cultural events that the church may sponsor.

2. The Administrative Assistant will serve as the liaison representative of the staff to the Special Activities Committee of the Women's Society, the Housekeeping Committee, and the Executive Committee in the development of programs where such committees or others of the Women's Society would be involved.

3. The Administrative Assistant will work with the minister in such areas of the church program as might not be foreseen at the present time, but which could conceivably develop, where organizational and administrative skills would further the work of the church.

C. The Administrative Assistant will serve as the liaison staff officer between the superintendent of buildings and the other members of the staff, the church organization and the congregation, as a whole, in matters that concern the physical maintenance of the church property. In other words, the Administrative Assistant serves as the single channel for suggestions, recommendations, to the maintenance staff, in so far as the organization, the church membership, and the acting staff are concerned. It is understood that there will be relationship in this activity both to the housekeeping committee of the Women's Society and to the Maintenance and Operations Committee of the church.

D. The authority of the Administrative Assistant comes from the governing board. It is understood that the Administrative Assistant is directly related and responsible to the board, through the minister who is president of that body, and also to the Minister of Education. The Minister of Education's line of responsibility to the board is through the Religious Education Committee, of which the Administrative Assistant shall be an ex officio member.

## The Membership Secretary

Some churches have found it advantageous to appoint someone to take charge of the membership roll, files, and related membership matters. The duties of the membership secretary include supervision of church office details.

The duties of the membership secretary of one well-administered church are as follows:

DUTIES OF MEMBERSHIP SECRETARY

*Baptisms*
1. Arrange time and date with minister.
2. Fill out forms and baptismal certificate.
3. Provide information for bulletin, Cradle Roll, and Beacon.
4. Enter in Chronological Membership Roll.
5. Make out certifications of past baptisms when necessary.

*Marriages*
1. Make necessary dates with minister, organist, chimes player, sexton.
2. Order carpet, canopy.
3. Arrange premarital conference with minister.
4. Confer with bride's mother on arrangements.
5. Conduct rehearsal and supervise wedding.
6. Fill out marriage book.
7. Record marriage in CMR.

8. Fill out license and send to issuing clerk.
9. Make out record card for anniversary letters.
10. Make entry on change sheet of new name and address.
11. Give charges to financial secretary for billing.

### Deaths

1. Coordinate dates with sexton, ministers, and organist, if necessary, for church funeral.
2. Enter data in CMR.
3. Make record card for anniversary letter.
4. Remove card from Alphabetical Membership File and make entry on change sheet.

### New Members

1. Arrange for letters of invitation and notices of new member classes to be sent to prospective members.
2. Talk to prospective members.
3. Send for letters of transfer.
4. Send reminders to prospective members re elders' meeting and coffee on Sunday morning.
5. Make sure letters are in order and contact those whose letters are not.
6. Attend elders' meeting and greet new members.
7. Contact those not at elders' meeting.
8. Attend Sunday-morning elders' meeting and New-Member Coffee.
9. Prepare name tags for new members at coffee.
10. Prepare list of new members for minister to read in church.
11. Enter new member names in CMR and index them.
12. Type list of new members for bulletin.
13. Fill out membership certificates.
14. Type AMF cards and insert strips.
15. Type letters of greeting from minister.
16. Add new members to change sheets.
17. Make Pledge History cards for new members.
18. Remove new members' cards from Prospect file.
19. File yellow sheets which new members filled out.
20. Notify churches from which new members came.
21. Send names of children under three years to Cradle Roll.
22. Send names of children of new members over three years to Church School Department.
23. Notify various organizations of interests indicated by new members.
24. Type letters to new members from finance chairman.
25. Send copy of Church History to new members.

### Maintenance of Membership Records

1. Search for addresses.
2. Write inactive members re their membership.

3. Prepare recommendations for elders' meetings.
4. Prepare change sheets—six copies—for changes of address, name, status.
5. Make out letters of transfer and type form letters to go with them.
6. See that changes are made in AMF, Addressograph files, CMR, Pledge History records, IBM Master Book.
7. Prepare statistical report for board meetings.

*Mailings*
1. Arrange for all addressographing (usually done by volunteers).
2. Supervise stuffing, sorting, tying into bundles all mailings, and deliver to post office.

*Church Magazine*
1. Prepare "Parish Points," that is, baptisms, weddings, deaths, list of new members.
2. Write occasional articles for magazine.

*Every Member Canvass*
1. Mail budget letter to members and adherents.
2. Check canvassers' cards against Pledge History records and add notations to canvassers' cards where necessary.
3. Mark district manager's lists and pull cards for special calls to be made by special canvassers.
4. Send pledge cards and mark district managers' lists where people have indicated they would not be at home and requested card be sent to them.
5. Remove cards and mark district lists where people have already made their pledge or a call should not be made because of illness, death, or some such reason.
6. Sort cards into districts and make up kits for each district.
7. Enter pledges on Pledge History cards.
8. Make notations for ministers' follow-up from canvassers' remarks.
9. Number pledge cards where envelopes are needed. Mail envelopes.
10. Type stickers for pledges for acknowledgments, pledge receivable cards, and offering envelopes.
11. Type Pledge Control.
12. Make daily reports showing the standing of each district.
13. Send daily reports to district managers indicating pledges received in each district.

*Directory*
1. Prepare membership list for annual directory.

*Compile Personal Information*
1. Post personal information to Pledge History cards from results of fi-

nancial drives, letters, telephone calls, church school records, and so on.
2. Post information to Prospect Cards regarding their interest in joining the church.

*General Office Work Coordination*

1. Spread work among the members of the staff to keep any one person from being bogged down or any job from being promptly completed.
2. Answer staff questions and advise.
3. Search for and interview prospective employees.
4. Confer with ministers on purchases and sexton help.

In view of the many contacts the membership secretary will have with the congregation, the employing group should not only consider a candidate's skills and dependability but should also look for a person who is understanding, responsive, and sensitive to people with requests, suggestions, and needs.

## The Financial Secretary and Treasurer's Office

In a small church the treasurer may, on a volunteer basis, take care of all financial matters, including the maintenance of the budget; monthly reports to the board; payment of bills, salaries and other obligations; notification of pledgers; counting Sunday collections; and bank deposits.

But as the numbers of those who pledge or contribute increase, and as the church activities and services multiply, the demands may become too great for one person to handle. Some churches in this position have added to the staff a financial secretary to work with the treasurer.

### DUTIES OF FINANCIAL SECRETARY

1. Responsibility for counting, depositing, and recording of all church moneys, via Sunday collections, mail, and other.
2. Keeping of pledge cards and pledge controls.
3. Setting up of pledge payment posting cards.
4. Recording of all pledge payments.
5. Acknowledging pledges and other contributions.
6. Distribution of offering envelopes.
7. Mailing of quarterly pledge statements.
8. Keeping records of all memorial and other unpledged gifts.
9. Seeing that gifts of securities are properly handled (that is, the securities

are sold, acknowledged, and payments credited to pledge account or other).

10. Keeping proper records of the various funds and accounts in General Funds, Building Funds, Endowment Fund, Nursery School, and Special Funds (which includes Church School, Ministers' Special, Deacons' Fund, Library, Sermon Publications, and so on).
11. Reconciling all bank statements for the several bank accounts.
12. Making out weekly, semimonthly, and monthly payroll checks.
13. Submitting quarterly and annual social security and withholding-tax reports to the Income Tax Bureau.
14. Keeping complete records on payroll, social security, taxes, group insurance, hospitalization, and so on.
15. Obtaining approval on all bills, invoices, and so on, submitted for payment.
16. Paying of all invoices, bills, and so forth.
17. Keeping files on all matters to do with finances—paid bills, payroll, correspondence, and so forth.
18. Payment of quarterly benevolences from the church and church school.
19. Sending of statements to people and/or organizations for charges for use of buildings, weddings, overtime services, and so on.
20. Ordering of all office supplies, stationery, and so on, and keeping inventory of same.
21. Keeping of all church keys.
22. Preparation of monthly financial statement for official board.
23. Preparation of monthly financial reports for committee chairmen.
24. Assisting treasurer, Finance Committee, and committee chairmen with preparation of annual budget.

The financial secretary should be bonded as the treasurer recommends. The governing body should rule whether or not the financial secretary may sign checks. The individual church should determine whether checks must be signed by one or two officers and should announce at a regular meeting which officers and/or employees of the church are authorized to sign them. The treasurer's office should establish the procedure for the payment of bills. Normally no bill should be paid without the approval, in writing on the bill or in connection with it, of the person authorized to place the order and therefore to approve the payment.

Bookkeeping procedures should be clearly established. The books should be audited periodically, and an annual audit should be made by a professional accountant.

All moneys contributed to the church, both loose and in envelopes, should be handled by two persons. Procedures in the treasurer's office may vary. There should be an established routine to ensure an orderly procedure. In the life of the church, what is called "pure business" should be kept from being just that. The soundly administered church should continually emphasize "spiritual stewardship." Custody of the church funds and of its material possessions should be regarded as a "sacred work and a hallowed responsibility." Dedicated to this task, the treasurer and the financial secretary will keep in the right direction and will engender the right spirit in the office.

### Superintendent of Buildings (Engineer)

Churches with substantial properties and complicated heating and electrical equipment can use the service of a superintendent of buildings, preferably someone with engineering experience. Many large churches steadily employ several persons to keep the rooms, corridors, and washroom facilities, as well as the sanctuary, in good order. The superintendent of buildings should supervise such employees and should be responsible for the operation and maintenance of the air-conditioning systems and other equipment.

One church outlines the duties of the superintendent of the building as follows:

DUTIES OF SUPERINTENDENT OF BUILDINGS

1. Oversee all phases of the church's physical equipment, and the maintenance of the church buildings.
2. Care for the oil burners, circulating pumps, plumbing, and electrical system.
3. Arrange and assist the sextons in placing tables, chairs, sewing machines, and so on, as required for various church functions.
4. In the summer, plan and oversee all seasonal work, such as waxing the floors, cleaning and painting where necessary in the interior of the buildings.
5. Supervise operation of all special machinery and equipment, such as mechanical ladders, snow-removal plow, acoustical systems, switchboard on stage, and so on.
6. Order, under prearranged plan with Maintenance and Operations Committee, all supplies needed in cleaning and repairing the church property.
7. In charge of the workshop—all tools, supplies, and equipment relating thereto.

8. Responsible for assigning work schedules for day, week, and season for janitors, and approving their time schedules.
9. In cooperation with the Music Committee oversee the operation of machinery in conjunction with the organ.

## Sextons and Janitors

The terms of employment and relationships of the sexton should be clearly established, including the following items: (*a*) hours of employment; (*b*) salary, vacations, holidays, increments; (*c*) duties: cleaning the interior of the church, supervising the grounds, mowing the lawns, and removing snow; (*d*) duties for special services or ceremonies, such as evening worship, pageants, weddings, and funerals; (*e*) responsibility regarding the interior and exterior of the church fabric, cleaning of gutters and special washing or painting in the summertime; (*f*) care of storage room and church equipment; (*g*) removal of garbage, refuse, and responsibility with regard to furniture or other items that need repair.

## The Housekeeper

In a church in which the women's society is very active or in which there are numerous activities involving the use of sitting or club rooms and of the church kitchen, it may be wise for the church to employ a part-time or a full-time housekeeper. The duties of a housekeeper in one active church are as follows:

### HOUSEKEEPER'S DUTIES

1. The prime duty of the housekeeper is to oversee the church kitchen and see that all equipment and supplies and utensils are in order.
2. Whenever basic supplies run low, it is the duty of the housekeeper to report such to the proper individual, that orders may be made in sufficient time for major church events.
3. The housekeeper is to order all supplies and food that may be used for teas, small receptions, and meals involving a small number of people.
4. The housekeeper is responsible to a designated individual of the staff. In one church that operates effectively, this individual is the administrative secretary. With that staff member, the housekeeper plans all dinners and is subject to the suggestions of the administrative secretary for all details of any church affairs.
5. All tablecloths, dishcloths, and towels are to be washed, pressed, and kept

in order. In fulfilling this responsibility, the housekeeper may notice certain linens that need replacing. A plan for reporting such, and for prompt replacement, will have been made.

6. Dishes are to be carefully checked after each using, and if there is any breakage, that should be reported immediately to the responsible individual.

7. The housekeeper shall take an inventory of all supplies and utensils in the kitchen, such as dishes, silver, glassware, pans, baskets, pitchers. There shall be a permanent inventory and a method approved whereby an accurate week-by-week inventory is established.

8. Beyond looking after the kitchen, there may be other responsibilities of the housekeeper, such as care of the minister's study. There should be a daily tidying of the minister's study and a weekly thorough cleaning. Annually all furniture should be given special attention; all books and bookshelves dusted and, where needed, oiled and waxed.

9. The housekeeper may be given responsibility for the care of certain other areas of the church, such as the sacristy and any memorial rooms that should have special attention.

10. When church dinners are held, the housekeeper, who is in charge of the kitchen, will instruct volunteers who may assist in food preparation, cooking, serving, and cleaning.

11. The housekeeper shall have sole oversight of certain major equipment, such as coffee urns, dishwashers, stoves, and refrigerators. With such machinery and equipment that requires special knowledge for operation, it shall be understood that the housekeeper alone will operate such equipment.

12. As it is needed and when time permits, the housekeeper will clean and properly wax the kitchen floors.

13. The housekeeper is responsible for arranging setups for all small dinners and teas.

14. Where there is particularly valuable plateware or silver, arrangement will have been made for such equipment to have special shelves or cabinets for housing. The housekeeper will see that such items are kept under lock and key.

15. The housekeeper will be particularly careful in utilizing "leftovers." The church rightfully will expect that the individual in charge of the kitchen and food will "be a good steward." Where possible, food that remains from a dinner or tea will be frozen, and all such, together with basic supplies, will be reported to and under the jurisdiction of the administrative assistant.

16. Seasonal work may include special attention to curtains, drapes, and any seasonal coverings for furniture. The housekeeper may be assigned the washing, ironing, and storage, where required, of such items.

17. An additional summer's task will be an annual inventory and a full report regarding all kitchen supplies, materials, and equipment. Shelves are to be cleaned, new shelf paper to be put down where needed; stoves will have a full and careful cleaning.

18. The housekeeper may be in charge of the minister's robes and vestments. These shall regularly be checked for any tears that should be mended, any buttons that need replacing, and so on. As needed, this clothing shall be cleaned and moth-proofed.

19. Attention should be given to rugs and other furnishings of the church that may be subject to ravages of moths. During the summer the housekeeper may be responsible for the cleaning and moth-proofing of all such materials.

20. A duty that certain housekeepers fulfill is that of assisting the women's communion committee in cleaning communion glasses, polishing the communion silver, and assisting in the storage in the sacristy of such precious equipment of the church.

21. Another duty that may logically come in the area of the housekeeper is assistance to the choir guild in the care of certain choir robes. In one church, the housekeeper is responsible for the appearance of robes worn by the senior choir.

22. The housekeeper shall be expected to provide refreshments, as may be required or needed, by small groups or individuals meeting in the church. For example, where a church may have two services, it may be extremely desirable to have a cup of coffee for ushers, choir members, and clergy who work the double shift.

23. A further duty may be the care of the First Aid kit. Certainly in the kitchen area of the church there shall always be sufficient first-aid equipment to take care of minor injuries, such as cuts and burns. The housekeeper shall see that bandages and agreed-upon medicinals are ever on hand and in order.

24. Particular attention shall be given to "keeping the kitchen in order." It will be understood that, if volunteers assist in the kitchen, the housekeeper will instruct them as to where dishes, cups, cooking utensils, and so on, are to go, and it will be expected that all will cooperate with the housekeeper in the principle of "a place for everything and everything in its place."

25. The housekeeper alone shall have a key or keys that shall be used to lock drawers or cabinets for silverware, any silver tea service, or other valuable serving equipment of the church. She alone shall have access to these drawers and cabinets. A duplicate key, however, shall be in the church office and kept in an inaccessible place, such as a safe. The only individual who shall have access to such duplicate keys shall be an officer of the church or a member of the staff so authorized by the official board.

## Secretaries

Every church needs a secretary. One congregation with almost 3,000 active communicants has a broad, diversified program, both for Sunday worship services and for weekday activities, and needs four secretaries and a switchboard receptionist. The duties of these employees are specified and are revised as responsibilities are modified.

The outline of their duties may serve as a guide for any church that employs a secretary:

### DUTIES OF SENIOR MINISTER'S SECRETARY

*Daily*

Put out mail for office. Open minister's mail and arrange with most important letters on top.

Take mail to his office and pick up anything in "out box."

*Monday*

Type Sunday's sermon from record. Use sermon notes as guide. (Typing should be triple-spaced.) Type pastoral prayer from Sunday.

Type form letters that include letters to those who gave flowers for Sunday service; letters concerning any baptisms listed in bulletin; letters concerning deaths listed in bulletin; letters to people in hospital—this list will be supplied by assistant minister's secretary.

*Tuesday*

Take book of staff minutes to lunch and put on table where the minister sits. Take staff lunch minutes and type them on Ditto as soon as possible after lunch. Distribute copies to each member of staff, first punching holes for three-leaf notebook.

Also, type hospital letters if the list was not completed on Monday.

*Wednesday*

Any regular unfinished work, such as dictated correspondence.

*Thursday*

Newspaper clipping letters—read the paper for names of church members, clip articles concerning them and then write short letters enclosing clipping. The minister will sign.

Change postage meter. Watch switchboard during lunch and get refreshments in order for coffee break. Watch switchboard during coffee break.

*Friday*

Regular work.

*Form letters*

Other than those mentioned already, wedding cards and funeral cards are received from the membership secretary. These are kept in a file in the desk and a letter is written to the person or persons involved a year after a wedding or funeral takes place. These are filed under "Wedding Letters" and "Funeral Letters" in the desk.

Church school parents receive a form letter from the minister when their children first enroll in the church school. This form letter is written by the minister's secretary.

*The Governing Board*

The governing board meets the second Thursday of every month excluding July and August. An agenda is typed by the minister's secretary. The Monday before the meeting a reminder of it with a form to be filled out should be given to the ministers, and also a reminder should be given to the membership secretary.

The minister's file "Board" should be put in his office on Wednesday morning. He will probably have dictated material for the board agenda by Thursday morning, and this should be typed on a Ditto, all pages stapled together, and put in the Club Room Thursday evening, together with the board file.

*January*—Send postcard to all board members giving them dates of board meetings for the coming year.

*February*—Remind the minister that new board committee setups are needed by April 1. He should get to work on this in February if possible, so the tentative setups can be presented to the Board in March at their meeting.

*Lent*

As soon as Lent is over start writing letters to speakers for Lenten series for the following year. Form letters are in folder marked "Lenten Speakers."

In early December write to all Lenten speakers for the year coming up, asking them for glossy print and biographical information for Lenten brochure. When brochure is printed send copy to each speaker.

*Communicant Class*

The minister instructs this class on Sunday afternoons during Lent. Make sure he has all the supplies he needs (printed cards of Ten Commandments, and so on).

A few weeks prior to the start of the class, get a list of all eligible children, and the minister writes them a letter informing them of the class. A copy is in the Communicants' Class file in the filing cabinet. A few days prior to the start of the class a reminder is sent out. Make up a list of the children who said they would attend so that the minister can mark their attendance. After the number of children is well established (after about four weeks) make out a list of the children, with the proper spelling of their names, so that Bibles may be ordered with their names printed on them.

## Communion Services

On the Monday prior to a communion service in the church, the chairman of the Communion Committee will give you the names of the elders who will serve Communion. A listing of the names is made and sent to each person involved, plus the mimeographed directions. This should be done on Monday. The same procedure holds for the communion service on Maunday Thursday prior to Easter.

## Church Magazine

Publication dates are set up in June by the minister's secretary in conjunction with the receptionist in charge of the church calendar. Choose dates that seem to fit in best with upcoming events. Send copies of the tentative dates to the editor of the magazine, the ministers, and so on. Discuss dates at a staff lunch, and then, if all agree, ditto copies listing dates. Send one to editor and one to printer, and distribute copies to all in church office and on staff.

Get names of publicity people from Annual Directory for coming year and make up list. These people comprise magazine staff. They should get list of dates with instructions concerning writing of articles, and so on.

Two weeks prior to magazine deadline, a post card should go to each reporter informing them that the deadline is coming up and when the mailing date is. This should be brought up at staff lunch also.

On the Thursday magazine deadline, take all copy to the editor, saving a carbon for yourself. If any more copy comes in on Friday, take it to the editor.

Proofread any articles sent in by people not on the church staff when proof is returned by the printer. When everything has been proofread, return it to the editor.

## Sermons

Any sermon that is to be published should be in the hands of the printer at least three weeks prior to publication. It is the duty of the minister's secretary to make sure it is prepared in time.

## Christmas Card

The minister uses the same cut that the church uses for its Christmas card. It is good to start working on getting the cuts during the summer. Try to have all information on this by November and send to the printer. The card is usually mailed out at the beginning of December.

The minister's card goes to all persons on his personal address list. Volunteers should address these, starting the first of November. Ask the membership secretary about getting the volunteers.

*Binding*

Early in January the church magazine, the Board Agenda and Minutes are to be arranged for binding. These should be put in consecutive order. This is done every two years.

*Staff Conference*

The minister's secretary takes most of the notes for this conference and compiles the notes that everyone else has taken upon her return to the church. She then prepares the staff conference minutes, making several copies and routing them around the office so everyone who attended can read them for changes, corrections, et cetera. After this, the final copy is typed up and dittoed copies made. Enough copies are made so that each member of the board can have one and also each member of the staff. Also extra copies should be made to distribute before the conference on the following year to use as a guide.

### DUTIES OF RECEPTIONIST

Main responsibility: receptionist and switchboard operator. Maintenance of church calendar, including booking of rooms, arrangements for use of buildings, and so on. Prepare billing cards for the financial secretary. Send form, with letter, to group requesting space in the church.

Prepare Sunday bulletin. File copies for future use and binding. Prepare bulletin for special church services. Inform organist and superintendent of buildings of sermon topic, hymns, and so on, for hymn board and outside bulletin boards. Inform minister of pulpit announcements.

Send publicity notices to newspapers.

Prepare weekly sexton and housekeeper schedule.

Prepare daily listings of events and rooms to be used for bulletin boards.

Prepare calendar of events for church magazine.

Maintain schedule of girls for switchboard duty Saturday mornings.

Type stencils for monthly financial statements.

Compile church attendance figures for monthly board report.

Record staff lunch reservations.

Assemble material for annual directory.

Record pledge numbers on payment tapes and glue in cash book. Post church pledge payments from cash book. At end of each month, total and prove pledge controls.

Prepare stickers for new pledges to be used on posting card, offering envelopes, acknowledgment. Mail same. Add new pledges to respective control and file cards.

## DUTIES OF ADMINISTRATOR'S SECRETARY

Main responsibility: secretary to administrator.

Do all mimeographing.

Keep narthex and all literature racks supplied with literature.

In charge of "Lost and Found." Put articles in closet for weekends and bring back to office for the week.

Cull newspapers for articles concerning our members and send form letter from minister.

Maintain church scrapbook.

Prepare bulk mailings for post office (fill out pink slips and tie bundles of cities and states when necessary).

Keep schedule for ministers for Prayer Phone and Daily Prayer service. Give them reminders. Select names of members to be remembered in daily prayer service, and give minister list of names.

Send acknowledgments for sermon publication gifts.

Sort church offering envelopes on Monday mornings.

Cradle roll.

Membership Coffee letters.

Tuesday for post office, stamp meter, telephone.

Help housekeeper when needed for Tuesday's staff lunch.

Take care of closets as to food supplies for the different departments. Type monthly list for financial secretary as to all provisions used by the different departments in the church for activities that are being held.

Write Sunday-school absentee cards, together with list and follow-up list for Parents Association.

Check on mailbox every week on the side door near the board room.

Keep published sermon list up to date.

Keep record of articles published in the different magazines for the minister's personal file.

Sell library books during the week for the chairman of the library committee.

## DUTIES OF ASSISTANT MINISTER'S SECRETARY

Main responsibility: secretary to assistant minister.

Pick up mail at post office daily.

Enter all changes of address, name, status, on change sheets. Enter such information from change sheets to the Alphabetical Membership File, Prospect File, and IBM master book (this entry should be made at time of preparation of change sheet in order to see all individuals in a family involved in one address change).

Keep prospect file up to date, entering comments from the visits by the assistant minister.

Make appointments for the assistant minister to visit prospects. Enter fact of appointment made on prospect card. Also, enter comments gleaned from calls made by her.

Prepare lists of prospects to be invited for each joining.

Visit hospital Tuesday and Friday mornings to get names of new patients. Make up hospital lists for distribution.

Process new church school parents from interoffice enrollment sheet. If not already on mailing list, make prospect. Indicate proper church school tabbing. If on mailing list, put tabbing information re church school on change sheet. Add new church school parents who are not members in that section of IBM book, Send letter from minister to church school families who are new to us.

Post church school pledge payments.

##### DUTIES OF SECRETARY OF THE DIRECTOR OF RELIGIOUS EDUCATION

Main responsibility: secretary to director of religious education, secretary to assistant minister.

Assist counting of church school money on Monday mornings.

Maintain shut-in list. Send bulletins to shut-ins on Mondays.

Prepare interoffice church school enrollment form from names supplied by director of religious education. Enter information in following places from this form:

Church school permanent enrollment card (new one or from inactive file).

Church school parents' file.

Send offering envelopes. Set up posting cards.

Maintain file of students away at school and in armed forces. Prepare stickers for these for church mailings.

Prepare church school bulletin.

Type daily letter to those remembered in daily prayer service.

Type form letters for minister: Guest book letters, appreciation for flowers in Sunday service, baptisms noted in bulletin, deaths noted in bulletin, those on hospital lists Tuesday and Friday.

Cradle Roll: Send letters to children on Cradle Roll at birth and at each birthday. Make up white cards and permanent record cards for Cradle Roll.

Christian Education Minutes: Type and send out to the committee.

## The Nursery School

If the local church finds a need for a daily nursery school, the quality of the program will be determined largely by the professional leaders of the program. With the governing board's approval, the selection committee should engage a leader, following the employment procedures outlined earlier. It should select a woman with academic background and adequate experience who has a love for children and an interest in children's work together with religion and the ability to impart religious truths to small children.

The superintendent of the nursery school should be given the utmost freedom in the operation of the school. She should report to the overseeing board or committee on the activities of the school, its needs, its progress, and so on. As an employee of the church she should be responsible to the governing body.

Additional teachers should be employed only with the superintendent's assent. The superintendent should interview all the candidates, and teachers should be responsible to her as head of the school. Confusion may result in a nursery school, as in other departments if the superintendent is by-passed by a committee or a church officer. If there is a question regarding a particular employee, the superintendent is the one to be consulted.

### DUTIES OF SUPERINTENDENT OF NURSERY SCHOOL

1. Complete direction and supervision of the school's program.
2. Cooperation with the Mothers' Board and the Director of Christian Education.
3. Admittance of children.
4. Supervision of teachers.
5. Presiding at and planning staff meetings.
6. Attendance at meetings of the church staff.
7. Ordering of supplies.
8. Keeping records of attendance and health reports of the children.
9. Conferences with parents.
10. Checking teachers' yearly reports to parents.
11. Public relations, through supervision of articles for newspaper, church magazine, and school paper.
12. Recommendations for staff appointments.
13. Visiting and keeping in touch with other church-sponsored nursery schools.
14. Attendance at meetings of the County Nursery School Council.
15. Yearly conference with kindergarten teachers of the local school.
16. Teaching prayers, hymns, and helping in the music program of the four-year-old group.

### The Nurse

Many parents of infants and preschool children will be gratified if the church provides a trained nurse to supervise or to be available for their children. Local and state laws vary with regard to the nursing or medical care that may be given at a nursery school. Church policy should comply strictly with the law, and parents should be told what service the church is prepared to render.

The local church should consider providing nursing care for infants and toddlers while their parents are attending the church service, and during special events or meetings.

One parish located in an area where many mothers are employed during the day provides a nurse care service during the week on a nonprofit basis. Each mother contributes to the compensation of the nurse. Where such service is available, it is usually on a part-time basis.

The brief items that should be considered and covered are: (1) hours and compensation; (2) duties; (3) fringe benefits, such as social security and employment insurance; (4) means of informing parents that the nursing care service is available.

### Principles of Flexibility in the Church

The majority of American parishes, both urban and rural, are affected by movements of population, changing needs within the parish, and the pressures of present-day living.

As the minister should be constantly addressing himself to the needs of his parishioners and strive to answer their personal questions, so should the church program be responsive to the needs and problems of the congregation. Doing this will entail changing programs and emphasis to serve the various age groups.

The need and importance of flexibility should be stressed to every new employee. Today his duties may be thus and so, but six months from now, as the governing board and the ministerial leadership study the church program, they may have to be modified to meet other requirements. The employee must be ready and willing to adjust and to take on new tasks, as necessary. Within the church office particularly an employee may be asked to put aside his assigned duties and assist in a program that is urgent. It is advisable, therefore, that more than one employee be familiar with each office or staff task. In the case of an employee's illness or protracted absence, someone will then be prepared to take over. The policy of flexibility, permitting each employee occasionally to perform part of another's work also prepares the church staff to fill vacancies and offer promotions within the organization.

The cooperative spirit that makes for flexibility in the staff should originate with the minister, who should demonstrate by word and action that there is no duty or phase of·the church life that he is not familiar with and willing to enter into.

## STAFF ORGANIZATION

On the facing page is the staff organizational chart of one well-administered church.

In this organization every committee is responsible to the governing body, and the senior minister superintends every department and every individual on the staff.

The organization in any church may be modified from time to time, but the lines of responsibility must be clearly established and maintained. The administrator should be in touch with all members of the staff and should have them report to him. The governing body should be informed of the staff organization, and any modifications in the relationships should be approved by it.

## ANNUAL EVALUATION OF PERSONNEL

The governing body, through an outside person or a small committee, should review and evaluate from time to time the services of employees, their competence, their well-being, and their contribution to church programs as a whole. Of course the personnel committee should have continual oversight of the employees. Many of our larger congregations probably have among their members efficiency experts or engineers. One such expert who is sympathetic and understanding toward the church program may offer constructive suggestions for improving the staff organization and increasing the efficiency of certain operations and procedures.

Employees should be advised, preferably at the time of employment, that there will be an annual review and evaluation of their work. For example in its letter engaging a director of religious education one parish stated that the senior minister and the chairman of

STAFF ORGANIZATIONAL CHART—CHRIST CHURCH

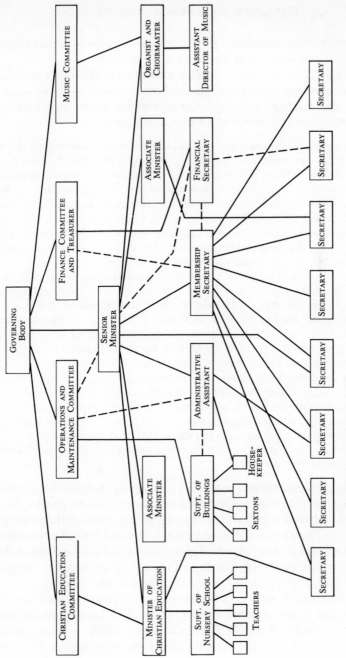

represents direct relationship and responsibility

--- represents partial relationship or limited, but specific, responsibility

the religious committee would review his work annually to see whether everything was mutually satisfactory.

Suggestions or counsel resulting from an evaluation survey, even of the most informal kind, should be put in writing. In the case just cited the minister and the chairman of the committee sent to the director a letter which read in part as follows:

We would like to repeat what we have shared with you on several occasions during the past months and prior to your coming. Our church needs the vital and continuous leadership of an able religious educator who can develop and administer and inspire an ever-growing and developing program here. As you look into the immediate year ahead, you face many practical opportunities which should be met. All of us want you to go forward in developing the strongest, wisest program that it's possible to conceive. It is vital that you lay out a plan and a program. Set aims and objectives that will be stimulating to the faculty and to the entire Church School program.

We've covered in conversation and in memoranda a number of items that need particular improvement. The conduct of the Every Member Canvass for the children, education in the field of stewardship, the development of family participation; the improvement and vitalization of the total public relations program; the development of more telling extracurricular activities, such as the Father-Son Banquet and the Mother-Daughter Banquet are items of significant concern; the increase in church school attendance; the enlargement of our enrollment; the closer and more intelligent relationship between the music program and the Christian education program; increased parental participation in the church school; the development of an attendance award methodology; the thinking-through of a program for memory work—these are some of the many areas, as you know, that need development.

We want you to go forward. We are with you on it. Counsel and confer with us as you develop plans.

The persons engaged in making a survey or analysis should proceed as follows: (1) Employees should be advised that an analysis is to be made and should be assured that it is being made in their best interests. (2) The analysis should be objective and free of personal bias. (3) It should be held in confidence and should not be discussed with other parishioners. (4) The report should be delivered to the proper authority. (5) A report should be given to the employee. (6) Any modification in duties or suggestions for improvement should be discussed promptly with the employee with recommendations for putting it into effect. (7) There should be a follow-up at a suitable time to check whether the modifications recommended have been made.

## FILE OF JOB RESPONSIBILITIES

Considerable time, thought, and effort go into outlining the responsibilities of each position. Job specifications should be kept in permanent files (1) by the personnel committee, (2) by the senior minister, and (3) in the church office. If there is an administrator or other supervisor, he should be responsible for keeping the file up to date. Any change in responsibility or outlined procedure should be recorded in the master file and notice thereof be sent to the department concerned. Every paper in the file should be dated.

If several changes have been made during the year, they should be incorporated in a new job-specifications sheet for the employee, previous outlines being placed in a "dead" file for possible future reference. Each employee should have in his desk the outline of his duties and note thereon every modification. All modifications should be called to the attention of the immediate supervisor.

On the occasion of a worker's leaving the church's employ, the personnel committee and those in charge of the staff may reevaluate the responsibilities of the position to be filled. This will be helpful in the approach to a new employee.

## WAYS TO DEVELOP EFFECTIVENESS OF THE STAFF

Besides recognizing the staff, making their names and backgrounds known to the congregation, introducing them to fellow workers, and orienting them in their work, the minister or other administrator can help them to become effective workers.

### Welcome Ideas and Suggestions

The chief administrator, probably the senior minister, should be receptive to suggestions made by staff members. He should, in fact, invite such suggestions. In weekly staff luncheons and in conference with individuals or with small groups, he will have excellent opportunities to ask "How can we improve our services? What can we do to make our work more efficient?"

The administrator has the prerogative of deciding which ideas and suggestions are valid. He should be quick in expressing commendation and appreciation and equally prompt in pointing out why a suggestion is not valid.

The personnel and finance committees should welcome any suggestions as to how the church may administer with greater economy and greater efficiency. Respect for their opinions and ideas gives staff members a feeling of direct participation and responsibility in the over-all church program. Good ideas and suggestions should be passed on to the proper committees. The minister should see that credit goes where credit is due.

## Minutes of Staff Meetings to Each Staff Member

Decisions or major announcements concerning the staff should be distributed in multigraph form to all members. Each staff member should have a loose-leaf binder or folder in which all minutes and records are to be filed permanently in chronological order. One church office requests that each staff member keep in the file also a page of memoranda for his or her personal attention. If, for example, at a staff luncheon or conference it was decided that the minister's secretary should telephone the editor of the church magazine two weeks before publication date, she should note this on her personal sheet in the front of her staff folder, adding for easy reference the page number or the date of the staff minutes. Such a file is a necessity for a new employee taking over and is also an easily accessible body of material for an occasional review of a person's work.

## Reports of All Departments to the Staff

If the church staff is to function effectively, each member should be familiar with all the phases of every department. Sending copies of memoranda and important announcements to each staff member is one way of giving this information.

The parishioner may seek answers from the sexton, the switchboard operator, or any other staff member to a variety of questions, such as—"Who is in charge of the Cradle Roll Department?" "Whom should I contact to have my child enrolled in the Junior Choir?" "Who is in charge of wedding arrangements?" "When does the confirmation class start?" It is important, therefore, that everyone on the staff be informed about the entire church program.

Besides announcements, major communications, and memoranda,

the following procedures may be helpful in keeping all staff members properly informed:

*a.* At the weekly staff luncheons, each staff member should make announcements regarding the current and future activities or plans of his department.

*b.* Each staff member should be urged to read the Sunday bulletin and the church magazine carefully.

*c.* Departmental planning conferences should invite representatives of other departments to participate. For example, when the Christian education department is making its plans for the year, representatives of the church office and the music department not only may assist in the planning but will also be better informed as a result of their participation. Occasionally, at staff meetings extra time may be granted to the leader in one department to outline the program of his department. One church staff decided that once a year an entire staff meeting should be turned over to the leader of a particular department. For example, the superintendent of buildings may discuss the work of his department, and the other staff members may have an opportunity to ask questions about the music program for the entire year. Such meetings increase the knowledge of all staff members so that they are better able to assist parishioners that desire information.

### Stress "Write It Down"

Written memoranda and instructions produce more prompt and efficient service than oral remarks. All messages, ideas, suggestions, and so on, should be put in writing. One oral statement may be forgotten entirely or be misunderstood.

One may say to the staff, for example, that the superintendent of buildings should be notified of any needed repairs. But prompter service will result from the following typewritten instruction: "Please report in writing as soon as they are noted any broken, worn-out, or damaged items that need replacement or repair." Telephone and other messages should be written down. For example, the switchboard operator may say to the minister: "Mrs. John Smith telephoned. Please call her back. Her number is WHitehall 2-6784." The operator should write down the message, adding the time at which it was received and any pertinent information she has obtained to expedite or facilitate the minister's return call.

The value of putting on paper an outline of plans and procedures is well illustrated by the chart (opposite) that one church gives to each staff member. It shows the hours when secretarial and custodial staff members, identified by their initials, are on the church property engaged in church services. This chart tells each staff member when contact can be made with other employees.

### The Staff to Be "Observers and Listening Posts"

Since many staff members are in contact with parishioners, they are in a position to gain information regarding the parish as a whole. They should report to the senior minister or to the leader of the department concerned any complaints, suggestions, and problems of the parishioners. During the every-member canvass, church members will react in various ways. Each employee should be requested to pass on to the administrator any constructive suggestions or any questions that are raised.

### The Minister's "Door Is Open"

The morale of the staff will be good if each employee feels that the senior minister, as chief administrator, is interested in his work. The minister should demonstrate his interest by being available. He should impress upon each staff member the idea that he desires and expects good work but also has a sincere interest in and appreciation of the persons who do the work. In the course of the years almost every employee will have personal difficulties and doubts and problems with regard to his work. When there is need for counsel and support, the minister should indicate by word and deed that he is willing to be a confidant, guide, and friend as well as "the boss."

## THE PERSONNEL COMMITTEE'S RECORDS

Besides a record of the work assignments of each employee, the personnel committee should keep, for present and future needs, confidential files and records of church personnel. When a staff consists of several members it may be desirable to have a folder for each employee to hold correspondence and confidential memoranda, and a standard mimeographed form may be used to record such infor-

SECRETARIAL AND CUSTODIAL SCHEDULES FOR 19– CHRIST CHURCH

| Name | K.D. | E.E. | E.M. | J.H. | F.M. | H.M. | F.E. | T.R. | E.P. |
|---|---|---|---|---|---|---|---|---|---|
| Sunday | | 8:45 to 12:45 | | | | | | | 8:00 to 4:30 |
| Monday | 8:30 to 5:00 | | 8:30 to 5:00 | 9:00 to 2:00 | 8:00 to 4:30 | 9:00 to 5:00 | 9:00 to 2:30 | | |
| Tuesday | 8:30 to 5:00 | | 8:30 to 5:00 | 9:00 to 2:00 | 8:00 to 4:30 | 9:00 to 5:00 | 9:00 to 2:30 | | |
| Wednesday | 8:30 to 5:00 | | 8:30 to 5:00 | 9:00 to 2:00 | 8:00 to 4:30 | 9:00 to 5:00 | 9:00 to 2:30 | 10:00 to 5:30 approx. | 9:30 to 6:00 |
| Thursday | 8:30 to 5:00 | | 8:30 to 5:00 | 9:00 to 2:00 | 8:00 to 4:30 | 9:00 to 5:00 | 9:00 to 2:30 | 9–12 approx. | 10:30 to 7:00 |
| Friday | 8:30 to 5:00 | | 8:30 to 5:00 | 9:00 to 2:00 | 8:00 to 4:30 | 9:00 to 5:00 | 9:00 to 2:30 | | 10:00 to 7:00 |
| Saturday | | 8:30 to 12:30 | | | | | | | 8:00 to 4:30 |

mation, as the name, address, telephone number, social security number, date of employment, salary, salary increments and dates, vacation provision, hospitalization group insurance, pension, and so on.

The importance of a confidential file for each employee cannot be overemphasized. In such a file should be placed, for future reference, the committee's comments and observations resulting from its annual evaluation of the employee, which are usually strictly confidential. If possible, confidential files should be kept apart from the church office, preferably in a safe under the care of the clerk of the governing body. Under this plan the documents will be in the keeping of the governing body. However, some committees may prefer to keep the files in the office or in the home of the chairman. Under this arrangement some materials may be lost, or the files may not be turned over promptly to a new committee. Each parish should adopt a plan suitable for its particular situation.

## STAFF ETIQUETTE

When a new employee joins the staff, a senior employee can help him by explaining office etiquette. From time to time the administrator should address the staff on the importance of good public relations. Friends and parishioners may be impressed favorably or unfavorably in their contacts with staff members. Thoughtlessness on the part of a church employee may adversely affect the attitude of a parishioner toward the church.

The administrator should call attention to improper conduct in the office, such as, for example, too much personal visiting during office hours, by speaking directly to the "guilty" person. From time to time he should address the entire staff on this or any other matter of office propriety with a view to improving efficiency and public relations.

The staff should be invited to offer suggestions for improving church office etiquette. The staff of one church which has a fine reputation for responsiveness to its congregation devoted some time at an annual conference to a discussion of courtesy technique. The result was the following statement:

### OFFICE ETIQUETTE

1. It is always important to remember that our main function in the office is to be helpful to the ministers and the members of the congregation.
2. Telephone technique: be courteous and patient, but brief. Avoid personal telephone calls. The receptionist will type instructions on how to handle various out-of-the-ordinary situations on switchboard to be given to those who operate the switchboard.
3. Do not discuss office problems or problems of parishioners outside the office.
4. Keep the voice low at all times. In asking questions go to the desk of the person to whom the question is directed.
5. Be businesslike and efficient at all times, and present such an appearance to anyone coming into the office.

6. Do not look at papers on other people's desks.
7. Person responsible for switchboard should stay in office during coffee break.
8. Call personnel by last name when with other people.
9. Maintain the dignity of the office in connection with sextons and housekeeper.
10. When parishioners, especially older people, come to the desk, stand and greet them.
11. All visitors should be announced via switchboard to the person they are visiting. Those visiting the senior minister should be escorted to his office by his secretary if they are not familiar with the building.
12. If anyone wants to see a minister, every effort should be made to contact one. If no minister is available, take the person's name and telephone number and have minister call as soon as possible. If a visitor seems reluctant to state his reason for seeing a minister, do not press him for this information.
13. Ministers should let switchboard know when they are away from their desks and, if away from the church, when they will be available.

# The Church Fabric and Furnishings

A study of a representative sample of 200,000 Protestant churches indicates the supplies, equipment and furnishings used and maintained. The survey shows that the properties of the 200,000 churches include 54,800 chapels, 120,800 parlors or social rooms, 63,600 reading rooms and/or libraries, 166,600 offices, and 179,800 kitchens. Analysis of equipment reveals that equipment and furnishings owned by churches were as follows:

| EQUIPMENT | TOTAL CHURCHES EQUIPPED |
|---|---|
| Motion-picture projectors | 120,800 |
| Slide or film-strip projectors | 127,000 |
| Motion-picture films | 27,000 |
| Film strips | 137,800 |
| Sets of slides | 73,600 |
| Screens for projection | 124,600 |
| Room darkeners | 25,200 |
| Tape recorders | 58,400 |
| Phonograph record players | 112,000 |
| Phonograph records | 90,600 |
| Public address systems | 83,000 |
| Pew hearing aids | 33,800 |
| Organs | 164,000 |
| Pianos | 174,200 |
| Carillons, bells or chimes | 81,200 |
| Bell ringers—automatic | 9,400 |
| Tower amplifiers | 29,000 |
| Thermostatic heat controls | 169,200 |
| Automatic stokers | 15,200 |

| EQUIPMENT | TOTAL CHURCHES EQUIPPED |
|---|---|
| Vacuum cleaners | 162,800 |
| Waxing and buffing machines | 61,600 |
| Floor waxing machines | 12,600 |
| Washbasins | 186,800 |
| Toilets | 186,800 |
| Urinals | 80,600 |
| Paper towel dispensers | 152,800 |
| First-aid kits | 54,800 |
| Fire safety equipment | 105,600 |
| Minister's vestments | 107,600 |
| Choir robes | 154,000 |
| Altar sets | 119,400 |
| Flags: Christian | 131,400 |
| Flags: national | 135,200 |
| Refrigerators | 155,400 |
| Freezers | 10,000 |
| Dishwashers | 17,600 |
| Automatic garbage disposals | 9,400 |
| Kitchen stoves | 162,800 |
| Hot water heaters | 149,000 |
| Steam tables | 25,200 |
| Bun ovens | 11,400 |
| Coffee urns | 157,800 |
| Institutional-size cooking vessels | 91,200 |
| Serving trays | 72,400 |
| Pews | 186,800 |
| Chairs (all types and areas) | 200,000 |
| Tables (all types and areas) | 173,000 |
| Carpeting (for all reported areas) | 119,400 |
| Outdoor bulletin boards | 122,600 |
| Indoor bulletin boards | 112,600 |
| Memorial tablets | 49,000 |
| Portable coat racks (in all areas reported) | 297,044 (total units) |
| Room dividers | 106,200 |
| Metal lockers | 19,400 |
| Blackboards | 158,400 |
| Stage equipment | 42,000 |

| EQUIPMENT | TOTAL CHURCHES EQUIPPED |
|---|---|
| Rheostats | 18,200 |
| Air-conditioning systems | 54,000 |
| Drinking fountains | 107,600 |
| Soft-drink dispensers | 27,000 |
| Typewriters | 179,800 |
| Postage meter machines | 2,600 |
| Addressing machines | 88,600 |
| Duplicating machines | 178,600 |
| Folding machines | 13,200 |
| Steel files | 154,000 |
| Safes | 51,000 |
| Office desks | 177,400 |
| Office chairs | 164,800 |
| Posture desk chairs | 66,000 |
| Upholstered office chairs | 69,200 |

These figures readily indicate that the majority of parishes have properties and equipment that need maintenance and care.

## PRINCIPLES OF CARE

Any church building and its equipment, however simple, must be properly maintained. The governing board should appoint an individual or a committee to supervise such maintenance.

Volunteers or paid employees, depending on the size of the parish and its programs, will carry out an established program for the oversight and maintenance of the church property.

### Cleanliness

The first aim in church maintenance should be cleanliness. The cleaning schedule should be determined by the extent to which the property is used. For example, if the sanctuary is used only on Sunday, the pews need be dusted only on Saturday. The pew cushions should be vacuumed periodically as necessary; the floor should be mopped, vacuumed, swept or waxed when necessary. The chancel equipment, too, must be cleaned regularly. Besides the weekly and seasonal routines there should be one annual or a biennial cleaning, painting, or washing. The principle that "cleanliness is next to godliness" should prevail. Never should a parishioner coming to worship find the pew dusty or the white woodwork smudged.

### Decently and in Order

The maintenance and operations committee should see that all supplies needed in the conduct of worship or of any activity are available and that the appearance of the church is conducive to work, worship, and study in a pleasant, orderly atmosphere.

*The Chancel.* If a special committee is made responsible for the orderliness and the appearance of the chancel, it should see that: (1) the altar or communion table is properly covered and equipped; (2) brass or silver accessories are burnished; (3) offering trays, if of brass, are polished weekly. (4) Vases of flowers or other floral arrangements, arranged according to established rules, should be used only to enhance the religious symbolism and to amplify the spiritual experience of the worshipers. (5) Hymn numbers should be in place on the hymn board before worshipers enter the church. (6) The Bible should be placed and arranged in accordance with the church tradition. (7) Seasonal ecclesiastical equipment should be in place. (8) The materials for holy communion should be ready and in place. (9) Hymnbooks, prayer books, and any other equipment needed by the clergy should be in their appointed places. (10) The choir stalls should be supplied with scores for the choristers. (11) A glass of water should be available for the clergyman. (12) The appearance of the chancel and all of its details should be checked before each worship service.

*The Pews.* The sexton, janitor, paid or volunteer, or a designated member of the maintenance committee should see that the worship materials are properly distributed for the convenience of the parishioners. The Order of Worship should be in the pew rack, or should be handed to each worshiper as he enters. In his pew the worshiper should find neatly arranged in the rack in front of him, a hymnbook, a Book of Common Worship, some pew cards, and a pencil.

If there are two worship services in the nave, the pews should be restored to order after the first service by designated persons, usually the ushers. Bulletins should be removed from the pews and from the floor. Glasses, purses, or any other personal articles left behind should be taken to the spot at which they may be claimed. Kneeling cushions should be distributed evenly and arranged neatly.

*The Narthex.* The worshiper gets his first impression of the church as he enters the vestibule, or narthex. The senior minister and the committee in charge of the property should consider the hopes and aspirations of parishioners attending worship service. The hour is sacred and quiet. People come to church to enter more fully into the life of God, to learn more about Jesus Christ, and to be inspired and directed by spiritual purpose. The narthex—which gives the first impression—should prepare the worshiper for this experience. If possible, it should be so planned as to permit an unobstructed view of the nave and the chancel with its cross or center of worship. At the entrance to the nave may be the baptismal font. There may be in the narthex memorial tablets or the Book of Remembrance. A visitor's table with a guest book and perhaps a rack for literature may be placed in positions accessible but not so conspicuous as to be obtrusive.

The narthex must always be kept clean. On rainy or snowy days mats must be laid down to absorb moisture and provide safe footing. If the floor becomes soiled between worship services it should be cleaned, if possible, before the second service. The heating and ventilation of the church should be taken care of by the maintenance committee and the ushers. During periods when the sanctuary is not in use, the heating ventilation should be adequate to prevent damage to property and equipment.

The ushers, sexton, or some other person should see that in the narthex or close to the sanctuary there is a quiet place to which a person who becomes ill may retire. First-aid equipment, a warm blanket, if possible an invalid's chair and a cot should be on hand. In some churches a small waiting room off the side of the narthex is used in emergencies. This room is used also by bridal parties and by funeral attendants. A drinking fountain and a washbasin may prove very helpful. Such equipment should be clean and in order for regular or emergency use.

### Repairs Made Promptly

Damage to church equipment should be promptly repaired. Burned-out light bulbs should be replaced at once. A damaged chair should be removed and replaced as soon as possible. If in a pew there is a splinter that causes runs in women's stockings, it should be planed off as soon as reported. Should the church steps crack or crumble because of frost, the maintenance committee should immediately take safety measures and repair the steps and remove any other hazard.

The governing board should anticipate deterioration and the need for the replacement of supplies and equipment, and should allocate funds in the annual budget for this purpose.

### Continuous Oversight by the Maintenance Committee

The maintenance committee should make a weekly check of the church property and report to the governing board once a month on the needs and the care of the physical property. Responsibility may be divided among the members of the committee, one member supervising the sanctuary, another the kitchen and the fellowship hall, and a third the educational building, the classrooms, and the church office. It is important that one member of the committee be responsible for the church grounds, and another for the exterior fabric of the church buildings. The chairman of the committee should keep in constant touch with the maintenance staff.

In many churches the storage room, workshop, and boiler room are allowed to become cluttered with discarded equipment that accumulate over the years. The maintenance committee should inspect every nook and cranny of the church and see that discarded materials and rubbish are removed from the premises. Some of the equipment may be useful to another church or institution. Storage rooms should be in good order.

The maintenance committee should have an inventory of the tools and supplies in the workshop and should check periodically to see that they are there and are in good working condition.

At least once a year the maintenance committee should make a survey of all the rooms and all the equipment under its care. The survey may be made effectively during the summer to serve as a basis for the recommendation of items to be provided for in the next annual budget.

## Annual Survey by Building Expert

Some churches have found it advantageous to employ, on a fee basis, a builder or a person experienced in the maintenance of property. There may be a qualified person among the parishioners. Appointed to the maintenance and operations committee and authorized to make an annual survey, he will be rendering a significant service to the church. Pointing of the mortar, repairing or painting the roof, improving the gutters, framework and foundation annually as necessary will obviate large expenditures for repairs later.

## Deterioration and Replacement Reflected in the Annual Budget

Too many churches proceed on the basis that their property will remain the same forever. But furnaces and boilers will deteriorate, and the best roof will leak in time under the ravages of rain, wind, and frost. Yet few churches seek to establish, through their annual budget, a fund for such major replacements. The governing board should adopt, if at all possible, a policy of accumulating funds for major repairs.

The maintenance and operations committee may profitably make a long-term evaluation of church equipment to estimate the number of years of service to be expected from it. On this basis the estimated cost of replacement can be prorated in the annual budgets. The majority of thoughtful parishioners will approve, realizing that providing annually for replacement in general is preferable to special drives or offerings for the replacement of specific items.

The music committee would do well to evaluate the useful lifetime of the organ. Will foreseeable major repairs, replacements, or modifications be needed in the immediate future? If a study indicates that the life anticipation of the organ is, say, fifteen years, has the official board adopted a budgetary program to accumulate annually moneys to replace it?

### Enlistment of Children in Respect for God's House

The religious education department, the senior minister, the maintenance committee should instruct and encourage children to participate in the care of church property. The Boy Scout room, the room used by young people, and the classrooms for religious education suffer heavy wear and tear. If the youngsters have been imbued with the idea that "this is God's house—this is my church," they may be more careful in preventing the accumulation of litter and may refrain from carelessly or deliberately defacing the walls and thoughtlessly scuffing or misusing the furniture.

The chairman of the maintenance and operations committee, the minister, or the director of religious education may enlist the cooperation of the young people by explaining to them at a group meeting the problems that the maintenance committee faces. The speaker should emphasize the fact that the church "is all of us."

Some churches have a junior maintenance and operations committee. Under the direction of the religious education department young people have organized themselves to assist the maintenance committee in the care of the property. They may serve as monitors on Sunday mornings or at meetings of young people's groups on church property. Their duties may include replacing hymnbooks, rearranging furniture before and after the meeting, and assisting in cleaning up. Perhaps the most significant by-product of such a program is the youngsters' feeling that they are sharing in the maintenance program.

## WOMEN'S CHANCEL AND HOUSEKEEPING COMMITTEES

In some churches the governing board delegates, through its maintenance committee, certain phases of the care and overseeing of the church to subcommittees. One of these subcommittees may be the housekeeping committee. Administratively speaking, this committee may be appointed by the women's association and have some responsibility to it, but it should be responsible directly to the maintenance and operations committee. In some cases the chairman of the housekeeping committee is *ipso facto* a member of the maintenance and operations committee. Depending on the needs and the program of the church, the duties of the housekeeping committee may include care and overseeing of the church kitchen and its dishes, supplies, and equipment, care of curtains and draperies, and overseeing of the women's meeting room and of the powder room.

The source of funds for the committee should be carefully determined. In some churches the women's society assumes the maintenance of the kitchen as its particular project. Whether dishes are to be purchased, or a large piece of equipment is acquired, the women's society will be the group to "pay the bill." If there is both a maintenance committee and a housekeeping committee, the procedure and responsibilities of each should be clear-cut and definite to avoid misunderstanding or friction.

In many parishes a chancel committee of dedicated women is in charge of the linens, silver, and glassware used for the sacrament of the Lord's supper, and of the cross, candelabra, vases, and other appointments. Though this committee may also be responsible for the flowers and the special decorations of the chancel, many parishes find it more satisfactory to have a special committee to handle this.

Though the chancel committee may be appointed by the women's society, it should be directly responsible to the senior minister and to the official board. It works closely with the pastor and should consult him on the needs of the special services and worship program.

There should be an understanding regarding responsibility for payment for new or additional chancel equipment. The governing board is responsible in such cases, but in some churches the women's society assumes the obligation as a loving service to Christ's church.

## FLOWERS AND DECORATIONS

The well-administered church should have a definite policy regarding the decoration of the church, particularly regarding the placing of flowers within the chancel. The maintenance and operations committee should make rulings regarding the use of thumbtacks, nails, and Scotch tape in connection with floral decorations. In written form, and approved by the governing body, the rulings should be in the hands of the flower committee.

Many churches find it spiritually significant to invite the congregation to place memorial flowers in the chancel on specified Sundays. Since the flower committee will see to this, the name, address, and telephone number of the committee member in charge should be made known to the congregation.

The floral committee shall give to the person responsible for the Sunday bulletin details regarding the flowers provided for the worship services. The committee should plan in advance how the flowers are to be distributed after the worship service. It should arrange the flowers in attractive bouquets and deliver them promptly to parishioners who are ill or to those who would appreciate receiving flowers from the church. A card should accompany the flowers to express the thoughts and feelings of the clergyman and the committee. A card signed by the minister may read simply: "These flowers are from the chancel of Christ Church and come to you with our prayers and affection." Another card, unsigned, may read: "These flowers come to you from Christ Church that we may share with you the fellowship of the morning service." One congregation sends a card with the following message: "These flowers have been in the chancel of Christ Church. They have heard the hymns that have been sung, the prayers that have been offered, and the sermon that has been preached. Now they have come to you and, in their silent way, are telling you all about it. God bless you!"

It is advised that the person responsible for the placing of memorial flowers prepare an annual calendar listing the Sundays and the names of individuals who have requested particular Sundays. A copy of the list shall be given to the receptionist or to some other staff member in the office. It will show at once on which Sunday flowers are to be given, by whom, and in memory of whom.

If there are particular problems or if special arrangements are necessary for a funeral service a member of the flower committee may be helpful both to the bereaved family and to the funeral director in making the most suitable arrangements of flowers and floral pieces. Or for a wedding, a member of the committee may serve the bride's family by suggesting the most effective and, if necessary, the most inexpensive decorations for the chancel and the church.

Either the minister or a staff member should be responsible for notifying the flower committee of any change in the usual procedure for handling memorial flowers. The committee should know in advance when the flowers are to remain in the chancel for special Advent vesper service.

The memorial flowers should not overpower the primary spiritual symbolism of the chancel. In one church in which the communion table with the cross on it is the focal point of worship, memorial flowers are placed in vases on each side of the cross. The committee has ruled that the bouquets shall not be higher than the arms of the cross. Thus the cross is always taller than the flowers and has due prominence in the chancel for the worshiping congregation.

The method of handling payments or contributions for memorial flowers should be established. Should individual families order flowers from any florist, or does the flower committee prefer to order all floral arrangements from the church florist? In the latter case, should the contributions for the flowers be made to the committee, which will keep a separate account through the treasurer, or should the donor pay the florist directly?

The church may invite contributions exceeding the cost of the memorial flowers and put the excess money into a tribute or memorial fund for a humanitarian or benevolent purpose. One church, developing a program along this line, has specified that a certain amount shall be paid to the flower committee for the memorial floral arrangements in the chancel. One half of the contribution pays for the flowers; the other half goes into a landscaping fund with which plants and trees are purchased for a permanent "memorial garden" on the church grounds.

Not only the chancel but also other areas of the church should receive attention from the flower or decorating committee. The assembly areas for religious education may be enriched, and a dignity of spirit may be conveyed to boys and girls, by flowers or green plants or leaves placed at or near the worship center. The matter should be discussed with the committee on religious education. This committee may be of the opinion that such decorations are unnecessary. On the other hand, if it feels that floral decorations will enrich its program, it should appoint its own committee, or perhaps one individual to be responsible for the project. Some churches have found it worth while to invite the children themselves to provide the flowers in their department on a given Sunday.

In communities where parishioners have gardens and a supply of plants or flowers, the church may welcome at certain seasons of the year gifts from the gardens of parishioners. However, a committee in charge, with its principles as to the aesthetics and arrangements within the chancel, should supervise and control this project.

## THE FABRIC AND MEMORIALS COMMITTEE

Active parishes with expanding programs should have a small committee known as the fabric and memorials committee. Guided by and responsible to the official board, this committee should have the following duties:

1. It should see that modifications made in the church fabric are in keeping with the architect's plan. Many a church has, over a period of years with decorating programs, the addition of furniture and furnishings, and structural repairs or additions, so modified and changed the original structure that from the aesthetic standpoint it is a potpourri.

2. It should approve every gift, whether for addition to the fabric or special furnishings, before it is accepted by the church.

3. It should consult, for advice regarding the church fabric, the architect that designed the building.

4. It should have access to the archives where blueprints, plans, and records regarding the church fabric are kept.

5. It should file all plans for memorial windows together with the related correspondence, and should confer with prospective donors of memorial windows, learn the details, and make the arrangements for ordering, installing and maintaining them.

6. It should look after memorial plaques, furnishings, or furniture presented to the church, and should keep in its archives a record of each memorial placed in the church, including the date of the gift, the name of the donor, and any stipulations, verbal or written, made upon presentation. This material is important, especially if, as times change, the church should find that a particular memorial is no longer appropriate to its program. Under such circumstances the committee should seek the approval of the donor or of the family of the memorialized to modify or dispose of the memorial.

7. The chairman of the fabric and memorials committee should be a member of the maintenance and operations committee, or the chairman of the maintenance and operations committee should be

an ex officio member of the memorials committee, so that each committee will be familiar with the work of the other.

8. The committee should suggest, in a list, memorials that would enhance the beauty or improve the program of the church. This list should be distributed to the congregation, and their inquiries be invited. For special dates in the church year, as, for example, All Saints' Day, the committee may publish an attractive leaflet telling about the memorials in the church. There is a stabilizing and ennobling spirit in a parish that respects and honors those who have loved the church and the congregation and whose memories therefore are perpetuated in tangible form in the furnishing or fabric of the church.

9. The memorials committee may suggest to the governing board, and perhaps later to the congregation, the mounting in the church of a "founders' table." The committee may cooperate with the religious education department in conducting an annual tour of the church, pointing out to children and young people for educational as well as inspirational purposes the memorials in the church.

## THE BOOK OF REMEMBRANCE

The major religious publishing houses issue various kinds of books of remembrance for recording memorials and special gifts. The memorials committee should provide the parish with such a book.

1. The book of remembrances should be as fine and beautiful as the individual parish can afford.

2. A member of the official board or a member of the memorials committee should be responsible for making entries promptly to keep the book up to date.

3. So that there will be no doubt as to what is to be entered in the book, the governing body should determine what constitutes a memorial. Is it a gift with a certain monetary value? Must it be a gift "in memory" of someone? These and other questions must be specifically answered.

4. The book of remembrance should be suitably housed. Some churches keep this book in an attractive shrine. The book may be displayed in a cabinet placed in the narthex, in a chapel, or at some

other spot where the atmosphere is quiet and sacred. The cabinet should have a glass door through which the book may be easily seen but not touched. The door should have a lock.

5. If there is no permanent public display case, the book of remembrance may be exhibited on special occasions, such as All Saints' Day, in a side room with an officer of the church in charge to show it in detail to interested parishioners.

6. The book should have permanent care. One person should be in charge. It would be wise to have a duplicate of the book of remembrance. If it is not feasible to have two books, an exact copy of the contents should be kept by the archives committee in a fireproof place. The memorials committee too may suitably have in its files a duplicate copy of all entries made in the book of remembrance.

## A WORK SCHEDULE FOR THE DAY, WEEK, AND SEASON

To ensure the proper care of the fabric and furnishings of the church and suitable arrangements for the church program the maintenance staff must have a work schedule. At the beginning of each week the sexton or the superintendent of the building should receive the schedule of the church activities involving the use of any part of the church. He should then plan the work program so that all the rooms to be used are in proper order and are equipped with the necessary supplies and facilities.

The maintenance and operations committee should schedule the tidying of the sanctuary, the dusting of the pews, the mopping of the floor, and the cleaning of washrooms.

The maintenance staff will work most effectively if it has a monthly schedule of special services to be rendered, such as waxing floors, cleaning or dusting windows and window sills, and burnishing interior and exterior equipment. Certain equipment and perhaps machinery should be checked periodically. All such items should be put in writing.

The seasonal or annual work program should schedule such projects, as painting, repairing steps in stair wells, cleaning storage rooms and disposing of things no longer needed, washing walls and woodwork, cleaning or repairing gutters, raking and removing leaves, and pruning and spraying trees or shrubs.

### Organ Maintenance

The organ should be serviced regularly under a contract with an organ service company. With the approval of the governing board the chairman of the music committee should enter into a contract satisfactory to the organist and the choirmaster. The contract should be kept in the music committee's files, but the governing board should know the terms, and, if necessary, additional copies of the contract should be furnished for the files of the clerk of the board.

In addition to the regular tuning, pitching, and cleaning and the replacement of worn parts by the service company, other provisions for the maintenance of the organ must be made by the organist, choirmaster, and music committee. (a) Someone must be responsible for maintaining in the chancel throughout the week the temperature range recommended for the console and the organ chamber. (b) If possible, a staff member who understands the whole mechanism of the organ, including the blowers, should be readily available on all important occasions when the organ is played. (c) It is usually advisable that only the organist and his assistant be given a key to the console and be permitted to play the organ. Some churches, in their contract with the organist, stipulate the terms on which the organist's pupils may play the church organ. The music committee should permit no organist to play the organ without approval of the organist in charge. (d) The sexton or the maintenance department should have specific instructions for cleaning the console and any parts of the mechanism.

### Piano Tuning and Maintenance

The music committee should provide for the regular tuning of the piano or pianos owned by the church. A specific arrangement should be made with the piano tuner to check and tune the pianos periodically (about once every three months), particularly those in continual use. The maintenance staff should be instructed as to the cleaning and care of the instruments. The committee on music should provide written instructions for the piano players, advising them to report promptly any defect in the piano, to close the piano before they leave, and to lock it if it is in an area of the church where that seems advisable.

### Room Setup Specifications

Every organization or group that wishes to use the church facilities should be given a mimeographed floor plan of the church. If it requests the use of the dining room, for example, it can easily indicate on the dining-room plan the desired position for the speakers' table and the preferred seating arrangement for the guests. With this information the sexton or the maintenance person responsible should have no difficulties in setting up the room. Additional information should be supplied regarding specific requirements, such as a lectern, a speakers' table, or a public address system. If motion pictures are to be shown the sexton should be told who will provide the equipment, where it should be placed, and who will operate it.

### Window Washing

In the seasonal work program particular attention should be given to the cleaning of windows. If the maintenance staff finds it difficult to do this work within the regular program, the maintenance and operations committee should have it done by a window-washing firm or an independent window washer. The windows should look as clear as the local atmosphere permits. Often, cleaning of windows on the inside may be part of the regular work program of the sexton. In that case the chairman of the maintenance committee should make sure, as he inspects the church property, that the windows have not been overlooked. Every week or two the chairman of the maintenance committee and the sexton together, using a check list, should inspect the church property, including the windows.

### Cleaning of Gutters

Clogged gutters and downspouts are often responsible for damage to church buildings. It is the sexton's job to see that the gutters and downspouts are clear and in good condition, especially in the spring and fall, when the hazards are greatest. The maintenance committee should provide safe, suitable ladders and any other equipment needed for this work. Dry wells should be checked annually, and any condition that might cause water to back up should be corrected immediately.

### Light-Bulb Replacement

In the storage room, under lock and key, there should be a good supply of light bulbs. If the church uses a great many bulbs it should purchase them wholesale, preferably on a bid basis. One person only, usually the sexton, should have access to the bulb supply. He should keep a record of the bulbs used and notify the maintenance and operations chairman when a new supply is needed. There should be a strict rule that a burned-out bulb must be replaced immediately. Staff members should inform the sexton promptly when a bulb is burned out.

### Washrooms

In churches where there is daily activity the washroom facilities should be tidied every day. With the advice of the maintenance and operations committee, the sexton should purchase and have in the supply room disinfectants and deodorants necessary to make the washroom facilities immaculate.

If there is a day nursery school, that department may make additional arrangements for cleaning the washroom facilities each day. Toilet bowls and washbowls should be disinfected.

The maintenance and operations committee should consider installing automatic disinfecting devices. The maintenance staff should see that there is always an ample supply of toilet tissues, soap, and paper towels, and that there are adequate disposal receptacles. For the convenience of the maintenance staff, a service closet should be located near the washrooms so that cleaning equipment and material will be easily accessible.

### Storerooms

Storerooms require careful management.

a. The storeroom should be locked. One key should be in the church office in the care of a staff member. A second key should be in the hands of the sexton or the superintendent of buildings normally in charge of the room.

b. The contents of the room should be prepared for long-term storage. Materials likely to be moth-eaten should be sealed in mothproof bags. Articles that cannot be covered should be placed where they will be least exposed to dust.

*c.* The temperature of the room should be low and should be checked from time to time for steadiness.

*d.* Boxes and packages should be labeled in large, clear letters with heavy black crayon legible from a distance.

*e.* A list should be made of the contents of the room, and an inventory should be taken annually to bring the list up to date. One copy of the list should be tacked to the inside of the storeroom door and another copy should be filed in the church office.

*f.* The above procedure should be followed, in general, by the women's society, the archives committee, or any other group in charge of special storage articles.

*g.* A food storeroom should be the responsibility of one duly appointed person.

*h.* If necessary, the storeroom should be cleaned periodically to remove dust and to prevent damage by moths or rodents, and should be ventilated now and then.

## PLANNING THE SUMMER'S WORK

During the summer, when there are comparatively few activities, the church may profitably give its attention to repairs, major cleaning, and the improvement of furnishings and facilities.

Before planning the summer program the maintenance and operations committee should consult the chancel and flower committee, the housekeeping committee, and other committees, and departments about needs for improvement of the church's physical facilities. The chairman or another member of the maintenance committee should confer with individuals and groups to obtain specific suggestions. For example, if the office of the director of religious education needs painting, the maintenance chairman, having received suggestions from the fabrics committee, should invite the director of religious education to state his suggestions or wishes regarding the freshening up of the office.

### Painting

The best time for painting is the summer. Particular attention should be given to entryways, hallways, stair wells, and washrooms. Areas where the traffic is heaviest and the wear and tear greatest should be painted first. The painting should be done with the minimum inconvenience to the parish. If, for example, one entryway is blocked because of the painting, another means of entry must be arranged for the parishioners' convenience. Offices, classrooms, and clubrooms may be painted next.

The sanctuary, fellowship or recreation halls, and the chapel and assembly rooms for children may need attention less frequently than other portions of the church. These major areas may best be redecorated under a contract with a professional. The maintenance committee should solicit competitive bids and submit its recommendation to the official board for approval.

Some of the painting may be done by the maintenance staff. The maintenance chairman may find that paint and hardware stores offer the church substantial discounts on paints, brushes, and other supplies. It should seek the best-quality products at a reasonable price.

The painters should be instructed as to where and how they should keep their equipment. When the painting is finished, brushes should be properly cleaned and stored for future use. Before approving the bill for payment, the chairman should check whether the cost of the paint and the amount used were reasonable, and whether unused paint was returned.

The maintenance committee should plan, if possible, to have the painting done by the staff so as to minimize disputes with the local painters' union and its regulations.

### Annual Cleaning

The dust and insect excretions that accumulate on light fixtures, rafters, drapes and hangings, and in other places that are not cleaned weekly or monthly, must be removed during the annual cleaning of the church. The maintenance committee must decide whether it is more advantageous to have the annual cleaning done by professional workers or to purchase the equipment with which it may be done by the maintenance staff of the church. The boiler room, the heating system, and the kitchen should be included in the annual cleaning program.

### Furniture Repair

Pews, chairs, tables, and upholstered furniture should be checked in the spring. Necessary repairs should be made while most of the church activities are suspended. The maintenance committee together with the sexton should determine the most convenient and most economical procedure for the repair work. With adequate work space and the necessary tools and equipment the sexton or the maintenance staff should be able to make minor repairs during the church year.

Slip covers to protect upholstered furniture between May and November prove economical in preventing wear and tear. For the rebuilding or recovering of furniture, the committee in charge should solicit competitive bids from reliable upholsterers. The color and types of material to be used should be approved by the memorials committee or by the authorized interior decorator. All renovations, redecoration, and reupholstering should be in keeping with the original plan for the church and its appointments.

### Waxing and Wood Feeding

The maintenance committee may find within the parish persons who are adept at caring for furniture and woodwork. In some churches a volunteer committee, responsible to the maintenance and operations committee, repairs all the wooden furniture and woodwork, and oils, waxes, varnishes, or shellacs the wood as necessary.

In some churches there are very fine wood carvings in the chancel. In many cases the communion table, lectern, pulpit, and perhaps the cover for the baptismal font are beautifully constructed of exceptionally fine wood. The maintenance committee should obtain the advice of an expert cabinetmaker or a maintenance specialist on the proper care of such important woodwork and carved equipment. The process, together with any specific instructions for the mixing of feedings for the wood, should be known by the sexton and the maintenance and operations committee. Usually maintenance can be taken care of by the church staff. But some wood carvings, such as organ screens, may need the services of a professional woodcarver or cabinetmaker.

For this reason the sexton, the maintenance committee, and the church office should have on file the names, addresses, and telephone numbers of persons qualified to do special repair or maintenance work, and also the name of the company or craftsman that originally made the important pieces of ecclesiastical furniture, whose advice might be valuable.

## WATCHMAN AND MASTER KEYS

Provision should be made for having the church premises watched when there are no activities in progress. Insurance rates may be lower if a sexton or a watchman lives on the premises or makes regular tours through the property than if property is left unattended. There should be precautions against fire, vandalism, and damage by weather due to windows being left open or by water from taps not properly turned off. The maintenance committee should make an absolute rule that, except during scheduled activities or programs, any unauthorized person seen on the church premises must be regarded with suspicion and questioned. Police protection and advice should be sought in handling intruders.

Sections of the building not in use during the evening should be locked by a responsible person, especially when young people's groups are meeting in the church.

Discrimination should be used in the distribution of master keys to avoid suspicion in case of a theft or a loss. The maintenance committee should make the following regulations:

1. No key is to be made or issued to an employee or officer of the church without approval of the maintenance committee.

2. A record of all keys shall be kept by the maintenance committee and an appointed staff member.

3. A set of duplicate keys to all lockable areas and cabinets shall be kept, preferably in a safe. Each key shall be identified by a label or tag, under the care of a staff member.

4. Master keys shall bear serial numbers or identifying marks, which shall be recorded.

5. An employee or officer leaving the service of the church shall surrender his key promptly.

6. Such keys shall be reissued only with the authorization of the maintenance committee.

7. The number of keys in circulation is to be kept at a minimum.

8. In the event that there are too many keys unaccounted for, possibly unauthorized duplicates, the committee should consider changing all the locks.

9. Every person holding a key should receive instructions, possibly in writing, as to his responsibility. The key should never leave his hands. He should open locked places only to authorized em-

ployees or officers and should be responsible for the conduct of the person he admits and, after the completion of the errand, for re-locking the door.

## THE MINISTER'S RESIDENCE

Most churches provide, as part of the minister's compensation, a residence called the "rectory," "manse," or "parsonage." Normally the official board assumes the "landlord's responsibility" for the care of the minister's residence. But the details of that care as regards the church and the minister should be stipulated by the governing board.

1. The maintenance and operations committee should be responsible for the care of the manse. It may appoint a subcommittee to confer with the minister's family periodically and make a report.

2. The maintenance committee should recommend annually the amount of money to be provided in the budget for the upkeep of the manse.

3. The insurance covering the residence should be adequate. The matter of whether the church or the minister should assume responsibility for insuring the household goods should be discussed.

4. The maintenance committee should welcome from the minister's family reports as to their immediate needs.

5. Responsibility for the payment of water, light, heat, gas, and telephone bills should be determined.

6. Responsibility for the maintenance and repair of such equipment as the hot-water heater, range, and refrigerator should be specified.

7. Responsibility for the care and maintenance of the grounds surrounding the manse should be allocated by agreement between the maintenance committee and the clergyman. Whether the minister or the church assumes the responsibility, the care of the grounds, shrubbery, trees, and garden should both meet the standards of the maintenance committee and be satisfactory to the minister's family.

Because the minister's family may be reluctant to make requests, a representative of the maintenance committee should periodically take the initiative in consulting the minister's wife as to her needs and wishes for the residence.

A careful survey of the minister's residence should be made annually. On the basis of such an inspection the maintenance committee may make a realistic budget recommendation for the coming year. The committee should inspect the fabric of the house, examining interior and exterior decoration, roof and gutters, foundation, basement, and heating equipment. The advice of a builder or a professional maintenance man may prove valuable. The church has an investment in property and an investment also in the morale and good will of the minister and his family. Care and cooperation in the maintenance of the manse property are therefore as necessary as in the maintenance of the church itself.

The maintenance committee should bear in mind that the parsonage is the home of the minister and his family, and should make every effort to ensure the privacy of his home and his family. The parsonage should be the minister's "castle," not another meeting place for the parish.

## METHOD OF PURCHASING SUPPLIES

The procedure for purchasing materials, supplies, and equipment needed by the parish should be systematic and efficient.

1. Under the supervision of the maintenance committee or a committee designated by the official board, a purchasing agent should be appointed through whom all orders are to be placed and by whom all bills are to be checked and payments approved.

The purchasing agent should be responsible to the treasurer or to the treasurer's office. The financial secretary may function as purchasing agent. If no staff member is eligible for the work, a layman should be appointed after due consideration of his availability, his willingness to serve, and his ability and experience.

2. When a department needs supplies or equipment, a written request should be sent to the purchasing agent.

3. The purchasing agent will have developed a file of suppliers and service firms. For example, the church may deal regularly with a printer whose services have been satisfactory. An order for printed matter should therefore be sent to that printer.

4. The purchasing agent should check, before placing an order, whether the budget provides for the item requested. If there is no such provision, special approval should be sought by the established procedure. Usually requests for "over-budget" items should be made through committee chairmen to the official board. Only with the approval of the board should over-budget items be ordered.

5. The maintenance committee should assist the purchasing agent in finding the best sources of supply, where the best service and the most reasonable prices may be obtained. Among the parishioners there may be businessmen that have contacts with firms that will offer the church substantial discounts on office supplies, cleaning materials, and so on. The purchasing agent should be informed of such contacts and should heed the recommendations of the maintenance committee when placing orders.

The purchasing agent should keep a carbon copy of all orders, and on receipt of the goods should have the department head who ordered them approve the bill for payment.

6. Before placing an order the purchasing agent should check the situation in each department to verify the need for the supplies requested.

7. Through the maintenance and operations committee the purchasing agent should convey to the staff and to the various departments any request for economy in the use of supplies and any suggestions for effecting savings.

## MAINTENANCE EQUIPMENT

To maintain its property, the church will probably have such equipment as lawn mowers, snow-removal machines, and waxing and buffing equipment, as well as supplies for daily use, such as mops, buckets, ladders, photographic equipment, and so on. Equipment should be cared for as follows:

1. Printed instructions for the care of each item of equipment should be kept by the sexton or the superintendent of buildings in an active file where it is accessible to the maintenance and operations committee and to any employee responsible for the care of equipment.

2. On the purchase of new equipment all the persons who will

use it and be responsible for it should be instructed in its use and care. For example, if the church purchases a power lawn mower that is to be used by the sexton and a part-time helper, both persons should witness a demonstration of the use and care of the mower.

3. Seasonal equipment, such as power equipment used in the summertime, may require special preparation for storage. The maintenance committee should see that there are housing facilities for important, and often expensive, pieces of machinery or equipment.

4. Equipment should be stored in inconspicuous places, out of the way of church activities, and should have the maximum protection against heat, cold, and dirt.

5. One person should be responsible for the care of equipment.

## OVERSIGHT AND CARE OF THE CHURCH KITCHEN

The oversight of the church kitchen equipment should be delegated to the women's society. Rules regarding the kitchen and plans for its care should also be in the hands of the maintenance committee.

Answers to the questions below should lead to the development of a sound policy and program for the use of kitchen facilities.

1. Rules must be established as to who has access to the kitchen. May the kitchen, its equipment, and supplies be used by outside organizations without the presence of a member of the kitchen committee or the housekeeper?

2. If there is a breakage of china or other equipment, what is the obligation regarding replacement?

3. To whom shall keys be issued?

4. Shall the cabinets housing silver and china be locked?

5. If there are storage cabinets or freezers for food supplies, who shall have access to them? What arrangements are there for purchasing foodstuffs wholesale, and how shall such foods be distributed to groups for activities involving the use of the kitchen?

6. How is the inventory of china, glassware, silver, table settings maintained? What is the plan for replacing broken and lost equipment?

7. If there is specialized equipment, such as dishwashing apparatus, coffee urns, or complex equipment or machinery, have complete instructions for its use been given to the persons appointed to operate it?

8. What about a check on the cleanliness of the kitchen after its use?

9. Are there adequate garbage disposal facilities? Is there regular and prompt pickup of refuse?

10. Where are the files containing instructions for the use of kitchen equipment?

11. What of seasonal or annual cleaning of such major appliances as the range, refrigerator, freezer, and so on.

12. What are the provisions for scrubbing, mopping, and waxing the floors and for washing the walls?

## INVENTORY

To serve as a source of information in the event of fire or destruction by some other act of nature or man, a complete inventory of the church equipment, furnishings, and supplies should be made annually. One copy should be filed by the clerk of the official board and another by the maintenance and operations committee.

Not only to supply information in a disaster but also to promote efficient, economical operation, an annual inventory for each department is advisable.

### Equipment

The church inventory should list each item of equipment and, if possible, the date of purchase and the cost. For items not purchased but presented as gifts, such as a typewriter or a mimeographing machine, the fair market value should be recorded.

### Furnishings

Chairs, rugs, tables, blackboards, lecterns, ecclesiastical equipment, pictures, bulletin boards, and so on, should be listed and their value estimated as accurately as possible. Furnishings added, replaced, or renovated should be noted. An experienced appraiser may be of great assistance in making estimates of value. His estimates might be used as a basis for insurance claims if valuable antiques or ecclesiastical furnishings should be lost. They may also focus attention on the need for greater care and better protection of valuable furnishings. They should also enter into the determination of adequate insurance coverage for the parish.

### Supplies

An inventory should be taken periodically of hymnbooks, prayer books, printed forms, letterheads, envelopes, mimeographing paper, notebooks, pencils, leaflets that are regularly used in the church program, and so on. Each department should be responsible for its own supplies. But one person appointed by the maintenance and operations committee should be authorized to make an annual and/or periodic survey of all the supplies of every department. Certain principles should be operative:

*a.* Sufficient supplies should be ordered to meet the needs, but ordering excess supplies may be unwise. It is better to have fresh material that can be quickly utilized than to stock large supplies that may deteriorate in time.

*b.* Supplies that are not needed and are not likely to be used should be turned over to the purchasing agent for distribution to other departments. If there is no need for them anywhere in the parish, the maintenance committee should sanction their disposal.

*c.* Before a supply is exhausted a replacement should be ordered. Placed near the end of a supply, a little reminder to reorder may obviate the inconvenience of running out of the item.

*d.* All supplies should be carefully guarded. Stationery, letterheads, mimeographing paper, and so on, may well be kept in a locked closet, with one person responsible for their distribution. This applies also to the maintenance department's supplies of toilet tissue, paper towels, soap, and floor wax.

*e.* Officers and staff members should regard the supplies in their care as church property. Conscientious stewardship should dictate that they are not to be used for personal purposes.

# RULES GOVERNING RENTAL OF CHURCH PROPERTY AND LOAN OF EQUIPMENT

The parish will, with great sensitiveness and with a feeling for stewardship, through its maintenance and operations committee, establish principles regarding the rental of church property and the loan of church equipment. The plan of one church is as follows:

### RULES FOR THE USE OF THE BUILDINGS OF
### CHRIST CHURCH
### PLEASANTVILLE, WASHINGTON

1. Christ Church of Pleasantville has followed and will continue to follow a long tradition of opening its doors to community groups that are devoted to the cultural, educational, recreational, and spiritual welfare of our area. (At this date in March of 19–, we note that some twenty different organizations use our facilities, beyond the many groups that operate under the direct sponsorship of the church itself.)

   The board, believing it expresses the will of the entire membership, wishes to hold to this tradition and, as we may be able to develop added facilities, to expand this outgoing ministry of granting the use of our properties and the services of our staff to yet other groups which are devoted to humanitarian service and the improvement of Pleasantville and our whole metropolitan area.

2. Through its Maintenance and Operations Committee, the board has recently studied the community activity in our church in relation to our constantly rising operational costs. This analysis shows that several thousand dollars of the annual budget of the Church are devoted to making possible this ministry to semiaffiliated and nonaffiliated organizations and groups in the community. In light of the fact that some of the groups now using the church facilities have inquired regarding policy and have asked for suggestions as to appropriate gifts which would help toward the cost of operation (light, heat, sexton service, cleaning, and so on) the following suggestions are being made:

   a. Application for the use of the building shall be made to the Church Office through the Executive Secretary and shall be approved by the minister and the Maintenance and Operations Committee of the board. It is urged that applications for the use of the church property be made as early as possible in view of the enlarging activity of the church itself and the necessity for careful scheduling of events.

   b. In light of the fact that the church policy tries to minimize money-raising projects, organizations using the property for such purposes should make clear in their application this intent and also give the reason for the money-raising project.

c. All organizations of Christ Church shall have priority in the use of the facilities of the sanctuary, the assembly hall, and the educational wing. Applications thereafter from other groups shall be granted in order of their receipt. In the event there are two applications for the same occasion, the application first received shall be given priority.

d. While the board does not set fixed charges for the use of the sanctuary or any of the rooms of the church, yet to offer a guide to various organizations, the board offers the following suggestions of gifts toward the payment of expenses, which would facilitate our operations and enable us to expand the role of community service.

(1) When the church is to be opened and one of the sextons is to be on hand for a regular meeting of a church organization, and an outside group meeting in the church numbers less than 25, no contribution would be expected.

(2) In the event an outside organization uses the church facilities during the day for a group numbering between 25 and 100, a contribution of $3 would be most welcome.

(3) In the event a group numbering 25 to 100 uses the facilities in the evening, it is suggested that a contribution of $5 be made.

To make the suggestions more concrete the following table has been drawn up for the guidance of groups using the Club Room, the Auditorium, and the kitchen. The schedule follows:

| Room | Day | | Night | |
|------|-----------|----------|-----------|----------|
| | *25 to 100* | *over 100* | *25 to 100* | *over 100* |
| Auditorium | $7.00 | $9.00 | $10.00 | $12.00 |
| Kitchen | 5.00 | 7.00 | 7.00 | 9.00 |
| Club Room | 3.00 | 5.00 | 5.00 | 7.00 |

If stage lights are used in the production of a theatrical, it is suggested that an additional contribution of $3 would be helpful.

(4) Outside caterers serving food in the church should be approved by the House Committee of the Women's Society, and the kitchen should remain under their supervision.

(5) Hot-water urns and coffee urns and the dishwasher in the kitchen should not be used unless the regular employee of the Women's Society or the church housekeeper is on duty in the kitchen.

(6) Applications for the use of china, glassware, and silver should be approved by the House Committee of the Women's Society.

(7) The board wishes to make it clear that these are not hard-and-fast rules. The board recognizes that some organizations with limited budgets, particularly those working with children and young people, might find such contributions difficult to make. We point out that in terms of the over-all cost the suggested contributions above are but a minimum of the operational cost involved in opening the church, providing utilities and a sexton.

(8) In the event organizations use the church property for an unusual number of hours or the meeting runs later than 11:00 P.M., additional contributions might very well be considered.

(9) The contributions suggested above should be made payable to Christ Church and placed in the hands of the Executive Secretary. Through the office of the Executive Secretary, compensation will be made to the sextons and other employees for added service. Therefore organizations using the Church are requested not to make individual direct gifts to any member of the staff, but rather to make the gift through the church office.

3. In addition, when the church proper is used for such distinctly religious services as christenings, weddings, and funerals, and to facilitate proper use, the board has established the following regulations:

*Christenings*

There shall be set times during the year for the public christening of infants during the morning service, but those parents desiring to have their children christened privately may do so by special arrangement with the minister and may use the church for this purpose without charge.

*Funerals*

There shall be no charge for the use of the church for funerals, whether of members or nonmembers, but the extra services of the organist and sexton shall be paid for at the following rates:
Organist—$25.00
Sexton—10.00

*Weddings*

In the case of weddings it is felt that it is only fair that some distinction be made between the families of members and families of nonmembers.

*Large Weddings with Rehearsal*

> Organist—$35.00
> Sexton—10.00
> Use of the church:
>   *a.* Members—no charge
>   *b.* Nonmembers—$25.00

*Large Weddings (over 50) with No Rehearsal*

> Organist—$25.00
> Sexton—5.00–8.00
> Use of the Church:
>   *a.* Members—no charge
>   *b.* Nonmembers—$10.00

*Small Marriages,* involving simply the opening of the church

> Sexton (if required)—$2.00 (When attendance of sexton is not required, there is no charge.)
> Saturday afternoons—$3.00

*Wedding Receptions*

If the other facilities of the church are used for a wedding reception, the following charge shall be made:
Members—$25.00
Non-members—$50.00

4. The appointed organist of this church shall be expected to play at all services. Should individuals desire another organist, the request should be approved by the appointed organist of Christ Church. No payment, however, should be made to the organist of Christ Church when another musician is at the console.

    The above-suggested contributions are to be taken as covering the staff of the church. Additional gifts to staff members are not expected.

5. The equipment and furniture of the church shall not be lent to any individual or group where the desire is to take that equipment or furniture away from the church premises. Exceptions are discouraged and require the joint approval of the minister and the chairman of the Maintenance and Operations Committee.

Another church that permits groups or properly qualified persons to take church furnishings or supplies off the premises has adopted the following form to be kept by a designated staff member:

---

CHRIST CHURCH

Date _____

Articles borrowed:

_____

_____

For What Group? _____ Date of Event _____

By Whom Borrowed? _____ Phone _____

Date Returned _____

By Whom Returned _____

Loaned by _____

---

Another church, noted for its competence and care in the supervision of all phases of the church life, has prepared the following instructions which are sent to all leaders of the church:

CHRIST CHURCH

October 18, 19–

To leaders of groups within our church:

In the past few years our church-affiliated groups have grown in number and activity. Of this we are justly proud. Our facilities are so much in demand that we are not able to accommodate outside groups.

With new groups, leaders, and committees it becomes necessary to reissue "Building and Equipment Use" rules, including some changes.

USE OF EQUIPMENT

*Audio-visual:* Public address, record players, tape recorders, projectors, stage spotlights, and so on, may be used within the church by competent operators, after the approval of the Director of Christian Education. The above equipment should not be removed from the church, except for church groups meeting outside the church, and then with the director's approval.

*Folding Chairs:* May be borrowed for church groups meeting in homes with the approval of the office.

*Kitchen:* See attached sheet "Use of Kitchen and Equipment."

*Dishwashing:* In fairness to our various-sized groups, and in consideration of the responsibilities of our church, the Trustees have adopted the following broadened dishwashing services plan:

"The church will assume the cost of dishwashing required by recognized church-affiliated groups for their regular scheduled religious meetings. Special meetings, parties, etc., of a social nature by all groups will be charged for dishwashing services at the rate of $1.00 per hour, at day rate, $1.10 per hour after 6:00 P.M. to midnight, and $2.00 per hour after midnight or on holidays."

Minutes, June 18, 19–

Please remember that failure to properly scrape, rinse, and stack dishes on West dishwashing counter places a greater burden on kitchen help and increases the cost of this service.

*Care of Properties:* Careless placing of cigarettes has marred the stage foot rail and the Fellowship Hall floor. Please use ash trays stored in the kitchen or smoking urns provided in Fellowship Hall. Carelessness with smoking and matches is a real fire hazard. Further misuse will necessitate prohibition of this privilege, which is now permitted only in the basement area and church offices.

Our custodians have been requested to reprimand persons causing abuse or misuse to church property and report such persons to the Trustees. Please care for your church property as you do your home. Report damaged furniture and equipment to the custodians immediately.

### USE OF BUILDING

*Scheduling:* Rooms, time, and date of use are now scheduled for regular meeting of present church-affiliated groups. All special meetings (other than small committee meetings) or social affairs must be scheduled with church office as early as possible, preferably at least one week in advance. Use only rooms reserved. Other rooms may be cleaned and arranged for another purpose. *Leave the rooms as you find them. Please close and lock windows before leaving room.*

Please observe the 11 P.M. closing hour, except by special arrangement with the office.

The following information is necessary when scheduling rooms:
1. Name of group.
2. Name of individual in charge of affair and his phone number.
3. Date of affair, including decoration and removal dates.
4. Start and closing time, including preparation.
5. Room or rooms required.
6. Number of tables and chairs and arrangement required. (*If possible furnish a sketch of table layout.*)
7. Kitchen facilities and dishwashing services required.

*Decorations:* Permanent wires are installed at rail level on the sides and rear of Fellowship Hall. There are also hooks placed at intervals below these wires. Please attach decorations to these facilities. Do not use tacks, staples, nails, or Scotch tape, as they mar the finish and pull paint loose. Do not fasten decorations to stage curtain. Wires may be suspended from overhead conduit pipe outside of curtain track.

House Committee of the Board
JOHN JONES, *Chairman*

### USE OF KITCHEN AND EQUIPMENT

*Coffee Urns:* Shut gas off. Empty and rinse urns. Do not adjust gas burners.

*Stoves and Ovens:* Start ovens and stoves on low and turn up gradually for best results. Do not turn all ovens and stoves on at same time, especially high position. Push damper rods in to heat ovens. Pull damper rods out to cool ovens. Shut electricity off when finished using stoves and ovens. Leave oven doors open.

*Dishes:* Scrape, rinse, and stack dishes properly in dishwashing unit along West wall. Keep shelf under the cupboards clear. If there are too many dishes to stack on the dishwashing unit, use carts for stacking. Do not use relish dishes as ash trays.

*No dishes, utensils or any equipment whatsoever can be taken from the church kitchen, with the following exception: When needed at either manse.*

*Silver:* Silver service, trays, and so on (used for coffee hours and teas) must be washed, placed in cupboard, and cupboard locked. When using the silver service, please put place mats under the coffee and tea pots to avoid scratching the tray. These place mats should be stored along with the silver service.

*Flatware:* Knives, forks, and spoons should be rinsed but *not soaked.*

*Cooking Utensils:* Put to soak.

*Table Coverings:* Lace tablecloths used for coffee hour and teas. Linen tablecloths used for banquets and special luncheons must be folded ready for laundry.

Place mats used for Association lunches, Circle lunches, and some dinners. White paper used for University of Life dinners, Canvassers' dinners, Laymen's dinners, All Twos suppers.

*Food:* All left-over food in kitchen and refrigerator must be disposed of. Food should not be taken out in kitchen dishes. If left-over food is to be taken home, use paper plates, foil, or waxed paper. Put all garbage in garbage containers, all cans and broken dishes in separate containers.

Special Instructions: Boards are provided—do not cut vegetables, and so on, on metal or Formica surfaces.

Report all breakage to House Chairman.

Supply cupboards must be locked.

See that all electrical equipment is disconnected when not in use. Be sure the exhaust blower in kitchen is shut off; switch marked *"fan"* is to right side of East door in kitchen. Candle boards should be cleaned after using.

Any groups arranging for outside caterers, please get instructions for this use of kitchen from the House Chairman of the Women's Association.

MRS. GEORGE STERLING
*House Chairman, Women's Association*

In such definite statements the church staff and those who have active responsibility in the life of the church have clear direction for ordered programs.

## SPECIAL CHURCH EQUIPMENT

Most Protestant churches have certain equipment that requires special attention and care.

### Vestments

The type and extensiveness of clergy vestments are in keeping with ecclesiastical tradition of the church. Some churches provide vestments for the active clergy and for visiting ecclesiastics. In other churches the vestments are the personal property of the clergyman. Whether the vestments are owned individually or by the parish, they must be properly cared for.

*a.* There should be a suitable place on the church property for storing ecclesiastical vestments. It should be accessible, clean, and, in some instances, temperature-controlled and free from dampness, bright light, and insects.

*b.* The vestments should be checked periodically for cleanliness, proper pressing, and needed repairs.

*c.* A woman, perhaps a member of the chancel or the choir robing committee, should be put in charge of the vestments and ecclesiastical accouterments.

*d.* For the comfort of the clergyman, vestments of different weights suitable for cold and hot weather should be considered.

*e.* If the clergyman is likely to be exposed to drafts when greeting parishioners in the narthex after the worship service, he may appreciate an ecclesiastical cloak. The person in charge of the vestments should see that the garments are at their proper place when needed. The sexton or an appointed usher may help the clergyman at the time of worship services by seeing that the proper vestments are available and, if necessary, assisting him in robing himself for worship service. In many Scottish churches this role is filled by the beadle. American churches may profit from this ancient custom of giving attention to the comfort and appearance of the clergy.

### Choir Robes

Under the direction of the music committee and with the concurrence of the minister of music, the following items should be considered in formulating a policy regarding choir robes.

*a.* Suitable robes should be provided for all choristers. The type of robe, the color, quality of material, and so on should be determined by the music committee, preferably with the advice of an interior decorator. The color and style of the robes should harmonize with the color scheme and architecture of the church. The comfort of the choristers and the wearability of the robes should be taken into consideration. It should be borne in mind that robes that tend to fade soon lose their freshness and attractiveness.

*b.* Before the robes are ordered, a plan for payment should be approved by the official board through the music committee.

*c.* Dustproof, lightproof, and mothproof storage facilities should be provided. They should be easily accessible to the choristers and conveniently near toilet facilities.

*d.* There should be separate dressing places for men and women. Someone appointed by the minister of music or under the direction of the choir guild should be in charge of the robes and, if possible, should be available when the choirs, especially the children's and youth's choirs, are robing themselves for a worship service.

*e.* Robes should be made according to individual measurements so they will fit properly. In the case of children and young people, growth in size must be taken into consideration.

*f.* At the beginning of the church year each singer should be assigned a robe identified by a number or a label inside the collar.

*g.* After the services, possibly under the supervision of the robing chairman, the choristers should hang their robes in the closet in a certain order so that for the next worship service each singer may quickly find his garment.

*h*. The music committee should see that there is budgetary allocation for the annual cleaning of robes.

*i*. A seamstress may be appointed to keep robes in good repair.

*j*. Choir vestments such as a white collar or cotta may require periodic laundering. A plan for such regular cleansing, pressing, and if necessary starching should be established by the music committee and be carried out by the organist and the choirmaster. In some churches each chorister voluntarily assumes responsibility for the cleanliness of his robe, cotta, and collar. Other churches find it more advantageous to have one person or a service group take care of cleansing all the robes and choir equipment.

*k*. Special attention should be given to the care of robes during the summertime or any other protracted period when they are not in use. The robes should be put in sealed bags, or other precautions should be taken against damage by moths.

*l*. It is advisable to keep the choir robes in closets that can be sealed and locked.

### Communion Plate and Ware

Some churches have valuable communion silver, and every parish has equipment for the sacrament of the Lord's Supper that should be treated carefully and reverently. The following plan should prove satisfactory.

*a*. Any exceptionally valuable communion plate must be kept in a safe place. If possible, every church should have either a sacristy or another area set aside for the housing, cleansing, and arranging of the communion plate and the elements.

*b*. The clergyman should inform the committee in charge of preparations for Communion which equipment he wishes used.

*c*. The chancel committee or a special committee may be appointed to supervise the preparation of the communion ware and the elements.

*d*. The committee should be informed of the dates on which Communion is to be administered, so that they may arrange the communion vessels on the altar according to the clergyman's instructions.

*e*. Observing the sacredness of the occasion, the committee should be unobtrusive in placing the elements in their appointed places and in removing, cleansing, and putting them away.

*f.* In parishes where the elements are passed to the congregation by the elders, the communion glasses should be returned to the serving trays or placed in the holders attached to the pews, and should be collected by the ushers after the congregation has left the sanctuary.

*g.* The committee should see that linens or cloths used in the administration of the sacrament are promptly laundered and put away spotless.

*h.* The silver should be burnished, the glasses or crystal should be sparkling clean, and there should be no finger marks. Glasses with chipped rims should, of course, be replaced.

*i.* If the elders assist the clergy in the administration of the sacrament, their chairman may serve as a liaison with the committee in charge of communion supplies and equipment and report to the official board the need for additional supplies or replacements.

*j.* Since Communion may be administered in more than one way, the clergyman is the person who should determine the form of the service and should recommend the persons who are to care for the communion ware and the elements.

### The Music Library

Since music is an important part in the church program, the music committee should plan to purchase scores and provide for their care. The following points should be noted:

*a.* Provision should be made in the annual budget for the purchase of choral music which should be in the care of the director or minister of music.

*b.* A music librarian may be of great assistance to the director.

*c.* Scores should be catalogued and preserved carefully. Special boxes or folios, obtainable from music supply houses, are the most suitable means of filing sheet music.

*d.* Under the direction of the minister of music, the scores for the selections to be rehearsed by the choir should be placed on the rehearsal seats by the church librarian before the rehearsal, and collected after the rehearsal. They should be in place for the worship service.

*e.* Each sheet of music should be stamped "The Property of the Music Department of Christ Church."

*f.* Music not in use should be filed in cabinets that are dustproof and moistureproof to prevent mildew.

*g.* The library should be situated near the office of the director of music and close to the rehearsal room.

*h.* A permanent file of all the compositions in the library should be kept in the office of the minister of music. A card for each box or folio of music should indicate the names of the composition and the composer and the number of copies on hand, and should have a reference number to the box or folio in the library. The cards should be alphabetized by composers' names.

*i.* The music library should have for each singer a folder in which the scores are arranged in the order in which they are to be sung at the worship service. The folders should be ready for the singers in the robing room.

### Stained-Glass Windows

*a.* If stained-glass windows are to be installed in the sanctuary, the official board, through a special committee, should consult a designer and craftsman. With the counsel and approval of the clergyman, the board should decide on the theme or motif to be expressed in the windows, and should request the artist to submit an over-all design, with detailed sketches, preferably in color for the approval of the board.

*b.* Some churches acquire stained-glass windows one by one over the years as memorial gifts from parishioners. If this is an acceptable program, the congregation should be so informed, and the memorial committee should be authorized to further the plan by conferring with interested parishioners.

All records, correspondence, plans, specifications, and sketches pertaining to the windows should be retained permanently by the church. While the project is under way the file may suitably be in the hands of the memorial committee, but upon its completion all records and correspondence should be placed in the church archives.

*c,* The official board should consider the preparation of a brochure describing the iconography, symbolism, and history of the stained-glass windows. This will be helpful in the education program with children and will be of great interest to visitors as well as to regular members of the parish.

*d.* Instructions for the care of the windows should be given by the artist and the craftsman to the maintenance committee and the sexton.

*e.* The insurance committee should see that the windows are adequately covered in the insurance policies.

*f.* The windows should be protected on the outside to avoid possible breakage.

*g.* The maintenance committee should plan for the proper cleaning of the windows, and should inspect them periodically and make the necessary repairs.

*h.* A specific craftsman approved by the original craftsman should be employed to repair a stained-glass window. His name, address, and telephone number should be on file with the maintenance committee and with a staff member.

### The Nursery School

Churches that operate a day nursery school or have a program for preschool children use equipment that requires special attention. Those responsible for the purchase and oversight of such equipment should be guided by the following considerations:

*a.* Before equipment is purchased the following questions should be answered in the affirmative: Has the nursery school requested the equipment? Is it safe? Is it sturdy? Are there sufficient funds to pay for it? Will it be used sufficiently to justify the cost? Is the cost of maintenance relatively low? Is there adequate provision for storing it when not in use?

*b.* Those in charge of the preschool program should make available to the children the only equipment to be used during that particular session.

*c.* Children should be taught to handle the equipment properly and to put it where it belongs when they have finished with it. Order and care should be stressed.

*d.* Because equipment used by small children suffers heavy wear and tear, provision should be made for repairing and painting it as necessary.

*e.* If there is an outdoor play area, it should be under constant supervision to ensure the safety of the children. Hazards, such as loose steps, stones, a jagged stump, or a damaged fence should be removed promptly. There should be no objects which, if thrown or swung, might strike and injure a child.

*f.* If there is an outdoor playhouse or equipment in the play area, it should be made inaccessible to children not permitted to use it.

*g.* Robes or blankets for use during the rest period, if not provided by the nursery school, should be brought by the mothers and should be labeled for identification. Such equipment, as well as aprons and other protective coverings, also labeled, should be kept in lockers when not in use.

*h.* Equipment of the nursery school or preschool program not to be used by other groups in the same facilities should be kept in locked closets. If equipment is to be used by more than one group, each group should assume proportional responsibility for its care, replacement, and storage.

### The Church School

The religious education program requires supplies and equipment. There should be an established procedure for their purchase, distribution and use.

*a.* The religious education committee should see that funds are allocated in the annual budget for supplies, curriculum material, visual aids, and any other materials needed in the administration of the Christian education.

*b.* The director of religious education, the superintendent of the Sunday school, or some other designated person should order all curriculum materials and supplies, and should approve all bills for payment by the treasurer.

*c.* The director of religious education should have an office with storage facilities for curriculum materials and supplies.

*d.* The Christian education program may appoint a secretary to see that each teacher and superintendent has the materials and supplies needed for his class or department.

*e.* Unused supplies or materials should be returned to the director's office.

*f.* Visual-aid materials, such as film strips, projectors, and motion-picture machines, may be put under the care of an appointed member of the Christian education program. Films and film strips should be catalogued, and they should be kept in labeled boxes or containers where humidity and temperature will not damage them.

*g.* Each teacher should be informed as to what visual-aid materials are available so that she may request the material she wishes for each session. Well ahead of time these materials should be in the classroom ready for use.

*h.* Teachers should be instructed in the use and care of motion-picture and film-strip projectors. For complicated equipment the service of an experienced operator may be advisable.

*i.* One person should be made responsible for such valuable equipment as projectors and recording machines to see that it is properly covered and stored when not in use, oiled according to factory instructions, and examined periodically to discover need for servicing or repair.

### Tape Recorders

Some churches use a tape recorder to advantage in their music, dramatics, and religious education program. In considering the purchase of tape recording equipment the following questions will arise:

*a.* Which departments and programs will use the equipment and under what conditions? Who will be responsible for it, and who will be authorized to grant permission for its use?

*b.* Where will the equipment be stored when not in use? Will the storage space be locked? Who will have the keys? Who will have access to it?

*c.* Who will purchase and pay for fresh tapes? Will each department file its own tapes, or is it more desirable to have a central filing section in the storage area where the recording equipment is kept?

*d.* Shall the machine be rented to individuals or to outside groups.

*e.* Shall there be only one authorized operator, or may each group have its own operator?

One church has the following form for requests to use its recording equipment:

AUDIO DEPARTMENT
REQUEST FOR SERVICE

☐ Record Special Program: Program _____ Date _____
Tape to be given to _____ ☐ Filed for future use—How long____

☐ Record Wedding: Names _____ Date _____ Time _____
Couple desires: ☐ Tape ☐ Records—How Many____Send to_____

☐ Copy: ☐ Tape   Original tape number _____ Program _____
Dubb tape at: ☐ 3¾,   ☐ 7½,   ☐ 15 inches per second
☐ Records ☐ 12 in., ☐ 10 in., ☐ 7 in. at ☐ 33⅓, ☐ 45, ☐ 78 rpm
☐ Soundscriber disc (for voice only) Give to _____

☐ Special Recording Session        Convenient Date _____
Purpose _____

Above service required by_____ Requested by_____

## Record Players

For use by young people's groups, for congregational dinners, and for other parish events, a record player may be very desirable. Questions similar to those raised with regard to a tape recorder should be raised with regard to a record player. Normally record players should be purchased by the groups in the church that have special use for them. If this is the case, they should be the responsibility of the purchasing group. But if the record player is bought with general church funds and for the use in over-all church program, responsibility for its use, care, replacement, and loan should be specifically assigned.

## Motion-Picture and Still Projectors

The conditions that apply to a record player apply also to motion-picture equipment purchased by the church for congregational use. Storage facilities should be adequate, and one or more persons should be appointed to operate the machine, especially in the case of expensive, complex sound and motion-picture equipment. Someone must be responsible.

To guard against the purchase of "fad equipment" the church should ask itself, "In terms of the program we visualize will our investment be warranted?" A church may rent equipment for a limited period or for special occasions and, in this trial-and-error experiment, determine intelligently whether it is justified in purchasing such equipment for the parish.

## ADDITIONS AND NEW BUILDINGS

The matter of making major additions to the church property or erecting new buildings is too complex for a full discussion here. Only a few general remarks will therefore be made.

### The Building Committee

When the official board is faced with the issue whether or not to invest considerable capital in additional building facilities, it should appoint a small cohesive committee to study the matter, make surveys, and submit its findings. If the findings indicate the advisability of building and if the congregation approves, the building committee should be authorized to carry out the project from beginning to end. Its duties will include recommending the architect, studying bids, letting contracts, supervising, on behalf of the church, all phases of the construction, consulting with various departments and church activities, raising funds, following through on capital fund pledges, and supervising dedicatory ceremonies and celebrations.

### The Architect

Some churches choose an architect as the result of an informal competition. The general requirements and specifications are conveyed to each of several architects and a deadline is set when all the architects' proposals and sketches must be in the hands of the committee. The architect whose work seems most satisfactory is employed.

Other churches consult several architects and select one to do their work. They take into consideration the architect's familiarity with church architecture and with the church program, and also his adaptability and cooperativeness, since he will be working closely with the building committee. They also investigate his reputation for living up to promises and agreements in producing plans and exercising supervision.

### The Builder

Many churches find it desirable to hire, at the same time that they engage the architect, a builder who will work closely with him and with the committee in completing the project. Contracts may be made with the architect and the builder to erect the buildings within a specified sum. The builder is then responsible for constructing the buildings at a cost not to exceed the stipulated one. This program has much to commend it compared with a carte blanche arrangement where the architect and builder can proceed on a "cost plus" basis.

### Fund Raising

The building committee should consider whether capital should be raised by an organization within the parish or whether a professional fund-raising agent should be engaged for that purpose. Where sizable funds are sought and the undertaking has major involvements, the services of a professional fund-raising organization may prove most satisfactory. Under such a procedure no committeeman will be subject to embarrassment by seeming to be too pressing in soliciting funds from fellow parishioners. Besides, a professional fund-raising organization has the necessary technical experience to organize and conduct a campaign under continuous supervision.

## FIRE PROTECTION AND DRILLS

The church should make every effort to prevent fires, and should take every precaution for the safety of its congregation and its building.

1. Representatives of the fire-insurance company should inspect the property, and their recommendations for improving the safety of the church should be followed. When the risk is reduced, the fire-insurance premium may be lowered. The local fire department should make periodic inspections.

2. Refuse that might become a fire hazard should be disposed of promptly. There should be no accumulation of paper, and inflammable materials should be used with caution.

Fire extinguishers should be placed in the kitchen, boiler room, and other places where a fire might start. The sexton, the staff, and the ushers should know where the extinguishers are and how to use them.

3. The ushers should understand their duties in case of fire. If the church must be evacuated, the ushers should go to their appointed stations and follow the established procedure for opening exits and conducting the congregation to safety.

4. A plan for evacuating the religious education building should be established with the approval of the local fire department.

5. Fire drills should be held periodically during the church school year, so that teachers and children will know which routes to follow to the exits in case of emergency.

6. Printed or mimeographed sheets indicating the route for exit, together with instructions to be followed in an emergency, should be posted in the corridors.

7. All exits should be conspicuously marked and, if necessary, be illuminated as the law requires.

8. Wherever possible, fireproof equipment and fabrics should be used, especially for stage properties.

9. Every effort should be made to prevent a fire from reaching stairwells and sections of the church from which it would spread rapidly. The maintenance staff should have explicit instructions regarding their duties and their stations in case of an emergency.

10. In the construction of a new building and in the remodeling of an existing one, fireproof materials should be used for walls, ceiling, and roof.

The following plan of one church may prove to be helpful to other churches:

FIRE DRILL INSTRUCTIONS

### Christian Education Building

Nursery Room 110
Nursery Room 107
Preschool Room 104
Kindergarten Room 101

These classes will leave the building through the outside back door in each room.

Classrooms

| | |
|---|---|
| 209 | 308 |
| 210 | 309 |
| 211 | 310 |
| 212 | 311 |
| 307 | 312 |

These classes will use the stairway at the north end of the building, descending to the first floor and will leave the building by the door at the north end of the first-floor hall.

Classrooms

| | |
|---|---|
| 301 | 305 |
| 302 | 306 |
| 303 | 314 |
| 304 | |

These classes will use the stairway at the south end of the building, descending to the first floor and will leave the building by the door at the south end of the first-floor hall.

Classrooms

| | |
|---|---|
| 201 | 205 |
| 202 | 207 |
| 203 | |

These classes will leave the building by the double doors at the main entrance to the Christian Education Building.

### The Chapel

1. The people in the last three or four pews that are occupied will move to the back of the chapel and to the right, leaving the building by the main entrance to the Christian Education Building.
2. The people toward the front on the right side will leave the building by the new door at the right front of the chapel.
3. The people toward the front on the left side will leave the building by the door at the left front of the chapel.

**Church House Rooms** 1 and 2 (in the basement of the Church House)

These classes will leave by the side door and the cement stairway on the outside of the building.

**Church House Room** 3 (in the basement of the Church House)

This class will leave by the outside door at the south end of the room.

**Fellowship Hall**

See special sheet with diagram for their plan of exits. Posted in each room will be instructions and a diagram showing how that particular group will leave the building.

# *The Church Grounds*

The exterior of the church and the property surrounding it may provide a spiritual ministry for all who pass by. If carefully planned and maintained, it may extend the influence of the church to those who never enter the sanctuary.

## OVER-ALL LANDSCAPING PLAN

The governing board should engage a landscape architect to draft, at a stipulated fee, a detailed plan for landscaping the grounds of the church.

1. Under a written contract, the architect should submit specifications to the governing body and to the grounds committee. The number of copies of the plan the landscape architect is to provide and the extent of the architect's commitment to supervise the planting and maintenance of the grounds should be stipulated.

2. If the church is not in a position to engage a landscape architect, it should appoint qualified or interested parishioners to develop an over-all landscaping plan. Whether prepared by a professional or a layman, the specifications and drawings should be in duplicate, one copy to be filed by the clerk or secretary of the governing body and the other to be used as a working plan by the grounds committee.

3. The governing board should instruct the landscape gardeners to follow the approved plan exactly. Changes recommended by the grounds committee should be approved by the board.

4. The congregation should be informed that a landscaping project is under way. This should obviate embarrassment when church members make suggestions or offer plants for the grounds. The officers and the committee can explain that "we have an over-all plan which has been carefully studied and approved and to which we are committed."

5. However, to help meet the expenses of landscaping, the board may authorize the grounds committee to invite gifts for shrubbery or plantings and perhaps undesignated gifts to assist in establishing basic lawn plantings and in the upkeep and oversight in the early stages of the landscape development.

6. If the landscaping cannot be completed in one continuous operation, the committee should adopt a step-by-step program, giving precedence to the plantings that will most quickly enhance the beauty of the church grounds so as to give the congregation a preview of the beauty that is to come.

7. The governing board may authorize the grounds committee to place in the pews on a specific Sunday special envelopes for contributions to the landscaping project. Contributions may also be made as memorial gifts in lieu of flowers at the time of death. Then, too, a portion of the memorial gifts from the congregation for the decoration of the chancel at Christmas and Easter may be allocated to the landscaping project.

### Supervision by the Grounds Committee

The over-all landscaping should call for the type of planting that will most improve the appearance of the church and meet other practical and aesthetic requirements of the parish. Once the plantings are begun, continual supervision will be necessary.

1. The official board should appoint a grounds committee for this purpose. This committee may be a subcommittee of the maintenance and operations committee. Since the grounds require specialized attention, persons interested in horticulture should be appointed to supervise the lawns and plantings.

2. Depending upon the resources of the parish, the grounds should be maintained either by volunteers, by the sexton or the maintenance staff, or, under contract, by a grounds-keeping and landscaping organization.

3. In any event, the committee should state in writing what constitutes "maintenance." Maintenance should include mowing the lawn at regular intervals and to a specified height, watering the lawn during the summer, pruning shrubs and trees, spraying particular plantings, fertilizing the soil around large trees, aerating the soil, cleaning sidewalks and trimming the edges of grass.

4. A member of the committee should periodically inspect the grounds to see that they are maintained as prescribed.

5. The governing board should receive regular reports from the maintenance committee on the condition of the grounds.

6. Prior to the preparation of the annual budget, the grounds committee should analyze its needs and recommend that they be provided for.

7. If necessary, the grounds committee may enlist young people and adults for certain maintenance jobs. Such a project requires careful planning and supervision.

8. The grounds committee should provide storage space for equipment and supplies used in the care of the grounds. If the church operates its own equipment, the committee should check it periodically, take inventory, and establish the rule that there is a place for everything, and everything is to be kept in its place.

9. The problem of snow removal varies from church to church according to geographical location and driveway and sidewalk areas.

10. The grounds committee should take precautions to avoid accidents on church grounds. Railings should be placed alongside steps and wherever necessary to guard against slipping on icy walks. The railings should be kept clean and should be painted or polished periodically.

11. The grounds committee should cooperate with the religious education committee in teaching children and young people to appreciate the beauty of the church grounds and in inculcating in them a feeling of responsibility for preserving it. Superintendents of departments and members of the grounds committee should address the young people on this matter at departmental worship services or at their meetings from time to time.

12. Where safety demands it, the grounds committee should request the police to direct traffic in the church area during worship hours. Together with the ushers or monitors the committee should see that there are no obstacles to prevent the orderly movement of parishioners on the church grounds themselves.

13. Defective walks and steps on church property should be repaired promptly.

14. The grounds committee should see that the church has adequate insurance coverage for employees and other persons injured on church property. It should follow the advice of the insurance committee for the removal of hazards on the church grounds.

## SYMBOLIC GARDENS

To further its educational and spiritual purposes, the church board, with its maintenance and grounds committee, may find it desirable to create symbolic or memorial gardens. There are innumerable possibilities.

1. A portion of the church grounds may be transformed into a topographical replica of the Holy Land.

2. The garden may contain mementos from the Holy Land that enhance Christian devotion, though Protestant churches in general do not erect shrines or grottoes. The grounds around some Protestant churches include areas fraught with spiritual significance in the form of statuary nooks that invite prayer and meditation.

3. Some churches find their grounds are spiritually enriched by plantings donated by families in memory of departed loved ones. In such cases a plaque or another permanent testimonial should be installed on the grounds to indicate that the plantings are memorials.

4. Where the grounds are suitable, an altar or an outdoor pulpit, or both, may enlarge the ministry of the church, serving as a setting for weddings, youth gatherings, and study or prayer meetings.

5. Every memorial for the garden and grounds should be duly acknowledged and formally dedicated, and a permanent record thereof should be kept both by the archives committee and by the memorials committee.

## PROVISION FOR SEASONAL REQUIREMENTS

The proper maintenance of grounds and plantings requires a program and proper equipment for the seasonal demands.

### Spring and Summer

Care of the lawn and special plantings during the spring and summer should include seeding, fertilizing, aerating, weeding, cutting where required, and training of certain shrubs and vines. If the church staff takes care of the grounds, the committee should provide the necessary tools and equipment, should furnish instructions as to their operation and care, and should inspect them from time to time.

The church should acquire only the tools needed for adequate maintenance. They should be selected for quality and durability. Equipment should include a lawn mower, clippers and edging devices, pruning shears, hoe, trowels, a wheelbarrow, shovels, rakes, and grass and sidewalk brooms.

The committee should be prompt in replenishing supplies and in acquiring needed tools. It should negotiate with a garden supply or hardware store for a discount on its purchases. The chairman of the committee should be authorized to approve for payment all bills for materials purchased within the grounds and maintenance budget.

### The Fall and Winter

In the fall the gutters of the church must be cleaned, and dead leaves and clippings should be raked into a compost heap to help fertilize the soil. During the summer and early fall the grass and plantings must be watered. Though expensive, a permanent recessed sprinkling system under the lawns may prove economical in the long run. The gardeners should cover shrubs that require such protection from winter cold.

Snow should be removed promptly from the church sidewalks and entrances. The grounds committee should provide adequate shovels and whatever mechanical snow-removal equipment is advisable. It should have a plan for emergency snow removal in case of a heavy fall on Saturday night or early Sunday morning. If necessary salt and other chemicals should be strewn on icy sidewalks and steps to prevent slipperiness. Heavy mats should be used on the church floors in wet weather to prevent slipping.

Where there is a great deal of snow to be removed from driveways, the committee may advantageously enter into a contract with a snow-removal service stipulating that snow is to be removed before worship services and before children are to assemble for their religious education.

The seasonal storage of equipment is important. The manufacturers' detailed instructions for the care and storage of equipment should be given to the person in charge of the equipment, and the committee should supervise the care. The instructions should be kept in the committee's files.

## SPECIAL CARE OF TREES AND SHRUBS

The grounds committee should have valuable plantings of trees and shrubs checked annually by a dendrologist or a nurseryman. The committee should be concerned especially about diseased and dead branches that might fall and injure someone. The periodic advice of an expert in the matter of fungus and other plant diseases may avert the loss of beautiful, expensive plantings. Spraying, particularly of large trees, should be done under his direction at a time when it will least disturb the regular church program.

In an emergency, such as severe damage to a tree that may necessitate its prompt removal, the grounds committee should have authority to proceed without consulting the official board. It should be stipulated that this authority is limited to emergencies affecting the welfare of the parishioners and the fabric of the church.

## RULES REGARDING THE USE OF CHURCH GROUNDS

The church organization may wish to hold special events on the church grounds. The following principles should be applied:

1. The grounds committee should be in charge and should be consulted.

2. The committee should cooperate with the church groups and organizations.

3. However, this cooperation is subject to the principle that the church grounds are to be maintained for the welfare of the church as a whole. Therefore, if a group of boys in the youth society desires to engage in vigorous games on the church lawn and if, in the

judgment of the grounds committee, this activity would permanently injure the lawn, the youth group should not be permitted to use the lawn.

4. Groups using the grounds for special events or purposes are asked to fulfill the ground committee's stipulations regarding the care of lawns and other plantings.

5. With regard to whether or not neighborhood children and outsiders may play on the church grounds, the grounds committee should be given authority to make rules that are in the best interests of the church and are not offensive to the community. Where feasible, passers-by should be invited to utilize the church grounds for rest and meditation. Situations in individual parishes differ so greatly that no one administrative policy can be followed in every detail. But the principle holds that there must be respect for the church property. In some situations a public notice may be posted regarding the use of the church grounds. In the spring, for example, when the lawn has been reseeded and the grass is tender, the grounds committee may put up a "Keep off the grass" notice. In the wintertime a snow-covered slope may tempt children to use it for sledding. But if at the bottom of the slope there is a stone wall with a drop-off of three feet to a public sidewalk and a busy street, there is danger, and the grounds committee, with the governing board's approval, should forbid sledding on the hill.

In some situations the supervision of the church grounds at night may be a problem. The assistance of the police may be needed in keeping loiterers away from the grounds after dark when there is no activity in the church. The ground committee, church leaders, and staff members should cooperate in keeping the grounds clear and preventing destruction to grass and plantings.

The grounds committee may be confronted with many delicate issues regarding the use of the church grounds. Its decisions should be directed toward the over-all welfare of the parish, with emphasis on the year-in, year-out appearance of the church property; the safety of all persons concerned; and cooperation with all members of the parish and the surrounding community.

# *Records*

## THE ARCHIVES COMMITTEE

The governing body of the church should appoint a permanent archives committee to file and maintain important church records, minutes, and other documents. Working closely with the clerk of the board, this committee should see that periodically materials accumulated in his office are turned over to it. The chairman should be punctilious in the care of records and memorabilia and should stimulate the interest of other parishioners in acquiring and filing all materials pertaining to the program of the church.

### Historical Documents

The archivist should give particular care to such important documents as the church charter, articles of incorporation, deeds to church property, and legal documents pertaining to church obligations. He should also keep all past membership books wherein are recorded the names of the ministers, elders, deacons and communicants as well as baptisms, marriages, and deaths. For safety reasons and also to save space the committee may advisedly microfilm certain documents and records. If documents are placed in a safe-deposit vault in the bank, the clerk of the board should have a list thereof, and the board should designate the staff members who shall have access to the vault.

If necessary, the archives committee should consult specialists as to the best means of caring for books and records. Documents should be placed in dust-free containers. Leather-bound books should be handled in accordance with the best advice available.

The archives committee should inform the senior members of the parish and the leaders of all the church activities that it is the depositary for historical documents.

### Current File

The church archives become valuable historically only if they include a continuous record of current activities. The following suggestions should be helpful in maintaining an interesting day-by-day record of church activities.

*a.* Photographs of church activities, church leaders, and groups within the church, should be kept in chronological order, in binders with glassine envelopes. Each photograph should be dated, and the names of the principals should be listed on the reverse. If the photograph shows a special occasion, the details of that occasion should also be mentioned.

*b.* Some churches avail themselves of the services of interested amateur or semiprofessional photographers in the parish to obtain photographs of the official body, the church school staff, the leaders of the women's society and the church staff as well as pictures of special events. Historical records are enlivened by pictures of church activities, such as the worship service, children receiving religious instructions, and young people participating in their special activities.

*c.* News items about church activities should be clipped from newspapers and pasted in a good quality, sturdy scrapbook properly identified by the name and the date of the source and accompanied by pertinent explanations or comments. The name of the person in charge of the scrapbook should be publicized so that all items concerning church groups or activities may be forwarded to him.

*d.* The Sunday bulletins, the church magazines, and the agenda and minutes of board meetings should be filed chronologically. For easy accessibility the church magazines and the Sunday bulletins may be bound annually in two volumes. There should be sufficient copies of these volumes for the archives, the church office, and the minister's study.

*e.* In order to establish a permanent file for all church organizations, the archives committee should request that each organization forward to it copies of its minutes and records, or that the secretary transmit such material at the end of the church year. The materials must, however, be accessible to the organizations if needed.

### Contents of the Cornerstone

On the occasion of the erection of a new church or another important building, records and items of historical interest are usually placed in the cornerstone. Duplicates of the contents of the cornerstone may advisedly be filed in the archives. In any event the archives committee and the clerk of the governing body should have a list of the contents of the cornerstone.

One church included the following items in its cornerstone:

---

CHRIST CHURCH

CONTENTS OF CORNERSTONE

Copy of brochure issued at the time the campaign for the building fund was started in May 1955.

List of contributors to the Campaign Fund.

Press clippings relating to the Church Dinner at Marta Island and the various progress reports during the campaign.

Press reports at the time of breaking ground for the addition.

Photographs of breaking ground and other photographs relating to the project since it was first announced.

Annual Church Booklet listing church membership, committees, etcetera, for the year 19– and ditto for the year 19–.

A photograph of the minister.

Reduced photographs of the two colored perspectives of the project, as originally suggested, made by the builders.

A list of the members of the Church Expansion Committee and of its subcommittees.

A list of the Sunday-school teachers and parent leaders and other committees in the Church School.

A curriculum prospectus for 19– and 19– for the Church School.

A copy of the Church History.

Photograph of the 19–/19– governing body.

Two issues of the church magazine.

Photographs of the former ministers of the church.

---

### Blueprints of the Church Building

All blueprints and drawings for the church property should be placed in the archives. The maintenance and operations committee should have copies of certain detailed blueprints. To maintain and repair equipment, the maintenance staff must be familiar with the heating, plumbing, and electrical wiring systems of the church, and should therefore have access to the original plans. This will avoid damage and save expense.

The architect's sketches and drawings will be helpful in the event of any structural repair or modification in the building.

The archives committee should place the blueprints in cardboard tubes or in flat dustproof containers sealed and carefully labeled. The archives committee should list the contents of each safe, vault, storage closet, and filing cabinet in which material is stored.

### Principles of Safety and Accessibility

Since church records are preserved for research purposes and for use on significant occasions in the life of the parish, they should be accessible when needed, and they should be taken care of properly.

*a.* The archives should be in charge of the archives committee, and nothing should be delivered into other hands without its approval.

*b.* Application for the material should be made to the chairman of the committee who should have authority to approve or referee its release.

*c.* There should be definite rules as to whether the material may be taken from the premises. If historical material is released, the chairman should request a receipt therefor.

*d.* All historical material should be kept under lock and key, accessible only to the archives committee. If the committee has a safe, the combination should be carefully guarded in the office of the clerk of the official board. Files and closets in which archives are kept should have locks, and the chairman of the committee should have the only "active" keys. Duplicate keys properly labeled should be kept in an office safe in charge of a church officer or a staff member approved by the board.

*e.* To prevent destruction by fire the committee and the governing board should consider using fireproof containers. The advice of the local fire department and of fire-insurance agents may be helpful.

Though there may be occasions in the life of the church when it is desirable to present historical exhibits under the supervision of the archives committee, individuals should be permitted to use the archives only for such purposes as the writing of a church history or for the clarification of past policies and programs that may have some bearing on the current program of the church.

The committee should use discretion with respect to the individuals to whom it grants access to historical materials for research purposes.

If the church cannot provide adequate care and fireproof protection for its archives, the official board might wish to investigate whether the denomination maintains a historical department in which the records of the local church may be stored under greater protection. This plan would offer safety but not accessibility.

Though the committee should fully protect the materials of the church, it should be cooperative in allowing the archives to be used for the edification of the parish, especially children and young people. At the request of the religious education department, the archives committee may prepare historical exhibits and give talks about certain phases of the church history, illustrating them with documents and photographs from the past.

### The Church Seal

The governing board should place responsibility for the seal either with its clerk or its secretary or with the archives committee. With the approval of the board, the seal should be kept in a "working safe" in the church office, under the care of a designated staff member, usually the minister or the financial secretary. It is to be used only for official purposes and is to be affixed to certain documents only by the authorized person. The minister may need the seal for the certification of a church membership, baptism, or marriage.

The seal should be kept in a container such as a lined box or a durable cloth bag in which it is unlikely to be damaged, marred, or broken and should occupy a spot in the safe or strong room where it is not easily bumped.

## MINUTES OF THE GOVERNING BODY

In view of the fact that the minutes of the official board are of great significance to the local congregations, to the overseeing ecclesiastical body, and to civil agencies, it is important that they be accurate.

1. The clerk or secretary of the official board should be responsible for the taking of the minutes.

2. For important motions and discussions which may become a permanent record an assistant clerk or another person should also take the minutes.

3. The secretary in consultation with the assistant should type the minutes and send the transcriptions to the chairman, president, or presiding officer for his approval.

4. The minutes should be mimeographed or duplicated and mailed to each officer.

5. They should be corrected and approved by the official board at its next meeting.

6. Members of the board should understand that the minutes are confidential and should treat their copies accordingly. Copies of the minutes should be filed in chronological order by the clerk of the board, and the minister should keep a permanent file of the minutes.

7. With the approval of the board a copy of the minutes may be placed in the working safe of the church office under the care of an appointed staff member.

8. The minutes should be made available to the church auditor and should be returned to the office in good condition.

9. The minutes should be kept in permanently bound volumes.

10. When required by the denomination, the minutes should be submitted according to schedule to the overseeing denominational agency for review, approval, and suggestions. The board should act on the suggestions and should correct any errors in the minutes.

11. By action of the official board, the archives committee should be made responsible for keeping all the minutes in a suitable safe or fireproof vault.

12. There should be rules as to who shall have access to the minutes and on what basis they may be lent for reading to parishioners, leaders of church organizations, historians, or others.

## ANNUAL REPORTS

In one form or another, the congregation should be given an annual report of the work of the church. This may be done at an annual congregational meeting at which each department, organization, and agency of the church presents a report on its activities and financial status. These reports should be distributed in multigraphed or mimeographed form.

Where there is no annual congregational meeting, a full financial report for the past year should be mailed to the parishioners and subscribers of the church. In addition, sound administration and good public relations would suggest that the official board address to the congregation in writing a modified report on the status of the church and a review of its spiritual and material stewardship. Copies of such statements and reports should be preserved by the clerk of the board, the archives committee, the minister, and the church office.

The annual report, which may be lengthy and bulky, should be issued in an attractive form. One church, using 9-by-11-inch mimeograph paper, staples the pages together under a heavier cover bearing a picture of the church. The body of the report, covering some forty pages, is mimeographed on different-colored sheets. A letter from the minister, together with a table of contents, enhances the interest and intelligibility of the report. The contents include:

| | |
|---|---|
| Introduction | Christian Education |
| Officers for 19– | Nursery School |
| The Church Staff | Youth Department |
| Membership Report | Community Church Women |
| Minister of Visitation | Community Churchmen |
| and Counseling | Homesteaders |
| Board of Trustees | Ionans |
| Financial Report | Kinsmen |
| Church Treasurer | Koionia |
| Benevolence Fund Report | Lamplighters |
| Benevolence Committee | Mr. & Mrs. |
| Outreach Committee | Prospectors |
| Board of Deacons | Schooners |
| Deacons Fund Report | Sojourners |
| Ministry of Music | Twigbenders |

Sketches drawn by parishioners may add considerably to the eye appeal of the annual report.

The official board may deem it worth while to combine the annual report with the church membership list in a yearbook to be mailed to all parishioners. In view of the expense involved, the yearbook should be as comprehensive as possible, including information about the church program, the church calendar, and items about each organization, department, and activity.

Annual reports should emphasize the dominant spiritual values and ends of the church life by using a religious theme and appropriate Bible quotations.

## STATISTICAL RECORDS

Whenever possible, statistics should be presented in tables, graphs, or charts. The minister and the officers of the church will then be able to see at a glance the development and needs of the church.

The record of church school enrollment on page 303 is a convenient summary of the changes over a six-year period in the number of children enrolled in each department.

This report indicates a significant increase in enrollment over a six-year period in the junior and senior departments, later called Youth Chapel. The same statistics are presented much more effectively in the table below, where the enrollments in each department during 1950–1955 can be compared at a glance:

CHURCH SCHOOL ENROLLMENT

| Month | Nursery Class | Kinder-garten | Primary Dept. | Junior Dept. | Junior High and Senior | Teachers and Officers | Total |
|---|---|---|---|---|---|---|---|
| 1950  February | 24 | 84 | 172 | 140 | 156 | 47 | 623 |
| 1951  November | 36 | 92 | 149 | 158 | 129 | 56 | 620 |
| 1952  March | 48 | 82 | 143 | 164 | 136 | 52 | 625 |
| 1953  February | 29 | 95 | 143 | 186 | 168 | 79 | 700 |
| 1954  February | 46 | 97 | 167 | 184 | 214 | 85 | 793 |
| 1955  February | 35 | 91 | 183 | 186 | 246 | 96 | 837 |

CHURCH SCHOOL ENROLLMENT

| | | | | | | |
|---|---|---|---|---|---|---|
| 1950 | February | | | 1953 | February | |
| | Nursery Class | 24 | | | Nursery Class | 29 |
| | Kindergarten | 84 | | | Kindergarten | 95 |
| | Primary Dept. | 172 | | | Primary Dept. | 143 |
| | Junior Dept. | 140 | | | Junior Dept. | 186 |
| | Junior High and | | | | Junior High and | |
| | Senior | 156 | | | Senior | 168 |
| | | 576 | | | | 621 |
| | Officers and | | | | Officers and | |
| | Teachers | 47 | 623 | | Teachers | 79 | 700 |
| 1951 | November | | | | | |
| | Nursery Class | 36 | | 1954 | February | |
| | Kindergarten | 92 | | | Nursery Class | 46 |
| | Primary Dept. | 149 | | | Kindergarten | 97 |
| | Junior Dept. | 158 | | | Primary Dept. | 167 |
| | Junior High and | | | | Junior Dept. | 184 |
| | Senior | 129 | | | Youth Chapel | 214 |
| | | 564 | | | | 708 |
| | Officers and | | | | Officers and | |
| | Teachers | 56 | 620 | | Teachers | 85 | 793 |
| 1952 | March | | | | | |
| | Nursery Class | 48 | | 1955 | February | |
| | Kindergarten | 82 | | | Nursery Class | 35 |
| | Primary Dept. | 143 | | | Kindergarten | 91 |
| | Junior Dept. | 164 | | | Primary Dept. | 183 |
| | Junior High and | | | | Junior Dept. | 186 |
| | Senior | 136 | | | Youth Chapel | 246 |
| | | 573 | | | | 741 |
| | Officers and | | | | Officers and | |
| | Teachers | 52 | 625 | | Teachers | 96 | 837 |

All statistical records should be filed both for permanent and for current use by the church officers, departmental leaders, and the staff. Each department should have an active file or folder for assembling statistical materials year by year. Obsolete material should be turned over to the archives committee for permanent reference.

A statistics file in the church office will be very useful to ministers and church officers in comparing the effectiveness of a program in one year as with its effectiveness in other years.


## CENTRAL FILING SYSTEM FOR CORRESPONDENCE

The minister and the clerk of the official board, together with the church secretary and other staff members, should establish a central file for all correspondence not confidential or personal.

1. Since the central file is open to all church officers and staff members, no personal or confidential materials should be placed in it.

2. The file should be easily accessible.

3. The material should be filed alphabetically.

4. All correspondence should be filed by one person.

5. All folders in the file should be properly labeled. Additional folders should be used to avoid overcrowding.

6. Usually material should be removed from the active files after five years.

7. Obsolete material, labeled by years, should be filed in chronological order in a "dead" file.

8. Certain correspondence may be valuable to the church. Such letters stapled to a carbon of the reply should be retained.

9. The person in charge of the files should be responsible for the removal of material from, and the replacement of material in, the files.


## MEMBERSHIP RECORDS

The maintenance of an accurate roll of church members and a file of their addresses, telephone numbers, and other information that may be helpful to the church requires careful planning and meticulous oversight.

We shall discuss here the keeping of a working record of church members. The permanent ecclesiastical roll book is discussed on pages 313–315.

The officers of the church should determine the form for an ac-

curate, usable membership record. The record card should be durable so as to withstand years of use. The entries on the card will vary
according to the needs and the program of the parish.

One church membership card records the following information:

Marital Status
Number on Roll
Date of this Card
District
Others in Household
  Name
  Kinship
  Church Relation
  Date of Infant Baptism
Joined by
Former Church
Occupation
Membership Ended by
  Certificate
  Suspension
  Death
Date
Date Restored
Home Address
Home Telephone Number
Business Address
Business Telephone Number
Communion Attendance
Offices Held—with Dates
  Elder
  Trustee
  Men's League

Women's Society
Youth
Young Adult
Church Services (Offered /)
               (Rendered x)
Sunday School Teacher
Sunday School Secretary
Sunday School Pianist
Sponsor Youth Group
Scouts
Food Preparation
Food Serving
Choir
Pianist
Typing
Phoning
Help with Mailings
Use Car
Painting
Woodworking
Care of Grounds
Financial Canvass
Home Visiting
Ushering
Nursery Care
Sewing

Another membership card may list only the name, address, telephone number, the date and means of affiliation, and the names of
members of the family.

Many churches maintain a family history card on which are recorded all pastoral calls and useful information received during the
every-member canvass.

The church may wish to keep a record of the parishioner's attendance of divine worship and participation in the Lord's Supper.

The every-member canvass committee may find it helpful to record each year the amount pledged and given to the church by individual members.

Some church supply houses sell membership record cards which by means of punched holes can be automatically sorted into desired categories.

The membership files must be accurate and always up to date.

1. One person should be responsible for keeping the membership records.

2. This person should receive all information regarding a member's change in status or address.

3. Information regarding church members should be obtained from the school organization and from the post office. The information should be verified before the records are changed.

4. The members should understand the importance of notifying the church office of a change of address. For this purpose the church may from time to time send, particularly to out-of-town or peripheral members, a change of address similar to the one below:

---

CHANGE OF ADDRESS

Date _____

Name: _____

Street or
P.O. Box _____ Zone No. _____
                    *New Address*

City _____ State _____

*Up-to-Date News From You:* _____

_____

Signed _____

---

Some churches have two membership record files, one alphabetical and the other by zone or district. In such cases both files must be corrected as necessary to be brought up to date.

In a more complex organization, perhaps Addressograph plates will have to be corrected, and the financial or educational secretary or others may require notification. One church uses a 5-by-3-inch card for this purpose:

```
                              Date _____19__ Initials
Correct Name _____
New Address _____
Old Address or Incorrect Listing _____
Source of this New Information _____
                    Change of Record Made on
Master Roll                   Affiliate Card
Office Copy                   Director Christian Education
Pastor's Copy                 Building Fund Record
Associate's Copy              Mail-Away Card
Aide's Copy                   Notations:
Finance Copy
```

Another church has an equally satisfactory form on a 3-by-5-inch card for notifying the persons concerned:

```
Date _____ No. _____
Change of Address _____
Transferred _____
Married _____
Deceased _____
_____

Member's name

New Address                              Street and Number

Old Address                              Street and Number

Zone                                     City

Please change your records, initial. and pass on to next office.
    Church Records _____   Assistant Minister's Office _____
    Pledge Card Records _____  Christian Education _____
    Deaconess' Records _____  Date-Line Office _____
    Board's Records _____  Building Fund Office _____
    Financial Office _____
```

Still another church uses a mimeographed sheet of about 9 by 5½ inches, called a "Route Sheet":

Date _____

ROUTE SHEET FOR

_____ Married
_____ Address Change    _____ New Member
_____ Dismissal          _____ Suspension
_____ Death              _____ Out of Town

NAME _____

OLD ADDRESS _____

NEW ADDRESS _____

_____ 1. Pull both file cards    old number.
_____ 2. Clip to this sheet and give to Mr. Jones, who will give new zone and district numbers.
_____ 3. Change both file cards, including zone numbers.
_____ 4. File both cards.
_____ 5. Pull old address plate.
_____ 6. Cut new address plate.
_____ 7. Ink new address plate and file.
_____ 8. Give this sheet to Financial Secretary.
_____ 9. Give this sheet to Educational Secretary.
_____10. File this sheet for permanent record.
_____11. Women's Association
_____12. Directory changes
                    *In*          *Out*
_____13. Men's List _____    _____

A certain church has besides an alphabetical membership file what it calls a family history card, an IBM book that contains the names of all members of the church with their registration number, date of joining, and other pertinent material. A change in the status of any member or prospect is noted on a "change sheet." The date and page number of the sheet are indicated. A change with sample listings is illustrated here:

## CHANGE SHEET

Page number _____

Date _____

Distribution

Wom. Soc. ☐    Addresso. ☐
Ch. Sch. ☐       Fin. Rcds. ☐
Music ☐         File ☐

Membership Control:

Brought forward _____
Added this page _____
Total _____
Removed this page _____
Carried forward _____

| Reg. No. | Date Joined | Name | Address | Dist. | A M F | I B M | F H C |
|---|---|---|---|---|---|---|---|
| | | CHANGE ADDRESS | | | | | |
| 001 | 8/9/59 | Doe, John | N. xx Sagamore Road, Anderson, N. Y. | 5 | | | |
| 002 | 8/9/59 | Doe, Mrs. John | O. xx Cross Roads, Boynly, N. Y. | 4 | | | |
| 003 | 8/9/59 | Doe, Janet | | | | | |
| | | CHANGE NAME AND ADDRESS | | | | | |
| xxx | 4/8/52 | N. Jones, Mrs. John | N. xxx Midland Avenue, Pleasanton, N.Y. | 10 | | | |
| | | O. Smith, Jean | O. X Lee Place, Smithville, N. J. | 2 | | | |
| | | ADD PROSPECTS | | | | | |
| PROSPECT | | Joy, Mrs. Robert | xx Pondfield Road, Yonkers, N. Y. | 12 | | | |
| | | Frank, Peter | x Columbus Ave., Mount Vernon, N. Y. | 9 | | | |
| | | REMOVE | | | | | |

Items regarding the change sheet and its follow-up are carefully outlined for the staff and are meticulously supervised by the membership secretary. Further details of such a program must be carefully itemized for those responsible for it. One church lists the following items:

Step 1. Look up each name in the Addressograph file to learn the status: Member (M) Prospect (P) Mailing List Only (MLO)

Step 2. *If Member or Affiliate:*
 *a.* Jot down Church District on returned letter or slip of paper on which name is written. This is on Addressograph card only.
 *b.* Look up name in Master Files and jot down Registration Number and Date of Joining.
 *c.* Check to make certain you have the complete and correct old address.

These cards may be removed temporarily from the Master File but, since these files are extremely "popular," it might be just as well to take down the information as suggested in order to leave the card for the next person.

 *d.* All the above information may be secured from IBM book.

Step 3. *If Prospect:*
 *a.* Look up card in Prospect File and jot down any information that you might need for Change Sheet.

Step 4. *If Mailing List Only:*
 *a.* Look up card in Mailing List Only file and jot down any information you might need for Change Sheet.

Step 5. Type an original and five copies on Change Sheet Form: General information:
 *a.* Under the Name column, type group heading such as CHANGE OF ADDRESS.
 *b.* Names should be last name first.
 *c.* Under the Address column type first the New Address—designate by capital N. Directly beneath it type old address designated by capital O.
 *d.* Be certain to copy Registration Number and date of joining for members. Affiliates will have only date of joining. In Registration Number column abbreviate Aff.
 *e.* District means *Church District*—not to be confused with Post Office district. Old Church District will have been jotted from Addressograph card; new one will have to be looked up in the olive-green notebook containing just this information—unless otherwise known. District 16 is used for all of our County ad-

dresses, 15 for all of the County outside Pleasantville, also New York City and Long Island addresses.

f. *All* members of a given family should be listed—unless information to the contrary has been given. See IBM book for this information. The new and old address typed once will suffice for family. Each one's Registration Number and date of joining must be filled in.

g. Under REMOVE PROSPECTS, you will naturally have only one line, generally speaking. Under the Registration Number column and Date of Joining column type in caps PROSPECT. This is so in case of MAILING LIST ONLY—type it in.

h. Under ADD NEW MEMBERS—Since new members are added only four times a year, the list may be fairly long. Put in alphabetical order; single-space for members of the same family; otherwise always double-space *all* entries.

*Very special and Important Information:—our only source of membership number.*

Note upper right of Change Sheet—Membership Control:

Added this page _____

Total _____

Removed this page _____

Carried forward _____

Ordinarily on the *Brought forward* line the figure from the previous page will be just that—brought forward.

*However,* if new members have been added to the page, they must be shown on the *Added this page* line and then totaled with the *brought forward* figure. In case of removals this number must show on the *Removed this page* line. This number will naturally be subtracted from *Total,* making the figure under *Carried forward* to be just that, namely, put in the following page line *Brought forward.*

*Page number*—simply look at previous page number.

*Date*—whatever it is.

## The Follow-Through on the Change Sheet

After a change sheet has been completed and distributed, the person in charge of the file copy will have certain very important steps to follow. Note the 3 columns on the Change Sheet: AMF, IBM, FHC.

The IBM book contains the names of all members of the church with their Registration Number, date of joining, address, pledge amount, if any, Symbol (1. Family name, 2. Member of family, 3. Person by himself) and Church District.

1. All necessary changes must be made in the IBM book. Since there is little room for such changes, they must be made neatly and accurately. Use a ruler and a sharp red pencil.

   *a. Change of address:* Draw a red line through the old address *only* and above it print in the new one.

   *b. Removals:* If family leaves Church for *any* reason, draw a red line through the entire line of information for each member.
   *Special note:* If family has pledged, their name and amount of pledge must be transferred to proper place in IBM book so as to keep our financial records straight.

   *c. Change of name:* Find former name in book, cross off and print in new. Generally this is in case of marriage, and name and address will both be changed. However, often young couple retains family address until further notice.

   *d. Change of name and address:* Find former name, draw line through entire line of information. Make the new name entry in proper alphabetical place, transfer all the information. Watch need for *Symbol change* and be sure to carry pledge, if any.

After each of the above has been done, check in IBM column of the Change Sheet.

Go to the files (AMF—Alphabetical Master File) and make all necessary changes.

Check the AMF column showing this has been done.

2. *Prospects:*

   *a.* Type in on yellow PROSPECT CARD name and address (last name first) and all pertinent information.

   *b.* File in ACTIVE PROSPECT FILE—check off AMF file column.

   *c. Prospect—Remove*

   Remove card from ACTIVE PROSPECT file, print across top REMOVE: write reason for removal with the date and sign your initials under the Information section. Place card in alphabetical order in DEAD PROSPECT FILE. Remove white Addressograph card, and destroy.

3. *New Members:*
   Since there are only four joining dates a year, there will be a number of new members each time. These names will eventually be printed in the IBM book the next time it goes "to press." Until such time, a typed alphabetical list must be made with number, date of joining, etcetera, exactly as it will be in IBM book. This list is to be clipped on the inside cover of the IBM book. Keep a duplicate list, just in case.

4. *Members—Deceased:*
Remove card from AMF files; write *deceased* on card with date, sign your initials. *This card must be given to Membership Secretary.* Remove Addressograph card, and destroy. If a Mr. and Mrs. card, mark off accordingly.

5. *Mailing List Only:*
When this is designated on Change Sheet, type up orange-colored MAILING LIST card and file in proper place. (At present, in the front of the Dead Prospect file.)

*The FHC column:*
This pertains to the financial cards—pledges for the given year which the financial secretary handles. However, the necessary changes must be made on these cards. The IBM book will show if these people have made pledges. Make note of these and then make changes in the Pledge Card file. Check the FHC column when completed.

Each person in charge of the other five copies of the Change Sheet will make necessary changes for his group and/or records.


# PERMANENT ECCLESIASTICAL RECORDS

The clerk of the governing body should be responsible for maintaining permanent ecclesiastical records. He may delegate detailed work to a membership secretary, but should supervise the record and send it, when required, to the ecclesiastical body.

### The Ministers

Names of the ministers, the dates of their installation and resignation or retirement should be recorded in a permanent volume. In addition, a permanent file should contain details concerning their educational background, the offices they held, the specific services they rendered, and any other outstanding details of their ministry. A photograph of the minister, his wife, and his family may be included.

### The Ruling Officers

The record book should show promptly the name, date of election, and ordination or installation of each lay officer of the church.

In some churches the governing board has a book that each officer signs on the occasion of his first attendance at a board meeting. The historian or archives committee may also record for future reference biographical information regarding each officer, elder, or deacon together with a list of the committees on which he served and the outstanding services he rendered.

### Chronological Membership Roll Book

On his reception into the church the new communicant's name should be entered with a number in a permanent roll book. The number will be useful for chronological reference and for the active files of the church office. The roll book should have columns for recording the member's full name, the date of his reception, and the method of reception, baptismal information and change in status.

### Baptism

The church should keep permanent records arranged in columns of all baptisms performed by its clergy, including the full name of the baptized, the date of birth, the place of birth, and the names of the father and mother. The records should be easily accessible for reference.

### Confirmation

The name of each person confirmed should be entered into the chronological membership record book. A photograph accompanied by the names of the members of each confirmation class will be of historical interest to the parish.

### Marriage

When a member of the parish marries, the permanent records and all active membership files should be corrected promptly. The names of the bride and the groom, the name of the officiating clergyman, and the place, date, and hour of the wedding must be permanently recorded. The couple's name and address must also be corrected on all active records. Each church will determine what further information is to be recorded. The names and addresses of the witnesses to the ceremony may be useful sources of information ten or twenty years later.

### Death

When a member of the parish dies, the date and place of death should be noted in the permanent records, and the name of the deceased should be deleted promptly from all active files and Addressograph plates.

### Change in Status

When a communicant requests a letter of transfer to another parish, the letter should be granted with the approval of the officers of the church, if its ecclesiastical regulations require such approval. There should be a permanent record of letters of transfer. A suitable book for this purpose is one in which a stub for each certificate of transfer contains the name of the person transferring, the date, the name and address of the church to which the letter was sent, and the name of the person signing the certificate. The name may be placed on an inactive roll or dropped from the communicant membership list. Such changes should be noted in the permanent records and immediately in the active list.

## SPECIAL FILES AND RECORDS

### Family History Files

Each family should be systematically recorded in an active church file. The size card recommended for comprehensive information is approximately 8 by 5 inches. In each case, the information desired will determine the size of the card needed. Items of information should include family names, given names of members, spouse, children and others, birth dates, date of baptism, date of reception into membership, how received, date dismissed, how dismissed. Talents, education, and work experience should be noted. The address, business affiliation, business and home telephone numbers should be recorded. If the church has a zone plan, the zone, district, and group identification may be helpful information. The card should contain remarks regarding calls made by the clergy and others, together with notations that may prove helpful. The annual contribution to the church may also be noted.

A separate alphabetical membership file may sometimes be advisable.

Cards removed from the family history files should be kept for several years in an alphabetical dead file.

### Prospect File

The church should establish a file of prospective members, beginning with the names signed on visitors' cards or in the visitors' book on Sunday. If the church has contact with the Welcome Wagon Service, it may obtain from that organization the names of families moving into the community. All the church organizations should be instructed to turn over to the office the names of new persons participating in their program. Particularly the church school should be alert in taking the names and addresses of persons who are not members of the church.

The procedure for the development of the prospect file of one church is as follows:

#### PROCEDURE FOR MAINTENANCE OF PROSPECT FILE

I. SOURCES

Guest Book (see further instructions VII)
Pew cards
Communion and Easter cards
Hospital lists
Church School enrollment slips (see further instructions VI)
Newcomers (bank lists, etc.)
Church organizations
Ministers

II. ADDING TO PROSPECT FILE

1. Check each name against—

   a. Membership File
   b. Prospect File
   c. Dead Prospect File

2. Prospect card will be typed.
3. List of new prospect names and addresses will be typed and given to person who makes plates and charge-out cards.

4. Add appropriate tabs as outlined below under Tabbing Instructions.
5. Cards will be date-stamped, initialed, and added to Prospect File.

## III. TABBING INSTRUCTIONS

1. Left-hand side of card—for ministerial attention.

   a. If there are children in the family, a *blue* tab will indicate that religious education director should follow through on it.
   b. No tab on left-hand side will mean that assistant minister should follow through.
   c. *A dark red tab* will indicate that an immediate call should be made by the ministers. (If accompanied by a *blue* tab, the director of religious education should call. If alone, the assistant minister should follow.)

2. Right-hand side of card—joining information.

   a. *Pink*—Invite to join Church on Palm Sunday.
   b. *White*—Invite to join in June.
   c. *Brown*—Invite to join in October.
   d. *Light Red*—Invite to join in December.
   e. *Dark Green*—Will definitely join.

3. Each new prospect card added to the Prospect File will be tabbed to receive an invitation to the next joining.
4. After each joining, the tabs for that joining will be removed from the cards remaining in the Prospect File, and those cards will be tabbed for inviting two joinings hence.
5. Invitations should be sent twice a year to each prospect unless we obtain information that would alter the situation. If, after one year of being on the mailing list and receiving two invitations to join the Church, there has been no response from a prospect, a letter will be sent to them asking if they desire to be retained on the mailing list. If we do not hear from them, or they reply that they do not wish to stay on the mailing list, they will be added to the Dead Prospect file with the reason for removing them and the date noted on the card.
6. When people have stated that they will join the church, that information should be given to the membership secretary and she will—

   a. Send for letters of transfer if necessary.
   b. Add to "Will join" list.
   c. Put green tab on Prospect card.

## IV. CHANGE OF ADDRESS OR STATUS

1. All changes of address must go to the secretary in charge.

2. She should make up change sheets listing all changes of address or status. As she types each change she should also make the change on the prospect card.

3. If someone moves from the worshiping area, she will list them on the Change Sheet under "Remove Prospects," indicating the fact that they have moved away.

4. Those prospects that have indicated that they are not interested in this church will also be added under "Remove Prospects." However, the Church School and Choir departments will have to investigate to see if this change of status affects their particular lists.

5. Change sheets will be distributed to—

    *a.* Church School Department
    *b.* Youth Choirs Director
    *c.* Bookkeeping Department
    *d.* Addressograph Department
    *e.* File

V. MAILING PURPOSES ONLY FILE

1. Those people who are interested in our church but who we know are not candidates for membership will be kept in a separate file, "Mailing Purposes Only."

VI. PARENTS OF NEW CHURCH SCHOOL PUPILS

1. Duplicate slips are made out by the registrar on Sunday mornings when a new pupil enters Church School.

2. The white copies are given to the membership secretary, who will follow the procedure listed under II.

3. She will then give the white slip to the Church School Department for

    *a.* Adding to class lists.
    *b.* Adding to Church School class parents.

4. Church School Department will then return the white slip to the membership secretary to file.

## Church School Membership File

The religious education department should carefully design, for permanent record, a card that will serve as a child's record as long as the department has any contact with it. Soon after a child is born its name should be entered on the card, and all pertinent information, such as the date of baptism, the date of confirmation, attendance at church school classes from the beginners through the young adult level, should be added, including the offices held in church school and youth activities.

The card will be particularly useful in following up children and young people who drop out of the religious education program. When a young person leaves the community to go to school or college, his card may be placed in a separate file. The church school membership files thus withdrawn form a separate record for an important department of the youth work.

### Parishioner's Vocations and Interests

When individuals join the church they should be asked to tell their skills and interests. Some churches have established a file of vocational abilities or avocational interests on 3-by-5-inch cards. In the upper left-hand corner of the card is the name of the activity or ability. Below this are entered the name, address, and telephone number of the church member, followed by such pertinent information as the name of the company with which the person is associated and any remarks that might interest those who might avail themselves of his skill or ability.

### The Music Department

The director of music should have an active card file giving the name, address, telephone number, and business address and telephone number of each person in the orbit of the music department. The musical background and experience of the individual may give helpful information. The date when the person began to participate in the choral program, the offices he has held in the choral work or the special services he has rendered should also be noted.

Where a music department has a series of choirs ranging from children's to senior, its file provides accurate and delightful information that can be used to develop morale among the choristers. Like other departments, the music department may desire to use Addressograph plates tabbed so that mailings may be made to the senior or chancel choir, the young adult choir, or the children's choir.

The music department should give special recognition to choristers who have outstanding attendance records. The names of these persons and their attendance records should be filed by the department.

### Files of Suppliers and Servicemen

The purchasing agent should maintain a file of suppliers of materials and a file of service people. The files should be so handy that anyone may quickly find the answer to such questions as "Who is the church electrician? Where can we get the best buy and most effective service for mimeographing paper and supplies?"

### The Financial Secretary's Files

The financial secretary should file canceled checks and other matter related to the payment of bills that may be requested by the auditors or by a particular church department. Pledge cards filled out during the every-member canvass should be filed alphabetically. Working files pertaining to all phases of the financial secretary's responsibilities should be arranged alphabetically, either in his desk or in a cabinet that can be locked.

The financial secretary should retain all vouchers and requests for checks in payment of bills. The following form is simple but will give all the necessary information:

---

CHRIST CHURCH

*Check Request*

Please prepare check
payable to _____ $ _____
This check is to cover _____
Mail to _____ Charge to _____
Requested by _____ Date paid _____
Approved by _____ Check No. _____

---

If the church makes a weekly summary of gifts and contributions, the financial secretary should file such summaries in chronological order. The form on page 321 is adequate.

The financial secretary should keep a record of checks drawn, together with such details as the name of the payee, the number of

CHRIST CHURCH

RECORD OF CONTRIBUTIONS COLLECTED

Checks and other identifiable payments not in church envelopes:

*Name*                                                          *Amount*

_____     $_____

_____     _____

_____     _____

_____     _____

                                            Total     $_____

*Loose Offering:*

    First Service: A.M.   $_____

    Second Service: A.M.   _____

    Third Service: A.M.   _____

                                            Total     $_____

*Contributions in Envelopes:*

| | Total Postings on Envelopes (a) | Difference a-c (b) | Total Money (c) | Amount |
|---|---|---|---|---|
| First Service | $_____ | $_____ | $_____ | |
| Second Service | $_____ | $_____ | $_____ | |
| Third Service | $_____ | $_____ | $_____ | |
| Total | $_____ | $_____ | $_____ | $_____ |

*Prepared by:*                          Grand Total   $_____

  First Service _____      Total Deposit   $_____

  Second Service _____      Difference   $_____

  Third Service _____      Date _____

the check, the amount paid, and the reason for the payment. A check in payment of salary to an employee should be accompanied by a statement itemized as follows: period ending; account number; hours, regular, overtime, total; gross pay; deductions, withholding tax, hospitalization, group insurance, annuity; net earnings. Such a statement provides the employee with a helpful record, and the carbon in the financial secretary's files serves as a record for his office.

The financial secretary should file a record of payments of pledges made by the individual church members. The form will vary from church to church. One card, 8 x 5 inches, is shown here:

| Name | | | | | | | | |
|---|---|---|---|---|---|---|---|---|
| No. | | | | | No. | | | |
| | 1958 | | | | 1959 | | | |
| | 1st quar. | 2nd quar. | 3rd quar. | 4th quar. | 1st quar. | 2nd quar. | 3rd quar. | 4th quar. |
| 1 Sun. | | | | | | | | |
| 2 Sun. | | | | | | | | |
| 3 Sun. | | | | | | | | |
| 4 Sun. | | | | | | | | |
| 5 Sun. | | | | | | | | |
| 6 Sun. | | | | | | | | |
| 7 Sun. | | | | | | | | |
| 8 Sun. | | | | | | | | |
| 9 Sun. | | | | | | | | |
| 10 Sun. | | | | | | | | |
| 11 Sun. | | | | | | | | |
| 12 Sun. | | | | | | | | |
| 13 Sun. | | | | | | | | |
| Total Paid Quar. | | | | | | | | |
| Bal. due | | | | | | | | |
| Bal. Last Quar. | | | | | | | | |
| Total Due | $ | $ | $ | $ | $ | $ | $ | $ |

| No. | | | | No. | | | |
|---|---|---|---|---|---|---|---|
| 1960 | | | | 1961 | | | |
| 1st quar. | 2nd quar. | 3rd quar. | 4th quar. | 1st quar. | 2nd quar. | 3rd quar. | 4th quar. |
| | | | | | | | |
| | | | | | | | |
| | | | | | | | |
| | | | | | | | |
| | | | | | | | |
| | | | | | | | |
| | | | | | | | |
| | | | | | | | |
| | | | | | | | |
| | | | | | | | |
| | | | | | | | |
| | | | | | | | |
| | | | | | | | |
| | | | | | | | |
| | | | | | | | |
| | | | | | | | |
| $ | $ | $ | $ | $ | $ | $ | $ |

### Church Windows and Memorials

The secretary of the board, with the assistance of a staff member, should maintain a special file for all records and historical matter pertaining to the church windows and memorials, the donors, memorial inscriptions, and correspondence with the designer and fabricator, as well as information regarding insurance, the care of the windows, and the names of craftsmen competent to repair or replace windows. There should be a separate file for memorials.

### The Endowment Fund

The correspondence of the endowment committee should annually be placed in a permanent file in charge of an officer of the governing body, preferably the chairman of the archives committee, or in charge of a staff member assisted by an officer in requesting correspondence and records from committee chairmen.

### Church Organizations

In a separate file in the church office, there should be a folder for each organization containing copies of its programs for the year, the list of members, officers, published materials used, and a copy of the by-laws. At the end of the church year the secretary of each organization should deliver to the office for permanent filing all materials that may have permanent value.

### Confidential Files of the Minister

In his desk, in a drawer that can be locked, the minister should keep confidential files to which he alone has access. In 9-by-12-inch manila folders, labeled according to his work and inclination, may be filed delicate counseling matters with memoranda for possible future assistance to the persons concerned.

### "Do Better File"

Every idea or suggestion for the development or improvement of any phase of the church program should go into the "Do Better File." Staff members should know that there is such a file in the church office, probably in the minister's study. Annually, perhaps at a staff conference, all the suggestions should be reviewed, and constructive ideas should be put into effect in the program for the next season.

### Methods of Operation File

All specifications regarding modes of operation in the church office or organizations should be permanently filed. This includes, for example, the procedure for changing addresses in the office, mechanical processes in the machine room, detailed procedure of the every-member canvass, and specific evangelistic emphases. When the file becomes inconveniently crowded, it may be subdivided by departments. The file should be accessible for reference, but no material should be removed unless there is a duplicate of it. One person should be responsible for the removal and return of folders.

### Photographs

Photographs should be identified by date, occasion, and persons pictured, and should be filed, preferably in albums with glassine envelopes to protect them and to facilitate their use. If this is not feasible the photographs should be filed in chronological order. Should the file become unwieldy, a separate folder may be used for each organization or activity.

## BINDING OF CHURCH RECORDS

The church office, the church library, and the official board as well as the staff members will appreciate the convenience of bound copies of the Sunday bulletins, printed sermons, the church magazine, and the minutes of the governing body. Bound annually, these volumes will constitute permanent records of the church. Copies should be distributed as needed to the church staff and departments.

## SECTION VII

# *The Church Office*

The church administration should constantly strive to improve the organization and operation of the church office in order to strengthen the ministration of the church to the congregation and the community.

## SWITCHBOARD AND TELEPHONE EQUIPMENT

The following suggestions are made regarding telephone service:

1. The telephones should be located where they will best serve the staff and parishioners.

2. Rules should be made regarding the use of the office telephones for other than church business. If personal calls should not be made by staff members and parishioners, a public telephone should be installed.

3. Regarding the switchboard, the following points are important:

    *a.* The switchboard should be located at a point where the operator may also serve as receptionist.

    *b.* The panel of the switchboard should be so placed that the operator may conveniently perform duties other than tending the board.

    *c.* When the switchboard is installed, provision should be made for adding trunk lines later on.

    *d.* A desk, with a typewriter and other necessary equipment, should be placed convenient for the operator.

*e.* The operator should be experienced.

*f.* One or two persons should be trained to serve as relief operators when the regular operator is away.

*g.* Because the incoming calls must be answered immediately, there should always be an operator at the board during office hours.

*h.* When the church office is closed, the switchboard should be set up for night use. Staff members should be told which extensions have outside connections when the switchboard is closed.

*i.* A notation regarding the setup for night use should be kept in the receptionist's desk, handy for relief operators when the regular operator is absent.

4. When an incoming call is not completed, the switchboard operator or a staff member should write down a message. If there is a call for the minister when he is not in the office, the operator should note the date, the hour of the call, the name of the person who called, the number for the return call, and any other pertinent information.

5. For every outgoing long-distance call staff members should record the date, the hour of the call, the individual or company called, together with the name of the town or city and the telephone number, and whether the call is a business or a personal call. This information is passed on to the person who pays the telephone bill. Personal calls should be paid for when the itemized bill is received from the telephone company.

6. Courtesy should always be exercised on the telephone.

*a.* The telephone should be answered promptly.

*b.* The switchboard operator should immediately identify herself by saying: "Christ Church, Miss Jones speaking." The person receiving the call should also give his name when picking up the receiver.

*c.* A pleasing voice, courtesy, and attentiveness to the caller's problems or needs are telephone etiquette. If the person called is not in the office, the operator-secretary should say, "Can I help you?"

*d.* Courtesy demands that a telephone message be written down to facilitate the return call.

## INTEROFFICE COMMUNICATIONS

The morale of the church staff is strengthened not only by personal conferences, staff and group meetings, and telephone conversations, but also by sharing important information with one another through office communication.

1. There must be a central mailbox with a labeled slot or pigeonhole for each staff member in which are deposited the notes, correspondence, and mailings addressed to him. The box should be checked regularly to avoid an accumulation of notes that may occur within a few hours.

2. One efficient way to communicate is to send staff members "blind carbons" of letters. If the secretary is instructed to send a blind carbon to, say, the director of religious education and the chairman of the maintenance and operations committee, she writes at the bottom of each carbon "bc" (blind copy) and the name of the person to whom the carbon is to go.

3. Staff members should report to other staff members conversations that may concern them. Often a note will suffice. For example, "Bill: Talked to Mrs. X. Her problem is serious. Give her special attention. Call me for further details."

4. Carbons of the minutes of committee meetings and reports should be shared with any staff member who may profit by them. They may be addressed in pencil in the upper left-hand corner, for example, "To Jim Smith" or "To Mary Jones".

5. After every special occasion, such as a congregational dinner followed by a special program, staff members should promptly send in writing to the person responsible for the program their suggestions for improvement in the future. These suggestions should be filed in the "Do Better File."

On the following pages are sample forms for interoffice communication.

The form for recording long-distance telephone calls is mimeographed on an 8½-by-5¼-inch sheet. It is shown at the top of page 329.

LONG-DISTANCE TELEPHONE CALLS

Date: _____

Phone call to _____
                              (City)

Number _____

Call made by _____

Charge to: Church _____

             Personal _____

The following form is used by the operator to deliver telephone messages:

To _____

Date _____ Time _____

WHILE YOU WERE OUT

Mr. _____

of _____

Phone _____


              Telephoned ☐   Please call him ☐

        Called to see you ☐   Will call again ☐

        Wants to see you ☐   Rush ☐


Message _____

_____

_____

_____

                              Operator

Often the minister's office is the nerve center of parish life. Some ministers attach a simple instruction sheet to the information they pass on to other staff members:

---

Date _____

To _____

_____

_____

    ☐  Please handle.
    ☐  Please note and see me.
    ☐  Please note and return to me.
    ☐  Please note and pass on.
    ☐  Please note and file.
    ☐  Please answer, sending me copy.
    ☐  Please prepare reply for my signature.
    ☐  Your comments, in writing.
    ☐  For your information.

Remarks:

From the desk of Dr. John Jones
CHRIST CHURCH
105 Walnut St.
Kansas City, Mo.

---

The following form may be helpful to parishes that wish to communicate with church and staff members concerning new people in the community:

CHRIST CHURCH
Fremont, Idaho

_____

The name given below has recently come to us through:
The Church School _____; Welcome Wagon _____; Church
Attendance _____

_____

Person has already been called on by:
Minister _____ Associate Minister _____
Director Christian Education _____ Parish Visitor _____
Name is being sent to:
_____ Women's Group
_____ Men's Club
_____ Couples' Club
_____ Clipper Club
_____ Central Club
New residents appreciate a friendly call of welcome. They like to attend a
church group with some member. Please report any further information to
the Church Secretary at (telephone number).

_____
(Parish Visitor)

To be noted by:
☐  Minister
☐  Director of Religious Education
☐  Membership Secretary

Often officers and staff members are not promptly or accurately
informed of a tragedy, difficulty, or emergency in the life of a
parishioner. To supply such information one church office circu-
lates daily a mimeographed "Rush Sheet" so that the staff may
bring their records up to date and may be promptly informed regarding the church membership:

RUSH SHEET

No. 21                                          February 1, 19–

*Death*

The Rev. Franklin W. Morton (non-member cont.), 231 West Fiftieth Street, died today. A memorial service will be held at a later date. Flowers will be sent to Mrs. Morton (member). Dr. Smith has spoken with Mrs. Morton.

*Illness*

John L. Barton (member), 4 Terry Place, is a patient in New York Hospital for surgery some time this week. Flowers will be sent and Dr. Meredith will be in touch.

## LIGHTING AND VENTILATION

The church office should be well lighted for efficient work, and adequately ventilated for health.

1. Windows should be clean to admit the maximum light.
2. Curtains, drapes, or blinds should be used when necessary for protection against strong sunlight.
3. Desks should be placed so as to receive maximum fresh air and daylight.
4. The office as a whole and all desks should have sufficient artificial light to enable the staff to work comfortably without eyestrain at all times of the day in all seasons of the year.
5. If possible, the office should be air-conditioned. Otherwise sufficient fans should be provided for the workers' comfort.

## THE PRINCIPLE OF PROXIMITY

The office personnel should be located with a view to efficiency and convenience in the execution of the daily working program.

Ideally the desk of the minister's secretary should be near his or within easy communication. If there is a director of the church office, his desk should be situated so that he can easily see all the workers and readily communicate with them.

If possible, storage closets for daily supplies should be near the office. Larger supplies may be placed in an inventory area not too far away. The machine room, with the mimeographing equipment and Addressograph plates, should also be conveniently near the office.

## FILING EQUIPMENT

At least three sets of files are needed in the church office: the files to be used by individual staff members for the daily program, the files for correspondence and for the weekly and seasonal program of the church as a whole, and the active files which should be readily accessible for reference. Eventually the "dead" files should be turned over to the archives committee to be disposed of or placed in the archives.

Filing equipment will vary according to the needs of the user. Some workers may find that a filing drawer in their desks will accommodate their material; others may need a two-drawer file the height of their desk. Another work program may require a mobile type of file. Correspondence and program material may well be filed in standard four-drawer steel cabinets.

Like other church files, the office files should be locked when not in use. The responsibility for special and individual files should be fixed, and access to the files should be limited. Anything removed from the files must be replaced where it belongs as soon as it has served its purpose.

The placement of the files should be determined by their appearance in the office as well as by their accessibility. Inactive files may be kept in older cabinets which should be placed in a storeroom or in some other inconspicuous spot near the church office.

Each folder in the files must bear an identification tab. For most church offices, simple, tabbed manila folders will suffice. Some church offices, however, paste typewritten labels on the tabs for the sake of uniformity.

## CHURCH VAULT AND FIREPROOF SAFES

Valuable papers, books, records, and documents, together with moneys in the church's care, must be thoroughly protected against fire and theft.

1. The moneys collected at worship services and on other occasions should be promptly placed by two church officers in a theft-proof vault or safe until the authorized person can count it, or until it can be deposited in the bank. Some churches make arrangements with the local bank to place their offerings in locked bags within the premises of the bank. Other churches have either a walk-in fireproof vault in the office or a heavy safe on the church premises where such valuables may be kept.

2. If the church has a vault, it should be used as a depository for: offerings and cash, the petty-cash box, the church seal, the chronological membership, the financial accounts, the record of parishioners' pledges, all important and irreplaceable papers of the official board, all confidential papers and items in the care of the church treasurer or of the secretary or clerk of the official body, important statements and working materials of the financial secretary.

3. Usually only one officer of the church and one bonded staff member should have access to the vault or safe.

4. If necessary, the clerk of the governing body may have a separate safe for his records and materials. He alone should have the combination, but a copy of it should be placed in the church's safe-deposit box in the bank. If there is more than one safe on the church premises, all the combinations should be in the safe-deposit box.

5. Access to the safe-deposit box and to all vaults or safes should be only with the authorization of the official board, and exceptions to this policy should be approved by the board.

## DESKS AND CHAIRS

The following principles should govern the selection of desks and chairs for staff members.

1. The aim should be uniformity in office equipment. Many churches and church offices have expanded gradually as the con-

gregation increased. Consequently the office equipment may be a hodgepodge. Uniformity may be approached by painting or refinishing used furniture.

2. Suitable desk chairs should be provided for the church secretary, and "posture" chairs improve the comfort, health, and efficiency of desk workers.

3. If the church is in a position to purchase new office equipment, it should acquire furniture that is simple, practical, harmonious, and attractive.

## THE RECEPTION ROOM

The reception room gives the newcomer his first impression of the church. A pleasant, gracious place makes the visitor feel welcome and kindly disposed to the church. Consideration should be given to the following items:

1. The reception room should be neat. The furniture should be dusted and polished.

2. The room should be tidy and free from litter. There should be nothing in the room that does not belong there.

3. There should be no accumulation of newspapers and no articles of clothing lying around.

4. One staff member should be responsible for the appearance of the reception room.

5. On a desk or a table should be placed copies of the church magazine and published sermons, as well as folders or pamphlets describing departmental programs or emphases of the church.

6. The décor of the reception room should be planned with the advice of an interior decorator and should be under the supervision of the housekeeping committee of the women's society.

## SUPPLIES

The church office should always have adequate supplies on hand. To ensure this, the following suggestions are offered:

1. The purchasing agent, usually a staff member, should aim to keep the outlay for supplies within the budgetary allotment.

2. When the supply of a particular item is low, that fact should be reported to the purchasing agent on a form for that purpose, such as the one shown below:

| OUT OF STOCK |
|:---:|
| Item: |
| Short Reported |
| Date _____ 19___ By _____ |

3. A running inventory of stationery, membership certificates, mimeograph materials and supplies, marriage books, baptismal forms, paper clips, pencils, rubber bands, typewriter ribbons, and other supplies should be maintained. The purchasing department should make periodic checks and should order the necessary replenishments.

4. The maintenance and operations committee should supervise all supplies and should provide a petty-cash fund for emergency and minor purchases.

## PRACTICING SMALL ECONOMIES

Every staff member should be a good steward of the church property, equipment, and supplies. He can cooperate in many ways, for example, by turning off electric lights not being used; limiting personal telephone calls and through courteous and attentive manner avoiding unnecessarily long, expensive conversations; using for notes the reverse of mimeograph paper; and practicing other simple economies.

## ADDRESSOGRAPH AND RELATED EQUIPMENT

A study of 200,000 churches indicates that more than 95 per cent have a pastor's study in which many types of equipment and machines are used. More than 45 per cent of these churches employ a secretary. Only 15 per cent of the churches with a membership of fewer than 250 employ a secretary; 50 per cent of the churches with 250 to 500 members need a secretary. In larger churches more than 90 per cent have the services of a secretary and the machines and equipment necessary for proper administration of the church. Of all the churches 90 per cent have typewriters, 3 per cent use a postage meter machine, more than 44 per cent have an Addressograph, more than 89 per cent have a duplicating machine. A large percentage uses the Mimeograph, a small percentage the Multilith. 6.6 per cent have either a built-in, vault-type safe or a standard safe.

The Addressograph equipment is almost a necessity when there are regular mailings to the congregation:

1. The best equipment pays in the long run,

2. The church should invite competitive bids to obtain the most favorable price for the equipment it purchases.

3. One person should be placed in charge of the Addressograph and the filing of the plates.

4. The Addressograph equipment should be located in a room that can be locked to exclude casual visitors.

5. If the church owns a Graphotype machine, it can save money and time by making its own Addressograph plates.

6. Addressograph plates should be tabbed so that they can be used for special mailings without being removed from their position in the file.

## MIMEOGRAPHING AND DUPLICATING EQUIPMENT

Most churches hand the congregation printed forms of the "Order of Services" and mail form notices of meetings and church affairs. For the preparation of such material a duplicating machine is a prime need. The person responsible for the work and the chairman of the maintenance and operations committee should canvass the market for equipment that will meet the church's needs, bearing in mind always that duplicating equipment is steadily being improved.

The servicing of equipment is so important that before buying a duplicating machine the purchaser should understand the terms of the guarantee and of the service contract, and should learn the name and address of the nearest service agent.

A spirit duplicator is efficacious in dittoing items for limited circulation.

The mimeograph machine should be of the best quality and should be guaranteed by a reliable manufacturer and with the assurance that servicing is available. Electrically operated machines are vastly more efficient than manually operated machines. Multilith equipment is more complicated than the Mimeograph. This fact together with the price and the extent of use should enter into a decision regarding the purchase of a Multilith.

## OTHER IMPORTANT OFFICE EQUIPMENT

### Dictating Equipment

The use of a dictating machine saves the time of both the minister and his secretary. The minister can dictate his letters into the machine while his secretary is engaged in other duties. In typing, the secretary can, if necessary, listen more than once to the dictated material and should, therefore, produce an accurate transcription.

Before purchasing dictating equipment the minister and the maintenance and operations chairman should compare the products of competing manufacturers. They should consider whether the equipment will remain in the minister's office or be transported to his home, and whether it can be used in the pulpit to record the sermon. If additional equipment is needed, it should be of the same type as the original machine so that parts may be interchanged. The equipment should be guaranteed and service should be available.

### Typewriters

Typewriting equipment ranges from used typewriters, which should have a guarantee, to the latest electric and automatic typewriting machines.

*a.* The person who uses the machine should be consulted as to any special requirements for her work and as to personal preference.

*b.* The typewriter should be covered when not in use.

*c.* The typewriter should be considered in relationship to other equipment already owned by the church.

*d.* The machine should be serviced regularly by a designated agency.

*e.* A typewriter with a wide carriage may be useful for special purposes.

### Letter-Opening Equipment

Many churches find that a letter opener makes for efficiency. A reliable office supply house will recommend one suitable for use in the church office.

### Adding Machines

The financial secretary's or treasurer's office of the church will find that an adding machine is an absolute necessity. The maintenance committee should study the requirements of the church office, and with the advice of the treasurer and financial secretary should acquire the machine that will best meet their needs. The machine should be in charge of one staff member and should be used by other members only with the knowledge of the person in charge.

### Folding Machines

A church that has frequent and heavy mailings will save time and money by using a folding machine. After analyzing its needs, the church should obtain the equipment that will best meet those needs.

### Coin-Counting and Other Machines

As the parish grows, the demands on the church office increase. When the mechanical operations are heavy and time-consuming, a coin-counting device and a sealing and postage meter machine will prove invaluable in easing the burden of the employees concerned.

### Duplicate Keys of the Church

Certain office supply manufacturers make a cabinet with hooks to accommodate the duplicate keys. Such a cabinet is especially useful during a building program, when there is need for duplicate keys to the various rooms and to the entrances of the church. Each key should be identified and should have a designated hook, and the cabinet should always be locked. One person should be accountable for duplicate keys and should make a record of every key handed out. Keys should be returned as soon as possible.

## STATIONERY

The church presents itself to its membership and the community in many ways. Even a simple matter such as the church stationery is important in its sphere. The person in charge of the church office should see that the proper stationery is on hand for every purpose.

1. The supply of stationery should always be adequate for normal needs. When supplies are low, they should be replenished well in advance of special mailings. Every staff member should have in her desk a sufficient supply of the stationery used in her office.

2. The business letterhead should state the name and address of the church, and also the telephone number, which is important.

3. Usually the letterhead gives the name of the ministers. The minister should express himself regarding the inclusion of the name of the director of religious education, the organist, and the choirmaster, or any others.

4. When a certain department is responsible for a heavy mailing, the letterheads should state the name and title of the head of the department.

5. There should be several types of stationery. The standard type is the 8½-by-11-inch sheet, but increasingly churches prefer for brief communications a letterhead half the standard size. Social stationery and post cards are also serviceable.

6. There should be an ample supply of mimeograph paper, both large and small, with the church letterhead. Whenever possible, the smaller paper should be used for the sake of brevity and economy.

7. Some churches find it profitable to enclose with certain corre-

spondence a self-addressed, postage-prepaid return envelope. Permission to use such a form must be obtained from the post office.

8. The church should have some very fine stationery on which to convey the resolutions of the official board and other memorials to people at a time of tragedy and in recognition of special services.

9. The church should provide the ministers with calling cards of simple design. Letterheads and calling cards are not intended to convey religious information or inspiration. This is accomplished more effectively by special material than by letterheads and calling cards.

## WORK SCHEDULE FOR THE CHURCH OFFICE

The director of the church office should plan the daily and weekly work schedule of each staff member. If the minister is the director of the office, he should confer with employees regularly regarding the program of their work.

If responsibilities are to be changed, the minister should confer with the persons concerned and should inform others who may be affected by such changes.

# Civil Matters

## A CHURCH LAWYER

The governing body of the church should designate the person who will look after the legal affairs of the church. Usually a member of the board or some other officer is qualified to act as the church lawyer. If there is more than one attorney among the parishioners, certain legal matters may be handled by two or more attorneys. Often attorneys render their services as a "contribution" to their church. The governing board must be careful, however, not to abuse this professional courtesy and should promptly and warmly acknowledge all services.

There are a number of areas in which the services of an attorney are needed. If, for example, the church contracts for a loan or gives a mortgage, the counsel and services of an attorney are needed. Or, if the parish is the legatee of a deceased parishioner, the lawyer may be asked to represent the church.

If the church is sued for damages in an accident on its premises, the church attorney will represent the defendant. The attorney should familiarize himself with local, state, and national laws regardgarding church property and its tax obligations. The attorney for the church is expected to serve the best interests of the church. He should be associated with the endowment committee and with other committees having civil responsibility.

## OBSERVANCE OF LOCAL AND STATE LAWS

It should be the policy of the church to comply promptly with local, state, and national legal requirements. The church attorney should be ready to contest any unfair discrimination or injustice against the church. He should also see that the church meets the legal requirements regarding the payment of social security taxes for its employees, and should inform and advise the clergy regarding changes in the law that affect the church.

If the church sells tickets on which a tax is to be paid, the official board should scrupulously obey the law in this matter. At least once a year the board should review the position and performance of the church with respect to compliance with the law. On the one hand, the church should meet all just requirements; on the other hand, it should expect equitable treatment.

## FIRE PREVENTION

Precaution against fire is a serious responsibility of the governing body. Every legal requirement for the safety of the church premises should be met. Fire-extinguishing equipment should meet the requirements of the local fire laws.

### Annual Inspection by Fire Department

To be sure that the church is meeting fire-insurance requirements and to fulfill its obligations to provide for the safety of the parishioners and the community, the board should request an annual inspection of all its buildings by the fire department. Recommendations for improving the safety of the property and the parishioners should be acted upon promptly. The insurance committee should consider the removal or reduction of fire hazards in expectation of lower insurance premiums.

### Fire Emergency Equipment

Following the recommendations of the fire department, the maintenance committee should place emergency fire-fighting equipment at every potentially dangerous spot in the church, particularly in the boiler rooms and the kitchen.

### Fire Drill

The laws or regulations of the fire authorities regarding the number of fire drills to be held annually in the interest of public safety should be obeyed.

## TYPES OF INSURANCE

The church should have sufficient insurance to cover the corporation in case of injury to persons or loss of property. The insurance program covering loss of church property by natural or other causes should be revised annually in accordance with an evaluation of replacements.

The public policies covering parishioners, staff members, and workers should be carefully reviewed periodically.

Special insurance against loss of or damage to stained-glass windows, objects of art, the organ, or other valuable equipment may prove economical in the long run.

The church should also be insured against loss by theft and vandalism.

The official board should appoint one individual or a small committee to supervise its insurance program. One such insurance committee is set up along the following lines:

### INSURANCE COMMITTEE

The purpose of the Insurance Committee is:

1. To protect the financial investment of church property through a well-planned and managed insurance program.
2. To establish the actual cash value of church property through the use of a competent appraiser.

   a. The actual cash value of church property in general is the replacement cash on the day of loss less depreciation, however caused.

3. To know the value of:

   a. Pipe organs—their attachments.
   b. Stained-glass windows.
   c. Valuable paintings, pictures, statuary, silverware, and so on.
   d. Motion-picture projectors, public address systems, and so on.

4. To hold public liability policies to protect the church against damages imposed by law for injury to persons using premises.
5. To hold automobile insurance covering bodily injury and property damage, fire, theft, and collision on all cars owned by church.

   a. Nonownership automobile liability insurance should be held to protect church when automobiles not owned by church are used in behalf of church.

6. Committee to review program regularly in order to keep abreast of the current situation and to approve the payment of premiums, as well as to keep in order the audit of policies.

## INSURANCE CLAIMS

The insurance committee, in consultation with the church attorney, should place the church insurance with one reputable broker. Though some parishioners may try to persuade the board to distribute the church insurance among the various companies they represent, it is advisable that only one agent handle all the claims against the church. The chairman of the insurance committee should immediately be apprised of any injury suffered by a parishioner or an employee while on the church premises. He should notify the insurance company and follow up the case until the claim is satisfactorily settled.

All correspondence pertaining to current insurance claims should be filed, and after settlement is made should be transferred to the permanent files.

## TAXATION ON CHURCH PROPERTY

The tax liability of religious institutions varies from state to state. The official board, through the church attorney, should pay all legitimate taxes but should claim any benefits granted to religious institutions, such as a reduction in taxes on a clergyman's residence. Where church-owned property is tax-exempt the church should petition for such exemption. If special taxes are levied on church or church-owned property, the board should seek, within the law, to free the church from undue obligation.

## LOANS AND MORTGAGES

In some parishes the treasury has authority to obtain short-term loans from a bank to meet the regular obligations of the church. During periods when income is lower than usual, as, for instance, to pay salaries during the summer, the board should be reluctant to grant blanket authority to borrow money. It may, however, annually authorize the treasurer to obtain such short-term loans as he deems advisable to meet the current obligations promptly.

Large loans for capital improvements or expenditures should be authorized by the finance committee and approved in each instance by the governing body. If the constitution requires, congregational sanction should be obtained. In making such loans the following points should be considered:

1. From which institution shall the loan be made?
2. Is the interest rate the most favorable that can be obtained?
3. Are the terms for repayment such that the church can meet them?
4. How will the funds be raised to meet the obligation?
5. When these matters have been decided the official board should authorize the church attorney or a finance officer to negotiate the loan.

Mortgages should be treated with even greater care than loans. Both loans and mortgages must be negotiated according to civil and ecclesiastical law. In some cases the local church must have the approval of its denominational judicatory before it assumes the obligation of a loan or a mortgage.

The terms of the mortgage should permit the church to complete the payment of its obligation before the due date. Generally speaking, the church will be wise to establish a time limit for repayment according to a preestablished plan.

# SECTION IX

# *Correspondence, Mailings, and Printings*

Through the written word the church maintains contact with its members, conveys information, stimulates interest, and strengthens the "ties that bind."

## THE PASTORAL LETTER

The minister may follow the old tradition of occasionally writing a letter to each member of the parish, to give him either information or inspiration. The letter should always be written for a specific purpose, as, for example, to initiate a parish-wide program for evangelism; to encourage attendance; to request support for a new service, such as a prayer meeting or a study group; to introduce a major project such as a renovation or building program; or to invite the parishioners to pray for the solution of a problem in the community. It should be prepared very carefully (see pages 351–353), and should be approved by a senior elder, and by the chairman of public relations before being mailed to the parishioners.

## SPECIAL NOTICES

Special announcements are conveyed less expensively on postal cards or in bulk mailings than by telephone and more accurately than by word of mouth. The parish should announce events well in advance of their scheduled dates, but should avoid mailing too many different notices. The women's society or the men's club, the couples' club and other major organizations should themselves mail notices of their regular meetings and special events.

Because everyone receives a great deal of mail, church notices should be brief, interesting, and, if possible, unusual and attractive to deserve attention.

## THE CHURCH MAGAZINE

To reduce the number of separate mailings, some parishes assemble all their announcements in one paper that they mail regularly to the church members. Church magazines are discussed in greater detail under "public relations."

Some churches enlarge the Sunday bulletin to include details of all parish activities and the order of worship for the coming Sunday, and mail this leaflet to the parishioners every week, Other churches mail once a month a magazine of larger proportions with a format different from that of the Sunday bulletin. Others, again, issue a bimonthly or quarterly magazine. Each church must determine the type of publication that will best serve its program.

## VARIOUS ADDRESSOGRAPH PLATES

On the mailings to parishioners all names must be correctly spelled and all addresses up to date. Otherwise, parishioners may be offended.

### Methods for Keeping Addressograph Plates Current

In the discussion of the church office (see page 306 ff.) is outlined the procedure for keeping Addressograph plates up to date. The person in charge of the plates should be notified promptly of any change in the status or the address of a parishioner. If the Addressograph plates are made by a company outside the church office, typewritten lists of the plates to be corrected and of the new plates to be made, together with the old plates if requested, should be delivered to the company as soon as possible.

Mail for persons whose Addressograph plates are being corrected should be addressed by hand from carbon copies of the lists of changes. Thus there will be no interruption in the delivery. If the Addressograph plates are made on the church Graphotype, corrections should be made promptly.

### Storage

The Addressograph plates should be filed in alphabetical order in special sealed drawers in the filing area of the office under the supervision of one person.

### The Labeling of Addressograph Plates

So that Addressograph plates may be used for various special purposes, they should bear a different color identification tab for each purpose; for example, a red tab for members of the women's society, a green tab for a member of the men's association, a yellow one for prospective members, a blue one for members of the young people's society, and so on. With tabs of the same color in the proper positions on the plates, the Addressograph can be set to run off addresses for any particular church group. The operation of the Addressograph should be in charge of one person.

## PRINCIPLE OF APPROVAL OF
## MAJOR COMMUNICATIONS

Before sending a major communication to the parish the minister and the head of the department should submit it to one or two persons with literary or public relations sensitivity for their reactions and comments. This practice may prevent the use of inept expressions or the possibility of misinterpretations. For the same reasons other staff members and organization chairmen should request the minister to read any communications they intend to send out.

## PRINTING

### The "Right" Printer

Parishes today use many printed letterheads and envelopes, and issue printed Sunday bulletins, announcements, perhaps a magazine, and possibly sermons. It is important, therefore, to employ a competent printer.

a. The printer should be located near the church, or else he should offer pick-up and delivery service.

b. The cost of printing should be determined by competitive bids for the entire printing program. It should be reviewed from time to time to ensure the official board that it is receiving the best service for the price paid,

c. The printing should be carefully scheduled, and the church and the printer should cooperate in keeping to schedule. Copy should be sent to the printer in time so that the printed matter will be available for distribution on the scheduled date. If there is a change in the schedule, the church should notify the printer, or vice versa, far enough in advance, if possible, to avoid confusion or unnecessary expense.

d. Both the church and the printer should make every effort to avoid overtime charges.

e. The church and the printer should agree on the amount of time to be allowed the church for the correction of proofs.

### Types of Printed Materials

The program of the church determines the types of printed matter needed. These may include envelopes, letterheads, calling cards, the Sunday bulletin, the church magazine, special notices, the annual directory, special brochures for some departments, sermons, and so on. The annual budget should provide for printed materials, with special allotments for such major items as the annual directory, the church magazines and the Sunday bulletin. The administrative leaders should see that printing costs do not exceed the budget. Additional costs should be approved by the official board.

## POST OFFICE—RATES AND REGULATIONS

The church should familiarize itself with the services the post office can render in bulk mailings. It should apply for a permit and arrange its mail according to postal regulations, so that it may be handled at the bulk rate for third-class matter. The church should consult the post office about notification of changes of address.

Many churches having a number of large mailings organize a volunteer committee under the direction of a chairman to assist in folding and in stuffing and sealing envelopes. The post office requires that bulk mail be separated into bundles according to destination. The person in charge of mailings would do well to ask the postmaster how delivery can be expedited. Church postage should not be used for personal correspondence. A refund may be obtained at the Post Office on unused prestamped materials and United States postal cards and stamped envelopes.

## PROPER FORM OF ADDRESS

The church office should be meticulous when addressing mail to a parishioner, in using his correct title—Mr., Dr., Mrs., Miss, or whatever title he requests—and in spelling his name correctly. Inaccuracies in these respects may unnecessarily irritate the recipient.

Every church office should have a leaflet giving the proper form of address and salutation for an ecclesiastical, political, or professional personage in ordinary correspondence.

## PRINCIPLES OF A GOOD LETTER

The failure of a church mailing to accomplish its purpose may be due to ineffective correspondence. Some of the basic requirements of good letter-writing are discussed below.

### Clarity

The letter must be clear. It should answer the questions, when? where? who? how? and why? If the religious leader finds it difficult to express clearly the spiritual message he wishes to convey, it is better to leave it unsaid than to express it awkwardly or unintelligibly.

### Brevity

Church communications compete for attention with hundreds of other pieces of mail delivered to every home. The shorter a communication is, therefore, the more likely it is to read, with certain exceptions. A letter consisting of a few sentences usually receives faster and better attention than a two-page, single-spaced letter with narrow margins. A letter should arouse interest and come to the point quickly, stating its information or message clearly and concisely. If the reader is expected to take some action, such as make a reservation by telephone, return an enclosed card promptly, or note the date of a certain function, the request should be stated briefly and clearly.

### Accuracy and Neatness

The appearance of a letter makes an immediate impression on the recipient. Wide margins and extra spaces between paragraphs make for an attractive appearance. Every letter should be typographically correct, of even color throughout, and free from mimeograph blurs and smudges. Defective copies should always be discarded, never mailed.

### One Topic

Each communication should deal with only one topic—the topic under which the correspondence will be filed for future reference.

## TYPES OF LETTERS

Church correspondence of necessity includes many personal letters involving individual situations and problems. The minister should acknowledge as promptly as possible all communications from the members of the church, and should instruct staff members, assisting them if necessary, to acknowledge services promptly and to fulfill, through correspondence, requests received from the parish.

There are several types of circumstances that call for substantially the same letter. For such purposes form letters, carefully drafted by the minister, the public relations chairman, and other competent persons, save considerable time and are highly satisfactory. They may be used for the following occasions and circumstances:

1. To greet local visitors.
2. To get in touch with a newcomer in the community.
3. To welcome new church school children and their parents.
4. As an invitation to join the church.
5. By the minister upon a person's reception into the church.
6. To invite financial support of the church.
7. To persons leaving the community.
8. To hospitalized persons.
9. To parents upon the birth of a baby.
10. Upon the placing of an infant's name on the Cradle Roll.
11. To parents upon the baptism of their child.
12. To couples married by the minister.
13. On the first wedding anniversary.
14. To students away from home.
15. To members of the armed forces.
16. To out-of-town visitors at the Sunday worship service.

Often an individually typed form letter may be sent to a number of people. In each case it should sound warm and personal, and perhaps have at the bottom a few words in the minister's handwriting.

The timing of a letter is often important. For instance, a warm personal letter from the minister to a new member within a week of his joining the church is more significant than one sent several days later. The invitation to pledge financial support to the church should also be thoughtfully timed. Some churches believe that two or three weeks should elapse before the finance chairman approaches the new member on this matter. In the main, promptness, courtesy, brevity, clarity, and warmth should be the guiding principles.

## SPECIAL NOTICES AND ANNOUNCEMENTS

The church makes several special mailings in the course of an active year. During the Lenten season, for example, there are announcements of special services and ministries. There are also announcements of the special activities of the various groups and organizations, and there are the parish programs for the entire membership.

The fewer the mailings, the greater the significance of the individual announcements. The church magazine (see page 362), which reaches the entire parish, carries notices of all activities.

Special notices should be interesting but succinct. Variety in the printing and the color of paper will help make them attractive. Notices should be printed and mailed as inexpensively as possible. They should reach the members on the most favorable day of the week, and always early enough to permit planning.

For notices of regular monthly meetings a form should be used that can be filled in by the church office. For example, "The regular monthly meeting of the official board will be held on _____ at _____ o'clock in the board room."

# Publicity and Public Relations

## THE LOCAL PAPER

The press is one of the best media by which the church can inform the parish and the community of its activities, services and ministries.

### Conference with Editor and Staff

The minister or the publicity director should, if possible, confer with the editor of the newspaper or, if the paper is large, with the religious news editor so that the editor may learn the significant emphases or progress of the church and so that the church may understand the paper's policy with regard to the publication of religious material. Information regarding the form and the deadline for submitting publicity copy should be passed on to the publicity chairman of the church organizations.

### Basic Principles

To ensure the best service, the relationship between the church and the press should be one of mutual understanding.

*a.* Church publicity personnel should be cooperative, courteous, and appreciative in dealing with the press. They should try to understand the problems of the newspaper and appreciate the efforts of the newspaper to serve them.

*b.* Copy should be sent to the proper person on the paper. If it is sent a day ahead of the deadline, the editor may be able to give the church news more space and a better position on the page.

*c.* The copy should be typed double- or triple-spaced, preferably 4 inches wide, on 9-by-11-inch paper to give the copy editor plenty of room for his changes.

*d.* The principles of news writing should be followed. Usually the questions when? where? who? how? and why? should be answered in the first, or lead, paragraph. The following paragraphs should elaborate. Arranged in this order the most important information comes at the beginning and will not be deleted if the article is too long, since cutting begins with the last paragraph, which should be the least important.

*e.* The material should have a "news flavor." The purpose in publishing an item is, first, to give information and, second, to be interesting.

## ADVERTISING

### Billboard and Street Signs

The cost of billboard advertising will prevent many individual churches from engaging in this form of publicity. However, a local council may pool the resources of several churches for advertising and may find it helpful to the Christian work of the community to utilize billboards or major roadside areas for such publicity.

Street signs giving the name of the church and indicating its location may be set up, with the approval of the local civic administration, at strategic points. Professionally designed, they should be attractive in appearance and brief in wording, and should be clearly visible to passing motorists. The signs should be painted from time to time. No advertising is preferable to slovenly advertising.

### Telephone Directory

For the benefit of our present-day transient and migratory populations the public relations committee of the church may deem it advisable, the budget permitting, to place in the classified telephone directory an advertisement giving the name and address of the church, the names of the ministers, and the hours of public worship and of the church school.

### Hotel Directories

In some metropolitan areas the publicity services post in hotel lobbies according to denomination the names and hours of worship of the local churches. In smaller communities the hotel manager usually cooperates with the churches by displaying invitations to worship.

### Newspaper and Magazine

In cities and other places where there is a large transient population the church may find it worth while to advertise in the local newspapers and perhaps in other periodicals with a wide circulation. Whether or not such an investment would be profitable depends mainly on the geographic location and the type of community in which the church is situated and the cost of the advertising.

### Other Forms of Advertising

In resort areas the public relations committee may distribute bumper signs for use on automobiles. In areas where the population is mobile and transient an invitation to the church may be placed in parked cars, and car cards may be used in public conveyances, especially in areas where there are servicemen.

## THE PRINCIPLE OF APPRECIATION

A healthy public relations program should express the Christian sensitiveness toward one's fellow man. Everyone wishes to feel that he is contributing a worth-while service to the parish and would like to know that it is appreciated. The administration should therefore acknowledge such services.

The minister should express his appreciation personally to individuals and groups engaged in outstanding programs of service and devotion, such as, for example, the choir and the staff of the church school. Below are two letters appropriate for such expression:

DEAR ——— :

As we come to the holiday time I want to say "thank you" for your loyalty in teaching in the Church School. No phase of our program is more significant than this.

I know what patience it takes. May you have the assurance that the impressions you are making and the truths you are teaching go much deeper than immediate evidence may suggest.

God bless you in the services you are giving Him and His children. My appreciation for you is very deep and real.

Yours gratefully and affectionately,

DEAR ———:

I know of the superb job you have done in getting Class Parents for the Church School, and this note is to extend my hand in a very wholehearted word of appreciation. What you have done and what you are doing will go a long, long way in strengthening our whole program not only for the children but also for the men and women of our parish. Fond wishes and deepest thanks.

Yours faithfully,

## Recognition in the Church Publications and Worship Services

Recognition of outstanding services should properly be made at specific times in the church year. One church annually acknowledges on one Sunday the ministries of the teachers in the church school, on another Sunday the services of the leaders in the music program, and on a third Sunday the efforts of the leaders of the every-member canvass. Sometimes the names of these people are published in the Sunday bulletin, and the minister may say a few words of appreciation from the pulpit.

Resolutions passed by the governing board in recognition of the services of individual church officers should be published in the church magazine or duplicated so that they may be available to all members of the church.

One minister expressed his appreciation of distinctive services in an open letter in the Sunday bulletin as follows:

Thanksgiving Season should be a time for writing many long-overdue letters of appreciation. Below are listed some who serve us, on a voluntary basis, and who deserve a word of appreciation:

*John and Ida Morgan,* who each week, for more years than we can remember, have done our mimeograph work.
*Frank B. Nelson,* who has handled the church's legal affairs during the past several years.
*Mary L. Markham,* who has made our Church Library one of the finest.
*Mrs. Walker Gilchrist,* who as our Children's Director, works behind the scenes helping keep our Church School staff and program functioning.
*Our Ushers* (over 50 of them), who look after our large congregations each week.

### All Contributions Acknowledged

The financial secretary or the treasurer should promptly acknowledge all pledges, contributions, and gifts. For pledges made during the every-member canvass a form card with the amount of the pledge typed in will usually suffice. But additional gifts for a specific purpose should be acknowledged promptly by letter. Memorials and other special gifts to the church should be acknowledged by an officer and should be recorded in the archives. In some cases the official board should express its appreciation of an exceptional contribution through its secretary by official action. In other cases, the minister should add his word of acknowledgement and appreciation.

## RADIO AND TELEVISION

A number of churches are finding that their ministries of inspiration and teaching can be expanded through radio and television broadcasts, where the local station allots a very limited time to the religious ministry. The broadcasts should be under the supervision of the radio-television committee of the local council of churches.

The minister of each church should cooperate in the common undertaking and should inform his parish as to the hour and the station over which the broadcasts or telecasts are made.

Some parishes may feel that they should have their own radio or television program for ministering to their shut-ins and others who cannot attend worship services. Whether or not a church should engage in such an undertaking should be determined by the answers to the following questions:

1. Is the minister interested in and capable of providing a suitable program?

2. Has the minister the energy and the time to prepare and execute a radio or television program? (Ministers interested in this field will find an increasing amount of literature on the techniques of radio and television presentation, and the Protestant Radio and Film Commission of the National Council of Churches conducts workshops and offers guidance in this area.)

3. Can the church obtain a good time slot for its program?

4. Can expenses, if any, be met, and does this form of ministry justify the expense?

5. How are listeners to be notified about the program? Notices may be sent to shut-ins, and announcements may be addressed to the hospitals. The Sunday bulletin and the church magazine should carry repeated announcements of the church's radio or television ministry.

## DUPLICATION AND DISTRIBUTION OF SERMONS

If parishioners request more copies of sermons than the minister can personally supply, the official board should consider the advisability of duplicating and distributing the sermons. The decision should be based on the answers to the following questions:

1. Do the parishioners desire such a program?

2. If so, should the sermons be mimeographed or printed? How many copies should be made?

3. Should copies be mailed to all members, or should they be available only on the literature desk or in the church office?

4. Should the project be financed by budgetary provisions, by subscription, or by annual voluntary contributions?

5. How and where should copies be distributed? They should be sent to hospitals and other institutions, to college students, members of the armed forces, and other church members out of the community.

6. If the program is to be a continuing one, a special sermon publication committee under the chairmanship of a board member should be appointed.

## REMEMBRANCE OF PARISHIONERS

As an expression of his warm interest in his parishioners the minister may wish to remember, by a note or telephone call, significant events in their lives, such as the anniversary of a marriage or a death or a birthday. He may evince his concern for special needs; for example, by addressing "To Whom It May Concern" a letter introducing a parishioner as a member in good standing in his church. Such a letter may be very helpful to parishioners who do a great deal of traveling.

## PLACE AND PURPOSE OF THE CHURCH DINNER

The congregational dinner should be used as an occasion to inform members of the work and needs of the church and to inspire greater dedication. A congregational dinner may also be planned specifically to deepen supportive friendships among the parishioners. If it enhances the love and understanding of the members for the church and enriches the spiritual life, it will serve a worthy purpose.

## "DIAL A PRAYER" PHONE

Local telephone companies will rent to churches equipment for recording a one-minute prayer that subscribers may hear by dialing a certain number. The minister records a different prayer for each day. In populous areas the minister's voice on "Dial a Prayer" has brought comfort and inspiration to the hospitalized, the shut-ins, the lonely, and to those who have acute problems. Whether or not to rent the telephone equipment is a matter for each church to decide on the basis of cost, potential use, and the minister's ability to record a different prayer for each day.

## DAILY PRAYER FOR PARISHIONERS

Often the spiritual ties between a clergyman and his parishioners are strengthened by daily ten-minute silent prayer services. If the service takes place early in the morning or a noontime, when the parishioners are widely scattered at their work, there may not be many persons in the church, but the thought that the spiritual leader, at a particular hour, is silently praying for his flock is deeply meaningful to many. In one such program the minister writes to a few persons each day telling them that he lifted them, their hopes, and their needs to the throne of grace in his period of silent prayer. This makes them feel closer to Jesus Christ and His church.

## THE CHURCH MAGAZINE

The following requirements should be met by a successful church magazine.

1. There should be a competent, devoted editor to supervise all aspects of publication.

2. The format should be interesting and attractive.

3. The writing should meet the standards of good reporting.

4. The magazine should be distributed to all parishioners.

5. It should be published at intervals that best serve the needs of the parish.

6. The cost of the magazine should be provided for in the annual budget.

7. The contents of the magazine should vary with the seasons and with the objectives and programs of the church. The magazine should convey information, increase understanding and loyalty, and inspire the parish. It should contain the following items:

    *a.* An editorial or message from the clergyman.

    *b.* Titles of books and leaflets recommended for inspirational reading.

c. Report of the every-member-canvass program.

d. A parish calendar for the week, the month, and the season.

e. Baptisms, deaths, and marriages.

f. Names and addresses of new members.

g. Notices of the programs and activities of all organizations.

h. Announcements of significant church events.

i. Personal items about the staff members and noted personalities in the church.

j. An explanation of staff responsibilities, and a statement of the hours when the minister is available and details regarding his various ministries in the church.

k. An editor's column in which decisions and activities of the governing board are summarized.

l. Resolutions regarding outstanding service in the church.

m. The magazine should have a masthead listing the names and titles of those who participate in its publication.

n. Personal items about parishioners.

o. A sermon occasionally.

p. Introductions of missionaries and accounts of the larger work of the church as a denomination.

q. Names and addresses of young people away at school and college.

r. Rules regarding the church grounds and buildings.

s. Condensed accounts of church activities in the world, the nation, and in the local area in which the parish may be involved.

t. Inspirational thoughts, religious poetry and epigrams.

u. Names of the officers of all organizations.

v. The organizational setup, together with all committees, of the official board.

The parish magazine should reflect the interest, the activities, the program, and the aims of the church, and should serve to further those ends.

## THE ANNUAL DIRECTORY

Many churches publish an annual directory listing the names, addresses, and telephone numbers of their members. An asterisk is sometimes used before the names of parishioners who make an annual pledge to support the church. Additional materials to be contained in the annual directory are:

1. Names of the members of the staff.
2. Historical material, including the names of previous ministers.
3. Appointments of the year, including Sunday worship services, the communion service, special services, such as Advent, Christmas, Lent, and Holy Week.
4. The annual meetings of the congregation.
5. The calendar of major events of the year.
6. Names of officers and standing committees of the official board.
7. Brief statements of purposes, together with the names of officers and dates of meetings of all major church organizations.
8. Names of the ushers for the year.
9. Details regarding the endowment fund.
10. A brief summary of the annual financial statement of the church.
11. Names of members who died during the previous year.
12. A form of bequest for the church, together with a statement regarding the endowment fund.
13. Names of outside organizations using the church property.
14. Rules regarding the use of the church property.
15. A statement regarding flowers in the sanctuary.
16. Benevolences.
17. A page for notes and additions to the annual directory.

## THE SUNDAY BULLETIN

The Sunday bulletin serves several purposes. It gives the order of the service for the guidance of worshipers. It announces parish activities and it should be used for inspiration and for spiritual and mental enrichment.

The following go to make up a satisfactory bulletin:

1. The editor should receive all notices and all details regarding the worship service.
2. There should be a deadline for the delivery of notices and the materials of worship.

3. If the bulletin is printed outside the church premises, arrangements should be made with the printer for the delivery of the copy and the delivery of the printed calendars.
4. If the material is reproduced in the church office, by mimeograph or other methods, defective or smudged copies should be discarded.
5. The layout of the front page may be the same or different every Sunday. Some religious supply houses supply Sunday bulletins with various pictorial designs on the first page.
6. The name and address of the church and the date of the bulletin should appear on the front page.
7. The bulletin should include significant religious thoughts of an educational or inspirational nature.
8. It should contain material of interest and help to strangers and visitors, such as the name of the minister and, if space permits, the names of the organist and choirmaster, and the treasurer, together with telephone numbers.
9. Some church bulletins have spaces to be used instead of pew cards, for such information, as the desire to join the church, name of a newcomer to the community, desire for a conference with the minister, illness, and so on.
10. If not each Sunday the bulletin should include from time to time the names of the official board, and the church staff.
11. The bulletin may well have a calendar of church events scheduled for the coming week.

## SPECIAL BROCHURES AND LEAFLETS

Among the special leaflets that may serve the needs and program of the parish are the following:
1. A leaflet describing the church school and the religious education program, and containing the names of the Christian education committee, the staff members involved, and brief statements regarding the aims and objectives of the program, as well as an outline of the church school program, its departmental organization, and the names of superintendents and other leaders with their addresses and telephone numbers.

2. A special pamphlet on the symbolism of the stained-glass windows.
3. Folders describing when additions to the church structure are dedicated, when a new chancel or an educational wing is built or a new organ installed. Besides the order of the dedication service, the leaflet may have photographs, specifications of the new structure for historical purposes, and the names of those who had a part in bringing the project to fruition. Leaflets for special Advent and Lenten services should be on hand.
4. Some churches publish occasional papers for church school teachers or for the choral program, depending on the needs of the parish.
5. Publications for special educational programs, a series of lectures, or a Lenten dinner series.
6. Leaflet inviting visitors and newcomers in the community may further the church's program and outreach. Such leaflets should be attractive in format and present the program of the church simply and interestingly.
7. A leaflet concerning the architecture of the church, especially if the church has historical associations or if the fabric and embellishments are interesting or outstanding.
8. A brochure on the history of the church, especially on anniversary occasions.
9. Brochures for the every-member canvass, describing special projects both material and spiritual.
10. An inspirational leaflet explaining the symbolism in the wood carving or stonework of the church.
11. Specialized publications for the programs of groups, such as the young adult society.
12. A newsletter for the servicemen of its parish and congregation.

## THE PEW CARD

To obtain information for the clergymen and other staff members a pew card may be simple, with places only for a signature and for such items as a request for a call from the minister, the name of the visitor's home church, or an indication of interest in joining the church.

One church places seven different-size cards upright in the pew rack so that only the title of each card is visible. There is a prayer-request card, a prospect card, a service card, a visitor's card, a subscription card, a call-requested card, and a communicant's card.

The prayer-request card asks for the name and the need of the person for whom prayer is requested. The prospect card asks for the names and addresses of people who might be interested in the parish. The service card, beginning with the words "I gladly volunteer my service to Christ and this Church in the following capacities when possible," lists such services as ushering, young people's work, sewing, and library work.

The visitor's card requests the name, address, telephone number, and the name of the visitor's home church.

The subscription card for nonmembers invites a pledge toward the "Great Kingdom Enterprise." The signer pledges a weekly, monthly, or annual contribution to be distributed as he indicates for benevolences and for the support of the church.

The call-requested card asks the signer to indicate the reason for the call by checking one of the following: sick, sorrow, need, stranger.

The communicant's card asks for the communicant's signature, address and telephone number and the date under the statement "I participated in the Lord's Supper at Christ Church." There is space for indicating whether the communicant is a member of the parish.

## THE GUEST BOOK

The guest book in the entryway or narthex of the church invites strangers, visitors, and newcomers to leave their names and addresses with the parish. The guest book should be of fine quality and should have a permanent binding. It should be in charge of a hospitable, trained member of the church. It is often desirable to have two members at the guest book to greet visitors, strangers, and newcomers. One church offers the following suggestions:

SUGGESTIONS TO HOSTESS AT GUEST BOOK
AND DEACON IN CHARGE

1. Be friendly! Your warmth is needed to overcome strangeness,
2. Obtain *full* name and *full* address of *all visitors*. *Correct* information is important.
3. Make note of special interests or other information, either in Guest Book or memorandum book provided.
4. Printing is suggested. Legibility is necessary.
5. Invite to coffee hour in the Club Room when available.
6. Hand them a copy of the church magazine and "You Are Invited" brochure.
7. Direct to literature table.
8. Inform yourself about church activities as a preparation for answering questions.
9. Telephone local residents on Monday. This gesture bespeaks the friendliness we want to extend. Inform the church office (telephone number) of the results of your calls by Wednesday.

## THE "COFFEE HOUR"

If the church has the facilities, the "coffee hour" after the worship service will serve as an occasion when church members may visit and become better acquainted with one another and may greet and welcome newcomers. If such a program is instituted, the following points should be considered:

1. How will the expenses be paid?
2. Who will appoint and instruct the hosts and hostesses?
3. How should the coffee hour be announced?
4. Will the stranger easily find the place where the hospitality is provided?

## THE CHURCH AND COMMUNITY SERVICES

### The Uses of Church Facilities by Community Groups

On general principles, the church should cooperate with the educational, humanitarian, and cultural groups in the community, but not with purely political or disputatious secular groups or organizations. The official board should establish a policy and make regulations regarding the use of church property, and organizations using the church property should be expected to cooperate.

As leader of the church the minister should improve public relations by a warm interest in and support of the local hospital, the Red Cross, the homes for the aged and the handicapped, and other enterprises dedicated to public service. As head of the church he must schedule his time properly to fulfill his first obligation, which is the spiritual and educational oversight of the church committed to his care. He cannot distribute his energies too widely, but the community should be aware of his interest in support of and cooperation with public welfare projects in keeping with Christian spirit of love and service to one's fellow men.

The local parish may assist such projects by posting notices on the bulletin board and placing announcements in the Sunday bulletin and church magazine.

## THE CHURCH AND OTHER INSTITUTIONS

### Schools and Colleges

The church should evince a cordial interest in local educational institutions. Many college students away from home appreciate the church's invitation to participate in worship and youth activities and to visit the homes of parishioners. Local needs and opportunities will determine the best program.

### Homes for the Aged

Through a social service committee the church may help local institutions for the aged, homeless, and handicapped by sharing with them music and youth activities and programs and offering them the service of the sewing group of the women's society and other resources of the church.

### Service Clubs

In towns and smaller communities, the church should cooperate with service clubs in projects benefiting young people and adults.

Though participation may be on a limited basis, it will indicate that the minister is interested in "good work" and that church and community are in rapport.

### Industries

The church may be able to provide specialized services and ministries to industrial workers, depending on conditions. But before engaging in such a project it should consult the executive and labor authorities.

### Hospitals

The minister should be in close touch with the local hospital. Besides ministering to hospitalized parishioners, the minister together with the church officers may express the thoughtfulness of the church to all Protestant patients in other ways. For example, they may deliver flowers from the chancel, which, accompanied by a card, may mean a great deal to an ill person. The organization of a hospital calling committee of devoted women and men may be in order. Where several churches have a cooperative program they may recommend to the hospital administrator the appointment of a Protestant chaplain.

## CHURCH BULLETIN BOARDS

Bulletin boards should be strategically located. The material on them should be legible, neat, and never out of date. The person responsible for the board should supervise it regularly early each week.

## SURVEY OF NEEDS

The church should annually engage in self-examination to determine the effectiveness of its ministry to the parish and the community. This matter is discussed more fully on page 38 ff.

The governing board should appoint a special committee to analyze all phases of parish life, internal and external. On the internal side the committee should examine the details of the worship services. On the external side it should investigate the outreach of the church to newcomers and to the community. The results of the investigation, together with specific recommendations approved by the minister, should be presented to the governing board.

## THE PRINCIPLE OF THE SECOND MILE

No policy will make for a happier and more harmonious spirit in the church than doing more than is expected in the way of personal concern for and prompt helpfulness to every member in the parish. From such attentiveness of church leaders to the spiritual welfare of each parishioner is developed the *esprit de corps* that strengthens the ties that bind parishioners to one another and to their Saviour.

## WELCOMING CONSTRUCTIVE SUGGESTIONS

At every opportunity the minister and the official board should let the parish know that they appreciate suggestions for strengthening and improving the church life. This "open-door policy" may be announced by the minister every so often from the pulpit, through pastoral letters, through announcements in the bulletin, and in statements of prominent laymen at annual meetings of the church and on occasions when they address the various church organizations. All suggestions should be acknowledged with appreciation and should be considered carefully.

## THE HOSPITALIZED AND SHUT-INS

To avoid hurt feelings and irritation the church should be very attentive to its indigent, shut-ins, and ill parishioners. Through repeated announcements, through pew cards, through a social service or a special calling committee, the church should maintain contact with these persons. They should be remembered at Christmas time, should receive communion, and should be visited by devoted lay people.

1. Someone should keep a list of hospitalized members, checking the hospital list twice a week, preferably each day, for new admissions.
2. The minister should call as soon as possible.
3. The church should keep a list of shut-ins, and changes in the list should be passed on to those in the attentiveness program.
4. At stated times during the year the sacrament of the Lord's Supper should be offered to those unable to attend church.
5. The Sunday bulletin should be mailed to shut-ins.
6. At regular intervals flowers should be sent to shut-ins and to those who are hospitalized.
7. A committee of church women may render a significant service by remembering shut-ins on their birthdays and by calling on them at other important occasions in their lives. Files containing pertinent information should be kept up to date.

## THE LITERATURE TABLE

The printed matter of the church may be distributed at a neat, attractive table located in an area of heavy traffic. The minister should approve the appointment of the literature-table committee and the selection of the literature. From time to time the location of the table and the materials available should be announced in the bulletin. The literature-table program is discussed more fully on page 111.

If there is any word that would serve as an overarching banner for the wisely conceived and carefully administered parish, it would be from the mind of St. Paul, "Let all things be done decently and in order."

# APPENDIX A

STANDING RULES
OF
CHRIST CHURCH
KALAMAZOO, MICHIGAN

As Adopted by The Official Board, March 2, 19__

## Article I

### Meetings of the Official Board

1. Unless otherwise fixed at a previous meeting, the stated meetings of the Official Board shall be on the second Thursday evening of every month, except July and August, at such hour as shall be from time to time appointed. The meeting shall be opened and closed by prayer.

2. A majority of the Official Board regularly convened shall be a quorum for the transaction of business.

3. The following shall be the order of business at all meetings, except that at a special meeting the business for which such meeting was called shall take precedence:

(1) The minutes of all previous meetings which have not been approved shall be read for correction and approval
(2) Report of the Treasurer
(3) Reports of Standing Committees
(4) Reports of Special Committees
(5) Report of Minister
(6) Unfinished Business
(7) Petitions, original communications and new business
(8) Approval of next meeting date

When not in conflict with these standing rules, business shall be conducted in accordance with Robert's Rules of Order.

4. All official acts of the Official Board, to be executed in writing and under its seal, shall be signed by the President and countersigned by the Clerk or Treasurer.

5. No person other than members and members of the Official Board

elect, the Clerk and the Treasurer shall be present at any meeting of the Official Board unless by its permission.

## Article II

### Elders and Deacons

1. The number of offices of Elder and the number of offices of Deacon shall each be fifteen. The Elders and the Deacons, together with the Minister, shall constitute the Official Board.

2. The offices of Elder and the offices of Deacon shall be divided into three classes of five each, and each class of Elders and of Deacons shall be elected for a term of three years commencing on the first day of April in the year of his election.

3. At the expiration of a term of three years, any Elder or any Deacon may be reelected for an additional term of three years, but after an Elder or a Deacon shall have served two consecutive terms commencing on or after April 1, 1956, he shall not be again eligible for election to the same office until one year shall have elapsed after the expiration of his last term of office. In determining eligibility for election, service as an Elder or as a Deacon for a term of office of eighteen months or more commencing on or after April 1, 1956, shall be considered as equivalent to service for a full three-year term and service for a term of office of less than eighteen months shall be disregarded.

4. Elders and Deacons shall be chosen by the Official Board not later than March 15th of each year from among the members of the Church in full communion. At the time of the announcement of the Official Board's choice of Elders and Deacons, the President of the Official Board shall appoint a Nominating Committee of seven members, consisting of two Elders or former Elders, two Deacons or former Deacons and three other members of the Church in full communion, who shall prior to the next succeeding annual choice of Elders and Deacons submit to the Official Board the names of suitable persons to fill any vacancies occurring in such offices.

5. Whenever any vacancy shall occur in an office of Elder or of Deacon through any cause other than expiration of a term, the Official Board may choose a member of the Church in full communion to fill such office for the unexpired term.

6. The name of each person chosen for the office of Elder or Deacon shall be published in the Church on three successive Sundays previous to his installation, to the end that any lawful objections may be presented to the Official Board and duly adjudicated by it.

7. Any of the foregoing provisions of this Article II to the contrary notwithstanding, the Official Board (*a*) not later than March 15, 1956, shall elect five Elders, each for a term of three years commencing on April 1, 1956, to

succeed the four Elders whose terms of office will expire on that date and shall elect seven Deacons, five for a term of three years and two for a term of two years commencing on April 1, 1956, to succeed the six Deacons whose terms of office expire on that date; (b) not later than March 15, 1957, shall elect nine Elders, five for a term of three years and four for a term of one year commencing on April 1, 1957, to succeed the eight Elders whose terms of office will expire on that date, and shall elect seven Deacons, five for a term of three years and two for a term of one year commencing on April 1, 1957, to succeed the six Deacons whose terms of office will expire on that date; and (c) not later than March 15, 1958, shall elect five Elders, each for a term of three years commencing on April 1, 1958, to succeed the four Elders whose terms of office will expire on that date, and shall elect five Deacons, each for a term of three years, to succeed the four Deacons whose terms of office will expire on that date.

### Article III

### President

1. The Minister of the Church shall be the President of the Official Board and shall preside at all meetings thereof. The Consistory may elect one of the Elders to be its President pro tem. in the absence of the Minister.

2. Special meetings of the Official Board may be called by the President or, in his absence, the President pro tem. when deemed by him necessary and must be called by him at the request of three members of the Official Board.

3. The President or one of the Elders shall open the meeting at the hour at which the members shall be notified to meet, or as soon thereafter as a quorum shall appear. He shall direct the proceedings, maintain order and dignity, confine the members to the question before them, and prevent interruption. He shall state and put all questions, when the members are prepared to vote, and declare the decision by the hearing of the yeas and nays, unless he or any member shall express a doubt of the decision, in which case a count shall be taken.

### Article IV

### Clerk

1. The Official Board shall annually elect a Clerk who need not be a member of the Official Board. The Clerk shall attend all meetings of the Official Board, of the Official Board of Ministers and Elders, of the Great Official Board, and of the congregation, and record the minutes of each in suitable books kept for that purpose. He shall have the custody and safekeeping of the records of those proceedings, the record of the baptisms, marriages and members of this Church, and all other books and papers committed to his

charge, and also the seal, and shall not suffer any of them to be taken out of his possession except on an order of the Official Board; but it shall nevertheless be his duty to deliver to members of committees, to the Treasurer and to delegates of the Church to the Classis and Synods, such books, papers and extracts as may be necessary for the discharge of their respective duties, taking a receipt for the same.

2. The Clerk shall keep a book in which he shall register the names of all members of this Church as they shall be admitted, with the dates of their admission; and the names of all members dismissed to other churches, and the dates of their dismission, and the Churches to which they are recommended. When a certificate of dismission from another Church has attached to it a blank form for the acknowledgement of the receipt of such certificate, he shall fill the blank and return the same to said church without delay. He shall from time to time enter in his book the death of members, so far as the same shall come to his knowledge, and the date of such death.

3. The Clerk shall notify each person elected to an office or appointed to a Committee of the Official Board of his election or appointment. He shall inform all officers and committee chairmen of any action of the Official Board affecting their respective duties. He shall notify the chairman of each committee of the Official Board of the names of the persons composing such committee and of the business committed thereto. He shall also send all notices required to be given to the Elders and Deacons.

4. Without an order of the Official Board, the Clerk shall not give copies of the minutes nor allow access to the same to any persons except members of the Official Board and the Treasurer.

5. The Clerk shall aid the President in the dispatch of business by preparing and laying before him at every meeting a list of the unfinished business, of committees to report, and of all other matters to be brought before the body, in the proper order, pursuant to the standing rules and other resolutions.

### Article V

#### Treasurer

1. The Official Board shall annually elect a Treasurer, who need not be a member of the Official Board. The Treasurer shall attend all meetings of the Official Board and shall be a member ex officio of the Finance Committee. Before he enters on the execution of his duties, he shall, together with two sufficient individual sureties, or a surety company, to be approved by the Official Board, execute a bond to "Christ Church of Kalamazoo" in the sum of ten thousand dollars, conditioned for his prompt and faithful discharge of the trusts reposed in him. The premium on any such bond shall be paid from the funds of the church.

2. The Treasurer shall have the custody and safekeeping of all bonds, mort-

gages, deeds, maps, and other papers and evidences of titles to lands and other property belonging to the Church, and shall not deliver the same, or any of them, out of his possession, except on an order of the Official Board and then only against a receipt therefor. He shall, however, aid the officers of the Official Board and the members of all committees, standing or special, with all such information as he may possess relating to the subjects committed to them.

3. The Treasurer shall, under the direction of the Finance Committee, collect and receive all the income and revenues of the Church; pay all taxes and assessments payable by the Church; effect from time to time fire or other insurance on or in connection with the property of the Church and pay for the same; pay the fixed salaries of the Ministers and employees of the Church; and make only such other expenditures as may be authorized from time to time by the Official Board.

4. He shall deposit in the name of the Church all funds of the Church in such bank or banks, trust company or trust companies of Kalamazoo as the Finance Committee shall approve. He shall keep proper and detailed accounts of all his receipts and disbursements, and all financial transactions, subject at all times to the inspection of the Official Board or any committees designated by it.

5. On the days of the stated meetings of the Official Board, the Treasurer shall balance his cash books and lay before the Official Board his accounts of receipts and expenditures, showing the balance in the treasury. At the stated meeting of the Official Board on the second Thursday in January in each year he shall render full and particular accounts of all his transactions as Treasurer for the preceding fiscal year.

### Article VI

#### Committees

1. The Standing Committees of the Official Board shall be the Committees on Finance, on Benevolence, on Music, on Pulpit Supply, on Operations and Maintenance, on Religious Education, on Communion, on Ushers, on Publicity and Public Relations, on Endowment and on Auditing.

2. The members of each Standing and Special Committee shall be appointed each year by the President with the approval of a majority of the members of the Official Board. The person first named shall be chairman, whose duty it shall be to call meetings of the committee. A majority of each committee shall form a quorum for the transaction of business.

3. The Finance Committee shall be composed of nine (9) members, at least three of whom shall be appointed from the new members of the Official Board each year. The Committee shall report to the Official Board at each regular meeting. They shall have the management and supervision of all the finan-

cial affairs of the Church. They shall ascertain the financial needs of the Church for the coming year and prepare a budget embodying the same and present it to the Official Board at its October meeting for its approval. Upon approval of the budget by the Official Board, the Finance Committee shall devise ways and means of raising the money to meet the same and take charge of the canvass of the congregation or any other plan that may be adopted by the Official Board to raise the needed funds.

4. The Auditing Committee shall annually select a Certified Public Accountant who shall in January of each year, or as soon thereafter as practicable, examine and report to the Official Board with respect to all accounts of the Treasurer for the preceding calendar year.

## Article VII

### Financial Rules

1. No debt shall be contracted by any Committee, Standing or Special, in excess of the amount appropriated to its use in the annual budget, unless such debt be specially authorized by Consistory. All unexpended balances of sums appropriated for a definite period shall lapse at the end of such period.

2. The several Committees receiving appropriations in the annual budget shall by October 1 in each year present to the Finance Committee in writing itemized statements of the estimated expenditures of such Committees for the ensuing fiscal year. The Chairman of the several Committees shall be entitled to be heard by the Finance Committee with respect to the statements so presented. The Finance Committee shall report thereon at the October stated meeting of the Official Board and submit an estimate of the receipts and expenditures of the ensuing year, and of the anticipated surplus, if any. Such proposed budget shall be filed with the Clerk of the Official Board and copies thereof prepared by him and furnished to each member of the Official Board prior to such meeting.

3. After adoption of the annual budget by the Official Board the same shall be submitted to the membership of the Church for its approval at a congregational meeting called for such purpose.

## Article VIII

### Miscellaneous

1. All minute books, books of account and books of record of any kind as they become filled, and other papers (except the deeds and other documents relating to the property of the Church, which shall be in charge of the Treasurer), after they shall be of no further use to the body or officer to which they relate shall be deposited with the Clerk, to be by him properly labeled and safely kept among the archives of the Church.

2. The fiscal year shall be the calendar year but in all other respects the Church year shall begin April 1 and end March 31.

3. No established custom of the Church, nor any of the standing rules of the Church, shall be altered or repealed nor any new rules adopted unless notice, stating the alteration proposed, shall be given at a stated meeting previous to that at which such alteration, repeal or additional rule shall be considered, and it shall be adopted only by a vote of two-thirds of all the members of the Official Board. No standing rule may be suspended except by unanimous consent at a meeting of the Official Board at which two-thirds of the members shall be present.

4. The standing rules of the Church shall be deemed in all respects subject and subordinate to the Constitution of Christ Church in America, as the same may be in effect from time to time, and to the extent that such standing rules may at any time be inconsistent with the provisions of such Constitution, the latter shall prevail.

## INDEX TO APPENDIX A

# APPENDIX B

CHRIST CHURCH
OLINVILLE, NEW YORK

*Details of Methods Used in Contacting New People and Prospective Members*

I. *Source of gaining names of new people who move to the community*

1. Contact with real-estate agencies. A note of appreciation is always sent to any new realtor who provides the names of new people who have purchased homes or moved into apartments.
2. A further source is through the lists made by the political parties of people who move to the community. Party leaders and ward workers are continually on the lookout for new people and are bringing their lists up to date.
3. Through contact with the public relations individuals in the local banks, the Church is further able to procure names of individuals who are new to the area.
4. The Welcome Wagon Service, through a cultivated rapport with its representative, has proved to be a further source of gaining the names of individuals who are moving into the area.

(In each instance, full cooperation and warm appreciation is always expressed by the Church.)

II. *Method of greeting to new people*

1. Whenever the church receives the name of an individual recently moved to the area, a general letter, individually typed, is sent to that individual or family welcoming them to the community, telling them of the various churches in the area and assuring them of the desire of the ministers and the staff to be of any service or help to them. The letter states that in the event they are Protestant and have a background closely affiliated with our Church, they would be most welcome.
2. The letter contains a return business reply post card on which the individual can indicate whether or not he or she desires to receive the Church literature or has any further requests.

381

3. A part of the plan, which, as yet, has not been organized on a regular basis for a week-in, week-out persistent program, includes a call on such individuals by an "Invitation Committee" of the Church. The committee will be made up of laymen and women whose primary responsibility will be to make a personal call, learn more about these individuals and report back to the ministers.

(Christ Church in Olinville has successfully used 150 laymen in a calling program of this kind, done on an annual basis. It is my judgment that the more effective method is through a smaller group who will be committed to doing such calling on a regular basis week-in and week-out and returning to the Church office pertinent information about individuals and families.)

4. The ministers are particularly on the lookout for such new people who may come to the Church Worship Services or who enter into some participation of some of its activities.

III. *Source of names of individuals who may be considered active prospects*

1. The names of newcomers to the community are kept in a separate file. When through any source of information we learn that they are Protestant and have manifested some interest in the Church, they are put on the active prospect list.

2. Further sources of gaining names of prospects are through individuals who come to Church for worship. Three means are stressed whereby we get their names and addresses.

   *a.* All worshipers are urged to sign cards at special occasions in the Church year, such as Communion Services and on Easter Sunday. These cards are separated, members from nonmembers. They provide an invaluable source of obtaining the names and addresses of individuals who are attending Church but who are not members.

   *b.* Sunday by Sunday, there are visitors' cards placed in the pews. An announcement appears in the morning bulletin urging visitors to sign the cards and to use them for any requests to the ministers or staff.

   *c.* In the Narthex of the Church following the service, a member of the Women's Society and a Deacon stand at a desk where is placed the visitors' book. The ministers and Elders greet the congregation at the close of the service and are particularly attentive to singling out strangers, to greeting them and to guiding them to the visitors' book where they are greeted by the Deacon and are invited to sign their name in the visitors' book.

3. The Sunday morning bulletin frequently carries a printed greeting to

strangers and visitors. From time to time, when announcements are made, the minister will make a verbal greeting to those who may not be members of the Church and who fall in the category of visitors and strangers. These announcements emphasize the desire of the Church to have their name and address, urges that they sign the visitors' book or a visitors' card and that they leave the Church not as a "stranger" but as a "friend."

4. Other sources through which the names of active prospects are gained are through the various organizations of the Church: the Church School, Women's Society, Men's Club, Couples' Club, the Choirs, Youth activities, and so on. At least once a year, the membership secretary of the Church should go over the rolls of all organizations, taking the names of individuals who may have been added to the rolls of the various activities during the past months and placing such individuals on the active prospect roll of the Church. All societies should be looked on as channels to feed the congregational life. Emphasis is made with leaders to be attentive to greeting of newcomers.

5. A Good Will Calling Society of the Women's Association is invaluable in procuring additional names of individuals who manifest an interest in the Church.

IV. *Methods used to cultivate and deepen the interest of prospective members in the life of the Church*

1. All who sign the guest book or who bring their children to Church School for the first time, and so on, receive a personal letter from the minister welcoming them to the Church and inviting them to share in its activities in a full way. To all such individuals an annual brochure describing the Church activities is sent. They of course are invited to let their desires be known to the ministers and staff.

2. The Women's Society, through its calling committee, makes a personal contact with all such prospects. The information gained is added to the prospect card on which appears the name, address, telephone number, and so on, of the prospect.

3. All such active prospects have Addressograph plates made for them and are then put on the active mailing list of the Church. They receive the monthly magazine, copies of printed sermons issued by the Sermon Publication Committee, and other literature of general interest.

4. It is the plan to include a call by a member of the "Invitation Committee" on all such active prospects prior to the reception of new members at a Communion Service. At the present time, this program is followed through only on an annual basis by laymen and through

such personal contacts as the ministers can create within the limited scope of their time.

5. At least a month prior to the reception of new members, a personal note goes from the minister to a selected group of individuals who through their participation in the Church activities, the worship services, and so on, may be considered as receptive to an invitation to join the Church.

6. A class in preparation for Church membership for adults is conducted on four consecutive Sunday afternoons by one of the ministers. The class covers a review of Church history, the essential doctrines of Protestantism, the ideal of the Christian life, and so on.

V. *Reception of new members and following their reception*

1. On the evening when new members meet with the Elders, the minister speaks to the group for about a half an hour, reviewing the teachings of the preparatory class and indicating specifically some of the programs and needs of the particular congregation into which they are coming. They are greeted individually by the Elders. Every effort is made to heighten the experience as one of the deepest in an individual's life.

2. On the Sunday morning when members are received into the fellowship of the Church, each is called by name to stand, and, if the group is small, comes into the Chancel where each is greeted by the minister. The congregation stands and joins in the singing of "Blest Be the Tie That Binds." This plan is adjusted, determined by the number of individuals received. But every effort is made to make the public reception at the morning Church service a warm and spiritual occasion.

3. A tea is held on Sunday afternoon for all new members who have been received. The presidents of all organizations of the Church, the staff of the Church, representative Elders, Deacons and their wives are present. The purpose of the tea is to let all new members immediately become personally acquainted with the staff and with the leaders of the various organizations of the Church, and also to become more intimately and happily acquainted with each other.

4. An engraved certificate is sent to all individuals who have been received in the Church.

5. The minister sends again a personal letter expressing his joy at their reception into the Church and pointing out that the Church will be no greater than their loyalty to it. The letter also expresses the desire to be helpful in any pastoral way at any time.

6. When the new members meet with the Elders, each fills out a detailed form giving name, address, birth date, business connection, and so on. The form contains a place for a record of past Church activity and

for current interests, avocations, and so on. The membership secretary carefully goes through these forms that have been filled out and notes any particular interest that has been indicated. That interest is passed on to the department or activity which would be most appropriately related to it.

Shortly thereafter, as an example, if the individual has expressed an interest in music, the choirmaster would get in touch with the individual inviting him or her to a choir rehearsal or begin to open up some need in the musical life of the Church where they may be helpful.

7. The names, addresses, former Churches, of all members received are printed in a Sunday bulletin following the reception of the members. From the pulpit, the minister urges all new members to look closely and carefully at the list to note individuals who may be their neighbors or friends and make a particular personal effort to greet the new members into the life of the Church and personally to be helpful in informing them of any Church activity.

8. The names of all members are published annually in a booklet which is distributed to all the active communicants of the Church.

The above is a cursory outline of some of the cold mechanics that go into the methods employed at Christ Church. These mechanical processes do not indicate what is the overarching goal and desire, namely, to express a warmhearted affection and concern to all people who come within the orbit of the Church life—to be interested in them personally in a loving and compassionate way—and gently to open to them a vision of what an enriched spiritual life can mean to them, to their family, to their community. Every effort in the spirit of love is made to be helpful to all individuals who come within the orbit of the Church life. Beyond the above, the ministers do all in their power to have new members meet other members of the Church through introducing them whenever they are in groups within the walls of the Church, through inviting them at every and any possible occasion to informal gatherings in the Manses, and so on. While we follow a program of aggressiveness in the sense of being immediately attentive to newcomers and strangers insofar as we can, we are motivated by the motto that "whatever is done in the spirit of love will always be right."

Overarching this program and all aspects of the Church life is the conviction that Christ is not dead—He is alive—a power to teach and guide, comfort and inspire "you"! This spirit is reflected from the pulpit on Sunday morning to the work of the visitor who takes a bouquet to a mother and baby at the time of birth.

# Index